HISTORY OF
*United States Naval Operations*
IN WORLD WAR II

★

V O L U M E   S I X

# Breaking the Bismarcks Barrier
22 *July* 1942–1 *May* 1944

# HISTORY OF UNITED STATES NAVAL OPERATIONS IN WORLD WAR II

## By Samuel Eliot Morison

I *The Battle of the Atlantic*, September 1939 – May 1943

II *Operations in North African Waters*, October 1942 – June 1943

III *The Rising Sun in the Pacific*, 1931 – April 1942

IV *Coral Sea, Midway and Submarine Actions*, May 1942 – August 1942

V *The Struggle for Guadalcanal*, August 1942 – February 1943

VI *Breaking the Bismarcks Barrier*, 22 July 1942 – 1 May 1944

VII *Aleutians, Gilberts and Marshalls*, June 1942 – April 1944

VIII *New Guinea and the Marianas*, March 1944 – August 1944

IX *Sicily – Salerno – Anzio*, January 1943 – June 1944

X *The Atlantic Battle Won*, May 1943 – May 1945

XI *The Invasion of France and Germany*, 1944 – 1945

XII *Leyte*, June 1944 – January 1945

XIII *The Liberation of the Philippines: Luzon, Mindanao, the Visayas*, 1944 – 1945

XIV *Victory in the Pacific*, 1945

XV *Supplement and General Index*

Also
**Strategy and Compromise**

*Rear Admiral Theodore S. Wilkinson* USN
Commander Amphibious Force, South Pacific

HISTORY OF UNITED STATES NAVAL
OPERATIONS IN WORLD WAR II
*VOLUME VI*

# Breaking
# the Bismarcks Barrier
## 22 *July* 1942 - 1 *May* 1944

### BY SAMUEL ELIOT MORISON

*With Illustrations*

LITTLE, BROWN AND COMPANY
BOSTON · NEW YORK · LONDON · TORONTO

20   19   18   17   16

KPT

*Published simultaneously
in Canada by McClelland and Stewart Limited*

PRINTED IN THE UNITED STATES OF AMERICA

*To*
*The Memory of*
THEODORE STARK WILKINSON
1888–1946
*Vice Admiral, United States Navy*

*Fas est et ab hoste doceri.*
It is right to be taught even by an enemy.
— OVID, *Metamorphoses*, iv 428


Counterattack is the soul of defense. Defense is in a passive attitude, for that is the negation of war. Rightly conceived it is an attitude of alert expectation. We wait for the moment when the enemy shall expose himself to a counter stroke, the success of which will so far cripple him as to render us relatively strong enough to pass to the offensive ourselves.
— JULIAN CORBETT, *Some Principles of Maritime Strategy*, p. 25


Unloading is the world-wide difficulty of amphibious operations.
— REAR ADMIRAL THEODORE S. WILKINSON

# Preface

BREAKING the Bismarcks Barrier is both the title and the theme of this volume. That Barrier was a very formidable obstacle. The Japanese air and naval bases that constituted it were disposed like a gigantic fish weir, the wing of which was the air-sea route from Japan through Saipan and Truk to Rabaul. The circular part was woven between a number of stout posts represented by Kavieng in New Ireland, the Admiralty Islands, Wewak, Madang, Lae, Salamaua and Buna in New Guinea; Cape Gloucester, Gasmata and Rabaul in New Britain. Of all posts that supported this weirlike barrier, Rabaul was the most powerful and the most important. The enemy's capture of that colonial town on 23 January 1942, with its airfields and roadstead, extracted far more blood and sweat from Allied forces than the loss of Singapore. Rabaul was the base for powerful air and surface strikes on Port Moresby and Queensland in the early days of the Pacific war; Rabaul had a commodious harbor, safe from Allied air attack until the outer bastions of the Barrier were surmounted. There the bombardment missions, cruiser strikes and "Tokyo Expresses" that so long bedeviled American efforts in the Solomons were assembled. Rabaul's five airfields supported a pool of air power, reinforceable at will from Japan, whence bombers and fighters flew east and south to attack Allied shipping and ground forces. *Rabaul delenda est* was the one essential condition of General MacArthur's advance along the New Guinea-Mindanao axis.

Too long had the Bismarcks Barrier and its eastern bastions confined the activities of Admiral Halsey's South Pacific Force to the lower Solomon Islands. Too long had that Barrier and its southern bastions prevented General MacArthur from commencing his return to the Philippines. But the operations to break the Barrier's outer bastions and penetrate its weirlike center were difficult and complicated. Including the struggle for Guadalcanal, which was the subject of our last volume, they extended over a period of twenty-one months, from 1 August 1942 to 1 May 1944. They were conducted under two separate commands, General Mac-Arthur's and Admiral Halsey's. They included every sort of fighting that occurred anywhere in World War II: naval battles such as Kula Gulf, Kolombangara, Vella Gulf, Empress Augusta Bay and Cape St. George; land fighting in the equatorial jungle at Buna, Cape Gloucester, Munda and the Bougainville Perimeter; strategic bombing; air-surface actions, including the Battle of the Bismarck Sea; almost daily air *vs.* ship, air *vs.* ground troops and air *vs.* air actions; brief but bloody brawls between barges and motor torpedo boats; and some of the most important amphibious operations in the Pacific War.

All these were Allied operations. Although the United States contributed the major part of every arm employed, a large part of the ground and air forces and a respectable component of the naval forces under General MacArthur were Australian. New Zealand contributed ships, planes and ground troops to the South Pacific forces under Admiral Halsey; the Royal Netherlands Navy and merchant marine also took part in the operations around New Guinea. Moreover, most of the operations in this theater were not only Combined (performed by the forces of more than one nation) but Joint (performed by more than one branch of the armed forces). The Bismarcks Barrier was eventually broken through close coöperation between units of the Fleet (surface, submarine, and air), ground forces (Army and Marine Corps) each with its own air component, and the semi-independent V Army Air Force. Thus it would distort history to confine this narrative to the work of the United States Navy alone. To show what that Navy accomplished is, to be sure, the main purpose of this book; but, in the spirit of unification, I have attempted to describe the part played by each element of the Armed Forces in its proper proportion. If I have described the ground operations in New Guinea, Bougainville and New Georgia in less detail than many readers would wish, I have also, for the same reasons of space, sacrificed many interesting small-craft actions and naval air battles.

I began the preparation for this volume in the spring of 1943 by gathering information at Admiral Halsey's headquarters at Nouméa, Vice Admiral Fitch's headquarters at Espiritu Santo, and at Guadalcanal. Next I visited the headquarters of Vice Admiral Carpender and of General MacArthur at Brisbane, spent several days at Port Moresby and at Milne Bay, and rode around the coast of Papua as far as Morobe in those enterprising but uncomfortable craft, the motor torpedo boats. During the summer of 1943 I participated in the Central Solomons campaign under Rear Admiral Ainsworth. Later that year Lieutenant Henry Salomon USNR of my staff visited Torokina, Brisbane and Manus collecting information. As early as July 1944 I began writing the narrative of Parts III and IV, and this draft, completed that year, was read by my friend the late Vice Admiral Wilkinson, to whom this volume is dedicated. With Mrs. Morison and Mr. Pineau, I visited Tokyo in 1950 in search of more material from Japanese sources. We were graciously received by General of the Army Douglas MacArthur and the Chief of his Military Intelligence Section, Major General Charles A. Willoughby. We discussed Japanese naval strategy and operations with several past members of the Imperial Japanese Navy and acquired much additional information from them, from General MacArthur's files and from the chief historian under General Willoughby, Dr. Gordon W. Prange, on the operations covered by this volume.

Of my assistants in preparing this volume, Commander James C. Shaw, who relieved Mr. Salomon in September 1947, has been the most important. He participated in the carrier strikes on Rabaul, as I did in the earlier runs "up the Slot," and he did much of the basic research for Parts I and II, as did Mr. Salomon for Chapters XXV and XXVI. Mr. Roger Pineau translated important Japanese documents and did basic research on the Japanese side of every operation. Mr. Richard S. Pattee, one of my students in naval history at Harvard University, did the basic research on submarine operations. Mr. Donald Martin prepared the task organizations and performed other bits of research. Miss Antha E. Card did a good part of the typing and, with her flair for *le mot juste*, improved the manuscript, as did Miss Elizabeth Humphreys of the staff of Little, Brown and Company. Many United States Army, Navy and Marine Corps officers, and several Australian and New Zealand naval officers, supplemented the records by oral evidence in answers to my questions. My wife, Priscilla Barton Morison (who joined the staff, as it were, in December 1949) entered into the spirit of the thing with great verve and by her tact and charm has helped me to surmount the obstacles that are constantly arising in a work of this nature.

The charts are mostly the work of Miss Isabel J. Gatzenmeier of the cartographical section of the Naval War College, Newport, which is under the direction of Mr. Charles H. Ward. Mr. Charles H. Fitzsimmons, the Archivist, and Mrs. Emily C. Heffernan, the Librarian, of the War College have been most helpful. As always we have enjoyed the support and encouragement of Rear Admiral John B. Heffernan, Director of Naval History, and his efficient staff. To the Honorable Francis P. Matthews, Secretary of the Navy; to Admiral Forrest P. Sherman, Chief of Naval Operations, and to his Deputy Chief for Administration, Rear Admiral Charles Wellborn Jr.; to Rear Admiral Felix L. Johnson, Director of Naval Intelligence; and to Vice Admiral Donald B. Beary, President of the Naval War College, I am indebted for the aid and facilities that have enabled me to carry this volume to completion.

Again I wish to assure the reading public, whose reception of these volumes has encouraged everyone concerned in preparing them, that this is not an official history in the ordinary sense of that term, but "Morison's history." Nobody in the Navy has even suggested that I cover up blunders or play down errors. But, knowing as I do from personal experience how great a part luck plays in naval warfare, and how easy it is for the most gifted officer to make a mistake when required to make an instant decision in the stress of battle, I am probably more charitable toward such mistakes than are many writers who never get their feet wet.

SAMUEL E. MORISON

HARVARD UNIVERSITY
*29 June 1950*

During the three years since the first edition of this volume appeared, many readers have sent in corrections and emendations. Captain John W. McElroy USNR of the Naval History Division has checked all such data, and those found to be errata have been duly corrected in this present edition.

NORTHEAST HARBOR, MAINE
*September 1953*

# Contents

Preface                                                                  ix

Abbreviations                                                         xxvii

## PART I

## THE PAPUAN CAMPAIGN

I   Strategic Planning in 1943                                          3
    1. Casablanca and the Pacific, January 1943     3
    2. "Trident" and "Quadrant," May–August 1943    7
    3. United States Planning in the Pacific        9
    4. The Japanese Command and Planning System    15
    5. Japan's "New Operational Policy" of September    22

II   Holding Papua, *May–September 1942*                               27
    1. Lay of the Land                             27
    2. "MacArthur's Navy"                          30
    3. Kokoda Trail and Milne Bay, 18 July–17 September    33

III   Naval Aspects of the Buna-Gona Campaign, *September 1942–January 1943*    41
    1. Lining Up                                   41
    2. "Toughest Fighting in the World"            45

IV   Papuan Pause, *February 1943*                                     51

V   The Battle of the Bismarck Sea, *2–5 March 1943*                   54
    1. Into the Jaws of the B–25s                  54
    2. The PTs Mop Up                              60

VI   Southwest Pacific Submarines, *8 February 1943–*
     *1 May 1944*                                        66
     1. Patrols from Brisbane                            66
     2. Patrols from Fremantle                           75


                         *PART II*

THE CENTRAL SOLOMONS AND HUON GULF CAMPAIGNS

VII  Preparing an Offensive, *February–May 1943*        89
     1. Planes, Plans and Prospects                     89
     2. Russell Islands Occupied                        97
     3. Mainyard and Button                             100
     4. Interim Actions                                 106
        *a.* "Tip" Bags Two "Bastards." *b.* Mining Of-
        fensives


VIII Yamamoto's Last Offensive, *April–May 1943*        117
     1. The "I" Operation                               117
        *a.* In the Solomons. *b.* In New Guinea
     2. Death of a Fleet Admiral, 18 April 1943         128

IX   MacArthur Moves Forward, *22 June–6 July 1943*     130

X    The Invasion of New Georgia, *21 June–5 July 1943* 138
     1. Plans and Preliminaries                         138
     2. Task Organization                               144
     3. "Musket-He-Fire-Up," 30 June                    146
     4. Squaring Away for Munda, 1–5 July               153

XI   The Battles of Kula Gulf and Kolombangara,
     *5–16 July 1943*                                   160
     1. The Battle of Kula Gulf                         160
     2. Jungle Interlude, 6–12 July                     175

Contents                                                           xvii

3. The Battle of Kolombangara, 12–13 July              180
4. Rescue Mission for *Helena*, 6–17 July              191
5. Conclusion to Kula Gulf and Kolombangara            194

XII   Conclusion of the New Georgia Campaign, *13 July–
      20 September 1943*                               198
      1. The Siege of Munda, 13 July–5 August          198
      2. Air-Surface Actions, 17 July–3 August         206
      3. Motor Torpedo Boat Actions, 23 July–2 August  209
      4. The Battle of Vella Gulf, 6–7 August          212
      5. Mopping Up After Munda, 6 August–20 Sep-
         tember                                        222

XIII  Vella Lavella, *15 August–7 October 1943*        225
      1. Leapfrog to Barakoma, 15 August               225
      2. Securing the Island, August–September         233
      3. The Blockade of Kolombangara, 25 August–
         3 October                                     239
      4. The Battle of Vella Lavella, 6–7 October      243

XIV   Lae and Salamaua, *16 June–15 September 1943*    254
      1. Vitiaz and Dampier: the Vital Straits         254
      2. Lae Punched Out, 4–15 September               261

XV    Finschhafen and Beyond, *16 September–20 October
      1943*                                            269
      1. Finschhafen Falls, 2 October                  269
      2. Tucking in the Pennants, 1–20 October         271

                    *PART III*

          *THE BOUGAINVILLE CAMPAIGN*

XVI   The Seizure of Empress Augusta Bay, *12 October–
      2 November 1943*                                 279
      1. Bougainville in Pacific Strategy              279

2. Forces and Preparation, 12 October–2 November 288

3. Treasuries and Choiseul, 27 October–6 November 293

4. Cape Torokina Landing, 1 November 296

XVII The Battle of Empress Augusta Bay, *2 November 1943* 305

XVIII Carrier Strikes on Rabaul, *5–18 November 1943* 323
1. Action of 5 November 323
2. Action of 11 November 330

XIX Securing the Beachhead, *2–13 November 1943* 337
1. LSTs and Second Echelon, 2–7 November 337
2. Counter-landing and Koromokina, 7–8 November 341
3. Three "Air Battles of Bougainville," 8–13 November 342
4. Beachhead Secured 347

XX Busy Thanksgiving, *15–25 November 1943* 350
1. Activities in and around the Perimeter 350
2. The Battle of Cape St. George, 25 November 352

XXI Perimeter Defense and Development, *26 November– 27 December 1943* 360

PART IV

*RINGS AROUND RABAUL*

XXII Moving Into New Britain, *December 1943–January 1944* 369
1. Problem, Objective and Strategy 369
2. Arawe 373

Contents                                              xix

    3. Cape Gloucester                                   378
    4. Saidor and Sio                                    389

XXIII  Airsols' Assault on Rabaul, *17 December 1943–*
     *1 May 1944*                                   392
    1. "Festung Rabaul"                                  392
    2. New Year's Intensification                        398
    3. February Payoff                                   402
    4. Rabaul Reduced to Impotence                       405

XXIV  Northabout, *25 December 1943–20 March 1944*     410
    1. Holiday Express                                   410
    2. Occupation of the Green Islands, 10 January–
     15 February                                    412
    3. Destroyer Raids, 17–29 February                   419
    4. Occupation of Emirau, 20 March                    423

XXV  The Battle of the Perimeter, *January–March 1944*  425

XXVI  Admiralties Annexed, *29 February–1 May 1944*     432
    1. "Reconnaissance in Force"                         432
    2. Momote and Los Negros                             437
    3. Seeadler and Manus                                444

    Index                                                449

# List of Illustrations

*(Illustrations appear between pages 194 and 195)*

Rear Admiral Theodore S. Wilkinson USN          *Frontispiece*

Casablanca Conference, January 1943

Cincpac-Cincpoa Headquarters, Makalapa, Pearl Harbor

New Guinea Prizes:
Port Moresby
Milne Bay

Buna-Gona Campaign:
Lieutenant General Robert L. Eichelberger and staff
members at Buna
Native stretcher-bearers

Battle of the Bismarck Sea: Japanese destroyer under attack

Action off Vila, 6 March 1943:
Radarscope (U.S.S. *Denver*) showing situation at 0110
U.S.S. *Denver*

Guadalcanal, 1943:
Air raid
LSTs loading

Commanders in Chief Combined Fleet:
Admiral Mineichi Koga
Admiral Yamamoto: the Admiral is saluting pilots at
Rabaul about to embark on "I" operation, 11 April
1943. Vice Admiral Kusaka is on his left

Bombardment Targets:
Munda Point under air attack — looking west
Vila airfield, Kolombangara

Fighting Ships:
U.S.S. *Nicholas* firing at Vila, 12 May 1943
U.S.S. *O'Bannon*

Rear Admiral Daniel E. Barbey USN

Landings in the Southwest Pacific:
LCT at Kiriwina
PT and LCVP at Nassau Bay

Landings in the Central Solomons:
Rendova. Plane over beach is a P-40
Viru Harbor

Amphibious Supply:
LSTs approaching Rendova
LCIs unloading at Rendova

Battle of Kula Gulf:
U.S.S. *Helena* firing her last salvo
*Helena*'s bow floating next morning

After Battle:
Swabbing out the guns – U.S.S. *Honolulu*
Transferring U.S.S. *Strong* survivors from U.S.S. *Nicholas* to U.S.S. *Honolulu*

Battle of Kolombangara: U.S.S. *Honolulu* with damaged bow

Three Cruiser Commanders Relax: Merrill, Hayler and Ainsworth

U.S.S. *Selfridge* and U.S.S. *O'Bannon* after Battle of Vella Lavella

Bougainville Landings:
Torokina, looking north
Marines disembarking from transport

Barge Warfare, New Guinea:
Wrecked Japanese barge
PT sailors

Lae:
   Airfield, wrecked Japanese planes
   *LCI 339* damaged by bomb

Rear Admiral A. Stanton Merrill USN

Japanese Ships at Rabaul under Attack, 5 November 1943

Navy Planes:
   Liberator
   Hellcat
   Corsair
   Avenger

Destroyer Skippers:
   Captain Arleigh A. Burke
   Commander Frederick Moosbrugger

Jungle Mud:
   Bougainville
   Cape Gloucester

Rear Admiral Frederick C. Sherman USN, on flag bridge of
   U.S.S. *Saratoga*

Kavieng Raiders:
   U.S.S. *Bunker Hill*
   Saluting the dead with S-Turns in Ironbottom Sound

Beyond the Barrier:
   General MacArthur and Admiral Kinkaid
   Troopers going ashore

   *(All photographs not otherwise described are Official*
   *United States Navy )*

# List of Charts

Southwest Pacific Area   14

Eastern New Guinea and New Britain   29

Milne Bay, New Guinea   35

Buna-Gona-Sanananda Campaign, 19 November 1942–
22 January 1943   44

Battle of the Bismarck Sea, 2–4 March 1943   57

Solomon Islands Bases, 1 June 1943   91

Sinking of *Murasame* and *Minegumo* and Bombardment of
Vila, 6 March 1943   109

Minelaying in Blackett Strait, 7 May 1943   113

The Papuan Peninsula   135

New Georgia Landings, 30 June–1 July 1943   143

Battle of Kula Gulf, Main Action, 6 July 1943   164–165

Battle of Kula Gulf, *Nicholas* and *Radford*   173

Battle of Kolombangara, 12–13 July 1943   185

The New Georgia Campaign, 2 July–4 August 1943   201

Battle of Vella Gulf, 6–7 August 1943   217

Destroyers off Horaniu, 18 August 1943   235

Evacuation of Kolombangara and Vella Lavella   240

Battle of Vella Lavella, 6–7 October 1943   249

Lae, Finschhafen, Salamaua, September 1943   264

Bougainville and Adjacent Islands   285

Treasury Islands Landings, 27 October 1943 294

Bougainville Island Panorama 298–299

Cape Torokina Landings, 1 November 1943 301

Battle of Empress Augusta Bay, 2 November 1943: the Approach 309

Battle of Empress Augusta Bay: Hitting the Northern Flank 311

Battle of Empress Augusta Bay: Engaging the Main Body 314

Battle of Empress Augusta Bay: the Destroyer Chase 316

Battle of Cape St. George, First Phase 355

Battle of Cape St. George, 25 November 1943 357

Torokina Perimeter Expansion, 6 November–23 December 1943 361

The Bismarck Archipelago 371'

Taking Cape Gloucester, 26 December 1944 380

Fortress Rabaul 393

Green Islands Landings, 15 February 1944 417

Actions in the Admiralties, 29 February–30 March 1944 439

General Chart of the Pacific *Opposite* 448

# Abbreviations

Officers' ranks and bluejackets' ratings are those contemporaneous with the event. Officers and men named will be presumed to be of the United States Navy unless it is otherwise stated; officers of the Naval Reserve are designated USNR. Other service abbreviations are RAAF, Royal Australian Air Force; RAN, Royal Australian Navy; RN, Royal Navy; RNZAF, Royal New Zealand Air Force; RNZN, Royal New Zealand Navy; USA, United States Army; USMC, United States Marine Corps; USMCR, Reserve of same.

Other abbreviations used in this volume: —

A.A.F. — United States Army Air Force
Airsols — Air Solomons Command
AKA — Attack Cargo Ship; APA — Attack Transport
APc — Small Coastal Transport; APD — Destroyer-transport
ATIS — Allied Translator and Interpreter Section
Bu — as prefix means a Bureau of the Navy Department
CA — Heavy Cruiser; CL — Light Cruiser
C.I.C. — Combat Information Center
Cincpac-Cincpoa — Commander in Chief Pacific Fleet and Pacific Ocean Areas
C.N.O. — Chief of Naval Operations
C.O. — Commanding Officer
Com — as prefix means Commander. Examples: Comairsopac — Commander Aircraft South Pacific; Comcrudiv — Commander Cruiser Division
CTF — Commander Task Force; CTG — Commander Task Group
CV — Aircraft Carrier; CVL — Light Carrier; CVE — Escort Carrier
DD — Destroyer; DE — Destroyer Escort; DMS — Destroyer Minesweeper
div — as suffix means Division; Desdiv — Destroyer Division
H.M.A.S.; H.M.N.Z.S. — His Majesty's Australian *or* New Zealand Ship
IFF — Identification, Friend or Foe (a radio device)
*Inter. Jap. Off.* — USSBS *Interrogations of Japanese Officials* (1946)
JANAC — Joint Army-Navy Assessment Committee *Japanese Naval and Merchant Shipping Losses World War II* (1947)
J.C.S. — Joint Chiefs of Staff
Jicpoa — Joint Intelligence Center Pacific Ocean Areas

K.P.M. — A Dutch steamship company

LC — Landing Craft; LCI — Landing Craft, Infantry; LCM — Landing Craft, Mechanized; LCT — Landing Craft, Tank; LCVP — Landing Craft, Vehicles and Personnel; LSD — Landing Ship, Dock; LST — Landing Ship, Tank; LVT — Landing Vehicle Tracked (Amphtrac)

O.N.I. — Office of Naval Intelligence

O.T.C. — Officer in Tactical Command

PC — Patrol Craft; PT — Motor Torpedo Boat

RCT — Regimental Combat Team

SC — Submarine Chaser

S.O.P.A. — Senior Officer Present Afloat (or Ashore)

ron — as suffix means Squadron; Desron — Destroyer Squadron

Sopac — South Pacific; SWPac — Southwest Pacific

TBS (Talk Between Ships) — Voice radio

USSBS — United States Strategic Bombing Survey

VB — Bomber Squadron; VF — Fighter Squadron; VT — Torpedo-bomber Squadron. M is inserted for Marine Corps Squadron

WDC — Washington Document Center document, now in National Archives

YMS — Motor Minesweeper; YP — Patrol Vessel


Aircraft designations (numerals in parentheses indicate number of engines)


## United States

A–20 — Boston, Army (2) light bomber; A–29 — Hudson, Army (2) light bomber

B–17 — Flying Fortress, Army (4) heavy bomber; B–24 — Liberator, Army (4) heavy bomber (called PB4Y by Navy)

B–25 — Mitchell, Army (2) medium bomber; B–26 — Marauder, Army (2) medium bomber

Black Cat — PBY equipped for night work

C–47 — Skytrain, Army (2) transport

Dumbo — PBY equipped for rescue work

F4F — Wildcat; F4U — Corsair; F6F — Hellcat; all Navy (1) fighters

P–38 — Lightning, Army (2) fighter; P–39 — Airacobra; P–40 — Warhawk, Army (1) fighters

PBY — Catalina, Navy (2) seaplane; PBY–5A — amphibian

PV–1 — Ventura, Navy (2) medium bomber

SBD — Dauntless, Navy (1) dive-bomber

SB2C — Helldiver, Navy (1) dive-bomber

TBF — Avenger, Navy (1) torpedo-bomber

## Japanese

"Betty" — Mitsubishi Zero–1, Navy (2) medium bomber

"Emily" — Kawanishi Zero–2, Navy (4) patrol bomber (flying boat)

"Helen" — Nakajima, Navy (2) medium bomber

"Judy" — Aichi, Navy (1) torpedo-bomber

"Kate" — Nakajima 97–2, Navy (1) high-level or torpedo-bomber

"Pete" — Sasebo, Zero–0, Navy (1) float plane

"Sally" — Mitsubishi 97, Army (2) medium bomber

"Tojo" — Nakajima, Army (1) fighter

"Val" — Aichi 99–1, Navy (1) dive-bomber

"Zeke" — Mitsubishi Zero–3, Navy (1) fighter (called "Zero" in 1942–43)

## PART 1

# The Papuan Campaign

*East Longitude dates; Zone minus 10 time in the Southwest Pacific. West Longitude dates in Europe and the United States.*

CHAPTER I

# Strategic Planning in 1943[1]

## 1. *Casablanca and the Pacific, January 1943*

WHEN the Pacific war entered its offensive phase, the strategic planning that went on in the Joint Chiefs of Staff at Washington and the Combined (United States and British) Chiefs of Staff at their several conferences became very important. In 1942 Allied plans in the Pacific, if not improvised to meet particular Japanese offensives, resembled those elaborate football plays that are broken up by a strong opponent as soon as the ball is passed. But after the Allies had won their first success in the Old World — Operation "Torch" for the seizure of French North Africa — and after the Japanese spearhead had been blunted at Midway and broken at Guadalcanal, it was time to make long-range plans for victory in every theater of the war. The insistent questions were, "Where do we go from here?" and "How are we going to do it?"

The fundamental Allied strategic concept of World War II — beat the European Axis first — was never seriously challenged in these discussions, although it was severely strained by the British disposition to delay the "second front" in Europe. The President believed in it, the Joint Chiefs of Staff — Admiral Leahy, Admiral King, General Marshall and General Henry H. Arnold — believed in it; most of the lower echelons believed in it. General MacArthur, Chiang Kai-shek, and a number of flag officers in the United States Pacific Fleet, felt that it was a mistake. Certain newspapers and

[1] This chapter is based almost entirely on the records of the Joint Chiefs of Staff, and on conversations with American leaders from President Roosevelt down; other details are from General Marshall's printed *Reports* and from the papers of Harry Hopkins as printed in R. E. Sherwood *Roosevelt and Hopkins* (1948).

civilians put pressure on the Administration to reverse the decision, leave England and Russia to their fate, and throw everything America had into defeating Japan. Although there was never any real danger of so radical a reversal, the possibility that we might do it was a useful deterrent to the Anglo-Russian desire to have America apply her complete military power and resources in areas especially vital to them. The real danger was that the Nimitz and MacArthur commands would be given insufficient men, ships, planes and matériel to hold the initiative in the Pacific.

The first opportunity to thresh this matter out came at the Casablanca Conference in January 1943, attended by Roosevelt, Churchill, the Combined Chiefs of Staff and a host of staff officers and planners. Here the Chiefs of Staff had ample opportunity for discussion, while the planning committees argued about the needs of their respective strategic areas. The British Chiefs, who had ignored the Pacific when England was in danger, now learned for the first time how much America had accomplished with slender means, and how imperative it was to follow up Midway and Guadalcanal offensively.

In mid-December Admiral King had caused a rough estimate to be made of the percentage of the total war effort (men, ships, planes and munitions) of all the Allies, including Russia and China, then employed in the Pacific. He reached the surprising conclusion that only 15 per cent of the total Allied resources then engaged were employed in the whole of the Pacific, including the Indian Ocean, Burma and China. European and African theaters, the Battle of the Atlantic and the British build-up were getting the remaining 85 per cent.[2] At the Casablanca Conference King and Marshall brought these figures forward, insisting that the imbalance might be fatal. They agreed that Germany was the Number One enemy and renounced any expectation of defeating Japan before Germany was eliminated; but they said bluntly that unless the United States

---

[2] I have been unable to find on what basis this report was calculated; it must have been a very rough approximation; but nobody at Casablanca appears to have challenged it.

could retain the initiative against Japan, a situation might arise which would necessitate her withdrawing from commitments in the European theater. King and Marshall felt very strongly that our initial successes against Japan must be followed up promptly: that Japan must be given no opportunity to consolidate her gains and launch a fresh offensive against positions of her choice, while United States forces remained static. They insisted that the percentage of total forces deployed in the Pacific must be raised to at least 30 per cent.

The British Chiefs of Staff agreed, in principle, and the argument then shifted to ways and means. On this crucial point it appeared that one difference of opinion between the Allies which had existed since the beginning of the war was still acute. The Americans wanted the cross-channel offensive, for which they had been building up forces in Britain for a year past, to take place in 1943. The British, on the contrary, preferred "an all-out Mediterranean effort" in 1943, coupled with an intensification of strategic bombing of Germany, which the aviators, with their usual optimism, believed capable of breaking down German morale. If and when that much-desired state of things was attained, the British wished to be able to throw an invasion force across the English Channel at short notice; otherwise they believed that no major invasion of France could be mounted until 1944. General Marshall said that he was opposed to immobilizing a large force in the United Kingdom for 18 months; the United States could better apply her strength to the Pacific.

President Roosevelt, in a meeting of the Combined Chiefs which he attended, expressed regret that so little attention had been paid by the Chiefs of Staff to China. He also observed that the island-hopping strategy that we had hitherto pursued against Japan would take too long, "that some other method of striking at Japan must be found," and that he believed the attrition of Japanese shipping was one of our best means for victory. He observed that our submarines had disposed of one million tons of Japanese shipping — about one sixth of their merchant marine — during the first year of the war, that submarine warfare could and would be intensified, and that it should be supplemented by planes operating from Chinese airfields against shipping on the Japan and East China Seas. Roosevelt was a good prophet as to the submarines, but the Army Air Force in China never developed much skill at hitting merchant ships. Churchill left the Pacific war alone, and made it clear that he was mainly interested in the Mediterranean and the Axis "underbelly."

Casablanca concluded in a strategic bargain. The Americans abandoned their opposition to Mediterranean operations in 1943 and accepted the postponement of the Normandy invasion to 1944, knowing that this would release forces for a Pacific offensive. Nothing was said about percentages; but it seems to have been understood that new naval construction of types not wanted in the Mediterranean should go to the Pacific.

As outlined in the Combined Chiefs of Staff Report to the President and Prime Minister on 23 January 1943, which both accepted, the following operations in the Pacific were contemplated for 1943, in addition to the usual maintenance of lines of communication, protection of the British antipodes and submarine attrition of Japanese sea power: —

1. To continue Operation "Watchtower" up from Guadalcanal and New Guinea until Rabaul was taken and the Bismarcks Barrier broken.

2. To advance westward towards Truk and Guam.

3. To make the Aleutians as secure as possible.

4. To advance along the New Guinea-Mindanao axis as far as Timor.

5. To recapture Burma, in order to help China, by (*a*) amphibious assaults on the Ramree Islands and Akyab (whence one road led to Mandalay); (*b*) invasion of North Burma by British and Chinese ground forces to open a land route to China and prepare for (*c*) Operation "Anakim," the all-out offensive to reopen the Burma Road and occupy all Burma.

Of these operations, 1 and the beginning of 4 are the subjects of the present volume, 2 and 3 of Volume VII that follows. Number 5(*a*) was abortive, 5(*b*) not undertaken until 1944, and "Anakim," the most kicked-around operation in the war, never came off. The C.C.S. later agreed, in May 1943, that the Joint Chiefs of Staff should settle the details of Pacific operations in accordance with the changing situation and available material, and should not be subject to interference by the Combined Chiefs as to how far a given push should go. Any change of plans that required new allocation of fighting power had to go to the Combined Chiefs for approval; but as long as the United States kept her commitments in Europe and Africa, which she did, the British would not object to the J.C.S. running the Pacific war as they thought best.

## 2. *"Trident" and "Quadrant," May–August 1943*

After the Casablanca Conference adjourned on 23 January 1943, the problem of detailed strategic planning in the Pacific was thrown back to Washington. In response to a suggestion by General MacArthur, the J.C.S. called in March a "Pacific Military Conference" of which some of the most important members were Generals Sutherland and Kenney representing MacArthur, Admiral Spruance and Captain Forrest P. Sherman representing Nimitz, General Harmon and Captain Miles Browning representing Halsey. A J.C.S. Directive of 28 March, issued as a result of this conference, became the basis of a "Strategic Plan for the Defeat of Japan," which was presented to the "Trident" conference of the Combined Chiefs of Staff at Washington in May 1943, there somewhat revised, and approved by Roosevelt and Churchill.

The Plan of May, pointing toward China, differed in several important respects from the one subsequently followed. As soon as the Bismarcks Barrier was broken and the Burma bridgehead secured, massive forces under MacArthur's command would roll over the back of the New Guinea bird into the Celebes, Sulu and

South China Seas, while the Royal Navy recaptured the Malacca Strait and Singapore. From China, the strategic bombing of Japan would be increased, as of Germany from Britain. The two sea powers would reoccupy Hong Kong and develop it as a military base for the final assault on Japan.

This grandiose plan depended upon British coöperation to take Burma and open the Malacca Strait, and on Chinese coöperation to recover Hong Kong and protect General Chennault's airfields. Neither came forth. As early as the "Quadrant" conference of the Combined Chiefs of Staff at Quebec in August 1943, the British gave notice that there would be no Burma operation until 1944, if then; and in the late spring of that year the Japanese Army began capturing Chinese air bases, one by one. British absorption in the Mediterranean, the weakness and unreliability of Chiang Kai-shek's government, the difficulty of operating a navy in the South China Sea while Japan held the Philippines, and positive factors such as the brilliant success of American amphibious technique and of the fast carrier forces, wrought a complete change of plans in 1944, after the Bismarcks Barrier had been broken and the Marshalls secured. The eventual roads to Tokyo were two in number: Marshalls–Marianas–Iwo Jima and New Guinea–Leyte–Luzon–Okinawa; neither touched China. Burma remained in Japanese hands almost to the close of the war, and no attempt was made to recover the Netherlands East Indies.

All these possibilities seemed very remote during the months after Guadalcanal was secured. In May 1943, while the Combined Chiefs at Washington were charting roads to Tokyo that proved impossible to follow, Halsey was just getting ready to move into the Central Solomons, and MacArthur into the Trobriand Islands. A long, bitter struggle of almost a year lay ahead to breach and break the Bismarcks Barrier.

## 3. *United States Planning in the Pacific*

One of the outstanding achievements of the United States armed forces in the Pacific was the intelligence and perfection of their planning. One would hardly have suspected that, after perusing old "Rainbow 5" and other prewar plans for fighting Japan. But, by the end of 1943, the means at the production end had become so ample, and plans at the other end were so carefully drafted, that the need of fleet and force commanders to face unforeseen contingencies was reduced to a minimum. Planning and training are to naval operations what an architect's blueprints and a foundation are to a building. One needs courage, initiative and common sense to carry out an operation plan, but without a sound plan and trained forces no naval commander could conduct a successful campaign. "Luck," observed Admiral Nimitz, "can be attributed to a well-conceived plan carried out by a well-trained and indoctrinated task group." [3] Allied success in the Pacific owes so much to excellent planning that the reader may wish to know who was responsible and, in brief, how it was done.

At the apex of planning for the Pacific was Admiral King, who, as Cominch sat on the J.C.S., and as C.N.O., on the Combined Chiefs of Staff. His principal planning officer[4] from 1 July 1942 to 11 October 1943 was Rear Admiral Charles M. Cooke, who during the war amply justified his old Annapolis nickname "Savvy." When Cooke became deputy chief of staff to Admiral King in October 1943, his first assistant, Rear Admiral B. H. Bieri, succeeded him; and at that time Captain Edmund W. Burrough became Bieri's assistant. These two — first Cooke and Bieri, then Bieri and Burrough — were the naval members of the committee which did the strategic planning for the Joint Chiefs of Staff. And,

---

[3] Endorsement on Action Report of Bombardment of Shortland Islands, July 1943.
[4] Designated Assistant Chief of Staff (Plans). Rear Admiral R. K. Turner held this position until June 1942, when he left to take charge of the Guadalcanal operation.

as such, the same pair were ex-officio members of the Anglo-American Combined Staff Planners.

One very important planning function that Admiral King kept in his own hands was the allocation of new ship construction to the Atlantic and the Pacific Fleets. This was no small responsibility at a time when every command was clamoring for cruisers, destroyers, minesweepers, transports, cargo ships, beaching craft and landing craft, bombers and fighter planes. Fortunately, the Atlantic Fleet had not much use for *Essex*-class carriers, *Iowa*-class battleships, Avengers or SBDs. Admiral King's headquarters issued monthly a confidential list called *Assignment of Vessels and Aircraft in the Organization of the Sea-going Forces of the U.S. Navy* in which the composition of the two fleets was indicated. New construction was assigned where it would best support the plans which the J.C.S. and C.C.S. had approved.

The concept of a given Pacific operation might originate in Brisbane or Pearl Harbor or Washington. In any case the initial directive had to come from the Joint Chiefs of Staff, within the framework of resolutions previously adopted by the Combined Chiefs. The Joint Chiefs' Directive to MacArthur or Nimitz was generally very brief, ordering him to be prepared to take such-and-such positions by or on a certain date, and informing him how many ships and planes of what types, and how many divisions of ground troops in addition to what he already had, would be put at his disposal.

Admiral Nimitz's Cincpac-Cincpoa [5] staff was admirably organized for planning. It was a truly joint staff, with Army, Navy and Marine Corps officers in every section. The officers at the head of the planning section were Captain Charles H. McMorris until March 1942, Captain Lynde D. McCormick until 14 January 1943, Captain James M. Steele until 9 January 1944, and Rear Admiral Forrest P. Sherman (the deputy chief of staff) for the rest of the war. All four were intelligent, hard-working and conscientious officers, with strength of character and of conviction, who did

[5] Short for "Commander in Chief Pacific Fleet and Pacific Ocean Areas."

not hesitate to stand up to Admiral Nimitz and argue for what they thought was right or practicable.[6]

The changes in this office were not due to any dissatisfaction with the incumbents' performance. Admiral Nimitz believed that any planner (or, for that matter, any naval officer worth his salt) would go stale if tied too long to a desk, and that the staff would suffer without frequent infusions of new blood with combat experience. Moreover, the only way, under Navy rules, for a captain to get promotion to flag rank was to obtain a sea command. Captain McMorris, after serving as commanding officer of *San Francisco* at the Battle of Cape Esperance, was promoted Rear Admiral, won the Battle of the Komandorskis, and in July 1943 returned to Pearl Harbor as Chief of Staff Pacific Fleet.[7] As such he continued to influence planning throughout the war.

Upon receipt of a Joint Chiefs of Staff Directive at Cincpac headquarters, or in anticipation of it, J–2 section got to work on an "Intelligence Book" comprising all available information on the area to be invaded. Reconnaissance planes and submarines were sent out to obtain photographs and hydrographic information; Australians and others with special knowledge were brought to Pearl Harbor. At the same time, J–1 got to work on the basic operation plan. In the course of turning this out, it might well

[6] The organization of Cincpac-Cincpoa staff during the war, with the chief of each section during the greater part of it, was as follows:

J–1 (Plans) under a naval officer (see text).
J–2 (Intelligence) under Brigadier General Joseph J. Twitty usa. There were also British and Australian officers in this section. It worked in close collaboration with the Joint Intelligence Center Pacific Ocean Areas ("Jicpoa") and with Capt. Edwin T. Layton.
J–3 (Operations) under a naval officer, Capt. Walter S. DeLany, Capt. Thomas J. Keliher, Commo. James B. Carter. This section included the important Combat Readiness Division under Capt. Tom B. Hill.
J–4 (Logistics) under Maj. Gen. Edmond H. Leavey usa, working in close collaboration with Service Force Pacific Fleet, Vice Admiral William L. Calhoun.
J–5 (General Administration) under a naval officer, Capt. Lloyd J. Wiltse, Capt. Preston V. Mercer, Commo. Bernard L. ("Count") Austin.

[7] Capt. McCormick obtained command of a battleship, and then of a battleship division; Capt. Steele became C.O. of battleship *Indiana;* Rear Admiral Sherman became Commander U.S. Naval Forces Mediterranean in Jan. 1948 and C.N.O. in Nov. 1949.

appear that a part of the Joint Chiefs' Directive was impracticable. If Admiral Nimitz so believed, the differences were composed by flying a war plans officer to Washington, or by the Cominch or some member of his staff visiting Pearl Harbor. For instance, the original directive for the Gilbert Islands operation included the capture of Nauru Island some 380 miles west of Tarawa. The more that Cincpac's planners learned about Nauru, the less they liked it; but it was not until Admiral King visited Pearl Harbor and was confronted by a scale model of that island produced from contour plans brought from Australia that the Joint Chiefs' Directive was modified and Makin substituted for Nauru.

Much logistics planning, communications planning and other detailed work for lower echelons went on simultaneously with the basic overall plan, even before that had been "frozen." After a number of staff studies on "how to do it" had been prepared and discussed with Admiral Nimitz, he selected what he considered to be the best and issued it to all immediate subordinates who were to take part: to the fleet commander, the amphibious force and corps (ground troops) commanders, the land-based air commander and the staff communications officer, all of whom had previously been consulted if on shore and available. Each was given a copy of the "Intelligence Book" and each prepared plans on his level, allotting suitable parts — such as the employment of landing craft, weather prediction and underwater demolition — to the appropriate subordinates to work out for themselves. Because of time pressure, much detailed planning on such matters as logistics went on simultaneously with that of the overall plan. Throughout there was constant interchange of views among planners, rendered easy by close juxtaposition of Cincpac, Serforpac and Jicpoa headquarters at Makalapa, overlooking Pearl Harbor.[8] These subordinate plans were then coördinated into a workable pattern by J–1, a presentation was practised before Admiral Nimitz and key members of his staff, and the final operation plan was mimeographed and dis-

[8] Until the end of 1943 Amphibious Force maintained separate headquarters at Hospital Point, Pearl Harbor; but their planning officers then joined Cincpac's.

tributed. The entire process was an intellectual feat of high order worked out under great pressure. Cincpac staff could have used a year from the first directive to prepare for an operation, and would have liked six months; but it never had more than four months, and often not even that.

Operations in the South Pacific and Southwest Pacific areas were planned by Admiral Halsey's or General MacArthur's staff, after a joint conference at Brisbane or Nouméa. In Halsey's bailiwick the first opportunity for long-range offensive planning came in January 1943. Halsey's was a small and flexible joint staff, in which a number of members besides the war plans officer, Brigadier General DeWitt Peck usmc, helped with the planning. Rear Admiral Theodore S. Wilkinson, as Deputy Commander South Pacific, sat in on the important conferences and contributed many ideas. Halsey's chief of staff, the keen-edged and irascible Captain Miles Browning, had a finger in every pie. Captain Harry R. Thurber was operations officer from Christmas 1942 and acting chief of staff during Browning's absence in the crucial summer months of 1943. Energetic, sleepless, but always urbane, "Ray" Thurber contributed as much as anyone to South Pacific strategy and planning. He worked out the naval bombardments and mining offensives himself, organized all manner of fleet training, reconnaissance and logistic programs, and did much of the overall planning for the Vella Lavella and Bougainville operations. Halsey praised his "initiative, sound and courageous judgment, outstanding grasp of overall strategy, brilliant solution of operations problems."

Rear Admiral Carney,[9] appointed chief of staff on 26 July 1943, also became a tower of strength to Admiral Halsey. As Carney

---

[9] Robert B. Carney, born California 1895, Naval Academy '16, gunnery officer of *Fanning* when she captured *U-58* in World War I, C.O. of two destroyers, instructor at Naval Academy 1923–25, various duties in battleships to 1928, fleet training to 1930, gunnery officer *Cincinnati* to 1933, C.O. *Buchanan* and *Reid*, 1935–36, Office of Assistant Secretary, 1938–40, "exec." of *California* to Feb. 1941, chief of staff to Rear Admiral Bristol to Sept. 1942 (see Vol. I of this History pp. 85, 217) and C.O. *Denver*. Dep.C.N.O. (logistics) 1946, Admiral and C.inC. U.S. Naval Forces Europe & Med. 1950, C.N.O. 1953–55. Retired 1955.

had previously been commanding officer of cruiser *Denver* in those
waters, he knew them well and understood Halsey's problems.

Rear Admiral Richmond K. Turner, a glutton for work, planned
the amphibious phases of the Central Solomons operations him-

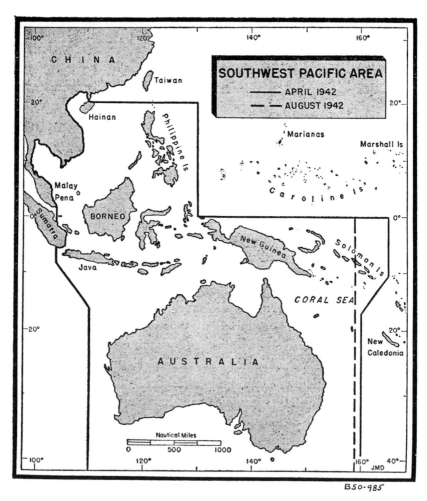

self, tossing out details for his subordinates to fill in. Rear Admiral
Wilkinson took over the III 'Phib from Turner 15 July 1943; his
"leapfrogging" strategy solved the riddle of Rabaul and his fine
hand was seen in the almost faultless landings at Cape Torokina

and Green Islands. A highly intelligent, industrious and conscientious officer, Wilkinson was also an excellent coöperator.

General MacArthur's command received planning directives directly from the Joint Chiefs of Staff via General Marshall just as Nimitz's received his via Admiral King. The Southwest Pacific staff was not a joint but an Army staff. That was natural enough during 1942 and the first half of 1943, in view of the nature of the operations and the few naval units available. Once this command really got moving — and the ground forces depended more and more on Admiral Barbey's VII 'Phib to keep them moving — there was plenty of joint planning between Amphibious Force and Sixth Army. Captain Bern Anderson, Admiral Barbey's chief planner,[10] found General Krueger's staff most coöperative. But, owing to the preoccupation of the Army Air Forces (the only air forces in this area) with strategic bombing, there was lack of coördination between them and the Navy. Fortunately, until the Philippines campaign began, Southwest Pacific operations were neither so prolonged nor so elaborate as to render this rift between air and naval planning a serious obstacle.

# 4. The Japanese Command and Planning System [11]

From the viewpoint of Washington or Pearl Harbor, the Japanese war planners had an enviably simple task in the years 1942 and 1943. In the first place, they had no allies to consider or to support; no Combined Chiefs of Staff to convert to what they wished to do. Germany and Italy were engrossed in their own problems on the other side of the globe and made no demands on Japan except for a little rubber and quinine, to be dispatched by

---

[10] Relieved in Dec. 1943 by Capt. Burton G. Lake. Capt. Anderson then became liaison officer with the Sixth Army.
[11] War Department Special Staff Historical Division translations of "Records on Supreme Command of the Imperial Headquarters," Nov. 1946, and "Southeast Area Naval Operations" Part 3; ATIS "Imperial General Headquarters Navy Staff Section Orders," Doc. No. 14016B; conversations with numerous Japanese officers. 1945-1950.

infrequent blockade runners, or service to U-boats in the Indian Ocean — which was grudgingly rendered. Germany would undoubtedly have welcomed a new front against Russia in Siberia, but Hitler never put pressure on Japan to establish one, so that the Japanese were unhampered by the "second front" propaganda that was constantly needling the Joint Chiefs of Staff. Nor did the Japanese strategic planners have to bother with political considerations. In time of war the military was the actual government of the Empire. No government committees scrutinized Army and Navy expenditures, no members of the Diet toured the Pacific and returned to sound off on naval strategy; no columnists or broadcasters dared try to prod the military into providing good copy; no armchair strategists ventured to express their views. Japan, too, had the advantage of interior lines. All roads from the outer rim of her expanded empire ran to Tokyo, and few of them were subject to attack except by the aggressive submarines of the United States Pacific Fleet. Yet for all that, Japanese planning was not very effective.

The primary reason for the inadequacy rested in the nature of the government. Military and absolutist regimes are undoubtedly well fitted to get the jump on an unsuspecting or unprepared enemy; but the history of modern warfare proves that they cannot win over representative governments in the long run, *provided* the people behind those governments have the heart to sustain initial punishment, and both the will and the resources to fight back. Japan was a military autocracy with a deified Emperor at the top; but the Emperor was a constitutional monarch, a mere figurehead like the little King of Italy, despite the fiction that he really governed. Neither the elder statesmen nor the civilians in the Imperial Cabinet could intervene in matters of higher strategy. The Emperor was given an accurate digest of the news, even if bad; but his most trusted civilian adviser, Marquis Kido, was not allowed to know what was going on or to have a short-wave radio to catch the Allied broadcasts.

The experience of Japan in World War II illustrates a maxim

attributed to Clemenceau: "War is too serious a matter to be left to the generals."

Imperial Headquarters (*Dai Honei*) was the real power in the government. This was the organ most closely corresponding to the American Joint Chiefs of Staff; and if the J.C.S. had conducted the war without reference to President, Congress, press or public opinion, the parallel would be closer. Nevertheless, Imperial Headquarters was not an organic body like the Joint Chiefs of Staff. It was rigidly divided into an Army Branch and a Navy Branch and it was the appropriate Branch, not *Dai Honei*, that issued orders and directives. Occasional deadlocks in our J.C.S. between Army and Navy points of view were indeed embarrassing, and made one of the strongest arguments for unification of the armed forces; but these disagreements were nothing to what went on in Imperial Headquarters. As a former Navy Minister put it, "Within the Imperial General Staff [Headquarters], as far as questions of Army operations are concerned, if the Chief of the Army General Staff says that we will do this, that is the end of it; and so far as the Navy operations are concerned, if the Chief of the Naval General Staff says we will do this, that fixes it; and should there develop difference of opinion between the two chiefs, then nothing can be accomplished." [12] Of course in the end there had to be a compromise because something had to be done; but the delay embarrassed the armed forces.

Thus, the two services were distinct even at the apex of *Dai Honei*. The Army Branch of Imperial Headquarters consisted of the Army Minister (General Tojo), the chief of the Army General Staff (Tojo doubled in this rôle after the beginning of 1943) and his vice chief. The Navy Branch included the Navy Minister (Admiral Shimada), the Chief of the Naval General Staff (Admiral Osami Nagano) [13] and his vice chief. These five or six war lords met twice

---

[12] Admiral M. Yonai in *Inter. Jap. Off.* II p. 328.
[13] Succeeded by Admiral K. Oikawa on 2 Aug. 1944, and by Admiral Soemu Toyoda on 20 May 1945. The Naval General Staff corresponded roughly to the Office of Chief of Naval Operations, U.S. Navy. The Navy Department in Japan was concerned almost wholly with administrative matters.

or thrice weekly in a room of the Imperial Household building (*Kunaisho*) of the Imperial Palace, Tokyo; but the actual decisions were made by each branch, separately. The Emperor attended these discussions only on very important occasions, such as the adoption of the new war plan of September 1943 and the decision to set on foot the "Sho" Operation which led to the Battle for Leyte Gulf. Only once, on the last day of 1942, when he was told of the decision to evacuate Guadalcanal, did the Emperor say anything. He asked General Tojo what he intended to do next? The General answered, "Stop the enemy's westward movement." Admiral Nagano explained that this meant to develop bases on Munda and Kolombangara, from which to inflict heavy damage by air strikes on Allied forces on Guadalcanal. That was the "I" Operation hereinafter described.[14]

Naval war plans were concocted in the Navy Building just outside the moat of the Imperial Palace grounds in Tokyo.[15] Normally plans were drafted by the operational section of the Naval Branch of Imperial Headquarters, with a senior staff officer of the Combined Fleet assisting,[16] and in close liaison with the operational section of the Naval General Staff. Combined Fleet Staff did a good deal of planning too; and if Imperial Headquarters delayed coming to a decision, owing to interservice squabbling, Admiral Yamamoto was apt to bring up a plan of his own — as in the case of Midway. Rear Admiral Sadatoshi Tomioka was chief of the operational section and, as such, head planner for the Japanese Navy from July 1941 to March 1943. His operation plans for the

---

[14] Told us by a former member of the Naval General Staff, who was in the next room when this conversation took place.

In order to obtain full political implementation of strategic decisions, there was a Liaison Council (*Renraku Kaigi,* later called *Senso Shido Kaigi*) between *Dai Honei* and the government, consisting of the members of *Dai Honei* plus the cabinet ministers concerned. The change came under the Koiso Cabinet. Another way of stating it is that the Supreme War Council (see Vol. III p. 20) took over the functions of the Liaison Council.

[15] This building was badly bombed in May 1945 and only a shell remains.

[16] Occasionally C. in C. Combined Fleet visited Tokyo for that purpose, but generally he sent a staff officer because under Japanese naval regulations a fleet commander was responsible for everything that went on under his command and could not delegate responsibility.

first great offensive in December 1941 worked so well that he was kept in the same position after Japan entered the unexpected defensive phase; and, as he ruefully admitted after the war, it is far easier to plan an offensive than a defensive. Admiral Tomioka was a young, highly intelligent and resourceful officer,[17] and Japanese naval planning deteriorated after March 1943 when he was relieved by Captain Chikao Yamamoto.[18] The American system of sending all planning officers to sea at frequent intervals and injecting new blood from the Fleet was not followed in the Japanese Navy, but Combined Fleet staff officers did participate in planning.

If the plan required Army participation, as it generally did, the corresponding section of the Army General Staff was consulted. And at this point there often occurred a deadlock, because General Tojo and other Japanese Army leaders discounted both the strength and the purpose of America. They were much more concerned over the chance that Russia would throw the Red Army against Japan. So firm was this obsession that Japan never molested the passage of Red Flag munitions ships between the American West Coast and Vladivostok during the entire war, lest Stalin be annoyed. Naval members of Imperial Headquarters had to argue for weeks with the Army members before agreement could be reached.

After a draft plan had been accepted by both Navy chiefs and had been discussed in Imperial Headquarters, the Naval Branch issued a directive. Thence the order or directive went to Commander in Chief Combined Fleet. As Admiral Yamamoto (or Koga) had previously been informed of what was going on, and had usually participated in the planning, they were able to issue an operation order without delay. Often, indeed, they had started planning on Combined Fleet and lower echelons while Imperial Headquarters were still wrangling.

[17] Born in 1897. His father, Baron Sadayasu Tomioka, was an admiral in the Russo-Japanese War.
[18] At the end of 1944 Capt. Yamamoto was relieved by Capt. Taro Taguchi and he, in June 1945, by Capt. Ohmae who had been in the planning section under Taguchi and was also liaison naval officer on the Army General Staff.

The great defect in this system was the want of joint planning. Discussions in Imperial Headquarters were not planning, in the ordinary military meaning of the word; and there was no joint planning below the discussions that preceded the issuance of a directive. On the American side, Army or Marine Corps (sometimes both) and Navy were represented on the staff of every commander subordinate to Admiral Nimitz, even in every amphibious group. But in Japan, Army and Navy made detailed plans unbeknownst to each other, unless (as at Rabaul) there happened to be a friendly sailor and soldier in juxtaposition.

In general, it may be said that the Army rather than the Navy controlled Imperial Headquarters. General Tojo, tripling as Premier, War Minister and Chief of Army General Staff, was the decisive figure. It was as if General Marshall had been President of the United States, Secretary of War and Chief of the General Staff at the same time; but the parallel cannot be pushed too far, because Tojo believed the prestige of the Army to be more important than the fate of the Japanese nation. Admiral Shigetaro Shimada had been selected as Navy Minister by the elder statesmen because of his reputed sympathy for the aims of the Army politicos. He followed Tojo so faithfully that Admiral Okada, one of the *Genro*, told him bluntly that he had lost the Navy's respect and should resign; but he hung on as long as Tojo did. Since civilian politicians and industrialists had no voice in the government, there was no effective coöperation from industry. The military chieftains wished public opinion to be uniformly optimistic, and so constantly proclaimed Japanese invincibility, suppressed bad news and deprecated Allied military potential. They were so successful that the hoodwinked citizenry saw no need for supreme effort on the home front. As late as the summer of 1943, American prisoners of war employed in Japanese shipyards observed Japanese laborers loafing on the job because, as they explained, "The war is won." Despite strong military traditions and their loyalty and docility, the Japanese people made no "total war" effort comparable to that of the American or British people.

Another grave defect arose from the excessive respect for rank and position in Japan. The initiation of suggestions about strategic plans, which any officer could venture in the United States, was in Japan the prerogative of Naval General Staff and Commander in Chief Combined Fleet,[19] and anyone who brought unwelcome information or intelligence to the top men was apt to be snubbed.

The following incident will illustrate this. Rear Admiral Yokoyama, the Japanese naval attaché at Washington in 1941, together with his assistant and a naval intelligence officer from the Mexico City legation, were interned at the outbreak of war. In addition to what they already knew, they had ample opportunity to learn more at Hot Springs, where they had full access to the American press. Returning to Japan by the first exchange ship on 15 August 1942, one week after the Guadalcanal operation began, they were received at the dock by an officer of the Naval General Staff, taken directly to headquarters, and not allowed to see anyone or read the papers. The idea was that they should use their fresh knowledge to play the United States team in a war game, with the Naval General Staff representing Japan. Since one of the premises of this game was that Japan had secured Guadalcanal, Admiral Yokoyama, doubling as Cominch and Cincpac, was forced to start his "operation" from no farther forward than Hawaii and Espiritu Santo. Yet, even with that handicap, the game, representing the next two years of the Pacific war, ended with the "Americans" retaking the Philippine Archipelago by 1 October 1944 — a pretty good prophecy. These officers, who so successfully anticipated Nimitz's and MacArthur's moves from the Solomons to Leyte Gulf, were, however, ignored. Nobody wanted their information or their views. We asked one of them if anything was said to his winning team by the Naval General Staff. "Yes," said he, "we were told to keep our mouths shut!"[20]

---

[19] The only operations, as my Japanese informants could recall, which were initiated from lower echelons, were the useless midget submarine attacks and the desperate *Kamikaze* business.

[20] Conversations of Lt. Roger Pineau USNR with the three Japanese officers. Bu⟨; another assured us that this game influenced the production of naval planes, which

By the same token, initiative on the part of junior flag officers was discouraged. During the war we wondered why Rear Admiral Raizo Tanaka, the destroyer squadron commander whose fine combination of sound training and resourcefulness won the Battle of Tassafaronga,[21] had no command after 1942. The reasons were twofold: he frequently pointed out that the poor quality of air coöperation with surface operations was causing unnecessary ship losses; and, as early as 30 August 1942, he declared to Admiral Mikawa, "Guadalcanal should be abandoned as its supply cannot be maintained." Mikawa replied, "The Highest Command have decided on recapturing Guadalcanal";[22] and despite Tanaka's loyal efforts in that direction he was "put on the beach," as we say in the United States Navy, after his prophecy had been proved correct.

## 5. Japan's "New Operational Policy" of September

In an earlier volume we have seen something of Japan's enlarged-perimeter or second-phase war plan of mid-1942.[23] This plan was suspended but not shelved by the Battles of the Coral Sea and Midway in May and June. Troops being assembled at Truk to conquer New Caledonia, Fiji, and Samoa were instead thrown into Papua for the transmontane march on Port Moresby. Guadalcanal airfield was started in order to protect the left flank of New Guinea and later to be springboard for the invasion of Espiritu Santo and New Caledonia. From these decisions, and the Allied decision to thwart them, resulted the Guadalcanal operation described in the last volume, and the Papuan campaign of 1942–43 which we are about to relate. The Naval Branch of Imperial Headquarters wished to write off Guadalcanal after the great naval battle of 12–15

---

did notably speed up after Sept. 1942. The average monthly production, Jan.-Sept. 1942, was 253 planes; for the next 6 months it was 461. By Dec. 1943 it haa passed 1000, below which figure it did not fall until Dec. 1944.

[21] See Vol. V of this History chap. xiii.
[22] Admiral Mikawa's personal diary.
[23] See Vol. IV of this History pp. 4–6, 10.

November, but Tojo and the Army stubbornly clung to the notion that they would capture the island and execute their original plans. It was the irrefutable argument of a steady drain of combat and merchant shipping into the Solomons' sink that caused them to change their minds.

The loss of Guadalcanal reverberated over the Pacific. Imperial Headquarters strengthened Indochina, scaled down a planned offensive in China, shifted air power from the Indian front and Manchuria where the Army wanted to keep it, reinforced western New Guinea and Timor with additional troops. The strategic initiative, which Japanese leaders had always considered essential, and to which they were accustomed in all previous wars, had been lost forever. And basic differences of strategic thinking between Army and Navy, submerged during the days of easy victory, now came out in the open and stalled decision.[24]

There was no dispute, however, about the clean-cut division of responsibility, which had been decided on as early as 18 November 1942, about Rabaul: that the Navy should protect the left or Central Solomons wing, the Army the right or New Guinea wing, of the Bismarcks Barrier.

In April 1943, while Imperial Headquarters were still discussing what to do next, Fleet Admiral Yamamoto was gathered to his ancestors, and the Emperor on the 21st appointed Admiral Mineichi Koga Commander in Chief Combined Fleet. In late May Koga visited Tokyo to discuss high strategy at Imperial Headquarters. A disciple of Yamamoto, Koga insisted that the only chance of Japanese victory lay in winning a decisive action with the United States Pacific Fleet and that this battle must be sought in 1943 to prevent the odds from being overwhelming. Imperial Headquarters were inclined to argue that everything be concentrated on defending this or that strong point, but Koga won them over to Mahan principles and obtained their consent to seek battle when an opening presented itself.

[24] Feeling between Army and Navy was so cool, Foreign Minister Shigemitsu assured the writer, that General Tojo was still ignorant of the score at Midway one month after that battle.

During the summer of 1943 the Allies took the offensive in New Guinea and the Central Solomons; and although, as we shall see, Japan contested every inch of ground and exacted a heavy price in men and ships, she lost her "so far and no farther" lines. Between 1 July and 1 October U.S. submarines sank 286,000 tons of Japanese shipping. There was no hope that Japanese shipyards could replace these losses, and slight prospect that anti-submarine measures could put a stop to them. American carriers romped westward to within a thousand miles of Tokyo. Intelligence reports from overseas indicated that by mid-autumn the Pacific Fleet would include ten fast carriers and as many battleships. All the news from Europe was bad. Italy capitulated and Germany's much-touted summer offensive against Russia turned into a retreat.

Imperial Headquarters sought frantically to divine the next enemy move, and provide against it. Discussion between the Army and Navy members at the bi-weekly meetings became acrimonious and bitter. Tojo, formerly advocate of holding Guadalcanal when holding was hopeless, now proposed to abandon the Bismarcks Barrier and set up a new perimeter running from the Marianas through Truk to Wewak, and to reinforce the Indian Ocean frontier. Thinking as usual in terms of continental warfare, he made the bad guess that the next Allied offensive would come from India.[25] Koga stoutly opposed, insisting that what did happen would happen — and that the Bismarcks Barrier with its outer bastions must be defended to gain time, both for a fleet action and for strengthening the inner perimeter that Tojo desired.

Koga won a reluctant consent of Imperial Headquarters to his point of view, and in late September that august body agreed on what was called the "New Operational Policy." The basic principle was to hold everything and prepare for an offensive in 1944. The agreement was embodied in Imperial Headquarters Army and

[25] Told me by a member of the planning section of the Naval General Staff. Tojo's bad guess was based largely on his expectation that the surrender of Italy would release British forces for the India-Burma front and bring an amphibious offensive in the Indian Ocean.

Navy Branch Directives of 30 September and of the next two months, the gist of which follows: —[26]

Imperial Army and Navy will fight off advancing enemy in southeast area, while building bases for later counteroffensives. Inflict telling counterblows against the attacking enemy and break down their fighting spirit by destroying them beforehand as much as possible.

1. Establish and fortify a new defensive perimeter, Marianas–Truk– Central Solomons–New Guinea–Timor.

2. With Rabaul as a nuclear bastion, stockpile munitions and use Japanese garrisons already posted in the Bismarck Archipelago, Bougainville and the Gilberts and Marshalls, to delay and wear out the expected Allied offensives.

3. Build 17 new airfields in western New Guinea in addition to the seven already under construction or "roughly completed." Particular efforts to be made to hold Dampier Strait and the north coast of New Guinea.

4. Maintain tenaciously the Indian frontier from western Burma through the Andaman and Nicobar Islands to Sumatra.

5. Maintain existing positions in and pressure on China.

6. Endeavor to avoid war with Russia but continue preparations for defense against possible Russian attack.

7. Improve home defenses and increase protection of shipping routes from the Indies.

8. Engage the United States Fleet in decisive action at an opportune moment, preferably when tied down to supporting an amphibious invasion.

9. Prepare to mount a counteroffensive beyond the perimeter, both in the Central and South Pacific, in the spring of 1944.

Number 2 is the most important for us; the present volume and the next tell the story of how it was overcome. Number 3 was realized only in small part, as General MacArthur got there first. The Indian Ocean line (Number 4) long held firm, and was broken only by the Anglo-American Burma campaign of 1944–1945. Little was done about the home front. The opportune moment for

[26] War Department Special Staff Historical Division translation of "Records of Supreme Command of Imperial Headquarters," Nov. 1946 p. 91; and "Southeast Area Operations" (Navy) Part 3 p. 2, supplemented by original file of Imperial Navy Directives at ATIS, translated by Capt. Ohmae. Especially Directives Nos. 280 (30 Sept.), 284 (11 Oct.) and 299 (15 Nov.) 1943.

the fleet action did not arrive until June 1944, after Koga's death, and resulted in a decisive American victory — the Battle of the Philippine Sea. And the opportunity for Number 9 never came.

Thus, as the Japanese themselves said, "The Southeast Area was changed from a crucial battle front to a holding front by decision of Imperial Headquarters." [27]

Such were Japanese strategic plans at the outset of the Bougainville and Finschhafen operations for breaching the Bismarcks Barrier, and of the Gilbert Islands invasion. Imperial Headquarters would soon have ample opportunity to test their holding policy. The story is a mournful one from the Japanese point of view, since it was impossible for the "New Operational Policy" to succeed against an enemy that was daily gathering strength, skill and determination. Yet, what else could the Japanese war lords do, unless they adopted the unthinkable policy of surrender? They might, to be sure, have withdrawn their defensive perimeter, as Tojo proposed, and concentrated on a new line of defense; but the strategy that they did adopt exploited the tenacious quality of the Japanese foot soldier and held up the Allied advance a good six months after 1 September 1943. That, after all, was just twice as long as MacArthur's Army, Hart's Fleet and the whole Abda Command had held up the Japanese offensive at the start of the war. And, if MacArthur and Wilkinson had not adopted the "leapfrogging strategy" of leaving key Japanese garrisons to "wither on the vine," it might have taken a year or more to break the Bismarcks Barrier. It would have been very discouraging for the Allies if, in the autumn of 1944, their armed forces had not yet penetrated the gigantic fishweir centering on Rabaul.

[27] "Southeast Area Operations," Part 3 (Navy), p. 4.

CHAPTER II

# Holding Papua[1]

*May–September 1942*

## 1. Lay of the Land

NEW GUINEA, one of the largest islands in the world, is
shaped like a prehistoric monster, half bird and half reptile.
The head, looking west, appears about to gulp down the Celebes,
while a swish of the tail 1300 miles eastward could hurl New
Britain over the Line. Until 1941 New Guinea had affected mankind's military arrangements no more than the reptile it resembled.
Yet in World War II this island became for the Japanese an in-
surmountable barrier, for the Allies a heaven-sent springboard.

Although discovered by the enterprising Portuguese in the six-
teenth century, New Guinea slumbered on for three hundred years.
In March 1700, Dampier sailed through the strait named after him;
D'Entrecasteaux passed by in 1793 and left a few French names
like the Louisiades, Capes Endaiadère and Sudest, besides the rumor
of sundry reefs that were to bedevil the Allied Navies in 1942. The
Netherlands in 1828 annexed the western half of the island — the
lizard's head and shoulders — but made no attempt to exploit the

[1] General Headquarters Southwest Pacific Area, Military Section General Staff,
Daily Summary of Enemy Intelligence (General MacArthur's G–2 report, prepared under the direction of Brig. Gen. Charles A. Willoughby USA) is the most
complete and informing daily report of any war theater, indispensable for the
history of the MacArthur command. George C. Kenney *General Kenney Reports,
a Personal History of the Pacific War* (1949) is a lively and informing story of
the Air Force in this area, but unreliable as to the damage it inflicted because the
author failed to check his aviators' claims and contemporary Intelligence estimates
with postwar assessments. Files of the Air Force periodical *Impact* are most useful,
as is Albert Harkness "Command History U.S. Naval Forces Southwest Pacific
Area," Office of Naval History. An ATIS translation of an official Japanese summary "Southeast Area Operations" Part 1 (Navy) gives the enemy side.

country or to tame its savage inhabitants. In 1873 Captain John Moresby RN discovered Milne Bay and ensured his promotion by naming places after contemporary Lords of the Admiralty. In general, the east and south coasts were ignored except by an occasional trader or blackbirder who risked (and frequently lost) his head when kidnaping natives to work the Queensland sugar plantations. Germany in 1884–85 annexed the haunch of the New Guinea bird as well as the northern archipelago (New Britain, New Ireland, New Hanover and the Admiralties), adding a new set of names such as Bismarck, Finschhafen and Seeadler. Farsighted Australians, recognizing the strategic threat, had repeatedly warned the British government of foreign encroachment, but it was only after this German move that the British belatedly annexed the lizard's tail and named it the Crown Colony of Papua.[2] Australia in 1919 was awarded a mandate to German New Guinea, which placed the eastern third of this great island under British control. A subsequent discovery of gold deposits in the interior brought a rush of men and machinery to extract "the precious things of the lasting hills," but only a small fraction of the surface was scratched; and by the start of World War II the European and Australian inhabitants numbered only 6000 as against an estimated half-million natives.

These natives, classed as Melanesians although diverse in color, size, language and customs, were completely primitive and highly warlike when the standard of Saint George was first raised over their land. Fortunately an enlightened and sympathetic administrator, Sir Hubert Murray, came upon the scene early enough to protect them from exploitation, and to win their confidence by respecting tribal customs and enrolling their chief men in a local constabulary. All matters concerning the natives were placed under a civil service called "Angau" (Australia-New Guinea Administrative Unit) which afforded a striking example of applying Christian principles and scientific intelligence to a primitive people. Angau

[2] *Papua*, the Malayan word for "wool," with reference to the woolly hair of the natives, was the first name given to New Guinea by the Portuguese. The term Papua is here used for the whole peninsula; but that part of it north of lat. 8° S (just south of Morobe) belongs, politically, to the Territory of New Guinea.

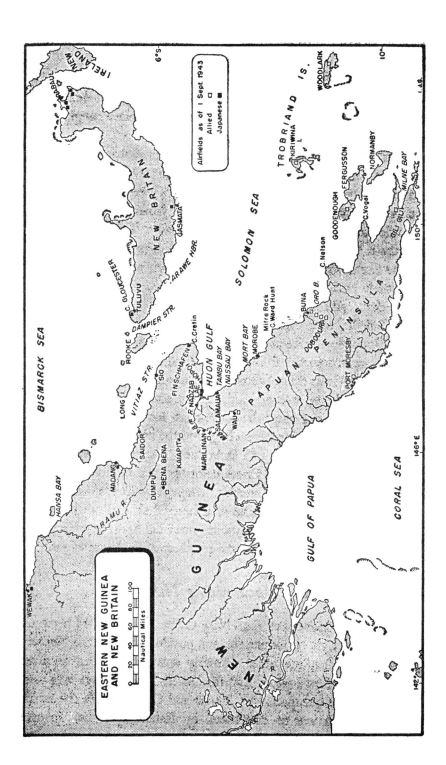

EASTERN NEW GUINEA
AND NEW BRITAIN

Nautical Miles
0  20  40  60  80  100

Airfields as of 1 Sept. 1943
Allied □
Japanese ■

was responsible for the loyalty of these "fuzzy-wuzzies" during the Papuan campaign. They were still primitive and dangerous, but these were valuable qualities in the New Guinea jungle when enlisted against Japanese invaders.

Port Moresby, the colonial capital of Papua, was the strategic key not only to that mountain-spined tail of the New Guinea monster, but to Torres Strait and northern Queensland. The Allies had to keep it as an advanced base; the Japanese had to take it in order to cut the America–Australia lifeline. Their first attempt to take it by an amphibious operation was frustrated at the Battle of the Coral Sea; their second attempt, which we shall now relate, was made both by land and by sea: a march over the mountains from Buna, and a swing around the lizard's tail, via Milne Bay. Both failed. Next came the American counteroffensive against Buna-Gona, first strike at the Bismarcks Barrier, first stage in Mac-Arthur's return to the Philippines. When the tail was secured as far as Huon Gulf, there followed half a year of air warfare while both sides gathered strength for the next struggle.

Note well on our chart the south-coast haven of Port Moresby, the forked tail enclosing Milne Bay, and the north-shore villages of Buna, Lae and Salamaua; and Dobodura. These were the prizes in what should have been an air-sea campaign; for distances by water were short, those by air shorter, whilst land routes were long, tortuous and difficult. Yet the weakness of air and sea power in the Southwest Pacific, coupled with uncertain hydrographic information, forced both sides into the toughest of land campaigns.

## 2. *"MacArthur's Navy"*

In the early months of 1942 New Guinea was pinched between two thrusts by the Japanese, the one pushing through the Netherlands East Indies, the other storming down the Bismarcks after establishing a firm base at Rabaul. Dutch New Guinea was outflanked by the occupation of Timor and Ceram, while the north coast of Papua was so dominated by Rabaul that the Japanese moved into Lae and Salamaua in early March unopposed, closing the Dampier and Vitiaz Straits. Wilson Brown's carrier-plane raid from *Lexington* and *Yorktown* across the Owen Stanley Range on 10 March [3] did some damage but also caused the enemy to reinforce Lae and Salamaua, creating anxiety lest Port Moresby become his next southward objective, as indeed it was.

That was the situation when the remnants of the Abda Fleet straggled into Australian ports. Vice Admiral Herbert F. Leary on 29 March 1942 could write the title Commander Allied Naval Force Southwest Pacific under his name, but of the few ships under his command only the overworked submarines were capable of a proper offensive,[4] and most of the others had to be employed in escort duty, especially after the midget submarine raid on Sydney and sundry sinkings of merchantmen off the Australian Coast. All this was cold comfort for General MacArthur, newly appointed Supreme Commander Southwest Pacific Area, who had to carry out a directive to "hold the key military regions of Australia for bases of future offensives against the Japanese homeland and to check further enemy conquests."

In May 1942, when the Japanese launched their sea attack for Port Moresby, they were stopped by Frank Jack Fletcher's task force built around carriers *Lexington* and *Yorktown*. After this Battle of the Coral Sea,[5] General MacArthur, who is perhaps the most enthusiastic advocate of carrier-based air outside the Navy, wanted at least two carriers turned over to his naval commander; but Nimitz had only three left after Midway to cover the whole Pacific, and the Admiralty refused to release British flattops from the Indian Ocean. In early September MacArthur asked for the old battleships that were milling around the Eastern Pacific, but Nimitz pointed out that there was no work for battleships in the Southwest.

The Guadalcanal campaign, begun of necessity "on a shoestring"

[3] See Volume III of this History pp. 387–89.
[4] Submarine patrols under this command in 1942 have been summarized in Vol. IV pp. 219–30.
[5] See Vol. IV of this History chaps. i–iv.

but protracted beyond anyone's expectation, absorbed most of the troops, supplies and new construction that the United States could spare from North Africa and the desperate anti-submarine campaign in the Atlantic. In worldwide Allied strategy, the Southwest Pacific led the list of "have nots" and "won't gets." On 11 September 1942, when Vice Admiral Arthur S. Carpender relieved Vice Admiral Leary, "MacArthur's Navy" consisted of only 5 cruisers, 8 destroyers, 20 submarines and 7 small craft.

The nature of the north shore of Papua was such that almost the only naval vessels that could profitably be employed there were motor torpedo boats and the new beaching craft – LSTs, LCTs, and LCIs. Of those, the Navy had only prototypes in the fall of 1942, and the new year was well along before even a trickle of the new, strange-looking tank and infantry carriers began coming across the Pacific into MacArthur's bailiwick, for which they were ideally suited. Admiral "Chips" Carpender had the invidious task of convincing the General that destroyers, cruisers and large transports should not be risked in the Solomon Sea. Not only were these waters under constant enemy air surveillance and within easy bombing distance of the Japanese airfields on New Britain; they were miserably charted. No adequate hydrographic survey had ever been made of the north coast of Papua between Milne Bay and Dampier Strait; the Admiralty charts merely threw in a few hypothetical hazards with such preposterous legends as "Reefs seen by D'Entrecasteaux" – in the eighteenth century. As it turned out, there were plenty of reefs that D'Entrecasteaux did *not* see, and it would have been foolish to expose troops to almost certain shipwreck at night, after air bombing by day. So amphibious operations in New Guinea had to wait until three needs were met: a supply of beaching craft, an aërial hydrographic survey, and at least partial control of the air. In the meantime, a number of small craft and steamers, mainly Dutch and Australian, managed to get through; but up to May 1943 every merchant ship of over 2000 tons which ventured around East Cape got bombed, and many were sunk.

## 3. *Kokoda Trail and Milne Bay*
## *18 July–17 September*

General Tojo and Imperial Headquarters strategists were as keen to secure Port Moresby and the whole of Papua as MacArthur was to keep them out. They considered their setback in the Coral Sea to be only temporary. Airfield development continued at Rabaul and elsewhere in New Britain; almost every day Allied planes and installations at Port Moresby were targets of Japanese bombs and bullets. The new Japanese plan now called for a pincer movement on Port Moresby; an overland march across the Owen Stanley Range, synchronized with a swing around the tail staged through Milne Bay. First targets were Buna and nearby villages on the north coast of Papua where the Kokoda Trail to Port Moresby began.

At MacArthur's headquarters it was suspected around 18 July that something of the sort was brewing. Members of his staff figured out that Buna would be the first Japanese target, and urged the General to make dispositions to occupy it first by airborne troops, for there was a small fighter strip nearby; but there were not enough seaplanes available to take in more than one or two hundred men, who would have been a useless sacrifice. So the enemy got to Buna both "fustest and mostest," and dearly it cost both Australia and America to get him out.

On 20 July 1942 the small and elderly light cruisers *Tenryu* and *Tatsuta* with three destroyers escorted a convoy of three transports from Rabaul. After passing through the deep waters of Huon Gulf, they put in at Basabua some eight miles west of Buna. Allied planes set one transport afire but she survived, and Colonel Yosuke Yokoyama's advance force of 1500 troops landed. Next day they marched to Buna, a small mission station and native village. Major General Tomitaro Horii and the main body of troops came in a big convoy on 18 August. By the 22nd, additional convoys gave the Japanese commander about 11,430 men.

By these unopposed landings the Japanese placed themselves in position for a transmontane march to Port Moresby. On the map it looked easy — a mere 100-mile hike and there you were on top of the Papuan capital, ready to grab the three big airdromes that General Kenney was developing. But the Owen Stanley Range is a jagged, precipitous obstacle covered with tropical rain forest up to the pass at 6500-foot elevation, and with moss like a thick wet sponge up to the highest peaks, 13,000 feet above the sea. The Kokoda Trail, suitable for splay-toed Papuan aborigines but a torture to modern soldiers carrying heavy equipment, was selected by the Colonel after a brief reconnaissance. The troops had also to contend with starvation and disease, and with stubborn rear-guard Australians. Day after day for six weeks they inched forward, and on 17 September the advance echelon reached Ioribaiwa, 32 miles from Port Moresby — only 20 air miles to the airdrome.[6] There General Blamey's Australians held fast, and on the 26th they began driving the Japanese back over the trail. The land threat to the Papuan capital and its airfields had collapsed.

One week earlier the seaward prong of the pincer had been stopped.

Milne Bay [7] is a cleft in the New Guinea lizard's tail, running 26 miles up into the land; a beautiful great bight over seven miles wide at the entrance and five miles wide at the head. Mountains clothed with heavy tropical trees march down to the sea for the first fifteen miles, leaving only a narrow strip of land fit for native gardens and coconut plantations; and this part of the bay is exceedingly deep. The head of it, which the Australians call "the frying pan," is

[6] Historical Div. G.H.Q. U.S. Army Forces Pacific *Chronology of the War in the Southwest Pacific 1941–1945.*

[7] Samuel Milner "The Battle of Milne Bay" *Military Review* XXX 18–29 (Apr. 1950); Lt. Col. J. R. Watch of 5th Australian Div. "Sequence of Events, Milne Bay Action, Aug.–Sept. 1942" written Feb. 1943; "Operations in Milne Bay, 24 Aug.–8 Sept. 1942 (Lessons from Operations No. 2)," mimeographed bulletin issued by General Blamey's Brisbane headquarters 18 Oct. 1942; conversations in June 1943 at Gili Gili with Cdr. Geoffrey C. F. Branson RAN (N.O.I.C. Milne Bay) and at Kona Kope with Cdr. Morton C. Mumma, both of whom were present throughout the action, the latter as liaison officer with the Australian Air Force; mimeographed pamphlet procured through the kindness of the Netherlands Embassy in Washington, "The K.P.M. Lines and the War in the Southwest Pacific."

fringed by a wide alluvial plain on which Lever Brothers had planted a big coconut plantation, Gili Gili. Between the plantation and the opposite shore there is anchorage for a large fleet in waters protected from the monsoons. A few miles from Gili Gili on the north side is a small mission station called KB (for *Kristian Brüder*).

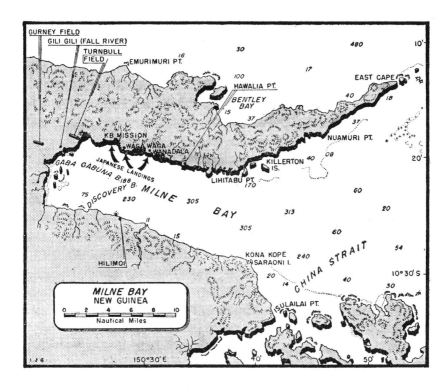

Both natural features and its position relative to New Britain and the Solomons made Milne Bay an ideal airfield site and naval operating base for either side. Whoever held it could prevent the other from nipping around the tail of New Guinea into the Solomon Sea or toward Port Moresby as the case might be; and as a staging point for offensive action it would be valuable despite the presence of millions of anopheles mosquitoes, enemies to all mankind.

Because of the short and protected sea route, MacArthur beat the

Japanese to Milne Bay. In early June 1942 a company of the 46th United States Army Engineers, a company of Australian infantry and an anti-aircraft unit, under the overall command of Colonel Frank L. Burns USA, were sent up in the Australian S.S. *Islander*. Promptly they started work on an airfield for fighter and bomber planes on the Gili Gili plantation. As the Colonel reported: —

> There were no wharves, no ships, and generally things could be described as chaotic. . . . The main problem was that of supplies . . . My first meal at Milne Bay consisted of a cup of tea, two musty biscuits and some syrup. The malarial rate was 400 per thousand per annum. . . . All the shipping resources, even the local mission lugger, were pooled, and work started with all personnel on a two-thirds ration of bully beef and biscuit.

At the end of six weeks, when the Milne Bay pioneers were down almost to their last bullet and tin of beef and had completely exhausted their aviation gas, engineers' and medical supplies, the Dutch S.S. *Japara* arrived with stores and reinforcements. Quoting Colonel Burns, she was: —

> . . . The first of many ships to brave, many of them without escort, the . . . unlighted and unbuoyed China Strait. . . . Two of every three ships which came in were Dutch. I'll never forget the *van Heemskerk*, the *Maetsuycher*, the *van Heutsz* and the *Tasman*. They were worthily supported by the Australian S.S. *Taroona, Katoomba, Duntroon* and others, and by U.S.S. *West Cactus* and *Bushnell*. A tribute must also be paid to the United States and Australian troops who unloaded these ships. This unloading was so urgent that it was decided not to sound any air raid warnings, lest they should prove false and hold up the work. . . . The first we knew of a raid was when bombs began to fall.[8]

The Dutch ships mentioned by the Colonel, and most of the others who served in these waters under the Netherlands tricolor, were freight and passenger vessels of the Koninklijke Paketvaart-Maatschappij (K.P.M.) and other lines that before the war plied among the islands of Indonesia. Altogether, 29 of them that had

---

[8] Radio message of Sept. 1942, quoted in the K.P.M. pamphlet (see note 7).

escaped the Japanese onslaught were allocated to General Mac-Arthur's command. Of 2500 to 4500 tons' burthen, they were officered by upstanding Dutch seamen, and manned for the most part by Javanese — whose stoical and fatalistic attitude toward air attack made for reliable crews. Five of these gallant "K.P.M. boats" were lost in this campaign.

A United States anti-aircraft battery was flown in on 19 August. Two or three days later, two K.P.M. boats and one Britisher landed the 18th Australian Infantry Brigade, a veteran outfit from the Middle East, with the Australian overall commander, Major General Cyril A. Clowes.[9] This brought ground strength up to 8500 Australians and some 1300 Americans. Air forces at this time comprised 34 Australian P-40s (Kittyhawks) on the one completed airstrip two miles west of Gili Gili, but two others were being built in the neighborhood.[10] Naval forces consisted of a few armed launches and auxiliary ketches.

The still overconfident Japanese mounted an amphibious operation against Milne Bay without adequate air or gunfire support, an omission that cost them dear. On 24 August the convoy weighed anchor at Rabaul and headed south through St. George Channel for Milne Bay. Cruisers *Tenryu* and *Tatsuta*, destroyers *Tanikaze*, *Urakaze* and *Hamakaze*, and *SC-22* and *SC-24*, escorted transports *Kinai Maru* and *Nankai Maru* carrying over 1900 tough Special Naval Landing Force troops.[11] A coastwatcher in the Trobriand Islands reported the convoy next day. At the same time, eight "Zekes" swooped over the Gili Gili field in search of grounded planes. Fortunately, the Kittyhawks were aloft and intercepted them. Now General Clowes knew that an invasion of Milne Bay was imminent.

[9] The 7th Brigade, a militia outfit, had already arrived.
[10] No. 2, afterwards called Gurney Field, and No. 3, afterwards called Turnbull Field.
[11] ATIS Doc. No. 19692A "Invasion of New Guinea," Japanese Monograph No. 851-101, pp. 25 and 28, gives what purports to be complete detail of the landing force, 1972 men; Capt. Ohmae states that the lower estimate in Crudiv 18 War Diary (WDC 160484), 1170 men, is the correct one, and so says Milner. Probably the convoy carried 1972 men but only 1170 were set ashore.

By midnight 25 August, the Japanese convoy was well inside the Bay, anchored off Wanadala about nine miles east of the Australian headquarters at Gili Gili. About 1200 men of the landing force poured ashore to fulfill their commander's orders to "kill without remorse." On Gili Gili airstrip the Kittyhawks lined up ready to fly to Port Moresby if the airfield were bombarded or assaulted by infantry. No such attack developed; so at daybreak the P-40s snarled aloft to cover several Flying Forts which arrived in the nick of time from their base on Cape York. The B-17s badly damaged transport *Nankai Maru*, then drove the other transport and her escorts out to sea, only partially unloaded. The Kittyhawks next turned their guns on the Japanese troops and supply dumps, giving the Australians opportunity to consolidate a line just east of the KB Mission.

Thenceforth the Battle of Milne Bay became an infantry struggle in the sopping jungle carried on mostly at night under pouring rain. The Aussies were fighting mad, for they had found some of their captured fellows tied to trees and bayoneted to death, surmounted by the placard, "It took them a long time to die." But General Clowes had the good sense to await attack on the edge of Airstrip No. 3 (Turnbull Field), instead of fighting the Japanese in the depths of the forest.

After their first attack on the airstrip was thrown back with heavy losses, they attempted to bring in reinforcements by sea, but Allied planes caught and destroyed seven large barges at Goodenough Island where their crews were resting. Japanese air power, depleted by the Guadalcanal fighting and baffled by foul weather, could not help the stranded troops at Milne Bay. Admiral Mikawa pushed through a relief convoy on 29 August, bringing 775 men under naval Captain Minora Yano, who joined the troops already there in a furious night attack on Turnbull Field. At dawn on the 31st they withdrew, leaving 160 dead. The Allies then took the offensive and pushed the dispirited Japanese back to KB Mission. Captain Yano radioed to Rabaul on 2 September, "Situation most desperate. Everyone resolved to fight bravely to the last." Mikawa borrowed a thousand men from the Army and directed a trouble-shooter, Captain Yoshitatsu Yasuda, to land them at Milne Bay, take command of all ground troops and capture the airfield. But on the 4th he canceled this plan and ordered evacuation. A light cruiser and three patrol craft took off the wounded that night and the remainder on the night of 5 September. About 1300, out of the total of some 2000 that had landed, got away, but these were in very bad shape physically. Australians and natives mopped up the stragglers leisurely, snaring the last one in November.

Japanese bombardment groups continued to heckle Milne Bay, and on 7 September *Tatsuta* and *Arashi* sank a British freighter at Gili Gili wharf. In order to stop these indignities, a Southwest Pacific task force under Rear Admiral V. A. C. Crutchley RN in H.M.A.S. *Australia*, with light cruisers H.M.A.S. *Hobart* and U.S.S. *Phoenix* and United States destroyers *Selfridge*, *Bagley*, *Henley* and *Helm*, took patrol station 300 miles south of the Bay, beyond Japanese plane radius yet near enough to strike if necessary. But the enemy had shot his bolt; he never showed up again in those waters.

The Battle for Milne Bay was a small one as World War II engagements went, but very important. Except for the initial assault on Wake Island, this was the first time that a Japanese amphibious operation had been thrown for a loss. It restored to Australian soldiers the self-confidence they had lost on the Malay Peninsula. The Aussies learned, as the United States Marines had already learned on Guadalcanal, that although the Jap would not surrender he could be beaten by sound jungle tactics and accurate fire power implemented by courage and discipline. Furthermore, the Milne Bay affair demonstrated once again that an amphibious assault without air protection, and with an assault force inferior to that of the defenders, could not succeed.

Goodenough Island, westernmost of the D'Entrecasteaux group, was unintentionally occupied by 353 Japanese, stranded when their small craft were sunk by air attack; and destroyer *Yayoi*, sent to rescue them, was also bombed and sunk by General Kenney's fliers. On 22 October General MacArthur sent up 800 Australians who landed on each side of the Japanese and commenced a pincer movement. The enemy fought a rear-guard action but was evacuated by submarine on the night of 26 October. Goodenough then became an Allied air base for the 1943 offensives.[12]

[12] "Operations Goodenough Island 22–26 Oct. 1942 (Lessons from Operations No. 4)," bulletin issued by General Blamey's headquarters 23 Nov. 1942.

# CHAPTER III

# Naval Aspects of the Buna-Gona Campaign[1]

### September 1942–January 1943

## 1. Lining Up

WITH THE ENEMY stopped on the Kokoda Trail and expelled from Milne Bay, General MacArthur was ready to take the offensive and throw him out of Papua. But Japanese troops are not readily dislodged nor their leaders easily discouraged. The retaking of Buna, Gona and Sanananda, three insignificant villages on the Solomon Sea, consumed six months' time, chewed up two or three Allied divisions, and required some of the nastiest ground fighting in any area of the war. Although fought within sight and smell of the sea, this campaign was not a naval operation; but without seaborne troop-lift it would probably have dragged out interminably. And it did drive the first wedge into the Bismarcks Barrier.

Anyone may wonder why Gona and Buna were so vital for the Japanese to hold and so difficult for the Allies to take. The existence of a little 1500-yard fighter airstrip between Buna and Cape Endaiadère, within flying range of Port Moresby, Milne Bay, Sala-

[1] Southwest Pacific Daily Summary (see chap. ii above, note 1); Cdr. Robert J. Bulkley "History of the Motor Torpedo Boats" in the Navy's Administrative Series (not printed); Lt. Gen. Robert L. Eichelberger "Our Bloody Jungle Road to Tokyo" *Sat. Eve. Post* 13 Aug.–24 Sept. 1949, and his Report issued immediately after the campaign. Two good books of 1943, George H. Johnston *The Toughest Fighting in the World* and Pat Robinson *The Fight for New Guinea*, are by war correspondents. The War Department (Military Intelligence Division) pamphlet *The Papuan Campaign* is still useful, but will be superseded by a volume in the Army's definitive series by Samuel Milner, who has kindly placed his information at my disposal.

maua and Rabaul, explains why the Japanese wanted this coast. But the Dobodura plain, six miles inland – key to a whole strategic area – was what the Allies were after. In order to secure it they had to wipe out Japanese garrisons in the vicinity.

Why, then, could not MacArthur's Navy nip around the corner, now that Milne Bay was secured, and with Kenney's planes flying over the mountains to help capture the strip; as later they captured a hundred beaches along the road to Tokyo? One answer was those reefs seen or unseen by D'Entrecasteaux; the other was the want of proper troop-lift. The VII 'Phib was still only a gleam in Uncle Dan Barbey's eye; there were no LSTs, LCTs or LCIs in the South Pacific; merchantmen could not be expected to dodge enemy air bombs by day merely to be impaled on uncharted coral pinnacles at night. There was, nevertheless, a naval aspect to the campaign: the logistic support rendered by small Dutch and Australian vessels manned by Papuans and Javanese.

The first thing was to see that the Japanese, forced to counter-march over the Kokoda Trail 26 September when almost on top of Port Moresby, kept right on going. General MacArthur sent one battalion of the 128th Infantry 32nd Division United States Army by the Kapa-Kapa Trail over the Owen Stanleys in order to out-flank the Japanese, and two more battalions, by 18 October, had been flown into a small landing strip on the north coast of Papua, at Wanigela on the Collingwood Bay side of Cape Nelson. Their first attempt to march toward Buna proved that the steep jungle valleys were impassable without extensive road building that would take months, even if bulldozers were available. Angau came to the rescue. It enrolled a thousand natives, including pearl fishermen and sailors from the Fly River in southern New Guinea. Some of them were sent north in ketch-rigged auxiliary fishing boats to help the Australians operate an impromptu troop ferry, which they did with efficiency and devotion. These "boys" provided ample evidence that intelligent treatment of the natives was bearing fruit.[2] Ameri-

---

[2] Information obtained from Maj. A. N. Baldwin, Maj. L. Austen and other officials in the Angau office at Port Moresby. I was there shown ample evidence

can soldiers with the latest twentieth-century equipment moved up the coast in nineteenth-century boats manned by Stone Age sailors! The boats dropped the Americans on the beach at Pongani in Dyke Ackland Bay, 25 miles south of Buna, where work was at once started on an airstrip as a focus for more reinforcements.

Meanwhile the Japanese retreat down the Kokoda Trail had turned into a rout. Thousands perished from starvation and disease; the commanding general, Horii, was drowned. As the Australians pushed Japanese down the northern slopes, MacArthur ordered the American troops at Pongani to move inland and effect junction with the Australians. Although bombed and strafed the entire way, the Yanks finally hallooed at the Aussies on 20 November in the level fields of kunai grass between Dobodura and Soputa. There they promptly began constructing an airstrip that developed into the great Dobodura airdrome.

Now let us turn our attention to the Buna-Gona objective. Buna has no harbor, and the sea approaches are difficult owing to the reefs that extend 25 miles out. From the land side it was approachable only by four native trails, hemmed in by swamps and obstructed by creeks. The most promising was the one traveled by the Japanese from Basabua southeast along the coast. But the enemy had planted a garrison astride it at Sanananda, and had also installed formidable blocks on the inland road between Soputa and Sanananda. A second trail followed the coast between Capes Sudest and Endaiadère. Here too the Japanese threw up strong defenses athwart the trail just short of Buna airstrip. A third trail from Dobodura via Simemi joined the coastal path south of Buna; the fourth ran from Dobodura through Ango to an inland point west of the airstrip and southwest of Buna. Anyone who strayed from these trails was soon enmeshed in a tangle of undergrowth or bogged down in mangrove swamp. All the Japanese had to do to defend themselves was insert stoppers where the four trails debouched into the coconut plantation just short of Buna. General

---

that the "boys" both commanded and handled the boats, although they had the assistance of Australians to run the engines.

Kenney's planes, flying bombs over the mountains, put the Buna airstrip out of operation by 1 October; but any easing of Allied pressure would allow the Japanese to repair it and fly more planes. The Japanese garrison might have evacuated from Basabua anchorage west of Gona, but they had been ordered to keep the

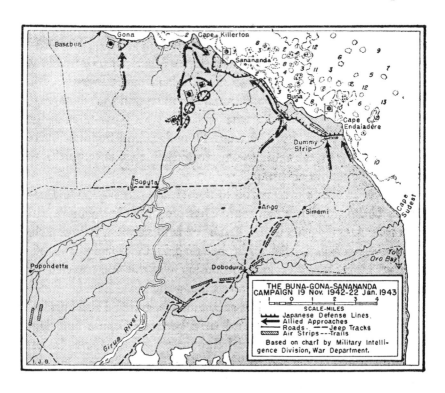

Rising Sun flying on the beachhead. These men were a fresh lot. Captain Yoshitatsu Yasuda, who had missed his chance at Milne Bay, commanded two units of the Special Naval Landing Force. Colonel Yokoyama, the Army leader who succeeded General Horii, had infantry, field artillery and anti-aircraft batteries well supported by service troops and labor gangs. All told, there were about 1800 combat troops and 400 laborers pressed into the tiny Buna perimeter.

The Japanese fortifications were as tough as their defenders:

coconut-log bunkers reinforced with sand-filled oil drums and concealed by fast-growing jungle bushes. The American soldier had first to find the enemy, uproot the bunker and then kill each diehard Nip. When one died, another promptly took his place, for the enemy had the advantage of interior lines.

The Allied attack on Buna began 19 November when the two U.S. infantry battalions from Pongani felt out the defenses on the eastern end of the perimeter. Japanese fire stopped them 400 yards short of a dummy airstrip which had been built to confuse our fliers; and the soldiers, foot-slogging in the muck under a downpour, heard truck motors bringing up fresh troops along the short Buna highway. A day later, the third battalion of the 128th splashed up through Ango and sounded out the Japanese northwest of the airfield. These troops, joined by a battalion of the 126th Infantry, formed a second front line entirely cut off by swamp from their friends to the eastward, a condition which remained throughout the campaign. The American lines had a left and a right, but no center.

To the northwest the Japanese not only blocked the road to Sanananda but established an 800-man garrison at Gona in order to protect Basabua Harbor. Fortunately for us, the only troops available at Sanananda were some three thousand survivors of the Kokoda retreat. On 19 November Australian patrols got into Gona village, but they were too few to hold it; the Japanese thrust them out. An offensive that began on the 23rd bogged down, as did that against Buna; but Gona was the first of the two places to fall.

## 2. *"Toughest Fighting in the World"* [3]

It was now apparent to both sides that a long and enervating campaign was in store. The attrition of Allied troops from combat, malaria and dengue fever mounted alarmingly. General MacArthur,

[3] The title of George Johnston's book. This writer is not prepared to agree that it was tougher than Italy, Tarawa, Iwo Jima, Okinawa, Peleliu or Guadalcanal; but it was certainly the nastiest.

who had set up headquarters at Government House, Port Moresby, enjoined Lieutenant General Robert L. Eichelberger USA on 30 November "to take Buna or don't come back alive." [4] From the following day, when this new commander of the American ground troops arrived at Dobodura, his fatherly but resolute figure was familiar at the front. While dodging bullets he cheered the weary, rewarded the brave and tossed out the incompetents. In the Gona-Sanananda sector, Major General George A. Vasey of the 7th Australian Division, who retained command of operations west of the Girua River,[5] welcomed the arrival of fresh American troops to help his weary veterans of the Kokoda push. The air force pitched in to drive off enemy convoys, bomb and strafe beleaguered Japanese and, most important, deliver troops and supplies over the mountains. Some supplies were merely dropped, but most of the airborne guns, food, medicine and clothing were landed at Dobodura and Pongani airstrips.

Stout commanders, fresh troops, air bombardment and air transport were major factors in the ensuing victory, but the campaign would have been longer and bloodier but for reinforcements coming by sea. During the summer and fall of 1942, some important hydrographic surveying had been done in Ward Hunt Strait between eastern Papua and the D'Entrecasteaux Islands. Three survey vessels of the Royal Australian Navy, small converted Burns Philp sloops named *Polaris*, *Stella* and *Whyalla*, covered by R.A.N. corvettes, laid out and buoyed a tortuous channel three miles wide from East Cape to Cape Nelson. Destroyers and big transports could have made Cape Nelson by daylight, but beyond there were too many saber-toothed reefs to risk valuable and tender hulls. So a "Lilliput Navy" was organized, consisting of K.P.M. ships, Angau vessels manned by natives, and small coasters manned by Australians. Several of the larger K.P.M. ships made ferry runs even beyond Cape Nelson to Oro Bay, from which Army engineers built

[4] *Sat. Eve Post* 14 Aug. 1949.
[5] Until 15 Jan. 1943, when General Eichelberger was designated commander of all forces north of the Owen Stanleys.

a coastal road of sorts up to Cape Sudest. The Lilliputs and K.P.M. boats carried approximately half of the supplies for the entire campaign.

Nobody slept on those voyages. At night the ships snaked through the reefs. By day they dodged Japanese bombs and strafing bullets. On 16–17 November 1942, four ships sank under bombing attack; the supply line was interrupted, and a planned advance of the 32nd Division was delayed three weeks. Enemy motor torpedo boats added to the havoc and made at least one kill. The supplies kept coming, although never enough. A Dutch train ferry, the 3000-ton *Karsik* that had formerly run out of Batavia, aided by the K.P.M. ship *Japara*, brought up a load of sorely needed Australian tanks. A trio of corvettes, H.M.A.S. *Broome, Colac* and *Ballarat*, carried three battalions of Australian troops to Oro Bay on 12 and 13 December. On another occasion General Harding and some of his staff, embarked in a small lugger, had it bombed and sunk from under them but swam ashore.

The principal contribution of the United States Navy to this campaign was the squadron of motor torpedo boats based on Milne Bay. General MacArthur, who had been evacuated from Corregidor in Lieutenant John D. Bulkeley's PT, had been impressed by the value of these craft and, as a result of repeated requests, entreaties and even threats by Admiral Carpender, tender *Hilo* (Commander F. A. Munroe) and four PTs, originally intended for another destination, were ordered into his command. *Hilo* with two boats in tow made Milne Bay via Cairns on 17 December. Two more boats, towed to Cairns by a Liberty ship, proceeded thence to Milne under escort of that tough old China hand, gunboat *Tulsa*. These two, *PT-121* and *PT-122*, jumped right in by firing torpedoes at a Japanese submarine off Milne Bay — unfortunately without effect — on the night of 18–19 December.

The radius of motor torpedo boat activity is so short, and their thirst for gasoline so consuming, that Milne, two hundred miles from Oro Bay, could serve only as a rear base. Commander Edgar T. Neale of the PT task group, searching for a suitable advanced base on Cape Nelson, found the ideal spot at Tufi, an Angau station on a deep, narrow and mountain-rimmed estuary, cool and clean and close to the fighting area. On 20 December *Tulsa* made the run safely with an initial load of supplies. At Tufi, easily camouflaged from enemy air observation, the boats could obtain pure water from falls emptying into the bay, and the men could see native life at its best. A sympathetic Angau director and staff offered hospitality and supplied native labor to handle gasoline and perform other heavy work.

Every night two or more PTs went prowling for supply submarines and troop barges. On Christmas Eve *PT–122* (Ensign Robert F. Lynch) stood up the coast beyond Gona in search of inbound Japs. Rain clouds rolled back from a bright moon in time for the lookouts to spot the silhouette of a conning tower. It belonged to a fully surfaced I-boat. Lynch drove in to half-mile range and fired two torpedoes for one hit. As the submarine did not sink quickly enough to suit him, he closed to 500 yards and let fly two more fish. After two explosions the I-boat appeared to break in two and disappear in a welter of flame and water. Lynch half saw, half suspected the presence of a second I-boat beyond his victim. Four closely-spaced torpedoes headed for *PT–122* proved his surmise to be correct; but he sidestepped them. We cannot identify these I-boats. On the same night *PT–114* and *PT–121* sank two barges loaded with troops for Buna.

This last encounter was symptomatic of two developments that went far. The Japanese armed forces, short on troop-lift (for which United States submarines were largely responsible) and not daring to risk valuable ships under skies or along shores dominated by their enemy, developed a construction program of wooden diesel-powered barges armed with machine guns, and a doctrine of traveling by night and hiding out in some wooded creek or cove by day. Native builders in China, Malaya and the Philippines turned out these barges by the hundreds, and the Japanese showed a skill in nocturnal close-to-shore navigation that aroused our reluctant admiration. On the other hand, the PT boats, originally intended for hit-and-run torpedo attacks on combat ships, were the barges' nemesis, and became so adept at machine-gun work that their torpedo function atrophied.

All through December the battle for Buna raged, with heavy losses on both sides. Every day Papuan stretcher bearers carried Allied sick and wounded through the jungle to waiting jeeps, where a painful journey over a corduroy road to Dobodura connected with evacuating air transport. Every day fresh troops plodded forward to fill gaps. One outfit entered the campaign with 1199 men and, six weeks later, had only 165 left. The great majority of the casualties were from disease. Men fought, lived and slept in mud and slime amid swarms of malaria-bearing mosquitoes. They broke out with horrible skin diseases and ulcers. But the state of their opponents was even more wretched. A captured diary recorded, "With the dawn the enemy starts shooting all over. All I can do is shed tears of resentment. Now we are waiting only for death. Even the invincible Imperial Army is at a loss."

On Christmas Day General Imamura ordered the garrison to evacuate, but they had no means to do so; on 2 January 1943 General Eichelberger's troops entered Buna.

As the Australians had already taken Gona on 9 December, the Allies could now turn their undivided attention to Sanananda, which was as strongly defended as Buna. The Japanese had established several roadblocks across the approaches. Australians in this section were tired veterans of the Kokoda Trail. Every Allied soldier still able to fight after the fall of Buna, and many who elsewhere would have been evacuated, were sent in to help. Before they finally closed in, *PT–120* caught three barges jammed with escaping Japanese officers, on the night of 17–18 January. The motor torpedo boat took on all three with her machine guns. The barges hit back in kind, and mortally wounded the boat's engineer, but two of them were sunk and the third set afire. Next day, 18 January 1943, Sanananda fell to the Aussies; and on the 22nd organized resistance ceased.

\* \* \*

The Papuan campaign, concluded two weeks before the parallel one at Guadalcanal, was far more costly in lives, relative to the forces employed. Out of 13,645 American troops engaged, most of the 32nd Division and part of the 41st, there were 2959 casualties. The Australian brigades that were engaged lost 5698.[6]

No troops fighting so resourceful and relentless an enemy under such miserable conditions could have done better. But the main reason for this heavy price in life and suffering was the want of Allied sea power in the Solomon Sea. General MacArthur had as many troops as the Japanese and more air power. But modern military strength is like a tripod, one leg being the ground forces, another the Navy, the third air power; with struts representing amphibious forces, carrier planes and the like connecting and strengthening all three. In this instance the naval leg was so much shorter than the other two that the whole structure tottered. If the Southwest Pacific command had been blessed with an amphibious force of shoal-draft beaching craft supported by carriers, cruisers and destroyers, the Japanese garrisons on that coast could have been cleaned up in a week. Supplies for the ground troops would have been ample. Carrier air strikes against enemy airfields on New Britain would have kept Japanese fliers grounded, and combat air patrol would have intercepted many who broke through. It will be instructive to compare this operation with that of Cape Gloucester in December 1943, when the tripod had legs of equal length.

On the Japanese side, Captain Yasuda of the Special Naval Landing Force, killed in action, "became the exemplary model for the Imperial Forces, teaching those units in isolated and supportless fronts the course of action to adopt." [7] A model indeed of tenacity and courage under hopeless conditions; but not of the sort that wins wars.

[6] U.S. Army: 671 killed in action, 116 other deaths, 2172 wounded; Australian Army: 2037 killed, 128 other deaths, 3533 wounded, 21 July 1942–31 Jan. 1943. The U.S. Army also had 7920 men "evacuated sick," but we have no corresponding figures for the Australians. (Data supplied by Mr. Milner in 1950.) They do not include casualties inflicted on ships in the service of supply, or on aviators.

[7] ATIS "Southeast Area Operations" Part 1 (Navy).

# CHAPTER IV

# Papuan Pause

## February 1943

IN WARFARE the shift from a defensive to an offensive posture is similar to the recovery from a long illness. Bitter memory and lack of confidence produce the same timid and uncertain gestures, a similar reluctance to venture from safety. With the collapse of Buna and Gona, as with the evacuation of Guadalcanal, the Allies in the Southwest Pacific suddenly found themselves recovering from a year of defeat and retreat, from one illness and relapse after another. Now, they could hardly believe they had the enemy on the defensive — wondered if it were not an hallucination which Tojo would promptly dispel.

Where was the medicine to continue the cure? Already on its way out from the States, but mostly in raw form which would need a lot of stirring and refinement before use. Many moons would wax and wane before the patient could really "go places."

We have seen how MacArthur's lack of amphibious force to support his Army made the going rough in Papua. The build-up of such a force began at very slow tempo, in January 1943,[1] under Rear Admiral Daniel E. Barbey. But how to hold the Japanese down until Barbey's boys got rolling? Commander Geoffrey C. F. Branson RAN, the stout little S.O.P.A. at Milne Bay, asked this question so loud and often, with no answer, that in late January he hopped a plane for Brisbane and sat down with Admiral Sir Guy Royle RN, Commander in Chief of the Australian Navy, Rear Admiral Crutchley RN, Vice Admiral Carpender, and some members of General MacArthur's staff. Branson insisted that Milne

[1] See chap. viii.

Bay must be advanced naval base for the next move, and pointed out that it was neglected and forgotten. His mission was fortunate, for it turned out that MacArthur's staff had not yet got around to thinking about advanced naval bases. Branson flew back to Milne Bay and for the next two months watched the Allied forces slowly move men, planes, boats and equipment into his malarial domain.[2]

The loss of Buna-Gona and of Guadalcanal, occurring almost simultaneously, warned Japanese Imperial Headquarters that the war had entered a new and unsatisfactory phase. They decided to reinforce and strengthen the line Munda–Rabaul–Lae, to step up air bombing of recently won Allied positions, and to wait for the Allies to take the initiative.

In January 1943 a Japanese infantry regiment moved into Lae and Salamaua in order to counter Australian activity at the inland air base of Wau; on the 19th, eight transports covered by two light cruisers and five destroyers discharged 9400 men at Wewak, 382 miles northwest of Lae.[3] Three months later the Japanese further extended their western flank by occupying in force Hollandia, Dutch New Guinea, of which they had taken possession the previous May. To be partially independent of the sea, they commenced digging out a road from Madang to Finschhafen. Their submarines and coast-hugging barges braved the Allied air and sea blockade in Papua almost nightly.

Motor torpedo boats maintained their unique position as sole surface representatives of the United States Navy in the Solomon Sea for another six months. During the hours of darkness they now had friends overhead, nighthawk PBYs built in the United States but manned and operated by the Royal Australian Air Force from a base at the head of Milne Bay.[4]

---

[2] Conversation with Cdr. Branson at "Target House," Milne Bay, in May 1943. One curious reason for the slow arrival of equipment was the unfortunate code name for Gili Gili, "Fall River." A lot of Milne Bay equipment was delivered at Fall River, Massachusetts, where nobody knew what to do with it.

[3] War Dept. Military Intelligence Div'n *Disposition and Movements of Japanese Ground Forces 1941–45* (Dec. 1945); ATIS No. 16268, War Diary of Japanese Naval Operations; Historical Div. GHQ *Chronology of the War.*

[4] For the inception of "Black Cats," see Vol. V of this History pp. 330–32.

During late January and February 1943, the PTs were constantly looking for action but seldom finding it. A few barges were sunk or driven ashore. Occasionally machine-gun and rifle duels were carried on between PTs and Japanese bivouacs. Once in a while an enemy submarine was sighted, but it usually submerged and got away because the boats had no sound gear for tracking underwater craft. Bad weather, flotsam and reefs made navigation a matter of luck; for the PTs were so fragile that even striking a log of firewood size might knock them out. Time and again the boats came in from patrol with jagged rents in hulls or propellers bent out of shape. Yet they served the purpose of a miniature fleet in being. The enemy knew and feared them and pared barge operations to the minimum.

In February, Commander Morton C. Mumma, former skipper of submarine *Sailfish* and recently naval liaison officer at General Kenney's headquarters, became commander of the New Guinea boats. Mumma had a better break than his fellows at Guadalcanal in that his boats were a recognized task group, not a sort of sea-going cavalry that could be ordered to charge by any flag officer who happened to be around. Furthermore, a steady stream of new boats from the States gave him a more effective force than any that had patrolled around Savo Island. On the southeastern shore of Milne Bay, in the tiny harbor of Kona Kope, which was free from the swarms of mosquitoes that infested Gili Gili, Mumma moored his tender *Hilo* and set about building a proper motor-torpedo-boat and PBY base. At first it did not amount to much; changing engines required a trip to Gili Gili to use a borrowed Army crane; dry-docking meant a cruise to Samarai in the Louisiades where natives, spurred on by raucous blasts from a conch shell, cranked the boats up a creaky marine railway. But gradually, faithful old China gunboat *Tulsa* brought in enough equipment to make Kona Kope more nearly resemble its Papuan meaning, "Place of Rest."

CHAPTER V

# The Battle of the Bismarck Sea[1]

## 2–5 March 1943

### 1. Into the Jaws of the B–25s

DURING February the only fighting ashore in New Guinea occurred in the vicinity of the Australian air base at Wau, 30 miles southwest of Salamaua. In this prewar mountain boom town near the gold mines, an isolated Australian garrison, supplied by air, stood off repeated and furious assaults by Japanese troops from Salamaua. The enemy regarded Wau as a close threat to the Huon Gulf that must be rubbed out. But their troops in New Guinea were inadequate in number and poor in equipment. General Imamura and Admiral Kusaka accordingly cooked up a scheme whose failure changed the entire complexion of the slow-moving New Guinea campaign. They decided to move 6900 soldiers of the Japanese Eighteenth Army into Lae, where the existing garrison numbered only 3500.

So large a force had to go by ship. Both commanders had distasteful memories of the disastrous air bombing undergone by Tanaka's Guadalcanal convoy in November.[2] But this time they might reduce the risk by blanketing the air with protecting fighters and by slipping in behind a weather front. There was much reason to

[1] Southwest Pacific Daily Summary (see chap. ii note 1). ATIS Enemy Publication No. 7, Nov. 29, 1943 "Bismarck Sea Operation" in 2 Parts, being translation of documents "contained in 3 briefcases and 1 mapcase, salvaged from Goodenough Island 8 Mar. '43," includes Adachi's operations order, complete list of ships and cargoes; Eighth Fleet War Diary (WDC No. 161259) translated by Lt. Pineau; USSBS Interrogations Nos. 511, 525, 526, 527; JICPOA Item No. 4986, "Captured Diary of Japanese Naval Officer"; General Kenney Reports.
[2] See Vol. V of this History pp. 266–69, 283.

expect they could get away with it. In January five ships had un-loaded at Lae with the loss of only two, both sunk by the V Army Air Force.[3] On 19 February a three-ship convoy had made an un-molested voyage to Wewak. Admiral Mikawa estimated that at the very worst a well-organized convoy could get half its ships through.

The convoy assembled at Rabaul. By the end of February, Simp-son Harbor had that crowded, pre-invasion look always so interest-ing to enemy aircraft. Sixteen ships — eight transports and eight destroyers — received their cargoes and personnel: 5954 troops in the APs, and 958 in the DDs. Escort commander Rear Admiral Masatomi Kimura, who flew his flag in *Shirayuki*, set midnight 28 February as the hour of departure. On board destroyer *Tokitsukaze* was Lieutenant General Hatazo Adachi, Commander Eighteenth Army, and staff. Lieutenant General Nakano with the 51st Division staff was in *Yukikaze*. *Teiyo Maru*, the biggest trans-port, carried 1923 men; "sea truck" *Kembu Maru*, the smallest, was filled with drummed aviation gas. *Nojima* was laden with provi-sions, much wanted at Lae.

The joint operation plan was as carefully thought out and as complete in every detail as anything given out by Kelly Turner. Every military unit and its matériel was divided among a number of ships, so that, even if half the transports were lost, a balanced force could be set ashore; but there was no precaution against total loss. Every ship was combat-loaded for the most expeditious unloading, and the men were ordered to continue discharging cargo at anchor right through an air raid. With plenty of boats on board, it was estimated that all the troops could be landed at Lae in six hours' time; all the supplies and matériel, within 48 hours.

The convoy formed, and sailed on schedule as February turned into March, under the darkling clouds of an approaching storm. It doubled the Crater Peninsula, steered north and then west into the body of water that would shortly be named the Bismarck Sea.

---

[3] *Nichiryu Maru* and *Myoko Maru.*

Here is its organization, together with the tonnage of each transport: —

LAE RESUPPLY CONVOY, Rear Admiral Masatomi Kimura [4]

ESCORT, Rear Admiral Kimura

Destroyers *Shirayuki,* *Arashio,* *Asashio,* *Tokitsukaze,* Yukikaze, Uranami, Shikinami, Asagumo

CONVOY, Captain Kametaro Matsumoto

| | |
|---|---|
| *Teiyo Maru* (6869) | *Taimei Maru* (2883) |
| *Shinai Maru* (3793) | *Kyokusei Maru* (5493) |
| *Kembu Maru* (953) | *Aiyo Maru* (2746) |
| *Oigawa Maru* (6493) | *Nojima* (4500) |

\* Sunk in this battle.

The skippers of these destroyers were old hands at dodging bombs on the Tokyo Express to Guadalcanal. Their gun crews were expert at shooting down Allied planes.

All through the night and well into the afternoon of 1 March, the ships plodded at 7 knots through the Bismarck Sea toward Dampier Strait. It was "dusty weather"; wind blowing a gale, air full of mist and rain. At 1600 Admiral Kimura's hope for a secret passage vanished when a B–24 pushed through the cloud veil and sighted his convoy. There was still the chance that he would not be attacked so long as the weather held foul. Mikawa had planned to mince up Allied planes on their fields at Dobodura, Gili Gili and Port Moresby, and had also promised an air cover of 200 Army and Navy fighter planes if and when the convoy came out in the clear.

But Mikawa grossly underestimated the strength of Allied planes in Papua, which had now risen to 207 bombers and 129 fighters,[5] and the same thick weather that protected the convoy also shielded them. The storm perversely shifted direction and passed over New Britain and into the Solomon Sea. And the Japanese air escort, jumping off from Rabaul, Gasmata and Lae,

[4] Eighth Fleet War Diary; names checked and tonnages added from ATIS "Bismarck Sea Operation" Part 1; confirmed 1945 by Col. Ichiji Sugita who made the operation plan, *Inter. Jap. Off.* II 498 (USSBS No. 511).
[5] See note at end of chapter.

had precious little gas or time to spend protecting the convoy.
Two other factors, unknown by either Mikawa or Kimura, completed the setting for disaster. In the last week of February, American air scouts had reported several convoy movements in New
Britain waters. Although none of these were Kimura's, the V Army

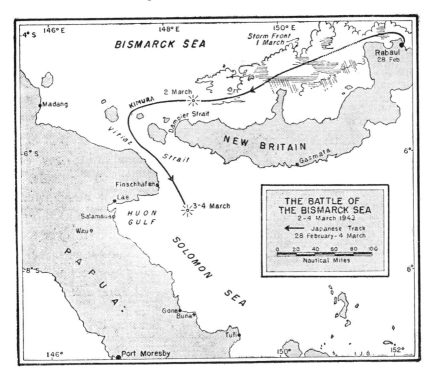

Air Force took the sightings as a portent, redoubled search efforts
and readied attack groups. The second item was a new and deadly
arming of certain attack planes. At General Kenney's command,
Major Paul I. ("Pappy") Gunn USA "pulled the bombardier and
everything else out of the nose" of his B–25s and installed eight .50-
caliber machine guns for strafing. These same B–25s carried 500-
pound bombs which were armed with a five-second delay fuze
permitting planes to come in almost at sea level and attack, with
no danger from their own bomb explosions. And Major William
Benn USA devised a new method of attacking with these bombs:

the plane to approach at masthead height, drop its bombs and be clear of the target before the five-second delay expired; the bomb, by exploding in the water alongside the ship, to inflict great damage by its mining effect. Flying Forts had recently tried this technique on Rabaul, but the enemy had not yet got onto it. General Kenney now decided to give "skip-bombing," as it is generally called, a full-scale demonstration.[6]

On the afternoon of 1 March one of Kenney's planes sighted the convoy and passed the word that General MacArthur's headquarters wanted to hear: "Convoy of 14 ships north of New Britain . . . westerly course . . . six of the vessels destroyers . . . The convoy was tracked until 2130, then contact was lost."[7] At 0815 March 2 it was again picked up, this time by a B-24, thirty miles north of Cape Gloucester. The convoy, then about to turn into Dampier Strait, was making 9 knots; Admiral Carpender's Intelligence Officer estimated they were headed for Finschhafen or Madang, and had some 4000 troops on board. Twelve B-17s and 17 other heavy bombers promptly took off, arrived over the convoy around 1015, and, disregarding both the combat air patrol[8] and anti-aircraft fire, made horizontal bombing approaches from 5000 feet altitude. By noon *Kyokusei Maru* was sunk; *Teiyo Maru* and *Nojima* were hit and damaged.

Mikawa at Rabaul should have read the air portents and ordered Kimura into safer waters. But he radioed not a word and Kimura went on to destruction. He altered plan in but one detail. Destroyers *Yukikaze* and *Asagumo*, which had rescued some 950 survivors from *Kyokusei Maru*, pushed ahead at high speed, steamed into Lae after dark and discharged the men there. An Australian PBY tagged the main convoy all night, dropping occasional bombs which kept the Japanese awake and worried.

The 3rd of March is the Girls' or Dolls' Festival in Japan, when little girls dress up their dolls and display them to friends and

[6] *General Kenney Reports* pp. 142–45.
[7] SWPac Daily Summary for 1–2 March.
[8] About 24 planes, said (in 1945) Col. Shinohara who provided air cover from Rabaul. USSBS No. 527 p. 3.

neighbors. So, to remind the troops of their homes and kid sisters, candy was issued to all hands.[9] But Huon Gulf was no place for girls or dolls that day.

Destroyers *Yukikaze* and *Asagumo* rejoined the convoy just in time for the start of Kenney's biggest air show. The convoy was in loose formation, sprawled nakedly under tropical sunshine. High above it — much too high to get skip-bombers — circled a meager air cover of some 40 "Zekes." Out of the southern horizon, at about 10 o'clock, came the one-two punch; a medium-altitude bombing attack by Flying Forts and a flock of A–20s and B–25s equipped for skip-bombing, darting in so low that their slip-streams ruffled the calm sea. Sixteen P–38s provided the top cover and kept their air escort busy, while 13 R.A.A.F. Beaufighters swept in at deck height, strafing fore and aft.

The veteran Japanese skippers ignored the B–17s as experience had taught them to do, but narrowly watched the B–25s and A–20s. It looked like one of those torpedo attacks the Avengers used to dish out at Guadalcanal. Helms were put over to present bows or sterns to the planes and comb the torpedo wakes. That was just what Major Ed Larner wanted. His skip-bombers lunged in two by two, each with eight forward guns hammering a deadly pattern down on the ships' decks from stem to stern. The victims could reply only with bow guns or stern chasers, if the gunners had survived. Next, like bullfighters tired of planting *banderillas,* the skip-bombers hurled their bombs at the targets, then swerved and climbed gracefully away. Never, since December 1941, had there been such a devastating air attack on ships. Out of thirty-seven 500-pound bombs, 28 scored. Each transport lurched, flamed and fell off her course, easy prey to the next wave of attackers. And more waves followed. By noon, over 200 bombs had fallen into and around the writhing vessels. High above the sea-level battle, P–38s and P–40s tangled with defending "Zekes." Vapor trails, tracer trails, and finally smoke trails arched across the sky. At middle altitude, the powerful B–17s muscled aside the "Zekes"; but

[9] Soldier's diary in ATIS "Bismarck Sea Operations" Part 2 p. 63.

one Fort lost a wing. Seven of its nine-man crew bailed out but were shot while hanging from their parachutes, and three P–38s which went to their rescue were shot down after disposing of five Japanese fighters. Over Lae, 38 more Allied fighters scotched enemy air traffic so that the "Zekes," now low on gas, had to retire before relief fighters appeared. Not a single ship got off undamaged; scarcely a plane was without a scar.

All through the afternoon the slaughter continued. First Lieutenant Roy J. Moore USA set down his B–25 at Moresby Field and made a report typical of the day: —

> When within strafing range I opened fire with my forward guns. The decks were covered with troops, lined up facing the attacking plane with rifles in hand. However, my .50-calibers outranged their small arms and I saw hundreds fall and others go over the side. . . . I then ceased fire and I made a gradual pull-up to clear the masts. My bombs skipped into the side of the ship and exploded, leaving a large hole at the waterline.[10]

The Japanese convoy was now scattered through the Gulf, most of the ships stopped, many sinking. Four undamaged destroyers fished out survivors and fled northward. Escape was foremost in everyone's mind. The sea was covered with life rafts, rubber boats and swimmers; there was no time to launch more than a few of the motor craft. "The Boeing [B–25] is most terrifying," wrote one survivor in his diary. "We are repeating the failure of Guadalcanal! Most regrettable!" [11]

## 2. *The PTs Mop Up*

Night should have brought respite to the unhappy Japanese, but here the Navy turned up in the form of motor torpedo boats. For two days the PT boys at Tufi and Milne Bay had been eagerly plotting Kimura's advance, waiting until he came within their

[10] *Impact* June 1943.
[11] ATIS "Bismarck Sea Operations" Part 2 p. 67.

short striking range. Commander Mumma brought three boats up from Kona Kope to join the seven already alerted at Tufi. In late afternoon the ten PTs, led by Lieutenant Commander Atkins, set forth to sweep through the Gulf after dark.

This was no picnic excursion. Unless absolute surprise was achieved, the PTs would be completely at the mercy of any Japanese destroyer which happened along. The boats designed for 42 knots were capable of only 32 knots, 3 to 5 knots slower than the destroyers of Kimura's convoy; and at any speed over 12 or 15 knots they showed a wake like a white rooster's tail. Their torpedo fire control apparatus was none too good, their one 40-mm, single 37-mm and two 20-mm machine guns made a meager counterfire to a destroyer's armament; and their thin plywood hulls splintered like matchboxes under impact. Two boats, in fact, hit submerged flotsam and were forced back to Tufi early in the run. The eight others, as follows, kept on: —

### MOTOR TORPEDO BOAT STRIKING FORCE
#### Lieutenant Commander Barry K. Atkins

*PT-66* Lt. (jg) William C. Quinby USNR    *PT-143* Lt. (jg) John S. Baylis USNR
*PT-67* Ens. James W. Emmons USNR    *PT-149* Lt. William J. Flittie USNR
*PT-68* Lt. (jg) Robert L. Childs USNR    *PT-150* Lt. (jg) Russell E. Hama-
*PT-121* Ens. Edward R. Bergin USNR    check USNR
*PT-128* Ens. James W. Herring

The PTs, plowing through heavy seas and rain squalls, arrived off Lae late in the evening watch, 3 March. At 2250 Atkins saw fire ahead and drove forward. Half an hour later *PT-143* and *PT-150* had closed sufficiently to make out the burning hull of abandoned transport *Oigawa Maru*. Each boat hurled a torpedo at the derelict and both scored; the transport went down in a welter of smoke and fire. Further search proved fruitless; there were only two enemy ships left in the Gulf, both damaged destroyers. At daybreak the V Army Air Force was back again, roughing up these two cripples. A single 500-pound bomb from a B–17 sailed into the forward stack of *Arashio* and tore a fatal gash in her hull. The second destroyer succumbed to masthead bombers in late afternoon. That did it. From the entire convoy of sixteen vessels only four destroyers, *Shikinami, Yukikaze, Asagumo* and *Uranami*, escaped destruction.

Meanwhile planes and PTs went about the sickening business of killing survivors in boats, rafts or wreckage. Fighters mercilessly strafed anything on the surface. On 5 March the two PTs which had sunk *Oigawa Maru* put out to rescue a downed pilot and came on an enemy submarine receiving survivors from three large landing craft. Torpedoes missed as the I-boat crash-dived. The PTs turned their guns on, and hurled depth charges at the three boats — which, with over a hundred men on board, sank. It was a grisly task, but a military necessity since Japanese soldiers do not surrender and, within swimming distance of shore, they could not be allowed to land and join the Lae garrison.

Japanese submarines and destroyers saved 2734 men from the convoy, but over 3000 were missing. Several hundred swam ashore, and for a month there was open season on Nips in Papua; the natives had the time of their lives tracking them down as in the old head-hunting days. Many boatloads, spotted by planes, were destroyed by the PTs. One group of 18 survivors made Kiriwina Island, only to be captured by the crew of *PT–114*. Another sailed 700 miles to Guadalcanal, there to be killed by an American patrol.

General Kenney's aviators believed, and General MacArthur's communiqués declared, that they had destroyed 22 ships, 55 planes and 15,000 men in this Battle of the Bismarck Sea.[12] But the correct score of 12 ships (including all eight transports), over 3000 men and 20 to 30 planes made a famous victory and at light cost; out of the 335 American planes engaged, only two bombers and three fighters had been lost. The enemy never again risked a transport larger than a small coaster or barge in waters shadowed by American planes. His contemplated offensive against Wau died a-borning. His troops already in New Guinea would in the future tighten their belts.

News of the battle shocked the Japanese high command, and the

[12] See note at end of chapter.

sinking of four freighters and a tanker [13] by United States submarines during the first eight days of March added to their grief. General Imamura's chief of staff flew to Tokyo to report to Imperial Headquarters, and, as a result, it was decided to send no more convoys into Papua; whatever reinforcements Lae and Salamaua required must come by barge from Cape Gloucester; or by submarines, at night.

The MacArthur command might have regarded this battle as a clue to easy victory by air power alone; but it was too wise to draw any such false conclusion. On the contrary, it correctly spotted the Japanese errors, realized that skip-bombing would henceforth be no surprise, and continued to rely on a balanced force to fight the war in this area. Unfavorable weather for the defense, Kusaka's failure to estimate Allied air strength accurately and reduce it on the ground, inadequate air cover for the convoy, poor anti-aircraft gunnery and slow speed of the ships, were important factors in this striking victory; and if two or three of them had been absent, Kimura's force would have been only scotched, not killed. The unbalanced Allied tripod stood up because of enemy ineptitude, and the superior skill of General Kenney and his pilots – together with a fair measure of good luck.

## NOTE ON COMPOSITION AND LOSSES OF THE LAE CONVOY

It is easy to trace from SWPac Daily Intelligence Bulletins how the American overestimate was made. The one for 3–4 March reported 13 to 15 ships sunk, and says that at least 20 ships were in the convoy – probably the two destroyers that landed survivors at Lae, and later rejoined, were counted twice. Same for 4–5 March says "Only one destroyer may have escaped," and "total ships involved were 22 . . . including 15 cargo/transport vessels." The one for 16–17 March, on basis of the documents captured at Goodenough, lists the destroyers and transports accurately by name but, on the basis of a second list, estimated to be an addition to the convoy, added *Kamo Maru* and *Shichisei Maru*. These had been in an earlier Truk-Rabaul convoy, but not in the one to Lae; *Kamo* was later sunk by a United States submarine off Sasebo 3 July 1944 and the other off the Palaus 29 December 1943, according to JANAC. It is equally certain that four destroyers escaped. *Asagumo* was sunk in the Battle of Surigao Strait, *Uranami* off San Bernardino

---

[13] JANAC p. 39, which also confirms the sinkings in the Battle of the Bismarck Sea.

Strait next day, *Shikinami* by a United States submarine in the South China Sea 12 September 1944; *Yukikaze* survived the war and was turned over to the Chinese Navy in 1947.

Correct information on the original composition of the convoy was in General Kenney's hands before the end of March (the ATIS document "Bismarck Sea Operation") and both composition and losses were checked by interrogations of Japanese officers at the end of the war, and from the Eighth Fleet War Diary (see footnote 1, above). So there is no excuse for General Kenney's stating, as he does on page 205 of his book, published in 1949, that the Japanese losses were "6 destroyers or light cruisers sunk, 2 destroyers or light cruisers damaged, 11 to 14 merchant vessels sunk (whatever the number actually in the convoy, all were sunk)." That, to be sure, was what the aviators reported at the time, and what was stated in the official communiqué; but such mistakes are common in war and inevitable in air war. It would be more creditable to acknowledge the truth, which is glorious enough for anyone, than to persist in the error.

## AIR GROUPS PARTICIPATING IN THE BATTLE OF THE BISMARCK SEA *

### 1-4 March 1943

### ALLIED AIR FORCES SOUTHWEST PACIFIC

Lieutenant General George C. Kenney

V ARMY AIR FORCE, General Kenney

ROYAL AUSTRALIAN AIR FORCE

Air Vice Marshal William D. Bostock RAAF

35th Fighter Group, Col. Richard A. Legg

| | | |
|---|---|---|
| 39th Fighter Squadron | P-38 | Capt. T. J. Lynch |
| 40th Fighter Squadron | P-39 | Capt. Malcolm A. Moore |

49th Fighter Group, Lt. Col. Robert L. Morrissey

| | | |
|---|---|---|
| 7th Fighter Squadron | P-40 | Maj. William P. Martin |
| 8th Fighter Squadron | P-40 | Maj. Mitchell E. Sims |
| 9th Fighter Squadron | P-38 | Capt. Jesse C. Peaslee |

3rd Bombardment Group, Lt. Col. Robert F. Strickland

| | | |
|---|---|---|
| 13th Bomb Squadron | B-25 | Maj. Harold V. Maull |
| 89th Bomb Squadron | A-20 | Maj. Glen W. Clark |
| 90th Bomb Squadron ** | B-25 | Maj. Edward L. Larner |

38th Bombardment Group, Col. Fay R. Upthegrove

| | | |
|---|---|---|
| 71st Bomb Squadron | B-25 | Maj. Eugene P. Mussett |
| 405th Bomb Squadron | B-25 | Lt. Col. Millard Lewis |

43rd Bombardment Group, Col. Roger M. Ramey

| | | |
|---|---|---|
| 63rd Bomb Squadron | B-17 | Maj. Edward W. Scott |
| 64th Bomb Squadron | B-17 | Maj. Kenneth D. McCullar |
| 65th Bomb Squadron | B-17 | Maj. Harry J. Hawthorne |
| 403rd Bomb Squadron | B-17 | Maj. Jay P. Reusek |

* All officers U.S. Army unless otherwise stated.
** Equipped for skip-bombing.

90th Bombardment Group, Col. Ralph E. Koon

| | | |
|---|---|---|
| 320th Bomb Squadron | B-24 | 1st Lt. Roy L. Taylor |
| 321st Bomb Squadron | B-24 | Maj. Cecil Faulkner |
| 8th Photo Reconnaissance Squadron | F-4, F-5 | 1st Lt. Frank S. Savage |

No. 9 Operational Group, Royal Australian Air Force,
Air Commo. Joseph E. Hewitt RAAF

71st Wing

| | | |
|---|---|---|
| No. 75 Fighter Squadron | P-40 | Squad. Ldr. W. S. Arthur RAAF |
| No. 77 Fighter Squadron | P-40 | Squad. Ldr. R. Creswell RAAF |
| No. 6 Bomb Squadron | Hudson (A-29) | Wing Cdr. A. A. Barlow RAAF |
| No. 7 Bomb Squadron | Beaufort | Wing Cdr. K. R. J. Parsons RAAF |
| No. 22 Bomb Squadron | Boston (A-20) | Wing Cdr. K. M. Hampshire RAAF |
| No. 30 Bomb Squadron | Beaufighter | Wing Cdr. B. R. Walker RAAF |
| No. 100 Bomb Squadron | Beaufort | Wing Cdr. J. R. Balmer RAAF |

CHAPTER VI

# Southwest Pacific Submarines[1]

## 8 February 1943–1 May 1944

### 1. Patrols from Brisbane

THIS PERIOD from February 1943 to May 1944 was one of transition in the submarine war against Japan. At the beginning only 47 fleet submarines were patrolling in the Pacific; at the end there were 104. Of all United States submarines available on 8 February 1943, Admiral King assigned 20 to the Southwest Pacific, and added four more in November. He raised the Seventh Fleet quota to "Two and one half squadrons modern submarines with associated tenders and rescue vessels, plus one of *Narwhal* class" on 12 January 1944. That meant a total of 31. While the Southwest Pacific quota was still 20 boats, about 12 had to operate in waters surrounding the Solomons, the Bismarcks and New Guinea.

In early 1943, there were still too many missions for too few submarines. Boats in need of major yard overhauls could receive only partial refits from a tender; crews in need of rest and relaxation had to be sent directly back on patrol; boats had to be pulled off the lucrative Japanese convoy lanes to perform special missions

---

[1] The research for this chapter has been done by Mr. Richard S. Pattee in the patrol reports in Office of Naval Records and History, in a file of Japanese replies to USSBS requests for information, and in the ms. compilation "Submarine Command" in the Administrative History series in that office; also the USSBS Report No. 54 *The War Against Japanese Transportation* (1947); the Comsubpac publication *U.S. Submarine Losses* (1946). Data checked from JANAC. Theodore Roscoe *U.S. Submarine Operations in World War II* (U.S. Naval Institute 1949), an excellent type history, appeared in the course of this research. It is based on the ms. "Submarine Operational History" mentioned in our Volume IV p. 187 note, and largely replaces it as a source.

or to scout for surface forces. This was especially true of the Brisbane-based boats of Task Force 72, commanded by Captain James
Fife.[2] Many of these boats carried out the functions of a fleet
scouting force, the type of submarine operation envisioned in prewar days when the Treaty of London almost prohibited attacks on
merchant shipping.[3] But Rear Admiral Lockwood's[4] submarines of
Task Force 71, based on Fremantle in western Australia, and the
few boats of Oahu-based Task Force 17 which operated on the
fringes of the South and Southwest Pacific, were able to carry out
unrestricted submarine warfare on the Japanese shipping lanes.[5]

The movements of the Brisbane-based boats were to some extent
integrated with the surface and air operations described elsewhere
in this volume. Before and during major amphibious landings in the
Solomons, Bismarcks and New Guinea, these boats were pulled in
from their patrol areas and formed into a scouting line between
Truk and the Bismarcks. As such, their primary mission was to
observe and report rather than to attack. When not scouting, the
South Pacific boats patrolled around Bougainville, New Britain
and New Ireland, and along the convoy lanes between the Bismarcks and Truk and the Palaus. In September 1943 an advanced
submarine base was set up at Tulagi. A boat would refit at Brisbane, cross the Coral Sea, making practice attacks on her surface
escort, top off fuel tanks at Tulagi and move up to her patrol area
along a "restricted bombing lane" off the east coast of Bougainville, in which Allied planes had to make positive identification of
any target before attacking.[6] Yet mistakes occasionally occurred.
The skipper of *Stingray*, after learning that a plane which had just
bombed him was "friendly," remarked, "No friend of ours!"

[2] Relieved 15 Mar. 1944 by Captain John M. Haines.
[3] See Vols. I and IV of this History pp. 8 and 189 respectively.
[4] Relieved by Rear Admiral Ralph W. Christie 7 March 1943, when Rear
Admiral Lockwood assumed command of Submarines Pacific Fleet.
[5] A few Dutch submarines operated from Fremantle, but most of the O- and
K-boats that survived the Abda command were attached to the British Far Eastern
Fleet operating from bases in Ceylon.
[6] Established as a result of a damaging attack on *Grouper* by an A.A.F. plane
on 30 July 1943.

At the end of 1943, after the Straits had been secured, the Brisbane-based submarines began to operate in the Bismarck Sea and along the New Guinea coast, shifting their advanced base to Milne Bay. A new restricted bombing lane was set up, running from Milne Bay through Vitiaz Strait to the Bismarck Sea.

By early 1943 all boats in this area had been air-conditioned and supplies of frozen foods were coming in, so that in 50-day patrols human endurance was not strained. All boats were now equipped with SJ radar, but performance was not always satisfactory because of operational failures, and it took eighteen months to train an electronics technician.

During this period of 15 months there were 75 war patrols, including special missions; and the total score for the Brisbane-based submarines was 47 *Marus* ranging from 50-ton trawlers to the 12,000-ton submarine tender *Hie Maru*, with a total tonnage of 204,000. In addition to these merchant ships and auxiliaries, light cruiser *Yubari*, three destroyers (*Oshio*, *Umikaze* and *Sazanami*), an unidentified vessel and submarine *I-168* were sunk.[7]

One of the first of the South Pacific boats to score in this period was *Albacore* (Lieutenant Commander Richard C. Lake), on her third war patrol. At 0330 February 20, in bright moonlight, Lake sighted three targets at 3500 yards, identified two of them correctly as destroyers and the third as either a frigate or a minelayer.[8] He took *Albacore* down, surfaced an hour and a half later, and at full speed made an "end-around" run until he was in a position to attack from ahead. At 0708, with the convoy in plain sight, he dove again, made his final approach and, just as the morning watch was ending, fired three torpedoes at the leading destroyer, followed a minute later by two at the third vessel. *Albacore* at periscope depth observed one torpedo hit the leading

[7] All torpedoings of over 500 tons here as elsewhere have been checked in JANAC. Owing to the few Japanese records on ships damaged, it is extremely difficult to assess correctly American claims of that nature.

[8] JANAC states that this ship was a frigate of 750 tons but does not name her; the ms. "Submarine Operational History" I 488 identifies *Albacore's* second victim as a 1345-ton minelayer of the *Shirataka* class. That is probably correct, since few of the Japanese frigates had yet been commissioned.

destroyer, *Oshio*, just abaft No. 2 stack and saw the other vessel, which had taken both "fish" destined for her, listing heavily with decks almost awash. After firing one more torpedo at *Oshio* and two at the other destroyer which was coming in fast, *Albacore* dove deep. During the next half-hour she heard 21 depth charges detonate, but none near her. When next she emerged, toward noon, there was nothing in sight; both targets had sunk.

*Drum* (Lieutenant Commander Bernard F. McMahon), in the course of transfer from the Pacific to the Southwest Pacific command, patrolled the Truk–Rabaul and Palau–Rabaul shipping lanes. On the morning of 9 April, following up a contact report from a V Army Air Force plane, she sighted a convoy of four *Marus* escorted by *PC-39* and fired three torpedoes at the leading ship. The escort kept *Drum* down for almost two hours, after which she surfaced and picked up a life ring which identified the victim as *Oyama Maru*. Pursuing the convoy on the surface, *Drum* caught up with it late that evening and made a night attack with three torpedoes, but sank nothing. McMahon now turned westward to the Palau-Rabaul route, where on 14 April he sighted a convoy whose air cover forced *Drum* down. Luck had not entirely deserted her, however, for on the afternoon of 18 April she sank the 6300-ton *Nisshun Maru* with two torpedo hits. *Drum* arrived Brisbane 13 May after disposing of over 10,000 tons of Japanese shipping en route.

During the entire war, Allied submarines sank 25 Japanese and 5 German submarines in the Pacific. *Scamp* (Lieutenant Commander Walter G. Ebert) on her third war patrol, accounted for one when patrolling southeast of Steffen Strait between New Ireland and New Hanover. On 27 July, while running submerged, *Scamp* sighted submarine *I-168* cruising on the surface. The Japanese saw *Scamp* too, and fired the first torpedo, which Ebert dodged just in time; he heard the torpedo passing overhead. At 1809 he brought *Scamp* up to periscope depth and fired four torpedoes at *I-168*. There was a flash, an explosion and a pillar of smoke at least 500 feet high as one of the torpedoes hit. Only an oil slick was left of *I–168*. Within eight minutes Ebert had taken his boat down to avoid a torpedo, returned to periscope depth, fired torpedoes, and sunk his antagonist.

*Silversides* (Commander John S. Coye) made a seventh war patrol which was one of the most successful in 1943. On the afternoon of 17 October, off New Ireland, she found her sister boat *Balao* engaged in chasing a convoy of three freighters, two tankers and two escorts. In the middle of the afternoon Coye heard *Balao* attacking. At dusk the convoy altered course in an attempt to shake off *Balao*, and ran right into the clutches of *Silversides*. She made an end-around run to get ahead and submerged at 2234. The convoy was steaming in three columns with one escort ahead and one astern. *Silversides* submerged about nine miles ahead of the convoy and at 0530 October 18 delivered an attack. Out of six torpedoes, two hit the leading *Maru*. Held down by the escorts' depth charges for almost two hours, *Silversides* emerged in time to see one escort picking up survivors astern of the convoy. She continued the chase over an ocean cluttered with debris for several miles. Coye made two later approaches, finally giving up on 20 October after a chase of more than 85 hours.

At dusk 22 October, *Silversides* sighted a convoy of seven freighters and two escorting patrol craft. She established communication with *Balao* and the two boats agreed to attack simultaneously on the surface at midnight. One of *Balao's* torpedoes prematured and the escorts, already jumpy, drove *Silversides* off before she could get into position. Coye again gave chase and late in the evening of the 23rd was rewarded by sinking a 5400-ton *Maru*. Next morning he found the convoy, which was milling about in confusion with two damaged and abandoned ships astern. One, with her bow blown off, obligingly sank without further assistance; but *Johore Maru* (6182 tons) was tough. Coye had to shell her and give her another torpedo which broke her back. The crew of *Silversides* were summoned on deck to see the sinking. Her patrol ended 8 November, with four *Marus* totaling over 15,397 tons to her credit.

*Scamp*, in company with *Balao*, *Albacore* and *Blackfish*, took position on the Truk scouting line to cover the landings at Empress Augusta Bay. They were unable to intercept the Japanese cruisers steaming down to Rabaul; but on the morning of 4 November *Scamp* sighted a convoy of three transports and three destroyers. Attacking late that afternoon, she fired six torpedoes for one possible hit, one dud and one premature explosion. This was her 15th premature in 17 salvos on her Pacific patrols to date. *Scamp*, with *Albacore* and *Blackfish*, was then ordered south of New Ireland to attack enemy ships fleeing from the 11 November carrier strike against Rabaul, and to rescue downed aviators. Before performing this mission Ebert de-activated the magnetic exploders of his torpedoes. On the morning of 12 November he sighted the new light cruiser *Agano* which had been hit by Admiral Montgomery's raid on Rabaul on the previous day, under way to Truk for repair. He made a cautious approach and fired six torpedoes, scoring, he thought, one or two hits on the cruiser; actually only one, but this hit rendered *Agano* "unable to navigate." [9] A glassy sea and the enterprise of escorting destroyer *Urakaze* prevented another attack during daylight, but *Scamp*, now joined by *Albacore*, decided to try again that night. Just as the two submarines were about to attack, destroyers and planes arrived from Truk and a heavy weather front closed in. When *Scamp* returned to Brisbane on 26 November, she could report that 5 of the 19 torpedoes she had fired on this patrol were prematures or duds.

*Raton* (Commander James W. Davis), fresh from New London, did very well on her first patrol. Passing through the Bougainville restricted bombing lane, on 25 November she reached a position west of Emirau Island in order to patrol the Palau-Rabaul convoy route. Next day she sighted two northbound *Marus*, whose surface escort and air cover prevented her from making a daylight attack, but she ran submerged at high speed for four hours to maintain contact — easy, because one *Maru* was a smoker. Surfacing for the approach at 1715, two hours before sunset, she dove as soon as the

[9] WDC Doc. No. 160623, log of Japanese cruiser movements.

masts were in sight, surfaced again to make a radar attack, and shortly before midnight was rewarded by putting three out of five torpedoes into 6600-ton *Onoe Maru*, which broke up and sank. The rest of the convoy escaped.

On the morning of 28 November *Raton* sighted a Rabaul-bound convoy of five freighters escorted by two PCs making 9½ knots. "We planned to get off six at the big one and four at one of the others," wrote Commander Davis, "but a radical change of course, just when we were ready to fire, made the range to the large one too great. However, the zig brought the remaining *Marus* into an overlapping line of bearing." The six torpedoes scored five hits on two freighters, both of which went down, depriving the Emperor of another 12,000 tons of shipping. The crew were brought up on deck in relays to "view the remains," and were gratified by the sight of two square miles of ocean littered with debris of every kind.

Pursuing the rest of the convoy, whose smoke was still visible over the horizon, *Raton* made a radar-directed attack shortly before midnight. All four torpedoes fired from the bow tubes exploded prematurely; one hit was obtained on a freighter, but it did not sink her. *Raton* outran the escorts on the surface, "pulled clear to take stock of the situation," sent out a contact report so that *Gato*, *Peto* or *Ray* could move up, and decided to attack again. She fired four torpedoes from her after tubes at 0300, but all missed and she was promptly chased away by a lively escort which opened up with gunfire and depth charges. "A very discouraging and disappointing night," concluded Davis. "Began to get worried late in the morning, as no one else had attacked the convoy. In checking back discovered I had left out the 'one' in the latitude report. Felt very badly."

He felt better on the 29th, when distant torpedo explosions were heard. This was *Gato's* work; and although she did not sink that *Maru*, it was not her last word, for in an attack on the same convoy next day she sank the 5618-ton *Columbia Maru*.

During the afternoon of 14 January 1944, *Guardfish*, *Scamp* and *Albacore* concentrated on one short section of the Palau–Rabaul convoy lane. Just after noon *Guardfish* (Lieutenant Commander Norvell G. Ward) sighted two destroyers which apparently were waiting for a convoy rendezvous. Again he met them at 1418, but in the meantime *Albacore* had torpedoed one of the destroyers, the 1950-ton *Sazanami*, leaving her on fire and sinking. Barely half an hour later, Ward heard *Scamp* attack the convoy that they were both after. A column of smoke announced her success as tanker *Nippon Maru* (9975 tons) exploded and burned. While the convoy's two escorting destroyers worked over *Scamp*, *Guardfish* closed to make a submerged attack on the two remaining tankers. Ward fired six torpedoes for five hits and one dud as tanker *Kenyo Maru* (10,022 tons) exploded and sank by the stern.

Between 23 and 29 January, 1944, *Guardfish* made a round trip to Tulagi for fuel. Just after noon 1 February, south of Truk, she sighted a convoy of two freighters escorted by destroyer *Umikaze* and two patrol gunboats. Unable to close the freighters, *Guardfish* fired four torpedoes at the destroyer; one demolished its stern, and *Umikaze* settled, rolled over and sank.

Besides warships and convoys, almost every submarine sighted trawlers, patrol boats and other vessels too small to warrant the expenditure of torpedoes. Most of these craft carried radio sets and many of them were heavily enough armed to make it a risky business to tackle them by gunfire. *Gato's* skipper, Commander Robert J. Foley, during her eighth war patrol, decided that the time had come to do something about these pests. On 13 February she was assigned to the Truk scouting line in preparation for the fast carrier strike on that Japanese base. On 15 February while south of Truk, *Gato* sighted a 150-ton trawler which she engaged with gunfire and set on fire so briskly that the crew abandoned ship.

*Gato* had her first major success of this patrol on 26 February. Early in the afternoon she sighted four freighters and two sub-chasers. She surfaced, chased this convoy and attacked during the night. Two of four torpedoes fired hit the leading ship, the 5200-ton *Daigen Maru No. 3*, and Foley's crew had the satisfaction of seeing her go down.

*Gato* now turned her attention to the northern coast of New Guinea, refueled at Langemak Bay, and on 9 March 1944 attacked and sank with gunfire a 50-ton trawler which had a Japanese Army crew and was trying to run in provisions for a by-passed garrison. Two days later, meeting a small "engines-aft" freighter and a 150-ton trawler, she surfaced and engaged them with her deck gun. The fight was short and ended with the freighter going up in flames and the trawler fleeing, badly damaged. *Gato* was now ordered to Pearl Harbor, which she entered 1 April after 70 days at sea.

Light cruiser *Yubari*, 20 years old and displacing only 2890 tons, had more than paid her keep by participating in the capture of Wake, the Coral Sea battle and the victory of Savo Island. Her single, prominent stack and amidships torpedo nests gave her so marked a resemblance to the new *Teruzuki*-class destroyers that she had repeatedly been reported sunk or at least damaged. But it was Lieutenant Commander Eric L. Barr who put the Indian sign on her. His submarine, *Bluegill*, on her first war patrol, on 27 April 1944 received a report from *Blackfish* that there were two targets about 150 miles south of the Palaus. The Japanese, alarmed by the Truk strike of 17 February, had begun to reinforce their southern islands, and *Bluegill's* contact was *Yubari* and destroyer *Samidare*, first of two units carrying 900 soldiers to Sonsorol, an island few had ever heard of and which certainly nobody wanted.[10] Barr headed that way at 17 knots, and at 0707 sighted topmasts through a rain squall and submerged. An hour later, emerging, he observed that the cruiser *Yubari* had stopped to land her troops and was being screened by destroyer *Samidare*. At 1014 *Yubari* steamed out from behind Sonsorol Island, maneuvering radically at high speed. Before *Bluegill* could maneuver, a bomb from a Japanese

[10] *Cincpac-Cincpoa Translations*, No. 11 (a compilation of Intelligence translations) 23 Dec. 1944 pp. 57–60.

plane forced her down. But at 1054 Barr found the cruiser, gave her six torpedoes at a range of 1900 yards, and got her. Two freighters also went into his bag on that patrol.

## 2. *Patrols from Fremantle*

"There is a ship." With these words and the implied addition "Sink it!" Admiral Ralph W. Christie [11] set the policy, strategy and tactics for the submarines of Task Force 71 which ranged the southwestern half of the Japanese Empire. The only operational orders given these boats were to sink enemy ships, preferably the biggest, but anything that floated was fair game. The Fremantle-based boats of Task Force 71 also did their share of special missions, such as minelaying, contacting Allied agents and supplying Filipino guerrillas; but these missions rarely interfered with normal patrolling.

Besides the main operating base at Fremantle, an advanced base was set up in April 1943 at Exmouth Gulf, where northbound boats could top off fuel tanks. Torpedo storage and refueling facilities were also provided at Port Darwin. The average patrol lasted 50 to 55 days, about 35 of which were spent north of the Malay Barrier. Principal patrol areas were the South China sea between Indochina and the Philippines, the approaches to Manila, and the Celebes, Molucca and Banda Seas.

From February 1943 to May 1944, Admiral Christie's boats, in 101 patrols, sank 96 *Marus* of over 500 tons for a total of 473,300 tons.[12] In addition they sank destroyers *Akigumo, Isonami, Sanae* and *Fuyo*, submarine *I-182*, and four smaller warships. At least 57 *Marus* and warships were heavily damaged and 55 small craft

[11] Rear Admiral Christie became CTF 71 as well as Commander Allied Naval Forces West Australia on 7 Mar. 1943 when Rear Admiral Charles A. Lockwood became Commander Submarines Pacific.

[12] These figures represent sinkings identified by JANAC, and due to the paucity of Japanese records represent a minimum assessment. These 101 include all patrols of CTF 71 ending after 10 Feb. 1943 and beginning before 1 May 1944.

of below 500 tons were sunk. The few patrols that we have chosen to relate are among the more important.

American torpedo shortage [13] reached its most critical point during the winter of 1942–43; the Fremantle command, at the end of the line, was almost starved. Unable to provide all his boats with a full allowance of torpedoes, Admiral Christie was forced in many cases to substitute mines. These minelaying missions were very unpopular with the submarine crews, as they meant going into shoal waters where the boats would be almost helpless if sighted and attacked. Submariners could never learn until after the war, if then, what damage their mines inflicted; and that was annoying.

*Tautog* (Lieutenant Commander William B. Sieglaff) carried out one of these minelaying missions. On the night of 6 March 1943 she laid 24 mines off the oil port of Balikpapan, Borneo. Glad to be rid of her "eggs," *Tautog* continued her patrol. On 10 March she shelled and sank two fishing boats and a schooner, and torpedoed and left burning a small tanker that had run aground. On 23 March at Pomalaa, New Guinea, she shelled an ore plant and a small coaster anchored inshore. *Tautog's* gun jammed, however, and as Sieglaff remarked, he "had to execute the classic naval maneuver" — an old Naval Academy euphemism for a quick retreat.

After sighting, chasing and losing contact with several small freighters, on 9 April Sieglaff sighted a convoy of five *Marus* and a destroyer near Buton Island just to the south of the Celebes. The initial contact was made at 0730, and half an hour later *Tautog* was in firing position. Sieglaff put two of three fish into *Penang Maru* but missed destroyer *Isonami* with another. Swinging his stern, he fired two more fish at another freighter and missed; but *Isonami* ran into the path of one and it "prematured" alongside her. *Tautog* was forced to go deep as *Isonami*, only slightly damaged, counterattacked. Three hours later, when Sieglaff brought his boat up to periscope depth, he found that the undamaged freighters had fled, but at 1145 he had the satisfaction of seeing *Isonami*, crippled by slow flooding, head for the beach, where she joined

[13] For reasons see Volume IV of this History, pp. 187–95.

*Penang Maru.* Now Sieglaff had a difficult problem, for the only torpedoes left were in his stern tubes and he had to take *Tautog* into very shallow water, turn and then fire. At 1306, just as *Isonami*, her damage temporarily repaired, was getting under way, he put another torpedo into her stern and she rolled over on her beam ends, a total loss.

*Gudgeon* (Lieutenant Commander William S. Post), on her seventh patrol, reached station off Surabaya 19 March and cruised back and forth for three days before sighting a target valuable enough to warrant revealing her presence in the heavily traveled Java Sea. Late in the afternoon of the 22nd she sighted a seven-ship convoy escorted by a destroyer and a patrol craft. Submerging, she moved into position, fired half a dozen fish at three freighters, and then was forced deep by depth charges. Only the 5400-ton *Meigen Maru* was sunk. The following morning, Post found himself in the kind of situation that makes submariners' hair turn gray. After making radar contact on another seven-ship convoy, he had submerged and started his attack when an escort picked him up on her sound gear. Post knew that he was in shallow water, but was surprised to hit bottom where the charts gave him over 26 fathoms. *Gudgeon's* crew had to sweat and listen while a Japanese patrol craft came barreling in and dropped seven depth charges very close. Luckily the skipper of that PC was an optimist and moved off to rejoin his convoy after only two runs.

*Gudgeon* got off the shoal, and, having sustained minor damage, decided to fight it out on the surface with a small subchaser sighted during the midwatch 24 March. Post fired four torpedoes which ran under, and then turned away and manned his 3-inch deck gun. On the fourth shot he put the subchaser's after gun out of action and scored three more hits before a Japanese patrol plane showed up. This was a time for discretion; he took the boat down. *Gudgeon* then moved up Makassar Strait and at 0210 March 29 sighted a large tanker in bright moonlight, surfaced, and immediately became the target for gunfire. Ignoring the shells splashing 50 yards away, Post fired torpedoes. Two hits stopped the gunplay, but did not sink the tanker; so Post pursued, put another fish into her, and then a fourth. After that, the 10,000-ton tanker *Toho Maru* went down. Just after noon the same day Post found himself in position to attack another tanker. Two torpedoes started her down, and five minutes later her boilers exploded and the crew abandoned ship.[14]

*Gudgeon's* next patrol, her eighth, was another blue-ribbon winner. After less than the normal two-week refit, she departed Fremantle 15 April 1944. Passing through Lombok and up Makassar Strait, she continued through Sibutu Passage and across the Sulu Sea to the Verde Island Passage. Here, west of Panay just before midnight 27 April, Post sighted the 17,500-ton passenger liner *Kamakura Maru*, pride of the prewar Japanese merchant marine. After working into position for an hour and a half, he fired four torpedoes and heard three hits. Believing the liner to be only damaged, Post started to swing ship to fire stern tubes; but before he could do so *Kamakura Maru* had gone down.

On 30 April *Gudgeon* landed one officer, three men and three tons of equipment for the guerrillas at Pucio Point, Panay, and evacuated two men for transit to Australia. After landing cargo, to restore correct balance Post shifted three torpedoes from the after to the forward torpedo room. Easily said but not so easily done, for the 14-foot, 2000-pound torpedoes had to be hoisted up the after torpedo hatch, lashed into the sub's rubber dinghy, floated forward and lowered down the forward hatch. On 4 May, Post "battle-surfaced" and shelled and sank a 500-ton trawler. The following morning a small coastal freighter was engaged, shelled and left burning. *Gudgeon* pulled clear, her 3-inch ammunition expended. On the morning of 12 May, Post sighted a freighter, camouflaged green and gray, moored north of Binorongan Point, Luzon. He brought *Gudgeon* in submerged, and fired his last two fish. Both missed and he saw them explode against the beach. Surprisingly, the postwar analysis credits *Gudgeon* with 5900-ton

[14] There is no record of this sinking in JANAC, but Post saw her with her decks awash and apparently done for.

*Sumatra Maru* sunk on this date and at that spot.[15] With no more torpedoes and no gun ammunition remaining, *Gudgeon* steamed through San Bernardino Strait en route to Pearl Harbor.

One of the earliest successful patrols was *Bonefish's* first. Under command of Lieutenant Commander Thomas W. Hogan, she left Darwin 15 September 1943 and on the 24th reached patrol station in the South China Sea off Cape Varella, the eastern bulge of Indochina. This was on the main oil line from Japan to Malaya, and Hogan did not have long to wait for targets. After sunrise next morning, he sighted a convoy of five *Marus* and an escorting *Chidori*-class torpedo boat.[16] He surfaced and started an end-around run to get into a favorable attacking position ahead of the convoy. At 0917 he sighted friends *Billfish* and *Bowfin*, both chasing this same convoy. *Bonefish* got in position at 1030, but the enemy zigged out of range and she had to surface and start over again. At 1315 the *Bonefish* crew saw *Bowfin* sink the 8100-ton transport *Kirishima Maru*, after which the whole convoy scattered. Hogan picked out a tanker target and gave chase. At dusk he pressed home an attack and at 1918 put two fish into her.

Hogan's next victim was the largest of four ships in a convoy sighted at 0208 September 27. *Bonefish* made a submerged attack at dawn and believed she got four solid hits, but was forced down, depth-charged and bombed for eleven and a half hours by the convoy's three escorts and a patrol plane. No matter — she had sunk the 9900-ton transport *Kashima Maru*, and the depth charges never touched her. After unsuccessfully chasing another convoy on 3 October, Hogan sighted three apparently unescorted *Marus* before dawn on the 6th. He made a submerged attack and split his torpedo salvo, hoping to hit every ship so that he could pick them off later. It worked all right with the two larger *Marus*, but the torpedo fired at the smallest prematured, and that ship turned out

---

[15] JANAC p. 41.
[16] The *Chidori*- and *Otori*-class torpedo boats (800 to 1000 tons; three 4.7 inch guns, 6 torpedo tubes, 28 knots, similar to American DEs) were among the most efficient and dangerous of Japanese anti-submarine vessels and were used extensively as escorts.

to be a well-armed escort which tried to ram *Bonefish* and then dropped depth charges. It was perhaps fortunate that the weather now turned foul and contact was lost in rain squalls.

On 9 October *Bonefish*, after four hours' tracking another convoy, made two hits on the 4200-ton *Isuzugawa Maru* which "blew apart" before her eyes, and two more on the 10,000-ton transport *Teibi Maru*, which went down stern first. An auxiliary gunboat then forced *Bonefish* deep and depth-charged her for two hours, doing no damage but preventing her from regaining contact. With all torpedoes expended, Hogan turned back to Fremantle, sinking en route a small schooner which topped off a record bag of 24,216 tons.

*Bluefish* (Lieutenant Commander George E. Porter) is another of the "big B's" that prowled the South China Sea that fall. On 8 November Porter divided his fire among four different ships of a convoy, obtained five hits, swung ship and fired stern tubes at two other *Marus*. But only a large tanker sank,[17] so he charged in again and got tanker *Kyokuei Maru*. After a depth-charging on 16 November which knocked out *Bluefish's* SJ radar, she started back to Fremantle. Off Borneo on the 18th she sighted a third tanker escorted by a destroyer. Porter trailed them all day and most of the evening, getting into position for attack at 2245. One of four torpedoes hit the tanker and three hit destroyer *Sanae*, which blew up and sank. Porter then fired his last torpedoes at the tanker, and missed; no more torpedoes, so he closed for a gun attack. The tanker crew had both guns and guts; they opened such rapid and close fire that *Bluefish* had to retire. On this patrol *Bluefish* had scored hits with all but four of the torpedoes fired.

Certainly there was as much luck in submarine warfare as anywhere; but luck has a way of rewarding skillful skippers and well-trained crews. *Bowfin* had both. Lieutenant Commander Walter T. Griffith, on three patrols, scored 9 ships totaling 46,000 tons torpedoed and sunk, 11 small craft destroyed by gunfire, and 6 ships,

[17] Not listed in JANAC, but Porter saw her blow up and go down.

including a destroyer and seaplane tender *Kamoi*, severely damaged.

On the morning of 9 November 1943, *Bowfin* opened her second patrol by shelling and sinking four schooners in the northern part of Makassar Strait. These small craft were apparently carrying some heavy cargo such as ore, for they sank like stones. Two days later, while *Bowfin* was moving through Sibutu Passage between North Borneo and Tawi Tawi, Griffith sighted two small tankers. Not wishing to attack in restricted waters, he circled and waited off Tawi Tawi Bay, inspecting his targets at leisure — which so unnerved their crews that they abandoned ship — and then sank them with gunfire.

At dawn 20 November *Bowfin* rendezvoused with *Billfish* to make a joint patrol of convoy lanes off Cape Varella. After six days of rain squalls, high winds and heavy seas, *Bowfin* almost stumbled into the midst of a big convoy at 0200 on the 26th. After two hours' maneuvering Griffith put two fish into the 5000-ton tanker *Ogurasan Maru;* her bow broke off and the crew abandoned ship, whistle blowing full blast. *Bowfin* put a single fish into a transport and then swung back to finish off the tanker. One torpedo did the job; a second missed astern but hit another *Maru*.

After 26 minutes of hectic action, Griffith pulled clear to reload, and an hour later *Bowfin* was ready for business. She started tracking the same convoy through rising sea and intermittent rain squalls. Her crew, an hour after bolting breakfast, and still at action stations, sighted a straggler from the convoy. *Bowfin* submerged, worked around for an attack position in the foulest sort of NW monsoon weather, and just before 1100 fired four torpedoes, which took the 5400-ton *Tainan Maru* apart; she collapsed like a house of playing cards and disappeared in less than two minutes. Griffith then surfaced and evaded an *Otori*-class torpedo boat. After eight hours of torpedo attacks, tracking and evading all the time in heavy seas with unknown currents under an overcast sky, Griffith became worried about his position, and pulled out to sea to get a navigational fix.

By next morning, 27 November, the wind had moderated to 30 knots and the sea had gone down. Griffith sighted and trailed a small coaster, the French S.S. *Van Vollenhoven*. She was small but legitimate game, as Indochina was under Japanese control; so, remembering Admiral Lockwood's words, "Subs must take what comes rather than wait for something better," Griffith sent the Frenchman down.

At 0225 November 28 *Bowfin's* radar picked up a five-ship convoy in a single column with two *Otori*-class torpedo boats ahead and one astern. Griffith planned to cut the column between the van escort and get the leading merchantmen. And he did just that — sank *Sydney Maru* with four torpedoes and the 9800-ton tanker *Tonan Maru* with two torpedoes. The third vessel, however, bore down on *Bowfin*, opening fire with a 5-inch gun at a range of 500 yards, and her second shot hit *Bowfin* aft. Believing he was "done for anyway," Griffith slowly and deliberately put his two stern fish into this enterprising ship, stopping her shooting and starting her toward the bottom. A quick assessment of *Bowfin's* damage showed that, although the main induction valve was flooding, the pressure hull was not pierced; therefore Griffith pulled ahead and started in for another attack, so informing *Billfish* with whom he had made contact. The attack was delivered, but one torpedo prematured and deflected the other for a miss.

Griffith now decided to pull away from the coast for a more thorough damage assessment. At 0612 he stopped and sent a repair party topside. The Japanese shell had ricocheted into *Bowfin's* superstructure, exploding between the main induction (flooding) valves and the pressure hull. The crew repaired this damage with plugs and patches by midafternoon and made a test dive. Everybody held his breath, but everything held. *Bowfin* entered Fremantle on 9 December, 1943.

*Bowfin's* success continued in her third patrol under Griffith. In Makassar Strait on 16 January 1944 she shelled and sank a white schooner which had a Malay fishing sampan rig and was obviously a "spotter." The following evening she raised a freighter escorted by a destroyer and a torpedo boat, but her attacks, spoiled by prematuring torpedoes, got only one hit which stopped the freighter. Griffith refused to abandon this contact. Starting in again at 0236 January 18, he evaded the escorts and put four fish into *Shoyu Maru*. She "was gone when the spray cleared." Later that morning, 18 January, *Bowfin* contacted a tanker and a destroyer [18] which he chased, but was unable to close before they entered Balikpapan River.

Having expended all his torpedoes, Griffith proceeded to Port Darwin, arrived 24 January, fueled and loaded torpedoes, and, with Rear Admiral Christie on board as observer, proceeded across the Flores Sea to the southern entrance of Makassar Strait.

Just before dawn, 28 January 1944, Griffith sighted seaplane tender *Kamoi*, tracked her all day although forced by the tender's seaplanes to dive five times, and in early evening conned *Bowfin* into attack position. Just as he was about to fire, Griffith sighted *Kamoi's* escort on a collision course with him. He fired anyway, but the tender avoided the entire spread. An hour later, at 2200, Griffith started in again and put two of six torpedoes into *Kamoi* just under her bridge. The tender turned her searchlight on *Bowfin* and opened fire. Griffith promptly retired; "searchlight crossed us twice, didn't pick us up." *Kamoi* spotted his wake and opened fire on that. Griffith pulled ahead and *Kamoi* turned up full speed, zigging, twisting and turning. At 2245 Griffith fired two fish which missed, but 45 minutes later he managed to get two solid hits on the tender. Ten minutes later, he fired again and missed; but a few minutes before midnight he put his last fish into her. *Kamoi* caught *Bowfin* in her searchlight and opened fire with her stern gun. Griffith found the illumination inconvenient and submerged. *Kamoi*, awash forward to her bridge, kept starting and stopping;

[18] This destroyer, at first identified as a *Tenryu*-class light cruiser, was subsequently found to be U.S.S. *Stewart*, captured in the Surabaya dry dock in Feb. 1942. The Japanese had salvaged, reconstructed and recommissioned her as a PC and used her throughout the war. She was finally recovered at Kure in October 1945, brought back to America and expended as a target off San Francisco. See Vol. III of this History p. 378.

when last seen her stern was out of the water with propellers thrashing, and the escort was alongside. With all torpedoes expended, Griffith cleared the scene to give his crew a little sleep and to let *Billfish* have the stage. *Kamoi,* although badly damaged, managed to make port.

During the last four months of 1943, submarines got 14 out of the 15 Japanese tankers sunk by American forces in the Pacific. Nevertheless, on 1 January 1944 the Japanese still had 300,000 more tons of tankers than on 7 December 1941. In January 1944 eight more enemy tankers went down, one to a Navy carrier plane and the other seven to submarines. Misfortune really overtook the Japanese oiler fleet next month. The 17 February carrier strike on Truk put five tankers totaling 52,183 tons under the surface; and then along came submarine *Jack* (Commander Thomas M. Dykers), *"Jack* the tanker killer," as she was known in the submarine fleet.

In the South China Sea at 0338 on 19 February, just after the moon had set, Dykers made a radar contact on an enemy convoy of five tankers and three escorts, in two columns. In a series of attacks that lasted all day and almost until midnight *Jack* attacked on the surface and sank four of them, totaling over 20,000 tons. On 29 February Dykers sighted an unescorted *Nachi*-class heavy cruiser, but as his engines were smoking he had to submerge. At 0100 next morning he made radar contact on a four-ship convoy. But *Jack's* only remaining torpedoes were in her stern tubes, which made attack difficult, for as soon as Dykers swung ship to launch the target would speed up or zig. He managed to torpedo two freighters but they did not sink. Outrunning the escorts on the surface, Dykers turned *Jack's* bow toward Australia.

The Japanese submarine fleet was diverted from its proper function, in order to supply garrisons cut off by Allied sea and air power. During 1943 several I-boats and some of the larger plane-carrying class were based at Rabaul to carry supplies to Lae and the upper Solomons. It was a very uneconomical method of transport, as even the biggest submarines could carry only small cargoes, and a round trip from Rabaul to Lae required ten days to two weeks.[19]

The same kind of mission was performed with much greater success by the Fremantle-based submarines of the Pacific Fleet to keep the MacArthur command in touch with the Filipino guerrilla movement.[20] During the period 8 February 1943 to 5 March 1944, 19 such missions were performed, seven of them by the big 2700-ton *Narwhal* which was especially assigned to this work, and the others by fleet submarines *Bowfin, Cabrilla, Grayling, Gudgeon, Tambor, Thresher* and *Trout.* These carried important contact men, such as Lieutenant Commander C. Parsons, to the guerrillas in Mindanao, Panay and Negros, together with arms, money, munitions, radio sets and miscellaneous supplies. *Narwhal* on one voyage took as much as 90 tons to Mindanao and Samar and, on another, evacuated 32 civilians from Panay. These missions were of inestimable value in obtaining intelligence of enemy ship and troop movements, keeping up the morale of the loyal Filipinos, supplying guerrilla forces with munitions and medicaments, and counteracting the Japanese propaganda to the effect that America had forgotten the Philippines.

In May 1943 *Tautog* received a very special assignment to land two pro-Allied Javanese agents on Kabaena Island in the Celebes. Both were pious Mohammedans; one had made seventeen pilgrimages to Mecca. Difficulties arose that had been anticipated neither by the *Submarine Officer's Manual* nor the Koran. Spam, ice cream, fried eggs and other staple submariners' food were tabu; canned tuna fish and salmon had to be provided; and the navigator acquired a new duty of giving the passengers the course for Mecca, four times daily. Thus history came full circle, for the science of celestial navigation evolved from this necessity that all Sons of the Prophet were under, to project their prayers in the right direction.

[19] Information from Capt. Watanabe, April 1950.
[20] List and incomplete summary of these missions in ATIS *Intelligence Activities in Philippines During Japanese Occupation,* Appendix iv; better summary in Roscoe *Submarine Operations* pp. 508–22.

## PART II

# The Central Solomons and Huon Gulf Campaigns

CHAPTER VII

# Preparing an Offensive

## *February–May 1943*

East Longitude dates; Zone minus 11 time, in the
South Pacific; West Longitude dates at Washington and Pearl Harbor.

## 1. *Planes, Plans and Prospects* [1]

IN THIS VOLUME we shall have to seesaw back and forth between the Southwest and the South Pacific, the MacArthur and
the Halsey commands, which had the common objective of breaking the Bismarcks Barrier. Now that we have followed Mac-
Arthur's Navy (after 15 March 1943, the Seventh Fleet), under
Vice Admiral Carpender, from Milne Bay through the Battle of
the Bismarck Sea, we may turn to the Solomons to see how
Admiral Halsey's South Pacific Force (after 15 March, the Third
Fleet) was faring.

As in the Southwest the fall of Sanananda (18 January), so in
the South Pacific the evacuation of Guadalcanal (8 February)
brought a pause in the fighting. A whistle had blown for "time
out" in the great game of war; both sides badly wanted a breather.
Yet the game must go on, even if at a less furious pace. Here was
Japan's chance to score, while her enemies were closely engaged
with the Axis in the Atlantic and Mediterranean. The Americans
must press their advantage over a scarce-cold Guadalcanal — "Keep
pushing the Japs around" said Admiral Halsey. For the time being,
only his air forces were in a position to do that.

[1] Cincpac, Comsopac, Comairsopac files; ATIS "Southeast Area Operations"
Part 2 (Navy).

During March and April 1943 the Americans had the advantage in quality aloft and sometimes in numbers too. Comairsopac, Vice Admiral Aubrey W. Fitch, had about 316 planes of all types on Guadalcanal by 1 March, and his force could easily be reinforced from a pool of over 200 more at Espiritu Santo and New Caledonia. General Kenney's Allied Air Forces Southwest Pacific helped by frequent raids on Rabaul and Bougainville fields. Many changes based on combat experience had been made in older models of American planes. They were now higher powered, more heavily armed and armored, and with longer range. New types, so excellent that most of them fought through the war unchanged, included the F6F (Hellcat), a heavier, faster and tougher fighter plane than its stubby brother the Wildcat; the F4U (Corsair), a gull-winged fighter which could climb faster than anything the enemy had and travel twice as far as the old Wildcat; the B–24 (Liberator) capable of carrying more bombs longer distances than the older B–17. American pilots, profiting by the instruction of veterans, were better trained than before and their briefing was based on "hot" photography and accurate interpretation. On the debit side, the only Allied air base in the Solomons was on Guadalcanal; even the new fighter strip in the Russells, completed in March, added little range to Allied raiders.

The Japanese advantage was mainly one of position. They owned a nicely spaced series of airstrips beginning with four at Rabaul, going down 166 miles to Buka, thence 105 miles to Kahili in lower Bougainville, thence a 102-mile jump to Vila, with Munda and Rekata Bay (the last a seaplane base) only a little farther. Munda was very convenient for staging planes from Rabaul or Bougain-ville for raids on Tulagi-Guadalcanal. The bombers stopped there only long enough to refuel, and after executing their mission re-fueled again and returned to Rabaul, beyond Henderson Field fliers' range. Against these air tactics, the American air bombings and naval bombardments which pitted Munda Field with holes were vain. The Japanese ground crews, on the double, filled in the craters with crushed coral, and in a matter of minutes or hours the strip was again operational. Instead of rebuilding destroyed structures, the ground crews went underground.

Munda, then, was only a whistle stop for the Tokyo Air Express, but an essential one because the same types of aircraft which had started the war were still bearing the burden. Every Japanese plane

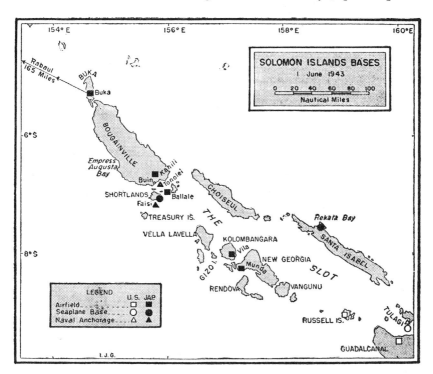

was highly inflammable for lack of self-sealing gas tanks. "Val," the dive-bomber with non-retractable landing gear ("pants down," we called it), was a slow and easy target for American fighter plane or anti-aircraft bullet. "Kate," the torpedo-bomber, lacked speed and endurance compared with the American TBF (Avenger). "Betty," the twin-engined torpedo-bomber, was fast and long-winded but horribly quick to catch fire. Japanese Army planes, seldom seen in the Solomons, were subject to the same defects. And the enemy made no provision for pilot survival. Many an aviator prematurely joined his ancestors because he was unprotected by cockpit armor. There was no rescue organization similar to our "Dumbo," [2] and aviators, like other Japanese fighting men, were indoctrinated to die rather than surrender. An air squadron was often kept flying until completely wiped out, instead of some of the veterans being saved to instruct young aviators.

While aviators continued their daily battles, staff planners in Nouméa and Pearl Harbor pored over charts and figures, sweating out studies and plans for the next move.

Even before their evacuation of Guadalcanal, the Japanese had decided on their next line for defending the Bismarcks Barrier — Munda to Salamaua. With Rabaul well-buttressed by Bougainville, the Shortlands, New Georgia and Choiseul, the air-sea "pipeline" to it from Japan via the Marianas and Truk should have been safe. As early as 18 November 1942 the Japanese Army and Navy concluded an agreement for the defense of Rabaul. The Army took over responsibility for the right wing at New Guinea, the Navy for Rabaul itself and the Solomons, and for overseas air operations against Allied shipping off the New Guinea coast.[3] This was a common-sense arrangement, consonant with each arm's theory of fighting the war. The Eighth Fleet, Eleventh Air Fleet and Special Naval Landing Forces were obviously the more capable of holding the Central Solomons against American air and amphibious attacks; the Army, whose air force was not trained to fly over water and whose leaders kept one eye on India and the other on Russia, was best fitted to fight over the large land mass of New Guinea. Japanese Army–Navy relations being what they were, this meant that General Imamura would seldom, and then with great reluctance, release soldiers to garrison the Solomons, and that Admiral Kusaka would not send bombers to pound General Kenney's airfields in New Guinea.

Fleet Admiral Yamamoto, Commander in Chief Combined Fleet,

---

[2] See Vol. V of this History pp. 332–33.
[3] Imperial Headquarters Navy Directive No. 159, Nov. 18, 1942 "Agreement between Army and Navy Branches," seen at ATIS, translated by Capt. Ohmae. There was a supplementary agreement of 22 March 1943, Directive No. 213.

husbanded his strength to engage the United States Pacific Fleet in a decisive action on the Jutland scale. He had tried it thrice (Midway, Eastern Solomons and Santa Cruz) and failed. Now he proposed to wait for Nimitz to overextend and give him the big break. But the loss of six carriers and 17 destroyers in less than a year required conservation of these two valuable types. Hence the carriers were safely tethered beyond range of American planes, and the Eighth Fleet at Rabaul was granted only a niggardly ration of destroyers.

On Christmas Eve 1942, Vice Admiral Jinichi Kusaka, Commander Eleventh Air Fleet at Rabaul, received the additional title Commander Southeast Area Fleet, which made him responsible for the Eighth Fleet and for all naval forces in the Bismarcks, Solomons and New Guinea. Knowing that he could expect little or no help from the Combined Fleet or the Army, Kusaka set about strengthening the air defenses of Rabaul. Airfield development at Munda on New Georgia and Vila on Kolombangara was speeded up; Santa Isabel was surveyed for additional strips. With the 200 fighters and bombers under his command he hoped to hold the Central Solomons with air power alone.

The Joint Chiefs of Staff at Washington could promise no reinforcements to the Pacific Fleet while Tunisia was still being fought over, while U-boats remained a major threat and when the invasion of Sicily was coming up. So, while awaiting the strength to launch a major offensive, Nimitz and Halsey planned. Shortly after New Year's Day 1943, Halsey sent two of his planners, Captain Browning and General Peck, to Washington to appear before the Joint Chiefs of Staff. And Nimitz, graduate and former staff officer of the Naval War College, demanded that every avenue be explored. On 15 January a 60-page estimate of the situation, outlining and comparing several courses of action, was completed by his staff. Assaulting Rabaul was considered and rejected as too costly.[4] Positions in the Upper and Central Solomons were studied one by one.

---

[4] As far as the record goes, Admiral King around 10 January first suggested taking the Admiralties and by-passing Rabaul.

Cincpac lingered longingly over "leapfrogging" New Georgia to Buin in southern Bougainville, and Ray Thurber at Nouméa contemplated by-passing Munda for Kolombangara. A startlingly bold new concept was presented at the same time: to assault Chichi Jima in the Bonins, only 523 miles from Tokyo. Any such operation would bring the Pacific Fleet into violent collision with the Combined Fleet, and Nimitz did not want that until the *Essex*-class carriers joined his Fleet; the logistic problems, too, were more than he could face at that time. So Nimitz regretfully set aside the Chichi Jima plan but recommended that it be kept alive until circumstances were more favorable, and "that continued study be made of plans to short-circuit the [present] campaign which now appears to offer Japan opportunity to remain on the defensive long enough to exploit the Far East, gain hegemony there, and force us into a stalemate."

On 23 January 1943 Nimitz met Halsey in Nouméa to discuss the next objective. The Japanese decision to evacuate Guadalcanal was already over three weeks old, but Halsey still knew nothing of it and estimated that the campaign would last some time yet. Nimitz made it clear that Guadalcanal was not to be made a permanent base — a decision infinitely comforting to everyone who had been there. "No permanent installations," he said; "only necessary construction; and there should be a reduction in rear areas. Everything should be predicated on a forward movement." [5]

Halsey's staff already had a minor forward movement in mind, to take the Russell Islands for a motor-torpedo-boat base, landing craft staging point and airfield, as a steppingstone toward Munda. "Sounds reasonable to me," said Halsey. Nimitz agreed and then bluntly asked, "When do you think you can move against Munda?"

[5] Admiral Nimitz's hope of rolling up rear bases as soon as a new forward base was established proved to be illusory. In preparation for the next offensive Efate, Funafuti, New Caledonia and Espiritu Santo went right on building up. In May, Halsey's headquarters were shifted from the old warehouse and stable on the waterfront at Nouméa to a French barracks building, placed grudgingly at his disposal by General de Gaulle, which had to be completely reconstructed for staff purposes. Airfields everywhere were being enlarged.

General Peck proposed 1 April as D-day; but it would be August before the first American set foot on Munda Field. Munda it was to be, if the Joint Chiefs consented. Everyone agreed that Munda must be the next big objective in the move on the Bismarcks Barrier. For the airdrome that the Japanese had built on Munda Point was one that we could use immediately; it had possibilities for development that were lacking at Vila, Ballale or Buin; and the logistic support of any one of these three, with New Georgia still in enemy hands, posed insuperable problems.

Admiral Nimitz insisted that the Navy should conduct this Central Solomons operation from Nouméa. Naturally this opinion collided with General MacArthur's equally firm conviction that the South Pacific belonged under his wing. The original Joint Chiefs of Staff directive of 2 July 1942 for Operation "Watchtower" had given the Navy responsibility only for taking Tulagi and Guadalcanal; all succeeding steps up to Rabaul were to be under MacArthur.[6] But in those days the South Pacific Force had been one of the "have nots"; now, after nine months' labor, Halsey had a well-oiled fighting machine, strong in all three elements and eager to climb up the Slot. So, since General MacArthur had his hands full in New Guinea and was developing a special amphibious force for service in those waters, why not let Halsey run the Central Solomons show?

Staff officers from both commands flew to Pearl Harbor early in March 1943 to discuss the matter with each other and with Admiral Nimitz. Halsey's representatives proposed that South Pacific forces assault Munda early in April. MacArthur's outlined Southwest Pacific plans for sweeping the Japanese out of Huon Gulf and asked that the Halsey offensive be timed, accordingly, for mid-May. The problem then went to the Joint Chiefs of Staff for solution. They judged it best for Halsey to wait until MacArthur had an air base in the Trobriands. Halsey agreed to the wisdom of deferring his operation, and on 29 March 1943 the Joint Chiefs issued a new directive, oriented toward Rabaul and "ultimate

[6] Vol. IV of this History pp. 260–61.

seizure of the Bismarck Archipelago." Tasks and command relations were set forth in the following terms: —[7]

## I. *Command*

1. The operations outlined in this directive will be conducted under the direction of the Supreme Commander, Southwest Pacific Area (MacArthur).

2. Operations in the Solomon Islands will be under the direct command of Commander South Pacific Area (Admiral Halsey), operating under general directives from General MacArthur.

3. Ships, planes and ground forces of the Pacific Fleet and Area, unless assigned by the Joint Chiefs to task forces engaged in the above operations, will remain under the control of the Commander in Chief Pacific Ocean Areas (Admiral Nimitz).

## II. *Tasks*

1. Establish airfields on Kiriwina and Woodlark Islands.

2. Seize Lae, Salamaua, Finschhafen, the Madang area and occupy western New Britain.

3. Seize and occupy Solomon Islands to include the southern portion of Bougainville.

MacArthur retained strategic command; Halsey obtained tactical control all the way up the Slot; Nimitz allocated fleet units subject only to J.C.S. rulings. Halsey, after reading the J.C.S. Directive, flew from Nouméa to pay a call on his "boss" in Brisbane. This visit proved a point made by Lord Nelson but often overlooked on the widely spaced fronts of modern war, that personal meetings between commanders are essential to military success. As Halsey later expressed his feelings: —

Five minutes after I reported to MacArthur, I felt as if we were lifelong friends. . . . I have seldom seen a man who makes a quicker, stronger, more favorable impression. . . . The respect that I conceived for him that afternoon grew steadily during the war. . . . I can recall no flaw in our relationship. We had arguments, but they always ended pleasantly. Not once did he, my superior officer, ever force his decisions upon me. On the few occasions when I disagreed with him, I told him so, and we discussed the issue until one of us changed his mind.[8]

[7] Summary of, not direct quotation from, "Cartwheel" Directive of 29 March.
[8] *Admiral Halsey's Story* pp. 154–55.

On this occasion MacArthur and Halsey concurred on the combined plans for invading New Georgia and the Trobriands and circled 15 May on their calendars as starting date. The operation was put off another six weeks, owing to unavoidable delays in building up the VII Amphibious Force; but the agreement on matters of principle was most important.

Shortly before this conference, on 15 March 1943, Admiral King instituted the new numbered-fleet system. Henceforth all Fleets in the Pacific were to be odd-numbered; all in the Atlantic even-numbered. The three Fleets and forces in the Pacific with which we are concerned were: —

Third Fleet (old South Pacific Force), Admiral Halsey; III Amphibious Force, Rear Admiral Turner, relieved 15 July by Rear Admiral Wilkinson.

Fifth Fleet (old Central Pacific Force), Vice Admiral Spruance; V Amphibious Force (set up in August), Rear Admiral Turner.

Seventh Fleet (old Naval Forces Southwest Pacific), Vice Admiral Carpender, relieved 26 November by Vice Admiral Kinkaid; VII Amphibious Force, Rear Admiral Barbey.

Each Fleet was further divided into task forces, newly shuffled for each operation, of which the first digit was the number of the Fleet; task forces were divided into task groups, with numbers following a decimal point, and the groups into task units, with numbers following a second decimal point.[9]

## 2. Russell Islands Occupied

The Russells, famous for mud, rain and coconut plantations, lie but 30 miles W by N of Cape Esperance, a scant 20 minutes' flight from Henderson Field. During the Guadalcanal campaign the Japanese used these islands as a staging point for barge traffic, and during the evacuation in early February 1943 they harbored several

[9] Thus, TU 31.3.2 in the next operation means the 2nd Task Unit of the 3rd Task Group, Task Force 31 (III Amphibious Force) of the Third Fleet.

thousand Japanese troops. Admiral Halsey, in the belief that these would stay put and fight, requested so many troops to get them out that Admiral King dispatched one of his typical caustic queries: "To what end are these operations a means?" The Russells occupation actually was an overstuffed affair, but it served as a useful dress rehearsal for bigger shows to come.

On 7 February 1943 Halsey ordered Rear Admiral Richmond K. Turner to take charge and land some nine thousand men on the Russells two weeks later. As the occupation force (elements of 43rd Infantry Division, 3rd Marine Raider Battalion, two Marine defense battalions, a Seabee battalion and a naval base organization) was mostly in New Caledonia, it had to be fleeted up in large transports for transshipment at Guadalcanal and Tulagi. The only fight of the entire operation occurred during this preliminary movement from Nouméa.

On the morning of 17 February a tanker and four transports carrying 4500 men, escorted by six destroyers,[10] were located and trailed by Japanese air scouts. The new Commander Eleventh Air Fleet at Rabaul, Rear Admiral Takaji Joshima, hoping to repeat his predecessor's exploit against *Chicago*, selected a dozen "Bettys" armed with torpedoes. The planes took off from southern Bougainville, and off San Cristobal were homed in after dark by snoopers. At 1911 a snooper dropped one of those intense white flares, the appearance of which was the prelude to a night air attack.

Captain Ingolf N. Kiland, task unit commander in *President Hayes*, had read the day's portents correctly and was not surprised. He increased distance among his bulky auxiliaries, stationed his destroyers in a bristling circle around them, and commenced a series of 45-degree turns. For the better part of an hour the Japanese planes pirouetted beyond gun range, tossing out brilliant flares and colored float lights. At 1943 the bellwether dropped a shower of sparkling green stars as signal to attack. A few minutes

[10] Transports *President Hayes, President Jackson, President Adams* and *Crescent City;* oiler *Tallulah;* destroyers *Drayton, Craven, Grayson, Lardner, Maury, Conyngham.*

later the twelve "Bettys" bored in against the convoy, now brilliantly illuminated by white flares. A full moon assisted, casting a diffused glow through thin streamers of cirrus clouds. Close to the convoy, the enemy fliers opened ranks to attack from several directions at once.

In Commander L. A. Abercrombie's escorting destroyers, radar tracked the planes and fed ranges, bearings and elevations to the gunners. Five-inch guns opened first, followed in quick succession by 40-mm, 20-mm and landing-craft machine guns manned by soldiers. The night flickered with muzzle flashes, tracers, flares, float lights and the flaming pyramids of splashing "Bettys." Below decks the troops could hear the boom of heavy guns, the chatter of light weapons and the shock of nearby torpedo explosions. Five planes in all were splashed and not one of their torpedoes hit, although several exploded in the boiling wakes of twisting ships. In 15 minutes the battle was over and by the time two PBYs from Henderson Field arrived with decoy flares the last shadower had left, the transports had resumed their march toward Guadalcanal and the soldiers had "hit the sack."

The tactics of this brief tussle were in happy contrast to earlier bungling at the Battle of Rennell Island.[11] American anti-aircraft defense coped successfully with the Japanese pattern of night air attack; Kiland's skillful maneuvering (worthy of Kelly Turner) and excellent anti-aircraft formation, in conjunction with fire control radar and the deadly proximity fuze, saved the convoy.

If Kiland's convoy was the only one to be molested during this staging movement to Guadalcanal, Airsols [12] was responsible. The Henderson Field airmen plastered Japanese bases at Munda, Vila, Bougainville and the Shortlands day and night with every type of airplane within reach — big, deep-chested Flying Fortresses and Liberators, hustling little Avengers and Dauntlesses, night-prowl-

---

[11] See Vol. V of this History chap. xv.
[12] The increasingly prominent rôle of Guadalcanal air power was recognized on 15 February when Rear Admiral Charles P. Mason arrived with the new title, Commander Aircraft Solomon Islands (Comairsols). He was relieved by Rear Admiral Marc A. Mitscher 1 Apr. 1943.

ing Black Cats, heckling Wildcats and Lightnings. It was the old Guadalcanal story — pilots and planes from New Zealand and three United States air forces coöperating to make the enemy's life unhappy and his airfields inoperable. Compared with the spectacular strikes on shipping in 1942, this was dull work but equally dangerous and vital. And it paid off. Nobody concerned in Admiral Turner's next amphibious venture got his feet wet.

A week before the Russells landings, reconnaissance parties found that all Japanese had evacuated the islands. Turner's task force departed Lunga Roads at nightfall 20 February to arrive at the Russells by daybreak. The landings, wholly unopposed, were repeated during the next few days until 9000 men and equipment for building a staging base·and airfield had been landed. The Japanese, ignorant of what had been going on for nearly two weeks, made their first air attack on the Russells on 6 March.

## 3. *Mainyard and Button* [13]

The delay in the start of the Central Solomons operations, first from 1 April to 15 May and then to 30 June, was unfortunate because it permitted the enemy to strengthen Munda. But it gave us time, too, to build for the immediate future. Let us take a look at Guadalcanal in the spring of 1943. No longer known in code as "Cactus," the Guadalcanal base is now referred to in dispatches as "Mainyard." And a main yard it is indeed, with a thousand mainland factories and a hundred other bases funneling matériel into the supply dumps around Lunga Point.

Take a tour now with Commander Mainyard, Captain Thomas M. Shock, as he inspects his military fief. To unfamiliar eyes all is a jumble; an office here, a workshop there, supply dumps everywhere. But the whole functions with the precision of the cruiser

[13] Besides personal experience, we have drawn on Commander Naval Base Guadalcanal *History of U.S. Naval Advanced Base Guadalcanal 1942–1945;* Bureau of Yards and Docks *Building the Navy's Bases in World War II.*

that "Tommy" Shock lately commanded. Here is the radio station, underground at last but damp and hot. Watch those dispatches grow on the spindle as the operators translate the whine of the high-frequency into the clatter of typewriter keys. Over there is a switchboard, the telephone exchange. Do you wish to call the air-field? Which one? There are several now besides Henderson. Suppose you want Public Works, as almost everybody in the Navy does. Which part of Public Works — the power plant, the road gangs, the Quonset hut builders, the telephone linemen?

We ride a jeep down lanes of coconut palms, past rows of green Quonsets. This is the armory, a small part of the Ordnance Department, which also runs an ammunition depot, demolition units, mine detail, torpedo "circus," and defense gun batteries. Supply Officer is another hard-worked sailorman. Food, clothing, tools and stores of all kinds pass through his worried custody. On the beach we find Port Director installed in a hut which affords him a good view of the crowded Lunga roadstead. A cranky "spitkit" fleet, part of which runs regular ferry service to Tulagi, is under his jurisdiction. They are the least of his worries. Scores of small craft need repairs and attention. Merchant ships anchored in the roadstead want lighters and tugs. Transport skippers scream for pilots, charts, berthing and unloading instructions. Unwanted visitors (like this writer) want transportation to Tulagi, Purvis Bay, Aola, the Russells. "Can't send you today, Commander; come 'round to-morrow." No use arguing; he's "fightin' the war."

Captain of the Yard, an old Navy title that brings memories of mellowed stone buildings and green parade grounds, means something very different on this island. Here he is boss of "boys" from Malaita, each dressed in a lava-lava with a hibiscus flower in his startling coiffure, who work on roads, tote cased supplies and build a fine mess hall out of palm leaves (much cooler than imported architecture), all for a shilling a day. Captain of the Yard is also chief of a fire department that proves to be necessary in spite of the prevailing damp; he runs a stockade enclosing the few Japanese prisoners; he supervises the homely services of mess cook, barber, laundryman and tailor, which are rendered under shrapnel-torn coconut palms.

The Medical Department, under a genial Harvard professor in uniform who is well named Colonel Friend, runs the hospital, pursues "bugs" in drinking water and mosquitoes in swamps and, for morale purposes, trains a fine brass band. He wins the battle against malaria and has tropical ulcers – figuratively and literally – on the run. When our troops move up to Bougainville where the mosquitoes are even more numerous and deadly than in the 'Canal, the incidence of malaria will be reduced almost to zero.

With no more necessity to push Japanese off Guadalcanal, there have come the good and the bad of ordered life: motion pictures, daily tabloid full of jokes and gripes, Sunday services, officers' and enlisted men's clubs, a police force, courts martial and boards of investigation.

Captain Shock must also treat with many units beyond his jurisdiction although on the same island. Three hundred planes of the armed forces roost nightly on the Lunga plain; nearby are encamped hundreds of men to serve them with bombs, bullets, fuel and overhauls. Camped in a cool, healthy area near Cape Esperance, the 43rd Infantry Division practises jungle tactics against the hour of the New Georgia landings. Not far away the 3rd Marine Division is limbering up for the next push.

Across Ironbottom Sound, Captain Oliver O. Kessing – better known as "Scrappy" – gives orders and dispenses hospitality at Government House, Tulagi. The sleepy old Chinatown, abandoned by its inhabitants early in 1942, has been completely razed and a city of huts erected; the cricket pitch of the former British residents has been turned into a baseball field; the golf links have been largely covered with buildings. Up-harbor, where there used to be a native village called Sesape, a swarm of motor torpedo boats is moored and new barracks for their crews have been built across the harbor at "Calvertville." On Florida Island, behind Gavutu and Tanambogo, which were captured only last August, Seabees are completing a seaplane base. Port Purvis, next estuary to the east, is now a fleet anchorage where "Tip" Merrill's and "Pug" Ainsworth's task forces may rest by day. Hard by the Lord Bishop of Melanesia's palm-leaf cathedral, a new officers' club, "the Iron-bottom Bay Club," is being built to provide interim refreshment for these night-riding sailors.

As the sun slips under the horizon by Savo Island, we pay social calls on some of the old-timers: Colonel "Harry the Horse" Liversedge, Lieutenant Colonel Griffith, Corrigan of the Solomon Islands Native Defense Force. They dispense liquid hospitality from a battered gasoline tin. Sergeant Vouza, hero of the native constabulary, comes out of the shadows clad in GI shirt, loincloth, Silver Star and George Medal.[14] He pays his respects to blond Sam Griffith and tells of hunting down stray Japs, a sport for which he feels proper sympathy is lacking among the newcomers. The talk harks back to Gavutu, the Tenaru and the Bloody Ridge, "the good old days" when we "fit" with General Vandegrift.

We leave the Marines singing their ancient songs, together with a new one, aimed at the Army, about "making things nice for our fighting men." And on the trail back to our Quonset we pass a crude signpost giving the mileage to Brooklyn and to Tokyo. A long way to go yet; why the hell don't we start? What's keeping us?

The same questions are being asked by all hands at "Button," which is still the incongruous code name for the advanced naval and air base at Segond Channel, Espiritu Santo, 560 miles SE of Henderson Field and 409 miles N by E of Nouméa. Six and a half degrees of southing make Button a much more salubrious place than the Lunga plain. The fleet anchorage is ample and well protected, the first of a number of wharves is completed by the Seabees in April, the shore installations are mostly on a slope facing the fresh trades, and the Pallikulo airfield, a few minutes' drive over coral-surfaced roads, is second in importance only to Henderson. Here are the headquarters of genial Comairsopac, Vice

---

[14] Hector MacQuarrie *Vouza and the Solomon Islands* (1948) is an excellent description of the prewar Solomon and Santa Cruz Islands, and includes a fine sketch of this interesting character.

Admiral Aubrey W. Fitch, who takes a fatherly interest in his domain and is beloved by the officers of visiting warships. Here experiments are being conducted in night bombing by radar, which will pay off next year; and here, located in a coconut grove near an enormous banyan tree, is Commander Robert S. Quackenbush's Photographic Interpreter Section.

Less than a year earlier, when we invaded Guadalcanal, "photographic intelligence" meant a few cloud-obscured aërials taken from great altitudes, and scenic snapshots torn from the albums of former residents. Since then the science of aërial photography has been revolutionized. Especially equipped P–38s, designated F–5, now carry Fairchild cameras daily over enemy bases. These cameras are of the Sonne continuous-strip type, in which the film's movement is synchronized with that of the plane over the ground. The F–5 flies so high that anti-aircraft fire cannot reach it, and so fast that pursuing "Zekes" are out-distanced. The planes return to Button, and within a few hours of when they were exposed, the films have been developed and are under scrutiny by Commander Quackenbush and his trained photographic interpreters. They prepare mosaics, grid overlays (photos marked in squares to indicate target areas) and vectographs which make a three-dimensional photo when viewed through polaroid glasses.[15] They study stereoscopic prints which nullify camouflage and separate real targets from dummies. Radar can show a shoreline clearly enough, but it cannot reveal the location of hidden batteries or supply dumps. Aided by photographs, the fire control men in warships can now lay their sights on some prominent radar landmark such as a point of land, then offset the guns to hit pin-point targets. This was another case in which American ingenuity beat the enemy at his own game. The persistent Japanese tourist with his Leica, snapping warships and shore installations before the war, was a mere figure of fun compared with the American aërial photographer.

[15] As a sample of the early work of this Unit, see the photographs of the developing Munda airfield, in Vol. V of this History p. 338.

These F–5s are a highly specialized squadron out of some hundreds of planes in the South Pacific engaged in search missions; and all search planes carry cameras as part of their equipment. One of the most important functions of Admiral Fitch is to plan searches in the South Pacific and to assign planes to them. The general idea is to cover all possible approach routes of Japanese air and surface forces. Sectors in which air opposition is most likely to be offered are handed to the far-ranging Liberators and Fortresses; others are covered by Catalinas, Venturas, or R.A.A.F. Hudsons. Sectors that cross the Japanese air-surface routes between Truk and the Solomons may be given to the combat air patrol of a carrier. Night searches are the prerogative of Black Cats; rescue missions of Dumbo. On paper a search pilot's task seems simple enough — take off from Guadalcanal, fly a straight course for so many hundred miles, cut over to the in-leg and return, making a "thin pie slice" track over the ocean. Some sectors are safe, but on others, enemy bases such as Munda are only fifty miles from the track. If that track is searched daily, eventually the Nips will spring a fighter trap for the scouts; so Admiral Fitch varies them frequently. But, fair weather or foul, "Zekes" or no "Zekes," a search pilot must push on to "journey's end . . . my butt and very sea-mark of my utmost sail." [16]

One might trace the progress of the Pacific war by bars as well as by airfields. Base Button, from which up-the-Slot surface raids now started, has now replaced Nouméa as the center of bustle and excitement. Ballfields, outdoor movie theaters, beer halls and the like have been provided for the bluejackets, and for the officers what was proudly hailed as the "longest bar in the Pacific," and would hold that record until an even longer one was set up at Manus. Drinks are rationed, so at the opening hour of 1700, when a task force is coming in, officers are lined up five deep. And, lest they forget what they are there for, a Seabee artist has constructed a glass wall of beer bottles, the brown ones in a pattern showing

[16] *Othello* V ii 267–68.

the name TOJO against a green-bottle background, and has set it
up as backdrop to the indispensable retiring room at the end of the
bar.

## 4. *Interim Actions*

### *a.* "Tip" Bags Two "Bastards"

Spring of 1943 found United States naval strength in the South
Pacific greater than ever before, except in fast carriers. There were
six task forces backing up the Guadalcanal line. Two, "Duke"
Ramsey's and "Ted" Sherman's, were built around *Saratoga* and
*Enterprise.* "Ching" Lee still flew his flag in *Washington,* and had
three more battlewagons of that vintage. "Harry" Hill swung im-
patiently around the hook at Efate with salvaged *Maryland,*
*Colorado,* and three *Sangamon*-class escort carriers. Halsey would
have no use for these before the summer offensive, if then; but he
counted on two cruiser-destroyer task forces under "Pug" Ainsworth and "Tip" Merrill to "keep pushing the Japs around." [17]
For there is nothing like action to improve morale and bring ships
to a high point of efficiency. The Japanese continued to expand
their air bases at Munda and Vila in spite of day and night air
bombings, so the obvious interim employment for the South Pacific
Force was to repeat the gunfire bombardments of these two air
bases that had been successful in January. [18] "Pug" had done that
job; now it was "Tip's" turn. This task force commander, a shy
and soft-voiced officer, concealed energy, drive and ambition under
a placid and modest exterior. He had trained his gunners well and
had confidence in them. [19]

[17] TF 67 (Rear Admiral W. L. Ainsworth): *Nashville, Honolulu, Helena, St.
Louis,* 8 DDs. TF 68 (Rear Admiral A. S. Merrill): *Montpelier, Columbia, Cleveland, Denver,* 8 DDs. Rear Admiral Giffen in *Wichita* was really the commander
of this task force, but Merrill was designated by Halsey to take charge of this
operation.
[18] See Volume V of this History pp. 325–30, 344–47.
[19] Aaron Stanton Merrill, b. Stanton, Miss. 1890, Naval Academy '12, World
War I service in destroyers based on U.K. ports and C.O. *Harvard;* aide to Rear
Admiral Bristol at Constantinople to 1923. Various duties in Asiatic Fleet, 1926–27;

Four destroyers under Captain Robert P. Briscoe, *Fletcher*, *O'Bannon*, *Radford* and *Nicholas*, were told to bombard Munda. They threw about 1600 five-inch shells into the airfield in the early hours of 6 March. It was rated a successful bombardment, but Munda Field was operating again next day.

Merrill's assignment, more difficult because farther from base, was prepared with more care. He had light cruisers *Montpelier*, *Cleveland* and *Denver* and three destroyers. Two submarines, *Grayback* (Lieutenant Commander E. C. Stephen) and *Grampus* (Lieutenant Commander J. R. Craig), were stationed along the Japanese retirement route to snare any ships trying to escape Kula Gulf. *Grampus* was never heard from after the evening of 5 March.[20]

It was a calm, moonless night when Merrill's task force entered the Slot. The three Black Cats assigned as spotters and scouts overtook him there. Changes of course and speed were made at prearranged times. The cruisers' bridges, without the accustomed chirp of the TBS, seemed strangely quiet. At 2230, Guadalcanal broadcast disturbing news: two Japanese light cruisers or destroyers had left the Shortlands at 1910 and were heading southeast at high speed. A few minutes later one of the Black Cats saw them.

Admiral Merrill was puzzled, but he had no need to worry. Destroyers *Murasame* and *Minegumo*, ignorant of his presence, were on a routine rice-and-bullet run to Vila. Their course took them through Vella Gulf and Blackett Strait. At 2330 off Vila they began transferring cargoes into waiting barges. Mission completed, they might have returned safely to the Shortlands by the

Office of Naval Intelligence; C.O. *Williamson* 1929; aide to Asst. Sec. Nav. 1933-34; Comdesron 8 1935, Naval Attache at Santiago de Chile 1936; Naval War College course, 1939; Comdesdiv 17 and Desron 8, 1939–41; Prof. Naval Science and Tactics, Tulane Univ. 1941–42; put *Indiana* in commission 1942; Rear Admiral from 11 Feb. 1943 when he received command of Crudiv 12. Director Office Public Relations Navy Dept. June 1944–Apr. 1945, Com Eight 1946, retired as Vice Admiral 1947, died 28 Feb. 1961.
20 No survivor or evidence was recovered. Her fate is still a mystery.

same route. Instead, they elected to go home the short way, via Kula Gulf. That was their undoing.

Merrill's force at this time was inside the Gulf making 20 knots on course SW by S, two miles off the coast of New Georgia. The Gulf was a bowl of darkness and Merrill's navigators relied on the SG radar. Points of land to port on New Georgia were plotted accurately, but radar indications on the starboard bow puzzled the operators. Radarscopes at 0057 gave bearing of Sasamboki Island southeast of Vila as 234°, which was all right, but distance 15,200 yards, which was all wrong. One minute later, the radarmen reported the "island" to be moving. Seconds later it split, indicating two ships. Radar plot [21] in each cruiser analyzed the situation and concluded that the problem was one for the gunnery not the navigation officer.

"Stand By to Commence Firing!" — the word rippled from flag bridge to conning towers, to gunnery control station, to gun mounts. There, nervous coughs, a shuffling of feet and an occasional low-voiced order scarcely scratched the consciousness of the gunners. In the aloofness of self, each thinks: Look at me — little Mac from back home. Sure I can dish it out, but can I take it? A Jap shell in my guts, or busting up 'cause I'm scared? . . . Voices are heard in gun plot: "Range One one O double-O; Range One O five double-O. Target course 335, speed 15. Solution! Range one O O double-O. Time 0101. Commence Firing!"

On board the unsuspecting Japanese destroyers, sailors secure

---

[21] Early in the war, digestion of radar intelligence was confined to fighter-director officers and enlisted radar operators. The night actions around Guadalcanal convinced everyone that radar contacts should be plotted and expertly analyzed in a quiet spot away from darkened bridges. Ships' crews equipped a compartment in the superstructure as "radar plot" and the executive officer gravitated thither. Gradually radar plot absorbed other functions, becoming a terminal for radio, radar and lookout reports. Information received would be correlated and passed to bridge, gunnery, flag or other stations depending on its character. Thus radar plot, as its scope and importance broadened, became the combat information center, C.I.C. By the end of the war C.I.C. was big business conducted in well-protected compartments below, manned by as many as 50 men; it may be said to have usurped Bridge as the nerve center of the ship. At the time of Merrill's raid, radar plot was in a transitory stage, its importance recognized but implements still primitive.

cargo lines as engineers bleed steam faster into humming turbines. The New Georgia coastline looms black and formless to starboard. Suddenly a lookout shouts. Pin-point flashes on the starboard bow, darting and blinking like sheet lightning! Lieutenant Commander

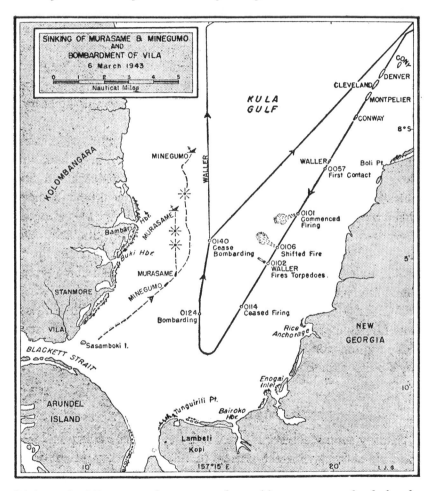

Tokuno in *Minegumo* shouts an order to his gunners as, dead ahead, he sees *Murasame* veiled in phosphorescent fountains of water. As usual in early radar-controlled gunfire action, the entire weight of the American cruisers' 6-inch fire falls on the nearer enemy ship. The sixth salvo hits *Murasame;* one of five torpedoes fired by destroyer *Waller* then crashes into her, and she explodes with a roar that is heard by Briscoe off Munda, 25 miles away. It is now about 0115 March 6.

*Minegumo* had turned northward and passed to the east of burning *Murasame*. At 0106 the American gunfire, still under radar control, shifted to her. Tokuno gamely replied, using American gun flashes as points of aim; but fire, flood and explosions soon stopped that and, within three minutes of Merrill's first salvo, *Minegumo* too was sinking. Tokuno took to the water with his shipmates and began a long swim to Kolombangara; next morning 174 exhausted survivors crept up on the sand.[22]

After this stirring ship action,[23] the bombardment came as anticlimax. It began promptly and lasted 16 minutes as scheduled, the three cruisers pasting supply dumps, runways, bivouacs and dispersed aircraft with thin-skinned, high-explosive shells. Enemy shore batteries kicked up a small fuss but were quickly silenced. Overhead in a Black Cat, Lieutenant Ned L. Broyles, who had observed the surface action with relish, spotted for a bombardment which he called "highly devastating." Then the task force scampered safely down the Slot at 30 knots.

Admiral Merrill, believing his targets to have been light cruisers, sent Halsey a jubilant dispatch, "Sank two light cruisers. What is 1943 bag limit on those bastards? Bombardment completed." Halsey's reply assured Merrill of an uninterrupted open season.

## *b.* Mining Offensives [24]

Hitting supply ships was one good way to put a crimp in Japanese air activity, but the enemy had become chary of exposing

[22] USSBS Interrogation No. 138; Comairsopac Intel. Bulletins; Eighth Fleet War Diary (WDC) states *Minegumo* sank at 0115, *Murasame* at 0130.

[23] Sometimes called "First Battle of Kula Gulf," but no name has been officially assigned. The Battle of Kula Gulf is Ainsworth's action of 5–6 July 1943. This Vila bombardment was followed up ten days later by another, led by Cdr. Francis X. McInerney in *Nicholas*, with *Radford*, *Strong* and *Taylor*.

[24] USSBS Naval Analysis Div. *The Offensive Mine Laying Campaign Against Japan* (1 Nov. 1946) pp. 62–3; Comairsopac Daily Intelligence Bulletins for the aircraft minelaying.

them. Another means remained, to mine the sea approaches to principal air bases. A mine is an insidious and nerve-rasping weapon, dangerous to ships even if it is known that waters are mined. You may not be able to avoid its explosive caress. You may think the enemy is sowing contact mines, only to find out after losing a ship that they are acoustics. Minesweepers often claimed to have disposed of them but failed to get the "counters," set to explode when the third or fourth ship passes nearby. The Japanese neglected this devilish branch of naval warfare because they never expected to fight a defensive war and failed to anticipate the possibilities of offensive mining. They had only four minesweepers at Rabaul, and Japanese sweep gear was inadequate — as we found to our cost after the war, when we had to sweep up our own mines around Japan.

Mining may be accomplished by any one of three agents: ship, submarine or airplane. The first two had already been used successfully by the United States Navy in the Pacific. Bougainville waters were too shallow and intricate for surface or submarine minelayers to enter. The alternative was the airplane, which both Germans and British had used to mine the narrow seas of Europe.

At dusk 20 March, 42 Avengers of the Marine Corps and Navy took off from Henderson Field, each carrying one ¾-ton mark-12 magnetic mine. Two and a half hours later, they were over Kahili checking landmarks in the hazy moonlight preparatory to starting their mining runs. Meanwhile, an Army diversionary flight of 18 B-17s and B-24s approached the field at medium altitude, dropping clusters of fragmentation bombs. When the field was well stirred up and Kahili "lit up like a Christmas tree" with anti-aircraft fire and searchlights as one aviator described it,[25] the TBFs dropped down to 1500 feet and disgorged their ugly cargoes into the harbor. Thanks to the Army diversion, not a single TBF was even scratched, and by midnight they were all back on Guadalcanal. The following night, 40 Avengers accompanied by 21 Army diversionary bombers gave Kahili an encore.

[25] Conversation with Capt. Frank E. Hollar USMC, pilot of a TBF.

It is difficult to assess the effects of an offensive mine field, but the Kahili plant had damaged destroyer *Kazagumo* and a merchantman within a fortnight, and it sank a 6400-ton *Maru* on 18 April. Halsey was encouraged to resume mining operations in May after Yamamoto's "I" Operation was over and Airsols could spare planes. During that month, nearly a hundred mines were sown in Bougainville harbors. Light cruiser *Yubari* was hit by one of these on 5 July, and submarine *RO–103* which disappeared in Solomons waters that month may also have been a victim. An officer interviewed after the war said, "In Munda, Buin and Kavieng the mines were very serious and there were many casualties." [26]

Repeated air strikes on airfields succeeded, in April, in establishing a daylight blockade of Munda and Vila against planes, but destroyer expresses still streaked in through Blackett Strait under cover of darkness. And a new motor highway starting at Bairoko on Kula Gulf gave the enemy an overland route for staging supplies into Munda. What could be done about it? Nightly raids by Black Cats lost the enemy sleep but cost him little. Cruiser and destroyer raids were too risky to be repeated often. The motor torpedo boats were still based too far away to be a threat. Night plantings of mines from Avengers appeared to be no longer paying dividends. So Halsey resorted again to ships to mine Blackett Strait.

The South Pacific Force included three little ships which had already served their country for twenty years and more: *Preble*, *Gamble* and *Breese*, four-stack destroyers converted into three-stack minelayers. They had practised coördinated minelaying together for years before the war.

On 4 May the three old-timers sailed from Espiritu Santo and were given destroyer *Radford* as consort because their radar sets were antiquated. Rehearsal runs were held en route. They refueled

---

[26] Ens. Toshio Nakamura's professional notebook, Jicpoa Item No. 4986; JANAC and *Campaigns of the Pacific War* p. 168; but *Yubari* may have been hit by a mine laid after May. Probably there was more damage, but the Japanese mine countermeasures officer in the Solomons was killed and took his knowledge with him. (Capt. Kyuzo Tamura in *Inter. Jap. Off.* I p. 16.)

at Tulagi, and continued into the Slot on the afternoon of the 6th. *Gamble* reported a leaky boiler tube which meant that her maximum speed would be 27 knots; but she stayed in the formation. They passed to the south of Rendova. At the same time Rear Ad-

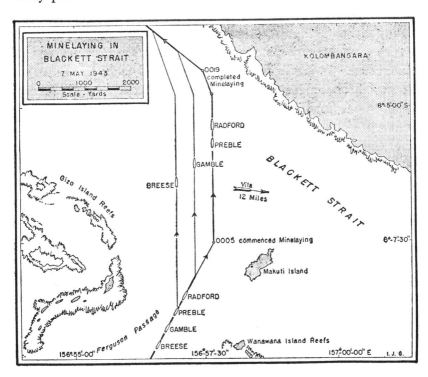

miral Ainsworth, with three cruisers and four destroyers, steamed up the Slot toward Vella Gulf to block enemy interference and get the old gals home if they got into trouble.[27]

One hour before midnight the minelaying group in column, *Radford* followed by *Preble*, *Gamble* and *Breese*, slowed to 15 knots and began the approach to Ferguson Passage, a reef-fringed channel between Gizo and Wanawana Islands. Lieutenant Com-

[27] Light Cruisers *Honolulu*, *St. Louis* and *Nashville;* destroyers *O'Bannon*, *Strong*, *Chevalier* and *Taylor*. The writer was with "Pug" that night and later interviewed the minecraft skippers, Lt. Cdr. Frederic S. Steinke of *Preble*, Lt. W. W. Armstrong of *Gamble*, Lt. Cdr. A. B. Coxe of *Breese*.

mander W. K. Romoser, *Radford's* skipper and task group commander, was uneasy when radar and sound gear showed the channel to be half a mile narrower than the 3000 yards indicated on his chart. A tropical deluge, descending when the group was in mid-passage, reduced visibility to absolute zero, but by good seamanship it managed to keep formation.

May 7 was but five minutes old when *Radford's* TBS announced the change of course to true North. As previously arranged, *Preble* followed in her wake, dropping the first mines as she swung. *Gamble* and *Breese* turned simultaneously so that the three mine-layers were spread out on line of bearing. A break in the storm disclosed each ship to the other in perfect formation, and the operation proceeded without a hitch. Still making 15 knots (then considered very fast for minelaying), each ship "laid an egg" every 12 seconds, so that in 17 minutes they had planted over 250 mines in three rows as neat as a cabbage patch.

Now it was time to retire northwesterly into Vella Gulf, a body of water into which no ship of the Navy had yet ventured except Ainsworth's cruisers and destroyers, which arrived a few minutes earlier. In his task force every pair of eyes topside peered through the darkness to pick up the familiar three-stacked silhouettes coming around Kolombangara. No sound had been heard, a good omen, but everyone was anxious for the little ships. At 0100, right on the dot, they were sighted; all four in a column smart enough for a Navy Day review, though their hulls were working and their engines groaning to keep up 25 knots. The two groups joined, steering parallel courses. Some Japanese night-hawk dropped a flare astern, spurring the black gangs to squeeze out a few more turns. High-speed prancing down the Slot in "Pug's" fast company so depleted the old-timers' fuel that they had to fall out and oil up at Tulagi before heading back to the "Button" barn.

Romoser's group not only deserved success after their fine feat of shiphandling, precise minelaying and radar navigation; they achieved it, and quickly. On the night of 7–8 May four Japanese destroyers swept into Vella Gulf and rounded Kolombangara. Dawn broke, and the crews were just congratulating themselves on a safe passage when three of the Blackett Strait mines tagged *Oyashio* and set her ablaze; a few minutes later three more crushed the hull of *Kagero*. Both floated, but *Kurashio*, hitting more mines within the hour, went down. Next morning a Kolombangara coastwatcher, Sub-lieutenant A. R. Evans of the Australian Navy, stared in delighted amazement at the two cripples flaming and floundering; undamaged *Michishio* was taking off their men. The news, too good to keep, was promptly relayed to Guadalcanal, which responded with a 60-plane strike. Bad weather kept all but 19 SBDs from getting through, but they cashed in on the afternoon of 8 May, plunking a thousand-pounder onto *Oyashio's* bow and landing near-misses alongside *Kagero*. Both ships sank. *Michishio* withstood a final attack by a trio of strafing Wildcats in the late afternoon and escaped, badly damaged.

With Blackett Strait effectively stoppered, the next thing on the mining program was to close the other entrances to Kula Gulf. One, the narrow Ferguson Passage, Japanese skippers were not expected to use at night. The wide entrance, following the northeastern quadrant of Kolombangara into Kula Gulf, now became the obvious route and so the place for a second minefield.

Halsey selected the night of 12–13 May for this operation and gave Admiral Ainsworth overall command of participating forces. In order to divert the enemy's attention from the minelayers, it was decided to bombard Vila and Munda the same night.

The two bombardment groups and the minelayers arrived early in the midwatch of the 13th. It was a clear, calm night. Ainsworth's three cruisers and five destroyers steamed down the west side of Kula Gulf and let go with a thunderous barrage on Vila airfield. Excellent aërial photos and SG radar enabled them to set gunsights accurately for the opening salvos. The enemy, preoccupied with tracking a Black Cat by searchlight, was astonished to hear shells dropping right in his camp. American sailors could hear the wail of the warning siren as searchlight operators and anti-aircraft gunners scurried into foxholes. After a 15-minute shoot on Vila, Ainsworth retired close to the New Georgia shore, so as to plaster Bairoko, terminus of the new highway to Munda. Cruiser *St. Louis* and destroyers *Jenkins* and *Fletcher* at the same time bombarded Munda.

In the meantime, the Romoser-led group of minelayers laid eggs in an 8500-yard line athwart the northwestern entrance to the Gulf. They then joined the cruisers, which had just slipped out through a five-mile gap still open on the New Georgia side.

This new mine field effected only a 24-hour blockade of Vila and Munda; the Japanese swept it up promptly. The bombardments were the last and most violent of the several gunfire visits to the two Japanese airfields. Ainsworth's was accompanied by several accidents, one of which cost the lives of 20 men.[28] Admiral Nimitz doubted that the risk of valuable ships and lives, and the expenditure of nearly 10,000 rounds of ammunition, were commensurate with results obtained.

Next time American naval guns visited the Central Solomons, they would be supporting an invasion.

[28] A turret explosion in *Nashville;* a powder cartridge "cooking off" in *Nicholas,* wrecking the gun mount; several 6-inch guns jammed; anchor carried away in *St. Louis* and punching a hole in the bow; steering engine breakdown in *Strong,* nearly resulting in collision with *Chevalier.* Engines, however, never have as much trouble as guns because, running continuously, the "bugs" are removed during shakedown. Guns fire too infrequently to determine defects before action, in spite of elaborate pre-firing "check-off" lists.

# CHAPTER VIII

# Yamamoto's Last Offensive

*April–May 1943*

## 1. The "I" Operation [1]

### a. In the Solomons

East Longitude dates; Zone minus 11 time.

A DMIRAL YAMAMOTO shot his last bolt in April. "I" designated the campaign promised to the Emperor as compensation for losing Guadalcanal. It meant a crushing, annihilating air offensive, to rub out one or more of the advanced bases recently won by the Allies, to set back their expected spring offensive, and to gain time for the defense of the Bismarcks Barrier. Why the "I" operation was not started earlier is not clear; probably for want of planes — Japanese naval plane production passed 500 monthly for the first time in March. Possibly it was because Imperial Headquarters took so long to decide whether Papua or Guadalcanal should be favored with the weight of bombs.

On 25 March, the war lords finally declared for Papua and ordered Fleet Admiral Yamamoto to take charge. Let him bring in the élite of Japanese aviation, the carrier pilots, to help the Eleventh Air Fleet strike.

First, several commands were shifted. Fleet Admiral Yamamoto and Vice Admiral Ozawa (Commander Third Fleet) set up headquarters at Rabaul in the same building with that of

---

[1] "Southeast Area Operations" Part 2 (Navy); USSBS *The V Air Force in the War Against Japan;* "History of Air Attacks on New Guinea Harbors," prepared by the writer in May 1943 on the basis of field notes; Comairsopac Daily Intelligence Bulletins; *General Kenney Reports.*

Vice Admiral Kusaka, the local naval commander. Vice Admiral Mikawa, whose record included the Savo Island victory and the Bismarck Sea defeat, went to Tokyo to advise and perhaps explain matters to the Naval General Staff; Vice Admiral Tomoshige Samejima, former naval aide to the Emperor, relieved him at Rabaul. General Hitoshi Imamura, Southeast Area Army Commander at Rabaul, sent his chief of staff to the capital with explanations.[2]

Admiral Yamamoto, after receiving a directive to concentrate his air power on Papua, undertook to split the "I" operation into two phases, the first to be directed against the lower Solomons. Perhaps the many targets anchored off Guadalcanal prompted this decision; possibly Merrill's cruiser-destroyer raid in March pointed up the vulnerability of Munda and the Central Solomons. Ozawa's Third Fleet carriers *Zuikaku*, *Zuiho*, *Junyo* and *Hiyo* together contributed 96 fighters, 65 dive-bombers and a handful of torpedo planes to assist the land-based force of 86 fighters, 27 dive-bombers, 72 twin-engined bombers and some additional torpedo planes [3] belonging to the Eleventh Air Fleet. All concentrated on the fields at Rabaul; then the medium bombers and fighters were fleeted down to Buka, Kahili and Ballale.

Americans at Guadalcanal had their first intimation of what was up on 1 April, when reconnaissance planes reported greatly increased plane strength in the upper Solomons. These reports had scarcely been tallied when 58 "Zekes" made a preparatory sweep down the Slot to reduce the number of American fighter-planes. Admiral Mason's fliers, warned soon enough by radar and coastwatchers, rose in time to intercept over the Russells. Forty-one Wildcats, Corsairs and Lightnings tore into the enemy force, knocking down 18 "Zekes" at the cost of six of their own number.

---

[2] Lt. Gen. H. Hyakutake, Com. Gen. 17th Army, and Lt. Gen. H. Adachi, Com. Gen. 18th Army, were still subordinate to Imamura.
[3] These are the operational numbers, checked by Capt. Ohmae.

Admiral Tomoshige Samejima, the new Eighth Fleet commander, took advantage of this diversion to push through a convoy to Vila, but it did not escape notice. Off the Shortlands, destroyer *Samidare* suffered a rivet-loosening near-miss, and that night a Black Cat and several Liberators attacked the ships ineffectively while they were unloading in Blackett Strait. Late on 2 April a number of P–38s caught a small transport north of Vella Lavella. The fighters dropped their gasoline belly tanks on her deck and swooped down to strafe with incendiary bullets, which kindled a merry blaze.

On 4 April the South Pacific intelligence officers noticed that enemy barges, transports and combat vessels also had taken a sudden upsurge. But they missed two runs of five destroyer-transports each into Vila, on 4 and 5 April. Rear Admiral Ainsworth's task force made six successive night runs up the Slot in the hope of intercepting the Vila Express, but reconnaissance planes failed to tell him in time to let him score. Japanese snoopers, on the other hand, kept Rabaul headquarters fully informed of Ainsworth's movements. Submarines were stationed along his track to report him, and night-flying torpedo-bombers were readied to fend him off.

One of the lurking subs, *RO–34*, tangled with Ainsworth's screen in the dark small hours of 5 April. Destroyer *Strong* made radar contact and doughty *O'Bannon*, only 1500 yards from the surfaced enemy, was ordered to attack. She first opened fire with 5-inch guns in radar control, then closed to point-blank range when the submarine became visible. Without radar, and crippled by the opening salvos, *RO–34* wallowed helpless as an old log. *O'Bannon* cut loose with machine guns and hurled depth charges right onto the enemy's deck; *RO–34* stood on her nose and slid under. She was sunk by *Strong* on 7 April off Lark Shoal.

This scrap, as well as the presence of snoopers, proved that a cruiser task force should be exposed only for some definite object. So Halsey ordered "Pug" to bombard Munda again on the night of 7–8 April, in the hope that he might incidentally bump into the Express.

This operation never came off. At high noon 7 April, *Honolulu, Helena, St. Louis* and six destroyers were standing out of Tulagi Harbor, when Guadalcanal radio broadcast "Air Attack." Ainsworth formed anti-aircraft disposition and headed for the open reaches of Indispensable Strait. And a good thing that he did; Yamamoto's "I" Operation was flying down the Slot, full strength. Japanese Intelligence had reported four cruisers, eight destroyers and 14 transports in Guadalcanal waters at 1100; and even though Ainsworth's task force was luckily escaping there remained nearly three dozen vessels of corvette size or larger, more than enough targets for the 67 "Vals," covered by the enormous number of 110 "Zekes," [4] now roaring toward Ironbottom Sound.

Bougainville coastwatchers had been the first to give warning; and photos taken by early-bird F–5s showed 114 planes at Kahili as against 40 the day before; 95 at Ballale as against none the day before. At 1226 a coastwatcher reported planes flying out of Buka; shortly thereafter, others described take-offs from Kahili and Ballale. Altogether, four waves flew against Guadalcanal shipping.

To intercept this massive onslaught – greater than any Japanese air attack since Pearl Harbor – 76 fighter planes were scrambled at Henderson Field.[5] Boring up through thin overcast to high cumulus clouds, they orbited in groups over and around Savo, stacked at varying altitudes. For a few minutes they had nothing to do but admire a typical early fall day in the Solomons – light southeast wind, occasional showers over the land, heavy black clouds and rain squalls over Florida Island which the enemy would be sure to use.

At 1400 the Russell Island radar screen became milky with traces of bogeys and Guadalcanal broadcast "Condition Red," followed shortly by an unprecedented "Condition *Very* Red." An hour later, "Zekes" whipped down on our fighters over Savo and the air battle was on. The Americans had the edge from the start;

---

[4] Of these all but 18 "Vals" and 21 "Zekes" belonged to the four abovementioned carriers. Numbers and composition checked by Capt. Ohmae.

[5] Thirty-six Wildcats, 9 Corsairs, 6 Warhawks, 12 Lightnings and 13 Airacobras.

but, while the fighters engaged, "Vals" slipped into the Sound unmolested.

In or near Tulagi Harbor were about 15 motor torpedo boats and their tender *Niagara,* tanker *Kanawha* awaiting an escort to depart, three tugs, the 3600-ton naval transport *Stratford,* six coastal transports of the APc class, and eight newly-arrived LCTs. Fueling from station tanker *Erskine Phelps* was the New Zealand corvette *Moa.* Minesweeper *Conflict,* net tenders *Butternut* and *Aloe,* several tiny auxiliaries and the old New Zealand coaster *Awahou* completed the Tulagi fleet. More ships were on Guadalcanal-side. All these vessels had anti-aircraft weapons, mostly small machine guns, while on the heights of Tulagi two quads of 40-mm guns pointed upward.

*Kanawha* had plenty of warning and was anxious to be off, but S.O.P.A. Guadalcanal (Rear Admiral Fort) directed her to await an escort and fuel it before departing. At 1445 she was finally ordered to leave. Her gunners looked to their weapons, the damage control parties blanketed the fuel tanks with $CO_2$, and the skipper, Lieutenant Commander Brainerd N. Bock, conned his ship out of the harbor. At 1502 she joined her escort, the lone destroyer *Taylor,* which Ainsworth (now well into Indispensable Strait) had released as to act as screen. Simultaneously, 48 enemy planes were sighted coming from the direction of Savo Island. Eighteen of them continued toward Tulagi; 15 made for *Kanawha.*

The sturdy old 14,500-ton tanker, making under 13 knots, with little room to maneuver and an inadequate anti-aircraft battery, was an easy bomb target. The first five planes hit an oil tank under the bridge, demolished the engine room and started leaks; the other ten planes then turned to other prey. Fires spread quickly on the tanker's oil-spattered decks; all pumps including the handy-billys were wrecked. The skipper of destroyer *Taylor,* who observed the damage, retired at 30 knots on the feeble excuse that he could render no assistance owing to the tanker's close proximity to the shore; the other ships stayed at a safe distance. Lieutenant Commander Bock showed good judgment in abandoning ship while there was still way on, in order to minimize the danger to his crew from burning oil on the surface. As soon as the crew was over the side — some on rafts but most in the water — tugs *Rail* and *Menominee*, sweeper *Conflict*, *LCT-62* and *LCT-58*, all came to her assistance. *Rail* pulled the navigator, Lieutenant C. W. Brockway USNR, out of the water; and, under his direction, volunteers returned on board and fought the flames with hoses amid exploding ready-box ammunition. They extinguished the fires and *Rail* towed *Kanawha* to a position on the west side of Tulagi, where they beached her around midnight. Unfortunately, she filled aft, slid off into deep water and sank before daybreak. Nineteen of her crew were lost.

*Kanawha's* assailants escaped, but not those who attacked shipping within Tulagi Harbor. A Wildcat piloted by 1st Lieutenant James E. Swett USMCR, chasing the enemy through "friendly" antiaircraft fire, knocked down three "Vals" during their dives, then pursued four more across Florida Island and downed them too. With his oil-cooling system shot up and his face scratched by windshield fragments, Swett managed to make a safe water landing in Tulagi Harbor.

Communications difficulties fouled up the defense. The raid warnings to some of the ships at Tulagi were delayed or incomplete. H.M.N.Z.S. *Moa*, one of those who did not get the word, was still fueling from *Erskine Phelps* when the enemy arrived. Two bombs aimed at the oiler slammed the corvette instead and sent her down in four minutes, fortunately with a loss of only five men. The LCTs were surprised, too; most of their skippers were on the beach, idle spectators as boatswain's mates conned and fought the little craft. They maneuvered skillfully and after the battle helped the salvage and rescue work.

As the Japanese bombers pulled out into the flat, they tried to make their getaway up the river valley which empties into the head of Tulagi Harbor. This was a bad choice, since it afforded good bird-shooting to *Niagara*, moored at the river mouth, and to a couple of tugs. Jungle foliage arching over the river formed a perfect blind for these ships' gunners, who splashed two or three planes and winged several others.

Another tanker drew Japanese bombs that afternoon. U.S.S. *Tappahannock* had been unloading aviation gasoline in Lunga Roads when the alert sounded. She got under way promptly and, escorted by destroyer *Woodworth*, had already threaded Lengo Channel when seven "Vals" zoomed in. Adroit dodging and effective anti-aircraft fire enabled both to escape, although some of the bombs fell very near.

Also in Lunga Roads were two naval cargo ships, two destroyers and three merchantmen. Only seven bombers went for these attractive prizes; none hit, although *Adhara* suffered sprung plates and minor hull damage from near-misses.

Survey ship *Pathfinder* had five boats out taking soundings in Lunga Roads when the bombers came in. Tugs *Vireo* and *Ortolan* and *SC-521* were nearby. Shortly before the attack, destroyer *Aaron Ward* escorting *LST-449* passed close aboard and all the small fry decided to snuggle under her gun protection. While the destroyer's gun directors were tracking enemy planes to the northward, three "Vals" broke cloud cover and glided unseen down the sun path. *Aaron Ward* had neither time to maneuver, nor chance to shoot, before her after engine room was torn apart by a bomb and both firerooms were flooded by near-misses. Several more "Vals" jumped *Pathfinder*. Stout sailors of *LST-449*, abetted by gunners in the other little ships, drove off the dive-bombers at no cost to themselves. *Aaron Ward's* skipper thought his ship was sound enough to make Tulagi under tow. He guessed wrong and, despite the best efforts of all hands, as well as of *Ortolan* and *Vireo*, she sank that evening less than three miles from her destination.

Ainsworth's task force, best equipped to deal with air attack, had but a fleeting glimpse of a few "Vals" high-tailing for home north of Florida Island. Still another group of ships, four large auxiliaries and three destroyers 15 miles east of Lengo Channel, sailed all afternoon under bombless skies.

What were our fighter planes doing all this time? Most of them were busy; of the 76 airborne, 56 made contact with the enemy. But, except in rare instances, as with Lieutenant Swett, they had to fight "Zekes," and, greatly outnumbered, on the enemy's terms. Captain Thomas G. Lanphier USA with three Lightnings reported splashing seven of the enemy fighters. A Marine pilot reported knocking down two more and then was shot down by "friendly" anti-aircraft fire; but he was rescued. One of the American pilots who bailed out fell a mile and a half before his chute opened, which it did with such a jerk that his shoes, wrist watch and ring kept right on going. Dozens of dogfights raged over Ironbottom Sound that day. It was amateur day, too. Few of these ships had ever seen combat; many had never even practised on towed sleeves. Everyone had a great time sawing away at the enemy planes, claiming kills and later painting Rising Suns on gun shields. Anti-aircraft gunners and fighter pilots made exaggerated claims that added up to a hundred or more; Air Intelligence finally credited them with 27 "Zekes" and 12 "Vals"; but Japanese records examined after the war, while confirming the dozen bombers' loss, admit only nine "Zekes" shot down. It is certain, however, that many of the cripples who fluttered into Munda that night never flew again. Allied air losses were 7 Marine fighter planes, and all but one of their pilots were saved. But a destroyer, a tanker and a corvette were sunk.

Air raids such as this were seldom effective unless accomplished by stealth as at Pearl Harbor, or repeated day after day as Airsols did the next year against Rabaul. The Solomons phase of "I" Operation did, however, throw American preparations off schedule for about ten days. Planned bombardments and minelaying ventures were postponed as the Americans warily awaited further onslaughts from the north that never came. For Yamamoto now pointed his javelin to the southwest, attacking Oro Bay, Milne Bay and Port Moresby.

# b. In New Guinea

Zone minus 10 time.

All during March, air attacks had been delivered on Allied shipping at Oro Bay, twelve miles south of Buna. United States Army transport *Masaya*, carrying high octane gas for the PT boats, and the 3300-ton K.P.M. ship *Bantam* had been sunk on this route 28 March by 18 "Vals" accompanied by 39 "Zekes." The most noteworthy counterstrike by General Kenney's bombers was on a Kavieng convoy, 1–2 April. *Florida Maru* (5854 tons) went to the bottom; a heavy cruiser, *Aoba*, back in service after her bad battering at the Battle of Cape Esperance, caught a bomb near the stern and remained a cripple for the rest of the war; destroyer *Fumizuki* had a boiler room flooded by a near miss.

On 11 April, as Yamamoto threw the "I" switch to New Guinea, several small ships were unloading supplies at Oro Bay for the Allied air bases at Dobodura. Shipping received but a five-minute warning at 1220 before the strike of 22 "Vals" and 72 "Zekes" came in. They netted one merchantman sunk, another beached and an Australian minesweeper damaged. Fifty fighters rose from Dobodura and knocked down six of the enemy with no loss to themselves.

Next day, 12 April, Port Moresby caught the biggest enemy air raid yet in the Southwest Pacific. Informed by a scout that there were 135 planes at Moresby fields and three transports in the harbor, Yamamoto's fliers in the unprecedented strength of 131 fighters and 43 medium bombers climbed over the Owen Stanley Range for a high-level bombing attack. Port Moresby, favored by a 38-minute warning, stacked 44 interceptors [6] to greet the onslaught. Since these fighters had many times their number of "Zekes" to deal with, the medium bombers got through. But they damaged only a few small craft in the harbor and a handful of

[6] *V Air Force in War Against Japan;* Gen. Kenney, however, says only 20.

planes on the Moresby strips. In the aërial fight two Allied and five Japanese planes fell, but not one ship was hit. Altogether a miserable score, compared with the raid on Darwin in February 1942.

Two days later the Japanese struck Milne Bay, where their scout planes had reported 14 anchored transports and over 50 planes on the Gili Gili strips. Actually, when Commander Branson RAN received word of the impending attack at 1100 April 14, there were but four or five corvettes, three transports and the 3500-ton British motorship *Gorgon* at the head of the Bay. The troop-filled transports (K.P.M. ships *van Heemskerk, van Outhoorn* and *Balik-papan*), which had been diverted from Port Moresby on the 12th, only to run into the same thing here, hurriedly discharged their men. As his anti-aircraft defenses were few, Branson dispersed the shipping, with characteristic energy dashing about the harbor in a crash boat to deliver orders. The Australian corvettes were told to get under way and assist any ship in trouble; an entering convoy to keep moving; *Gorgon* to clear the wharves; the Dutchmen to steam over to Waga Waga. By noon, Branson was back on the beach listening in on the fighter circuit, ready for the worst. Meantime, 24 Kittyhawks of the Royal Australian Air Force climbed to intercept a flight of 188 Japanese planes from Rabaul.

Shortly after noon the high-level bombers of this formation droned over Milne Bay, laying down a neat pattern of about a hundred bombs. An impressive water curtain half a mile long crossed the anchorage, which the ships had just left. Thirty minutes later, enemy dive-bombers set their sights on vessels zigzagging out in the bay. *Gorgon* took two hits which killed all but five men of her Chinese-Javanese crew, and the ship went out of control, but the indefatigable Branson rushed out a surgeon in his crash boat and summoned a corvette to give anti-aircraft protection and tow the motor ship in to the wharf. Together they claimed splashing three dive-bombers, and *Gorgon* was salvaged.

*Van Heemskerk* and her consorts, still carrying a touchy cargo of ammunition and gasoline, did not have time to clear the Bay before the Nips sighted them. As the Dutchman had inadequate anti-aircraft protection, the American troop commander, who had just landed, left 20 soldiers on board to help in her defense. These men, placing a jeep on each hatch, prepared to fight off the planes with their .50-caliber machine guns. *Van Heemskerk* survived four consecutive masthead-height attacks; then came a massive explosion in a hold containing ammunition and gasoline which caused the American jeeps and their crews to vanish from sight. Although the engineers remained at their posts and the Australian minesweeper *Wagga* closed to help with her fire hoses, the spunky Netherlander was a total loss.[7]

*Van Outhoorn* suffered near-misses which killed and wounded several men but did little damage to the ship. The Japanese fliers combed Milne Bay thoroughly, even picking on a little United States Army tugboat anchored at Kona Kope; but they failed to hit her, and tender *Hilo*, fortunately, was at sea during the raid. Three American planes were shot down as against seven Japanese. On the airstrips a small gasoline dump went up in flames and a few American soldiers were wounded.

Admiral Yamamoto on 16 April called a halt to the "I" Operation and ordered all Third Fleet planes back to their carriers. Too readily accepting the Japanese aviators' claims, he believed that the Bismarck Sea losses had been avenged by the sinking of one cruiser, two destroyers and 25 transports, and the shooting down of 175 planes.[8] Actual Allied losses in the Solomons and New Guinea combined were one destroyer, one tanker, one corvette, the two K.P.M. ships and perhaps 25 planes. But Yamamoto never lived to learn the truth. Faulty intelligence, dispersal of effort and, above all, failure to follow up, contributed to defeat the purposes of the operation. Air power without naval gunfire proved to be as ineffective as ships without air cover.

---

[7] This was the third of the Dutch merchant marine to be lost in 1943 in these waters, the others being *Bantam* and *'s Jacob*, hit by a bombing attack when returning from Oro Bay 8 March.

[8] "Southeast Area Operations" Part 2 (Navy).

## 2. *Death of a Fleet Admiral, 18 April 1943* [9]

Commander in Chief Combined Fleet now decided to visit Japanese bases in the upper Solomons to inspect defenses and to bolster troop morale. Admirals Halsey and Nimitz managed to learn of his intentions. To the top Intelligence Officers at Pearl Harbor and Washington, Nimitz addressed the inquiry: Would the elimination of Yamamoto help our cause? In other words, Did Japan have anyone as good or better to take his place? To the latter, the Intelligence answer was a decided "No!" Even before the war Yamamoto had had a high reputation among United States Naval officers, many of whom knew him personally, as an intelligent and resourceful leader.[10] So Nimitz "gave the green light" — and Rear Admiral Marc A. Mitscher, now Comairsols, was given the job of getting Yamamoto.

As had been predicted, Yamamoto and the most important members of his staff boarded two "Betty" bombers at Rabaul. At 0800 April 18, protected by six "Zeke" fighter planes, they took off for Kahili airfield, Buin. Sixteen Lightnings of the 339th Fighter Squadron from Henderson Field, led by Major John W. Mitchell USA, were already flying low up along the west coast of New Georgia. Yamamoto arrived over Buin at 0935. So did the Lightnings. Exactly as planned, the plane commanded by Captain Thomas G. Lanphier USA flashed in under the departing "Zekes" just as the two bombers were about to land. Lanphier shot down the one, Lieutenant Rex T. Barber USA disposed of the other. The

[9] 13th Fighter Command Detachment Action Report 21 Apr. 1943; Japanese and American communiqués; conversations with former Japanese officers, especially Capt. Watanabe of Yamamoto's staff.

[10] Yamamoto's alleged boast of dictating peace in the White House, though widely believed, had nothing to do with the decision. For his real attitude toward the war, see Vol. III of this History p. 46. What he said about the White House was, in effect, "To get the kind of peace the Japanese Army wants, one would have to dictate it in the White House — the Navy can't win it for them." A garbled and twisted form of this statement was let out by Japanese propaganda. (James A. Field Jr. in *U.S. Nav. Inst. Proc.* Oct. 1949.)

first, which carried Yamamoto, crashed in the jungle north of Buin; the other, carrying Vice Admiral Ugaki, his chief of staff, spiraled into the sea and sank. Yamamoto and five or six key staff officers were killed; Ugaki was critically injured. The American planes retired after nipping three of the "Zekes" and losing one P-38 piloted by Lieutenant Raymond K. Hine USA.

Next morning there was wild if restricted elation in Nouméa. Even dour Kelly Turner "whooped and applauded," [11] While Halsey sent a jubilant dispatch to Rear Admiral Mitscher at Guadalcanal: "Congratulations to you and Major Mitchell and his hunters. Sounds as though one of the ducks in their bag might have been a peacock." At Pearl Harbor, Nimitz with a beaming smile gave the news to his immediate entourage, swearing them to secrecy. Not until 21 May was the news of Yamamoto's death in "air combat" released by Tokyo. Until then we were not quite sure we had got the Fleet Admiral; the victim might have been someone else.

This neat, planned kill was equivalent to a major victory. Captain Watanabe of Yamamoto's staff, who had been delayed by unfinished staff business at Rabaul, recovered his leader's body in the jungle, cremated it, and carried the ashes to Tokyo, where they were given an impressive public funeral on 5 June. The spirit of the departed was invoked as a moral ally, and held up to the youth of Japan as a model. But his successor, Admiral Mineichi Koga, warned the Combined Fleet: "Our enemy is striving for ultimate victory by expanding his preparations for offensive action and devising plans for the strategic application of new weapons." [12] Everyone knew that there "could be only one Yamamoto and nobody could take his place." His loss "dealt an almost unbearable blow to the morale of all the military forces." [13]

[11] *Admiral Halsey's Story* p. 157. See that book, the *Washington Times-Herald* 7 June 1950 p. 2 and Allan Westcott *American Sea Power* p. 405 note for further details.
[12] Ens. Toshio Nakamura's professional notebook (Jicpoa Item No. 4986) copying "Address No. 4 to the Combined Fleet 23 May 1943."
[13] Vice Admiral Fukudome in *Inter. Jap. Off.* II 522; "Southeast Area Operations" Part 2 (Navy).

# CHAPTER IX

# MacArthur Moves Forward[1]

## 22 June–6 July 1943

East Longitude dates; Zone minus 10 time.

ON 15 March 1943, by a stroke of Admiral King's pen, the impoverished Southwest Pacific Force achieved fleet status. On its birthday, however, the new Seventh Fleet was still measured in tens rather than thousands. On paper it made a brave showing with seven task forces composed of strangely assorted surface, air and underwater craft scattered between northern Papua and southwestern Australia, under three different flags (Australian, American and Netherlands), but most of its strength was still listed as "upon reporting," which meant assigned ships en route or still in American waters. Planes, corvettes, minelayers and destroyers (Desron 4, *Selfridge* flag) were busy searching for Japanese submarines in Australian waters. Vice Admiral Crutchley's cruisers (H.M.A.S. *Australia* and *Hobart*, U.S.S. *Phoenix*) waited for their services to be required. There were a few tenders, only two tankers and but one transport; freight to New Guinea was hauled by the "Army's Navy" of small chartered Australian vessels, or the Dutch ships that had survived the Buna campaign. Most skeletal of all was the Amphibious Force, commanded by Rear Admiral Barbey, locally known as "Uncle Dan the Amphibious Man." [2]

The special problems of amphibious warfare had long been rec-

[1] Office of Naval History "Command History U.S. Naval Forces Southwest Pacific Area," "Command History Seventh Amphibious Force," Bulkely's "History of Motor Torpedo Boats"; Conversations with Capt. Bern Anderson, former planning officer under Admiral Barbey. For the Japanese, "Southeast Area Operations," Part 2 (Navy) and "Southeast Pacific Air Force Operations."

[2] TF 76: 1 APA, 22 APcs (upon reporting), 72 LSTs (upon reporting), 24 LCIs (12 more to report), 20 LCIs (52 more to report), 2 Australian corvettes (2 more to report).

ognized. As far back as September 1942 Admiral King had issued a directive for an amphibious training group in the Southwest Pacific. Rear Admiral Richmond K. Turner, in the midst of the Guadalcanal campaign, wrote a treatise on amphibious training, setting forth in strong words the necessity of speed in debarkation and handling of stores on the beach, efficient combat-loading of transports, proper types of craft and correct composition of forces, in shore-to-shore operations. Rear Admiral Barbey became interested in amphibious problems before the war, and had tried out various methods and matériel with the 1st Marine Division. During the second half of 1942, as a member of Admiral King's staff, he organized in the Navy Department an amphibious warfare section, which tested and developed the new beaching craft – LST, LCT, LCI –.[3] as well as the Landing Ship Dock (LSD) and all manner of amphibious vehicles: landing craft, amphtracs (LVT), dukws. Barbey's appointment as Commander Amphibious Force Southwest Pacific (which later became the VII Amphibious Force) was King's Christmas gift to MacArthur.[4]

Arriving 8 January 1943, Barbey set up headquarters on board *Henry T. Allen* in Brisbane River. Amphibious training centers for troops and sailors of both countries were established at Toorbul Point near the mouth of the river, and at Port Stephens near Newcastle. Captains K. J. Christoph and Bern Anderson started the training program immediately. In the spring of 1943 Anderson was relieved by Captain John W. Jamison, fresh from duty as beachmaster at Fedhala, North Africa; coastguardsmen, also veterans of North Africa, were sent over as instructors. "Red" Jamison tried his training techniques on the Guadalcanal veterans of the

---

[3] For landing craft types see Vol. II of this History pp. 29, 266–71.
[4] Daniel E. Barbey, born Portland, Ore. 1889, Naval Academy '12, "exec" of DD *Stevens* in World War I, aide to Admiral Bristol at Constantinople; engineer officer *Oklahoma* and *Cincinnati* 1922–26 (except two years' shore duty); "exec" *Ramapo* 1927–28; Naval Academy duty; C.O. *Lea* 1931–33; inspector of ordnance Mare Island, then 1st Lieut. *New York* and C.O. *Ramapo* 1934–37; C.O. *New York* 1940–41, chief of staff to Com Service Force Atlantic Fleet to May, Cominch staff to Dec. 1942. For rest of war career, see Vol. XV, Index. Com Seventh Fleet, 1945, Com Ten, Thirteen '47–50, ret. '51.

1st Marine Division and then went to work with the 32nd Infantry Division, which had been through the Gona-Buna campaign. Amphibious command courses were given to division, regimental and battalion staffs; specialists were briefed on communications, naval gunfire support, reconnaissance and shore-party duties; a troop-instructor school taught officers and noncoms the details of debarkation, boating and use of equipment. Actual landings were rehearsed, but there were only four assault transports allotted for training and these were frequently diverted to the New Guinea troop-lift. LCTs and LCIs were so few that soldiers were lucky to get even a look at one. On the practice beach there were never enough bulldozers, cranes, trucks or trailers; and the Army could spare no engineer specialists such as are required for effective shore parties.

Nevertheless, to the VII 'Phib fell the honor of making the first forward movement in this campaign. It was the weak left prong of a pincer, whose right prong was Halsey's Central Solomons operation.

The first objectives, as set forth by the J.C.S. Directive of 29 March, were two Trobriand islands, Kiriwina and Woodlark, in the Coral Sea to the north of Milne Bay. The only value of these islands in General MacArthur's eyes lay in their position as future Allied air bases. An airstrip on Kiriwina, 125 miles from New Britain and Woodlark and 200 miles from Bougainville, could afford fighter protection and bigger payloads for bombers raiding Rabaul, Kavieng and the Northern Solomons.

Admirals Carpender and Barbey considered this operation an opportunity to test doctrine and equipment of the VII Amphibious Force without the complication of enemy opposition. The last day of June was chosen as D-day; on the same date the III 'Phib was to move into New Georgia and General Eichelberger's troops would land at Nassau Bay 17 miles below Salamaua.

May and June were hectic months along the Australian and New Guinea coasts. Troops and ships moved forward to the final staging areas: the Kiriwina force to Milne Bay, the Woodlark force to Townsville in northeastern Australia. Reconnaissance parties gathered data on the two islands—giving rise to a ribald legend that unauthorized sight-seeing parties were picnicking with the attractive Trobriand girls. Landing craft staging into New Guinea grounded on coral reefs and some got off. Barbey borrowed four destroyer-transports [5] and six LSTs from Turner. Other LSTs fresh from the States were hustled into the task force before learning what they were expected to do. The only available salvage tug had to be manned by civilians. Repair ship *Rigel* was pressed into service as amphibious force flagship, although she had no room for an admiral and staff.

These were minor annoyances. The vital matter of drawing up plans and coördinating them with the Army went smoothly. For the first time in the Southwest Pacific, air, land and sea power operated as a balanced team. The newly organized Alamo Force of General Krueger's Sixth Army and web-footed boys of Admiral Carpender's Seventh Fleet drank from the same coffeepot and drafted plans at the same table, and Barbey's final plan became the template for future shore-to-shore amphibious operations in the Southwest Pacific.

The Trobriands operation itself was prosaic. On 20 June 1943 General Krueger set up Sixth Army headquarters at the KB Mission in Milne Bay, and there General MacArthur joined him. On the same day, Admiral Barbey flew in and hoisted his flag in *Rigel*. Next day destroyer-transports *Brooks* and *Humphreys* weighed anchor from Townsville, carrying an advance echelon of the 112th Cavalry to Woodlark. They arrived in the dead of night, 22–23 June, and discharged 200 troops without incident. Shoving off before dawn, they steamed back to Milne Bay and took a similar advance echelon of the 158th Regimental Combat Team to Kiriwina. Boats had trouble with the difficult beaches, and the APDs had to depart without completely unloading. Three nights later they came back and finished the job. On 25 June destroyers *Mug-*

[5] *Brooks, Gilmer, Sands, Humphreys.*

*ford* and *Helm* escorted north from Townsville half the Woodlark force, six LSTs and one subchaser. Destroyers *Bagley* and
*Henley* followed next day with a similar force. H.M.A.S. *Benalla*
(a survey ship) and two Apcs [6] set forth from Milne Bay on the
29th, together with 12 LCTs, 12 LCIs [7] and 7 LCMs screened by
four destroyers, for the main landing at Kiriwina.

On Woodlark the advance party laid out markers and prepared
the beaches so that unloading went forward with dispatch. Kiriwina, surrounded by a spiny necklace of coral, proved trouble-
some. Unloading dragged along discouragingly and a fortnight
was required to unsnarl all tangles.

Three weeks elapsed, but the Japanese offered no opposition to
this movement into the Trobriands, because simultaneous landings
at Nassau Bay and New Georgia seemed more important — as
indeed they were. During this time the VII 'Phib brought 16,000
men into the islands without the loss of a single man, ship or boat,
and the Seabees built an airstrip on Woodlark.

Kiriwina and Woodlark never paid dividends on the investment
of effort and matériel. Before either could be established as a strong
air base, the war had moved west and "fixed carriers" could not
up anchor and follow. But, regarded as an amphibious experiment,
the bloodless occupation was a thumping success. Good theories
were proved, bad ones discarded, confidence imparted to Uncle
Dan's webfeet. Before the war was over, VII 'Phib would have
over fifty amphibious landings to its credit.

Since the Battle of the Bismarck Sea, the Japanese situation in
Huon Gulf had deteriorated. The only reinforcements were 500

---

[6] Pronounced "apple-cart," APc is the abbreviation for "Small Coastal Transport." Many of them had been built in Maine like fishing draggers.
Wooden-hulled, and capable of only 12 knots, these ships proved too vulnerable
for combat operations. However, during the New Guinea campaign they acted as
navigational guides for landing craft and often as command ships for LST or LCI
flotilla commanders.

[7] Properly LCI(L), the designation of Landing Craft Infantry (Large), the
basic troop carrier. Other types by function were LCI(FF) flotilla flag, LCI(G)
gunboat, LCI(M) mortar, LCI(R) rocket. In this History, LCI will always indicate LCI(L) unless otherwise designated.

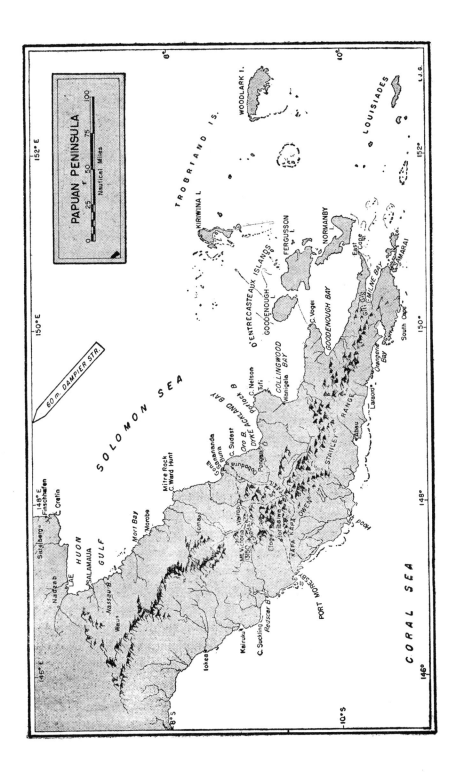

PAPUAN PENINSULA

Nautical Miles

0  25  50  75  100

152° E

150° E

148° E

145° E

8°

10°

10°S

8°S

WOODLARK I.

LOUISIADES

TROBRIAND IS.

KIRIWINA I.

NORMANBY

FERGUSSON I.

D'ENTRECASTEAUX ISLANDS

GOODENOUGH I.

C. Vogel

GOODENOUGH BAY

COLLINGWOOD BAY

Wanigela

Tufi

C. Nelson

East Cape

SAMARAI

South Cape

MILNE BAY

Orangerie Bay

Laragon

Tabeu

STANLEY RANGE

OWEN

KAFA KEPT

Goribali R.

Mt. Victoria

Waropi

IORBA

Elogi

Ponguani

DYKE ACKLAND BAY

Oro B.

C. Sudest

Gonananda

Buna

Ginpappo

Mitre Rock

C. Ward Hunt

Morobe

Mort Bay

SOLOMON SEA

60 m. DAMPIER STR.

C. Cretin

Finschhafen

Sialelberg

HUON GULF

LAE

SALAMAUA

Nassau B.

Waua

Nadzab

Iokea

Kairuku

C. Suckling

Redscar B.

PORT MORESBY

CORAL SEA

146°

148°

150°

152°

L.J.G.

soldiers brought into Finschhafen 30 March by four destroyers, and half as many men of the Special Naval Landing Force, who were carried to Salamaua by submarine. The campaign for taking the Wau airfield had fallen apart, and Allied pressure from that direction kept the Lae and Salamaua garrisons well occupied. The builders sweating out a road from Madang to Finschhafen were bogged down. Yamamoto's "I" operation had come to naught. In consequence, Allied shipping inched northward with equipment for Eichelberger's men, while Kenney's planes pounded Lae and Salamaua with little letup.

Imperial Headquarters admitted all these obstacles but clung desperately to the faint and foolish hope that Papua could be taken if only bases were established in the foothills of the Owen Stanley Range to support another transmontane thrust at Port Moresby and draw Allied troops within reach of Japanese jungle fighters. The Army and Navy vice chiefs flew down to Rabaul to sell this plan to the local commanders. Both Kusaka and Imamura opposed it as unrealistic; and while discussion of the next step forward was still hot, news of the Allied landings at Nassau Bay on 30 June ended all talk of an offensive.

General MacArthur expected nothing more of Nassau Bay than to ease the logistic situation. Supplies for the Australian 7th Division, then pressing down toward Salamaua, had so far been airborne to Wau and thence back-packed by native carriers. Commander Morton C. Mumma, admiral of the motor-torpedo-boat navy, pointed out the advantages of an all-water supply route with a terminus at Nassau Bay near Salamaua. The Australians liked the idea and were glad to have Mumma's PTs carry it out. To coincide with landings elsewhere and add to the enemy's befuddlement, the last day of June was selected.

On the eve of the landings, four boats under Lieutenant Commander Barry K. Atkins shoved off from Morobe for the embarkation point in Mort Bay,[8] 15 miles northward. At 1700 three of

---

[8] So named by Australian hydrographers after Cdr. Morton Mumma, who had explored it in a PT.

them came alongside a jetty, and troops from the Army's 41st Infantry Division commenced loading. *PT–143* and *PT–120* took 70 men each; *PT–142* managed to absorb ten more, but *PT–168* carried no passengers and kept her decks free for action. The Army contributed some three dozen landing craft manned by the 2nd Engineer Special Brigade. This unique invasion force put to sea in the teeth of a nasty southeast blow with heavy seas, high winds, lashing rains and low visibility. *PT–168* lost the convoy and patrolled independently. The other three sloshed along, averaging only 7 knots for the 40-mile run. *PT–142*, leading the first wave of landing craft, overshot Nassau Bay, reversed course and ran smack into *PT–143* with the second wave, and her landing craft scattered like frightened minnows. Lieutenant (jg) John L. Carey USNR, skipper of *PT–142*, chased them down, guided them in to the beach where they landed their troops, and then landed his own passengers. The second and third waves of landing craft broached in the surf and left the troops on board the PTs with no means of getting ashore, so the boats returned to Morobe at daybreak with their thoroughly miserable passengers.

Nevertheless, Japanese lookouts at Nassau Bay reported a large-scale invasion in progress and, as the 300-man garrison had not been ordered to stand and die, it turned and ran. Commander Tsukioka of the Special Naval Landing Force might have made a fighting bid for the beaches, but one of General Kenney's bombs killed him at his headquarters. So, despite the loss of much-wanted landing craft, the Allies had another beachhead. Two nights later, Lieutenant Commander Atkins covered the landing of reinforcements at Nassau Bay. He strafed nearby enemy villages while eleven landing craft came in under their own power, together with several more towed by trawlers. Still more troops were landed on 4 and 6 July. By this time, the beachhead was secure and the Australians were pushing eastward along the shore for an early junction with the Americans. Heavy artillery landed at Nassau Bay lobbed shells toward Salamaua.

Once more the motor torpedo boats had proved their versatility.

# CHAPTER X

# The Invasion of New Georgia

## 21 June–5 July 1943

### 1. Plan and Preliminaries

O N 3 June 1943 Admiral William F. Halsey signed a document which repeatedly mentioned such unrelated and fantastic words as "Aperient," "Armchair," "Blackboy," "Catsmeat," "Dowser" and "Jacodet." Bill Halsey and his staff had a reputation for humorous buffeting of word meanings, but this was a serious matter, the operation plan for the invasion of New Georgia; the odd words were code names for objectives. In the next three months American soldiers, sailors and Marines would see nothing incongruous in the use of these names in official correspondence or even conversation. For many, they still conjure up images of mucky jungles, mangrove-fringed shores and reef-studded waterways.

The overall operation, dubbed "Toenails," required that on the last day of June Admiral Turner's III Amphibious Force seize four primary targets so as to get within arm's reach of "Jacodet" —

---

[1] Operation plans, Action Reports and War Diaries of ships and commands involved; U.S. Army Historical Section *The New Georgia Campaign* (1946), Marine Corps Historical Section *The New Georgia Campaign* (by Maj. John N. Rentz) both seen in ms.; Cincpac "Operations in the Pacific Ocean Areas, 1943"; Rear Admiral T. S. Wilkinson's personal files; notes taken by the writer in the Solomons 1943; British Central Office of Information *Among Those Present* (1946); Comairsopac Daily Intelligence Summaries; Col. Temple G. Holland USA *The New Georgia Campaign*, Conference and Interviews at Infantry School Fort Benning, Ga.; Cincpac Secret Information Bulletin No. 10 *Battle Experience — Naval Operations Solomon Islands Area 30 June–12 July 1943*; Office of Naval Intelligence Combat Narrative No. X *Operations in the New Georgia Area*; ATIS No. 16268 "War Diary of Japanese Naval Operations"; "Southeast Area Operations" Part 2 (Navy).

Munda. "Armchair" (Wickham Anchorage on the southeast coast of Vangunu) would make a fine staging point for small craft from Tulagi. "Blackboy" (Segi Point) on the southeast cape of New Georgia, would be a fair site for a fighter strip. "Catsmeat" (Viru Harbor), a few miles up from Segi, would be another lay-over and replenishment depot for small craft. "Dowser" (Rendova Island), a cannon shot across Blanche Channel from Munda, in American hands would enable artillery to pound Japanese airfields on "Aperient" (New Georgia).

As the Joint Chiefs of Staff Directive for this operation was issued 29 March, and planning had been going on since January, there was nothing rushed or improvised about Operation "Toenails." Naval forces assigned to it were far better trained and more experienced than those which had carried out the Guadalcanal landings. Admiral Fitch's air staff had learned to coördinate air power with an amphibious force instead of pursuing the fruitless if spectacular strategic bombing concept. The 1st Marine Raider Battalion, which had taken Tulagi last August, would know what to do when it hit other Solomons beaches. Only the Army ground troops, despite intensive training in Guadalcanal, proved wanting.

While troops and ships waited for the signal to go, fighting continued in the air. One could easily fill a volume with stories of the individual conflicts; here we can merely allude to them. On 25 April Major M. K. Peyton usmc with four Corsairs engaged 16 "Bettys" and 20 "Zekes" making a raid on Guadalcanal. He lost two planes and one pilot, but destroyed five planes. Admiral Koga transferred 58 fighters and 49 "Bettys" from Truk to Rabaul on 10 May, and adopted the technique of sending 50 to 80 "Zekes" over the Russells to "entice" Americans into battle.[2] The biggest of these fights occurred 5 June, 81 "Zekes" tussling with 110 Allied planes; 24 were shot down against 7 American fighters lost — Japanese

---

[2] "War Diary of Japanese Naval Operations," ATIS No. 16568. There were also bombing raids on Henderson Field, where on 18 May 1943 14 men were killed and 20 wounded. At the end of May, Koga also started heckling Espiritu Santo. Tender *Curtiss*, that favorite Japanese target, had a stick of bombs laid close aboard; PT tender *Niagara* was sunk near San Cristobal.

pilots reported 41. They tried again on the 12th, with almost identical results.

On 16 June a large convoy commanded by Captain Paul S. Theiss, carrying troops to Guadalcanal, provoked the attention of Japanese bomber pilots. They were particularly excited about escort carrier *Suwannee*, which was defending the convoy. Six bold "Bettys" made for that gallant ex-tanker but fighter interception from Guadalcanal took care of them before she could fire a gun. Again, that night, 18 more "Bettys" were foiled by radical ship maneuvering. Admiral Kusaka then determined to get the troop transports in Ironbottom Sound. Two dozen "Vals" and 70 "Zekes" made the try and were wiped out almost to the last plane, at a cost of only six United States fighters. One Japanese pilot got home to tell his boss that six transports and one destroyer had joined the hulks on the Sound's bottom.

How wrong he was! The handful of "Vals" that broke through the fighter screen were disposed of by anti-aircraft fire from the ships, only two of which were hit. Freighter *Celeno* took two bombs but was beached and saved with the aid of tugs. *LST-340*, crammed with soldiers and loaded vehicles, was the principal casualty. Fire from a bomb hit was fed by gasoline, dunnage and ammunition; but the skipper, Lieutenant William Villella, refused to give up. He ordered his engineers, at the point of suffocation, to set the starboard engine at flank speed ahead (the port engine having been knocked out) and then to abandon the engine room. While his Army passengers were swimming to boats nearby, Villella steered for Lunga Beach and just made it as the starboard engine conked out. His flotilla commander, Captain G. B. Carter, then directed two other LSTs to give their sister a hand. Disregarding exploding ammunition and burning gasoline, they nuzzled alongside where their hoses could get at the flames, brought the fire under control by nightfall and saved the ship.

Since LSTs were still a novelty in the South Pacific, this little action attracted much favorable attention, and also demonstrated the weakness of the landing ships. They were literally what their crews nicknamed them, "Large Slow Targets." [3] With meager anti-aircraft armament and damage control facilities, concealment was their best defense, but the hundreds of LSTs which helped win the war certainly did not do so by hiding.

Japanese submariners accomplished even less than their flying countrymen in hampering preparations for the New Georgia invasion. Captain Theiss's convoy was not even sighted by four submarines lying in wait off San Cristobal. One of the group, *RO–103* did, however, sink Liberty ships *Aludra* and *Deimos* returning empty from Guadalcanal on 23 June.

So much for sea and air action. In the jungles of New Georgia, Allied patrols — mixed groups of soldiers, sailors, natives and civil servants of the British Protectorate — were already tangling with the Japanese, who had so antagonized the natives that they had to travel in large well-armed and noisy parties.

District Officer Donald G. Kennedy, a New Zealander coast-watcher who operated a radio station, intelligence post, downed-aviator haven and native guerrilla base at Segi Point, was a tower of strength for the Allies in this region. "These islands are British and they are to remain British," he declared in a message delivered to every native village. "The Government is not leaving. Even if the Japanese come, we shall stay with you and in the end they will be driven out." And he backed up these words by ambushing over a hundred Japanese soldiers who tramped too close to his hideout, and those who approached Segi by sea fared no better. Kennedy ran a unique amphibious force consisting of native-manned schooners. His "flagship," *Dadavata*, a ten-ton schooner, won a duel with a Japanese whaleboat in which the enemy was rammed and shot up, and his deck showered with hand grenades.

The Japanese tried to entice Kennedy to give himself up with the promise that he would be treated as a "first-class prisoner," and threatened him with a dire fate if he did not. On 17 June, one Major Hara set out from Viru with an infantry company and a

[3] 327 feet long, 50 feet wide, 11 knots maximum and 8 knots normal speed, armament thirteen .50-cal. and six 20-mm machine guns.

machine-gun platoon to capture Segi. Kennedy ambushed the party and captured the inevitable Japanese diary containing details of the expedition. He then faded into the hills and radioed for help. Admiral Turner, who never let a brave man down, sent two companies of the 4th Marine Raider Battalion tearing up the Slot on the night of 20 June, in destroyer-transports *Dent* and *Waters*. The Coast Pilot described the channel leading to Segi Point as "requiring ideal conditions for masthead navigation to ensure a successful transit"; and conditions were far from ideal that day. There was too little light for masthead navigation and the chart dismissed the bay leading to Segi Point with the ominous notation "foul ground." Kennedy had lighted bonfires on the beach and *Dent* carried a local pilot, but both ships scraped bottom. Fortunately they worked free without critical damage. While the transports eased gingerly toward Segi Point, Kennedy signaled a cheerful "O.K. here," and at daybreak the Marines started ashore. The unloading lasted two hours but the jungle-green camouflage of the APDs caused enemy airscouts to miss them. *Dent* and *Waters* wriggled out of the channel and made a safe daylight return to Guadalcanal.

Destroyer-transports *Schley* and *Crosby* duplicated this exploit a day later, bringing up two companies of the 103rd Infantry and a naval survey party.

These landings at Segi Point completed the preliminaries. Munda and Vila were already numbed by incessant air raids; no planes could now fly from their airstrips. But the enemy could still raid from Bougainville and Rabaul. Seven of Captain Fife's submarines idled along the equator, athwart the routes from Truk to New Britain and the Solomons. But Admiral Turner, with aching memory of Savo Island, did not feel that these measures were sufficient. This time, thought he, we shall make the surprise raids. That was done by Rear Admiral Merrill's support group on the night of 29–30 June. His cruisers and destroyers bombarded the Shortlands; his minelayers planted some 250 mines at a point ten miles east of these islands.

It was not Merrill who alerted the enemy. At 2400 June 29, submarine *RO-103*, patrolling west of the Russells, sighted and reported the American invasion force moving toward New Georgia. That was the first intimation to Tokyo or Rabaul that a big operation was imminent. The Japanese leaders had made a costly error in deducing American intentions, misled by their exaggerated belief in the effect of the "I" operation. They had watched ships and air-

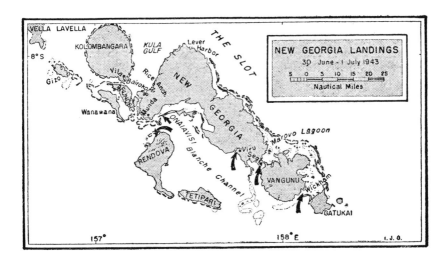

craft streaming into Guadalcanal and listened to the growing volume of radio traffic. But after 26 June they were deceived by fewer ship movements and less radio traffic into the belief that there was not going to be an offensive for the present, so Japanese planes in advanced airfields were moved back to Rabaul and no ships were sent there from Truk. The total surface and air force at Rabaul on 30 June was 1 cruiser, 8 destroyers, 8 submarines, 66 bombers and 83 fighter planes.[4] These were obviously insufficient to deal with the massive forces then converging on New Georgia, under the command of that versatile, seasoned and irascible veteran of the Guadalcanal landings, Rear Admiral Richmond Kelly Turner.

[4] Cdr. James C. Shaw "The Japanese Guessed Wrong at New Georgia" *Marine Corps Gazette* XXXIII No. 12 (Dec. 1949) pp. 36–42.

# 2. Task Organization *

## THIRD FLEET (SOUTH PACIFIC FORCE)

Admiral William F. Halsey, at Nouméa

Captain Miles Browning, Chief of Staff

### TF 31 AMPHIBIOUS FORCE

Rear Admiral Richmond K. Turner in *McCawley*
(Relieved by Rear Admiral Theodore S. Wilkinson, 15 July)
Major General John H. Hester USA, Commander Ground Forces

#### TG 31.1 WESTERN GROUP, Rear Admiral Turner

Rendova Attack Unit, Lieutenant Commander Charles C. Morgan

| | |
|---|---|
| TALBOT | Lt Cdr. Morgan |
| ZANE | Lt. Cdr. Peyton L. Wirtz |

Embarking 2 companies 169th Infantry, U.S. Army

Rendova Advance Unit, Commander John D. Sweeney

| | |
|---|---|
| DENT | Lt. Cdr. Ralph A. Wilhelm |
| WATERS | Lt. Cdr. Charles J. McWhinnie |

Embarking Companies C and G of 172nd Regimental Combat Team

1st Echelon, Rear Admiral Turner

Transport Unit, Rear Admiral Turner

| | |
|---|---|
| MCCAWLEY | Cdr. Robert H. Rodgers |
| LIBRA | Capt. William B. Fletcher |

Transdiv 2, Capt. Paul S. Theiss

| | |
|---|---|
| PRESIDENT JACKSON | Capt. Charles W. Weitzel |
| PRESIDENT ADAMS | Capt. Frank H. Dean |
| PRESIDENT HAYES | Capt. Francis W. Benson |
| ALGORAB | Capt. Joseph R. Lannom |

Embarking 1st Echelon Western Landing Force, most of 172nd RCT

Destroyer Screen, Captain Thomas J. Ryan

Division A 1 (also Fire Support Unit), Capt. Ryan

| | |
|---|---|
| FARENHOLT | Cdr. Eugene T. Seaward |
| BUCHANAN | Lt. Cdr. Floyd B. T. Myhre |
| MCCALLA | Lt. Cdr. Halford A. Knoertzer |
| RALPH TALBOT | Cdr. Joseph W. Callahan |

* The reader will find some repetition in this task organization because certain ships were used more than once.

Division A 2 (also Anti-Submarine Unit), Cdr. John M. Higgins
GWIN                Lt. Cdr. John B. Fellows
WOODWORTH           Cdr. Virgil F. Gordinier
RADFORD             Cdr. William K. Romoser
JENKINS             Cdr. Harry F. Miller

New Georgia Motor Torpedo Boat Squadron, Lt. Cdr. Robert B. Kelly; 12 PTs

2nd Echelon, Captain Grayson B. Carter

LST Unit, Capt. Carter
LSTs 395, 396, 472 and same LCI Unit as in 4th Echelon Western Force, embarking Landing Unit, Lt. Col. Charles W. Hill USA

3rd Echelon, Commander Paul S. Slawson

Destroyer-Transport Unit, Cdr. John D. Sweeney

Transdiv 12, Cdr. Sweeney
STRINGHAM           Lt. Cdr. Ralph H. Moureau
MCKEAN              Lt. Cdr. Ralph L. Ramey
also TALBOT, WATERS and DENT from the Rendova units

Transdiv 22, Lt. Cdr. Robert H. Wilkinson
KILTY               Lt. Cdr. Dominic L. Mattie
SCHLEY              Lt. Cdr. Horace Myers
CROSBY              Lt. Cdr. Alan G. Grant

LST Unit, Cdr. Slawson
LSTs 342, 353, 398, 399, embarking Landing Unit, Capt. C. W. H. Tripp, New Zealand Army

4th Echelon, Captain John S. Crenshaw

LST Unit, Capt. Crenshaw
LSTs 343, 354 and LCIs 61, 62, 64, 65, 66, 222, Cdr. J. MacDonald Smith, embarking Landing Unit, Maj. Luther R. Stebbins USA

Reserve Motor Torpedo Boat Group, Cdr. Allen P. Calvert; 12 PTs

Service Unit, Lt. Charles H. Stedman
Tugs VIREO and RAIL; two supply barges

TG 31.3 EASTERN GROUP, Rear Admiral George H. Fort

VIRU OCCUPATION UNIT, Cdr. Stanley Leith

1st Echelon, Destroyer-transports, Cdr. Leith
HOPKINS, Lt. Cdr. Francis M. Peters; also ZANE of Rendova Unit and KILTY and CROSBY of 3rd Echelon

2nd, 3rd and 4th Echelons, each one APc and 2 or 3 LCTs, embarking Landing Force, Capt. R. E. Kinch USA

TU 31.3.2 Segi Point Occupation Unit, Capt. Benton W. Decker

Four Echelons, each consisting of one APc, 2 to 4 LCTs; 5 LCIs, embarking Landing Force, Col. Daniel H. Hundley USA

WICKHAM ANCHORAGE OCCUPATION UNIT, Rear Admiral Fort

1st Echelon, Destroyer-transports, Rear Admiral Fort

MCKEAN and SCHLEY of 3rd Echelon, plus TREVER (Lt. Cdr. William H. Shea), and 7 LCI

2nd, 3rd and 4th Echelons, each one APc, 1 to 4 LCTs, embarking Landing Force, Lt. Col. Lester E. Brown

Russell Islands Motor Torpedo Boat Squadron, Lt. Alvin P. Cluster; 12 PTs

TF 33 AIR FORCE SOUTH PACIFIC, Vice Admiral Aubrey W. Fitch

SOLOMON ISLANDS AIR FORCE, Rear Admiral Marc A. Mitscher

Combat planes for the aërial offensive comprised 258 fighters, 193 bombers, 82 heavy bombers. Of these, 213, 170 and 72 respectively were ready to fly on the morning of 30 June.

The Air Search Unit, Captain Henry S. Kendall, included PBY Squadrons 23, 44 and 71, based on tenders at Tulagi and Santa Cruz Islands, plus a number of assigned A.A.F. heavy bombers based at Henderson Field.

Included in the Task Organization but not directly participating were the following groups of combat ships, organized as TF 36, covering force, under Admiral Halsey's direct command: —

Support Group A, 3 light cruisers and 5 destroyers,
Rear Admiral Walden L. Ainsworth

Support Group B, 4 light cruisers, 4 destroyers and 4 minelayers,
Rear Admiral A. Stanton Merrill

Support Group C, 2 carriers, 2 AA light cruisers, 4 destroyers,
Rear Admiral DeWitt C. Ramsey

Two Battleship divisions, Rear Admirals Glenn B. Davis and Harry W. Hill

Escort Carriers, Rear Admiral Andrew C. McFall

Eleven Submarines, under Captain Willard M. Downes

## 3. *"Musket-He-Fire-Up,"* [5] *30 June*

While Admiral Turner's troop-laden ships plod through the gloom of a dirty and moonless night, suppose we leap ahead and take a look at the coveted prize.

[5] Melanesian pidgin for "The gun goes off." For details we could not find room for here see Cdr. J. C. Shaw's article (note 4).

New Georgia Island, largest of the like-named group, is 45 miles long in a NW–SE line parallel to the Slot and separated from it by an almost unbroken coral-reef barrier. Between reef and shoreline is a series of blue lagoons such as Marovo, said to be the world's largest. On the opposite and southwestern side of the island the coral barrier is broken and steep cliffs rise abruptly from Blanche Channel, where the lead line has found 600-fathom depths within a mile of the shore. The rain-forest green of the serrated hills, the calcimine blue of the still lagoons and the lacy foam around the reefs, as seen from the ocean, suggest a tropical paradise; and ashore there is some substance to that elusive dream. Wild orchids bloom in extravagant profusion, bird-winged butterflies fly about, nearly as large as the screaming white cockatoos which keep them company; friendly natives ply graceful canoes along the quiet shores of the lagoons. Around the turn of the century an Australian pioneer named Norman Wheately established his headquarters at Lambeti plantation, Munda Point, on the shore of island-studded Roviana Lagoon. There he planted one of the few coconut plantations on the island; there too the Methodists founded a mission. And there, in 1943, Hirohito's "flying eagles" found good level ground for their nest. As long as Japan held Munda and had the planes, she could stop the Allies at the Russells. If, on the other hand, the Allies could base planes at Munda, they could deny everything below Bougainville to the enemy and would have another leg-up toward Rabaul.

The most important landings on 30 June were those on the north coast of Rendova Island, five miles across Blanche Channel from Munda. Admiral Turner, who always chose to be in the thick of things, took personal command in *McCawley* of the Western Group, whose first task was to occupy this island. But there were a few preliminaries before he arrived with the transports. Six miles east of Munda field are two small islands separated by Onaiavisi Entrance, a narrow passage which gives access from Blanche Channel to Roviana Lagoon. Here, during the midwatch of the 30th, destroyer-transport *Talbot* and minesweeper *Zane* hove-to, intent on disembarking two companies of the 169th Infantry Regiment United States Army. Heavy rain blotted out the land and *Zane* ran hard on a reef. While she struggled to free herself, the troops and supplies landed without opposition and assured a protected channel into the lagoon at such time as the invasion of Munda would commence. *Zane* perched helplessly on the reef throughout the morning, luckily unmolested by enemy planes or artillery; *Rail* pulled her off early in the afternoon.

A second pre-dawn landing also suffered from foul weather. Destroyer-transports *Dent* and *Waters* ferried to Rendova a jungle-trained and physically hardened outfit, the "Barracudas" of the 172nd Regimental Combat Team United States Army. These men planned to land in Rendova Harbor at a spot marked with a light by the advance patrol that had been there for several days. The rain quenched the signal and the troops landed in the wrong spot. Since they were supposed to wipe out the Japanese garrison before the main force arrived, this meant that the major landing would be opposed.

Out in Blanche Channel, as daylight crowded darkness from the sky, four transports and two supply ships edged into position off Rendova Harbor, and troops of the 172nd RCT, wearing packs that made them look like hunchbacked gnomes, stepped warily into the landing craft still hanging by their falls. Precisely at sunrise the first boats splashed into the water, cast off and scurried shoreward. The eight destroyers of the screen circled fretfully to seaward, looking for trouble.

In prewar days, Munda natives, commuting by canoe, had tended several coconut plantations on Rendova. The landings centered around these plantations on the northern part of the island under the wooded summit of Mount Rendova. Since the number of Americans disembarked on the island numbered thousands as against an enemy garrison of fewer than three hundred men,[6] the

[6] Japanese Navy garrison, 140 and one company of 229th Infantry Regiment, about 150 men. (Capt. Ohmae.)

landings were a pushover. The 172nd RCT, assisted by a party of Solomon Islanders under Major Martin Clements of the local constabulary, and by the "Barracudas" who arrived an hour late, dispatched about a quarter of the garrison and chased the remainder clear of the beaches. Enemy dead included the garrison commander and one shrewd diarist who had written, "I can't understand why Headquarters does not reinforce troops on Rendova which is a good landing place. A sad case!"

The only way for the enemy to disrupt the Rendova landings was to go after the transports. Munda shore batteries had that in mind, but since they expected a frontal assault on Munda beaches they held their fire, waiting for the transports to close. Only after the first wave of troops had hit the Rendova beach did the gunners realize their mistake and open fire, aiming at the nearest targets, four destroyers patrolling Blanche Channel. The first salvo straddled *Gwin* and, two minutes later, a 4.7-inch shell crashed her main deck aft, killing three men, wounding seven and stopping the after engine. The screen commander, Captain Thomas J. Ryan, ordered *Gwin* back to the transport area, and with *Farenholt* and *Buchanan* engaged in a spirited action with half a dozen enemy shore batteries. These were silenced and the destroyers were not hit. *Gwin* in the meantime laid a smoke screen to protect the transports unloading. That process went ahead with the precision of a dress parade. Even with the interruption of a false air raid alarm, holds were more than half empty by 1100.

So far, the American fighter planes which had been darting in and out of the partial overcast had not seen a single enemy plane. Here were six plump transports within sight of Munda field and 15 or 20 minutes' flight from the Bougainville bases. It was hard to believe. Actually there were no Japanese planes in the Solomons capable of making effective raids, owing to their premature withdrawal to Rabaul; and all Japanese radio circuits were clogged with reports of MacArthur's movement into Nassau Bay. What should the "eagles" hit first? Admiral Kusaka was in a jam; so was

General Sasaki at Munda, "completely baffled"[7] by the Rendova landing.

He felt a little happier at 1115 when 27 "Zekes," the only planes that Kusaka had ready, came down the Slot on a fighter sweep; but they were nearly annihilated by American fighters. The threat cost Turner one precious hour of unloading time, but there were no further interruptions, and at 1500 he ordered retirement. All but fifty tons of the supplies had been unloaded. General Sasaki on Munda, peering through his binoculars, regarded so speedy a debarkation as "absolutely miraculous." Two hours later he was treated to another miracle. A battery of Army 105-mm guns, emplaced on an island in Rendova Harbor, commenced lobbing shells across the channel at his outposts. A bombing raid by 43 planes on Munda at 1615 rendered him still more unhappy; but Sasaki's hour would come.

The transports had been under way but half an hour when their radars reported many bogies approaching from the northwest. Admiral Kusaka at last had a proper strike on the way, 25 torpedo-carrying "Bettys" covered by 24 "Zekes." They flew directly to Rendova Harbor, found no transports there, and searched along the coast of New Georgia. That gave defending fighter planes their chance. Fighter direction in destroyer *Jenkins* coached 16 F4Us of Marine Fighter Squadron 221 onto the enemy long before he found the transports. "Go get 'em, boys! Protect your shipping!" The Corsairs snarled down to pick off several "Bettys" before they reached Turner's formation.[8]

The transports and supply ships were in two columns flanked by seven destroyers. Turner pulled his old gambit, presenting long, high broadsides to the attackers until they commenced their run-in. Then he signaled "Emergency Turn Nine" (90 degrees right) which threw the ships' sterns toward the planes, narrowing hull exposure and giving anti-aircraft gunners more time to work

[7] This, and other details on Japanese movements, are from "Southeast Area Operations," Part 2 (Navy).

[8] This was the third flight that day for these planes. The speed of servicing by ground crews at Henderson Field rivaled the fast work of Turner's sailors.

over the enemy. About ten "Bettys" got through fighters and flak to drop their fish. Captain Rodgers of *McCawley* saw a torpedo approaching on his port quarter and vainly tried to comb the track, but the warhead hit amidships against the engine room and stopped "Wacky Mac" dead.

This was the only torpedo hit scored, and the Corsairs' and ships' gunners got 17 out of the 25 "Bettys" who made the try. For several days thereafter, ships steaming through Blanche Channel would sight green-jacketed bodies of dead enemy aviators.

*McCawley* did not catch fire but her engine room and after hold were flooded and another hold started to leak. Admiral Turner shifted his flag and staff to destroyer *Farenholt*. *Ralph Talbot* took off most of the ship's crew (of whom 15 had been killed and 8 wounded); *Libra* took *McCawley* in tow, with two destroyers as escort, and the other ships continued their retirement. At 1715 the enemy made his third and last aërial stab of the day. Eight "Vals" burst through the overcast and planted bombs ahead of *Libra*. Three of them fell to anti-aircraft fire, one to an after machine gun of still defiant *McCawley*, served by a Marine officer and a scratch crew.

*McCawley's* salvage crew fought a losing battle against flooding; by nightfall, when she appeared to be going down by the stern, all hands transferred to destroyer *McCalla*. Tug *Pawnee* arrived and took over the tow, only to have the line part. Admiral Turner was still debating whether to torpedo the ship or send another salvage party on board when, at 2023, two torpedoes smashed into her and down went *McCawley* to the bottom of the sea. The mystery was solved next morning when Lieutenant Commander Robert B. Kelly brought six PTs into Rendova and reported sinking an "enemy" transport in Blanche Channel. He had been informed by the Rendova naval base that no friendly forces would be there and so had assumed poor "Wacky Mac" to be Japanese. After this the PTs were placed directly under Turner's command and given a liaison officer to keep them properly informed.

The other landings that day had plenty of trouble, but none

from the air. At Viru Harbor, which we wanted as a small-craft base, the Japanese thwarted the first daylight landings completely. Companies O and P of the 4th Marine Raiders (Lieutenant Colonel Michael S. Currin USMC), who had made Segi Point 21 June, started toward Viru by rubber boat and continued on foot. Swamps, swollen streams and clashes with Japanese patrols put them behind schedule. So, when the Viru Occupation Unit (destroyer-transports *Hopkins*, *Kilty* and *Crosby*) headed into the gooseneck entrance of the harbor on 30 June, it was greeted by a Japanese 3-inch gun instead of by the Marines. After the troops had waited six hours, Admiral Turner ordered them to land at Segi Point. Next morning the marching Marines arrived at Viru and, as usual, "the situation was soon well in hand." Bombs from 17 SBDs helped disperse the hundred or more Japanese. The raiders combed steep lava cliffs and palm-fringed beaches, killing the foe in a series of rifle duels reminiscent of the old wild west films. Late in the afternoon they waved the landing craft of the second echelon in to the beaches.[9]

The southernmost of the landings, at Wickham Anchorage, demonstrated the danger of disembarking troops on strange beaches during darkness. Under the command of Rear Admiral George H. Fort, three destroyer-transports and seven LCIs came up from the Russells on the night of 29–30 June and at 0335 hove-to off Vangunu Island. Heavy seas urged on by high winds buffeted the landing craft; low, dark clouds inked out the faint starlight; it was impossible to see adjacent boats or pick up the beach outlines. Troops lost time and temper climbing in and out of wet, tossing boats while the destroyer-transports hunted for the proper disembarkation point. The LCIs barged into a formation of small boats, scattering them like a broken string of beads. In darkness and confusion the boats grounded along a seven-mile stretch to the west of the designated beaches, and six were lost in the heavy surf. Luckily there was no opposition and the troops were able to

[9] For details of Viru ground operations see Maj. Roy J. Batterton USMC "You Fight by the Book" *Marine Corps Gazette* July 1949 pp. 14–21.

reorganize before striking inland. Later that day they closed with the Japanese, some 300 strong, who were entrenched on a point of land to the east. Artillery, air strikes, bombardment by destroyers *Woodworth* and *Jenkins*, and four days of dirty jungle fighting, were required to eliminate them.

Since Segi Point had been taken before D-day, landing there was no problem except for the navigators. Before nightfall 30 June, the 47th Seabee Battalion began clearing away trees to make an airstrip. Rain dissolved the ground into a viscous gumbo, but the strip was ready for emergency landings in less than a fortnight.

## 4. *Squaring Away for Munda, 1–5 July*

Of the five initial landings in the Central Solomons, only the one at Rendova really paid off. Wickham Anchorage quickly became a refuge and breathing spot for small craft chugging up from Guadalcanal or the Russells, but never a base of consequence. Viru Harbor was found unsuitable for the proposed PT base and its only function was to repair small landing craft on a marine railway installed by the Seabees. Segi Point became an emergency air base, but the swift coursing of the war to the northwest reduced it to minor consequence. Onaiavisi had been secured merely to protect the eventual movement of amphibious forces into Roviana Lagoon, which started on 2 July.

Rendova was different. The 3400-foot mountain was an excellent observation post for us, as it had been for the coastwatcher; the beaches were good assembly points for boats, men and supplies embarking for the invasion of the enemy stronghold. Rendova Harbor became a base for PT boats to harass Japanese barge lines, and big Army guns emplaced ashore guaranteed support in the drive for the airfield.

All these factors were easily understood by anyone looking at a chart, but for the man domiciled on this valuable property, Rendova meant only mud and plenty of it.

On 30 June Seabees of the 24th Battalion felled coconut trees and laid out corduroy roads to bridge the mud, but so much of the heavy artillery mired down that the rest of it was emplaced on the firm coral foundations of adjacent islands. Supplies were left stacked in disorderly piles along the beach, adding to the confusion; lighters often grounded before hitting the shore, and their cargoes were soaked when carried by hand through waist-deep water. As usual, unwilling combat troops had to splice out the insufficient shore parties.

Next day, 1 July, the second echelon of the American landing force made Rendova without interference,[10] unloaded all supplies including 155-mm howitzers, and at nightfall headed for home down Blanche Channel. Enemy float planes attacked at 1923 but made no hits. Twenty-five minutes later, destroyer *Radford* of the escort picked up submarine *RO–101* on the surface, six miles distant. Commander Romoser conned her toward the boat. One mile distant, *Radford* opened gunfire and illuminated, surprising the submarine. Nineteen 5-inch salvos ripped off its conning tower and punctured the hull, machine-gun hits sparkled, and a torpedo was fired but missed. As Romoser closed to ram, *RO–101* went down in a pool of oil followed by *Radford's* depth charges. But she did not sink; was still afloat in September.

Admiral Kusaka now collected 24 Army bombers and as many fighters to team up with 20 "Zekes" for a noon assault on Rendova 2 July. They caught the beachhead flatfooted;[11] even search radar failed to give warning. The bombers skirted the peak undetected and were over the troops before "Condition Red" could be shouted, let alone set; soldiers standing in chow line were admiring the pretty formation of what they supposed to be B–25s when fragmentation bombs began to drop. Fifty-nine men were killed, 77 wounded; the hospital was wrecked and much damage done to boats and

[10] Admiral Kusaka sent 5 destroyers to stop it but they flinched from entering Blanche Channel in night rainstorms and retired. He then sent 6 "Vals" and 35 "Zekes" by daylight, but Allied fliers drove them off with a 50 per cent loss.

[11] Because of bad weather in the lower Solomons, Allied air patrol had been withdrawn.

equipment. And that night the Tokyo Express put in its first appearance in this campaign. Light cruiser *Yubari* and nine destroyers steamed into Blanche Channel and pounded Rendova heavily. Fortunately, every shell landed in the jungle.

Several miles to the southward the gun flashes were sighted by three PTs on patrol — Nos. 156, 157, 161. Their leader, Lieutenant Commander Kelly, with the *McCawley* incident fresh in mind, approached circumspectly and even crossed the enemy column, still doubtful of its identity. The Japanese squadron commander, untroubled by such doubts, detached four destroyers to steam in a tight circle around the PTs and sink them with gunfire. The boats escaped by making smoke and steering erratic courses; they even fired six torpedoes, which missed but scared the enemy off.

The danger point in an amphibious operation comes several days after the landings, when the enemy is able to counterattack in force. Halsey knew this, but the spotty Japanese performance so far tempted him to raise his guard. He ordered General Hester to ferry troops over to New Georgia on 5 July and take Munda Field.

Apparently it had not been decided, before the operation began, exactly where the troops would land on New Georgia. Army patrols after reconnoitering the shores of Roviana Lagoon reported that Laiana beach, only two miles from Munda, was heavily defended but that Zanana beach, over three miles farther to the east, looked like a pushover. With Turner's approval the General decided to land his force on Zanana and move on Munda through the jungle — a natural mistake but costly, since it put his army in a position similar to that of the unfortunate Japanese general who had attacked Henderson Field.[12] Advance units of the 43rd Division embarked in landing craft on 2 July and followed native guides through the reefs to Zanana. Subsequent landings by small batches of soldiers were more of an infiltration than an invasion. No resistance developed, and for the time being New Georgia was a safer place for Americans than Rendova where, on Inde-

[12] See Vol. V of this History pp. 189–90.

pendence Day, 17 Japanese Army bombers escorted by 66 fighters destroyed several landing craft and damaged two LCIs.

After this raid the Japanese Army refused to contribute more planes for the defense of the Solomons,[13] but agreed that New Georgia was a key outpost to be "held at all costs" and released 4000 troops for transport from Rabaul down the Slot. The first echelon was due to arrive at Kolombangara on the night of 4–5 July. As usual, the Japanese employed destroyers for troop-lift. Three ships left the Shortlands in early afternoon 4 July for a fast run-in to Vila Plantation.

As Admiral Halsey had been informed by scouts that the trails between Zanana and Kula Gulf were impassable, he had assembled an occupation force of 2600 troops under Colonel Harry Liversedge USMC to occupy Rice Anchorage and block reinforcements reaching Munda from Vila. The troops were carried in seven destroyer-transports, and were escorted by Admiral Ainsworth's force of three light cruisers and nine destroyers.[14] By chance, his timetable called for an entrance to Kula Gulf at the same time as that of the Japanese. Ainsworth's flagship, the lucky "Blue Goose," stuck her neck into Kula Gulf shortly before midnight, at the head of the bombardment group, shaping a course toward the Vila shore. Destroyers *Nicholas* and *Strong* pulled out ahead to search with radar and sound gear for surface and submarine foes. A dark, overcast night with a moderate southeast breeze pushing occasional rain-squalls over the Gulf gave radar more than its usual advantage over enemy binoculars. At 0026 July 5 *Honolulu*, *Helena* and *St. Louis* opened fire, lacing Vila with some 3000 rounds of 6-inch shell, while destroyers *Chevalier* and *O'Bannon* chimed in with 5-inch high-explosive. The formation than turned east and all

[13] Admiral Koga then moved into Rabaul 31 fighters and 13 bombers from carrier *Ryuho* (not to be confused with carrier *Ryujo* sunk at Battle of Eastern Solomons).

[14] Bombardment Group: CLs *Honolulu*, *Helena*, *St. Louis*; DDs *Nicholas*, *Strong*, *O'Bannon*, *Chevalier*. Transport Group: APDs *Dent*, *Talbot*, *McKean*, *Waters*, *Kilty*, *Crosby*, *Schley*; DMSs *Hopkins*, *Trever*; DDs *Radford*, *Gwin*, *McCalla*, *Ralph Talbot*, *Woodworth*. Troops: 3 battalions of 1st Marine Raiders, 3rd Bn. 145th Inf. Regt., 3rd Bn. 148th Inf. Regt. U.S. Army.

seven ships shifted fire to Bairoko Harbor, the New Georgia
terminus of the Japanese ferry line from Vila. The transports followed the New Georgia shore toward Rice Anchorage. At 0031,
when near Boli Point, *Ralph Talbot's* radar showed two surface
contacts heading west; by 0040 they appeared to be two ships
standing out of the Gulf on course NNW at 25 knots.

At that moment destroyer *Nicholas* of the bombardment group,
having finished shooting at Bairoko, was turning north. The rest
of the group followed in column. Admiral Ainsworth, who had
been notified by voice radio about the mysterious ships, was just
asking for their location at 0049 when *Strong's* gunnery officer,
Lieutenant James A. Curran, sighted a bubbling torpedo wake on
the port hand. Before he could even warn the bridge, the explosion
of a warhead tore open the hull on both sides, demolishing the
forward fireroom and flooding the engineering spaces. *Strong*
heeled to starboard and sagged amidships like a sway-backed
nag. As she staggered to a halt, her sister ships coursed swiftly
by.

This death-dealing thrust came from the Japanese destroyer
division, so many miles to the northwest that no American could
then believe that the torpedo came from that source. Ainsworth's
first salvo had alerted the destroyers as they stood into the Gulf.
Having no inclination for a close fight, they fired Parthian shots
with their "long lance" torpedoes, and then abandoned their transport mission and retired.

When *Strong* did not respond to radio query, Ainsworth directed
*Chevalier* and *O'Bannon* to her rescue. They found her about two
miles west of Rice Anchorage. Wellings, the skipper of *Strong*, had
kept his men on board, expecting that help would come before she
sank. *Chevalier* shoved her bow into the cripple's port side, manila
lines and cargo nets were quickly rigged between the ships, and
sailors were beginning to crawl across — for the sea was calm —
when Japanese shore batteries, quiet during the bombardment,
spotted the rescue group and opened up on an easy target. Four
150-mm guns at Enogai Inlet, which aërial reconnaissance had

failed to spot,[15] joined the batteries at Bairoko Harbor in a brilliant illumination (enhanced by flares from a plane) and brisk gunfire. After one shell (fortunately a dud) had hit *Strong, O'Bannon* belayed rescue efforts to deliver counterfire. *Chevalier* remained alongside for seven minutes while enemy salvos walked closer. Across her bows poured *Strong* survivors, 241 all told, while her stern mounts barked back at the shore guns. Commander McLean hauled clear at 0122, when *Strong* was settling like a punctured beer can. A minute later she went down with a monstrous death rattle as her starboard depth charges, under water since the torpedo hit, exploded.

*O'Bannon* and *Chevalier* now made for the nearest exit, pausing only to ask the other destroyers to look for floating *Strong* survivors. These had stepped off the ship just as she went down and so had borne the full brunt of the depth charge concussion, yet a number made the beach. Others, including Commander Wellings, were recovered by the destroyers; 46 were lost.

The transport group continued setting Colonel Liversedge's troops ashore right through the hullabaloo. At 0136 the first landing craft, towing rubber boats, started toward the beach guided by native canoes and a shore beacon. Darkness, rain, enemy artillery and a shallow bar off the beach produced the usual night landing snafu. *Gwin* and *Radford* silenced the shore batteries, although without air spot it was rather like the game of pinning a tail on a donkey, blindfold. By 0600 all the raiders and most of the soldiers and their gear had been landed, and the transports were executing Clear the Area. Ainsworth's bombardment group was already well on its way to Tulagi.

Colonel Liversedge, ordered to block land traffic between Kula Gulf and Munda, had ahead of him an eight-mile hike to be made on three days' rations. Leaving two companies of soldiers at Rice Anchorage to establish a supply base, he led his men into the jungle

---

[15] At the pre-sailing conference, Ainsworth had begged permission to bombard Enogai Inlet which on previous visits had harbored enemy artillery. Since air photos didn't show any guns, his requests had been denied.

at daybreak. Flight Lieutenant J. A. Corrigan RAAF and a corps of natives were supposed to have cut a trail toward the base of Dragon's Peninsula, as the area between Enogai Inlet and Bairoko Harbor is called, but they had not finished it; the troops only managed to slip and slide five miles that day, discarding blankets, packs and mess gear. It was midnight before the last man slumped into the muddy bivouac.

While the Marines dozed fitfully in the dripping forest, Admiral Ainsworth and the Tokyo Express collided full tilt in Kula Gulf.

# CHAPTER XI

# The Battles of Kula Gulf and Kolombangara[1]

## 5–16 July 1943

East Longitude dates; Zone minus 11 time.

### 1. The Battle of Kula Gulf

WHEN Ainsworth's ships shaped course down the Slot after the Vila-Bairoko bombardment, the Admiral could reflect that he had been sailing this route for half a year and no Japanese fighting ships except submarines had yet been encountered; he supposed that one of these had sunk *Strong*. Like all flag officers, Ainsworth had been schooled in battle tactics and was eager to test them. So, when in midafternoon 5 July word came from Halsey that the Tokyo Express was getting up steam off Buin, Ainsworth immediately came about in Indispensable Strait and bent on 29 knots; his ships' navigators began cutting in old tangents against the setting sun on the well-traveled road back up the Slot. Oil kings in the destroyers sounded tanks and reported fuel enough but none to spare.

[1] Action Reports of ships and commands involved, especially Rear Admiral Ainsworth's Action Report 3 Aug. 1943, Supplementary Report 15 Mar. 1944, O.N.R. & L. Recording 17 Jan. 1946; Capt. McInerney's Action Report; Cincpac "Operations in Pacific Ocean Areas July 1943" and Information Bulletin No. 10 "Naval Operations Solomon Islands Area, 30 June–12 July 1943"; Comairsopac Intelligence Bulletins; ATIS Doc. No. 15685 "Historical Reports: Naval Operations – The Battle of Kula Gulf" prepared by Cdr. Shiro Yamaguchi; ATIS No. 48464, Cdr. Mikami's answers to my questions on these actions; Jicpoa Item No. 5782 translation of captured Japanese Navy Torpedo School's "Battle Lessons Learned in Greater East Asia War (Torpedoes) Volume VI," pub. about Sept. 1943; Conversations with Rear Admiral Ainsworth and various officers under his

The task organization follows: —

TASK GROUP 36.1, Rear Admiral Walden L. Ainsworth

Crudiv 9, Rear Admiral Ainsworth

| HONOLULU | Capt. Robert W. Hayler |
| *HELENA | Capt. Charles P. Cecil |
| ST. LOUIS | Capt. Colin Campbell |

Screen, Captain Francis X. McInerney (Comdesron 21)

| NICHOLAS | Lt. Cdr. Andrew J. Hill |
| O'BANNON | Lt. Cdr. Donald J. MacDonald |
| RADFORD | Cdr. William K. Romoser |
| JENKINS | Cdr. Harry F. Miller |

\* Sunk in this action.

*Radford* and *Jenkins*, assigned to Ainsworth to replace sunken *Strong* and damaged *Chevalier*, were loading fuel and ammunition in Tulagi when orders arrived. *Radford* finished topping off at 1647 and scrambled madly to fill magazines. *Jenkins* spared her 200 rounds and pressed on ahead to the rendezvous; *Chevalier*, docked nearby, gave her 300 more and a hearty Godspeed. *Radford* got under way at 1837, and caught up with the formation.

Captain Bob Hayler, who had taken *Honolulu* through the Battle of Tassafaronga without a scratch, must have noticed the setup, ominously similar to that unhappy affair — a group of cruisers and destroyers summarily ordered to block, no time for a conference, destroyers joining late. But Ainsworth's skippers knew their task group commander very well, there had been plenty of time to practise and digest his battle plans, *Radford* and *Jenkins* were old teammates, and the Slot was as familiar to their navigators as Hampton Roads to those of the Atlantic Fleet. Moreover, every ship was equipped with SG radar and a combat information center.

Ainsworth's plan, built on the principles of concentration and surprise, envisaged two situations: a medium-range (8000–10,000 yards) engagement with full radar-controlled gunfire; or a long-range battle with star shell illumination. He assumed that the Jap-

command. Lt. Colton G. Morris USNR and Hugh B. Cave *The Fightin'est Ship* (1944), and James D. Horan *Action Tonight* (1945) contain vivid contemporary accounts of life on board *Helena* and *O'Bannon* but are not trustworthy for facts.

anese had inferior radar and that all their ships would carry torpedoes. But he still considered his cruisers' 6-inch guns the primary weapons.

A speed of 29 knots brought the seven ships off Visu Visu Point, the northwest knob of New Georgia, by midnight. They went to general quarters. As radar screens were still clear of bogeys, afloat or aloft, Ainsworth held to an anti-aircraft disposition. Topside gunners, ducking out of passing showers, viewed with satisfaction a cloud-blotted moonless sky, a calm sea and a gentle breeze. Below decks, engineers checked steam pressure and adjusted throttles when ordered to lower speed to 27 and then to 25 knots.

Three groups of enemy destroyers were tearing down the Slot to land supplies and troops at Vila for the Munda defense. They had left Buin after sundown. For missions of this sort the Japanese did not think much of the principle of concentration; they split up into three groups. The force was organized as follows: —

REINFORCEMENT GROUP, * Rear Admiral Teruo Akiyama

*Support Unit,* Rear Admiral Akiyama
Destroyers * *Niizuki, Suzukaze, Tanikaze*

*First Transport Unit,* Captain Tsuneo Orita
Destroyers *Mochizuki, Mikazuki, Hamakaze*

*Second Transport Unit,* Captain Katsumori Yamashiro
Destroyers *Amagiri, Hatsuyuki,* * *Nagatsuki, Satsuki*

* Lost in this action.

Despite the disparity in gun power and armor between Akiyama's force and Ainsworth's, and the presence of troop passengers, the Japanese Admiral had the edge. Bad weather had saved him from running the usual gauntlet of American bombs, and searching Black Cats had missed him completely. His battery of 24-inch torpedo tubes with reloads was a great leveler and, though Akiyama did not know it, Ainsworth was ignorant of the very existence of these giant torpedoes. *Niizuki* boasted a new radar set. And finally, the success of past transport operations gave Akiyama confidence. Only the night before, a single destroyer division had beaten off a powerful enemy task group. Tokyo was announcing a Japanese victory on the Fourth of July – mud in Halsey's eye!

At 0026 July 6, just as the Americans were slowing down off Visu Visu Point, Akiyama, already within the Gulf, detached Captain Orita's transport unit to close the southeast shore of Kolombangara en route to Vila. The seven remaining ships continued in column at 21 knots toward the foot of the Gulf. At 0118, Akiyama reversed course by column movement right and at 0143, sent Yamashiro's transport unit toward Vila roadstead. *Niizuki, Suzukaze* and *Tanikaze* headed north in that order.

At the very moment when Yamashiro was released, American radarmen were plotting the enemy track. They had made the contact at 0140 at a distance of 24,700 yards. Ainsworth's TBS was crackling with orders to shift from cruising to battle disposition and prepare for action. Destroyers abandoned screening stations to form column with the three cruisers, making the order of ships destroyers *Nicholas* and *O'Bannon,* cruisers *Honolulu, Helena* and *St. Louis,* destroyers *Jenkins* and *Radford.* At 0142 these changed course simultaneously from 292° to 242° to shorten range. Speed held at 25 knots.

For the next few minutes experts in the combat information centers puzzled over their radar plots. How many enemy ships – of what class – how disposed – on what course? Kolombangara's towering slopes blended into the picture, and plotting was confused also by Yamashiro's four destroyers peeling off. But by 0149 Ainsworth had assurance that there were two enemy groups totaling seven to nine ships. Wishing to keep the advantage of surprise, he then ordered ships 60° right, which brought them back into column on course 302°. The range was now 11,000 yards and Ainsworth had to act quickly. He decided to engage at medium range with full radar gunfire control. Since radar indicated that the larger ships were the four in the second (Yamashiro) group, he ordered *Jenkins* and *Radford* to join the cruisers in firing on them, while *Nicholas* and *O'Bannon* took on the nearer group, Akiyama's. At 0154 the Admiral gave Commence Firing to the

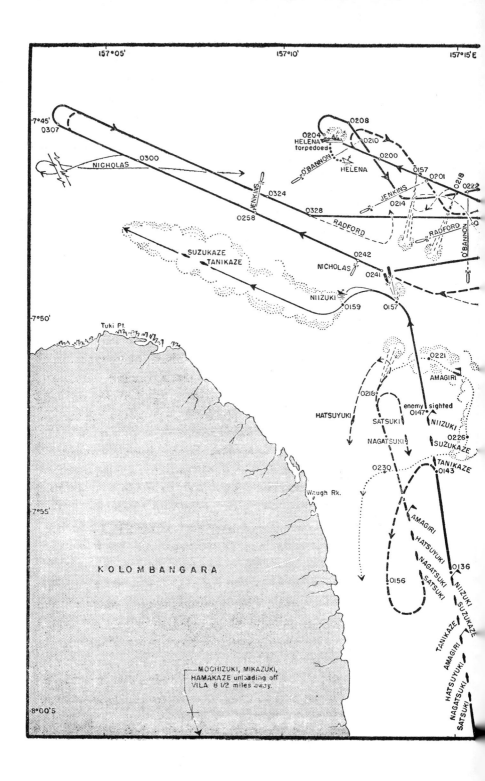

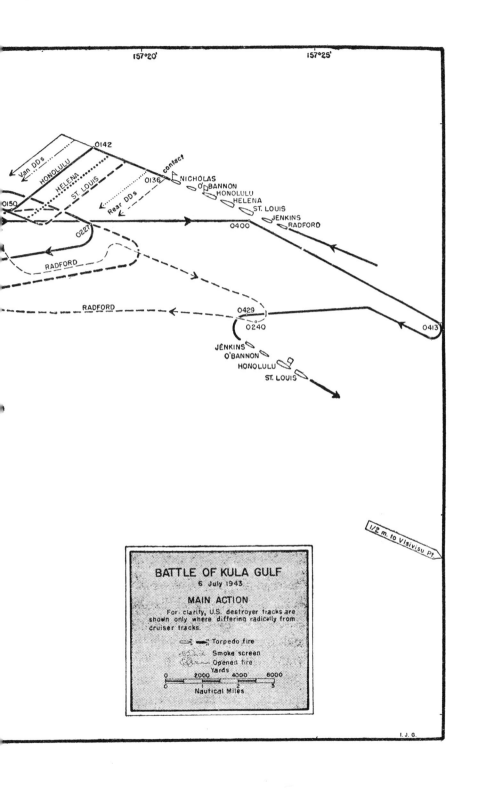

157°20'    157°25'

Van DDs
HONOLULU
HELENA
ST. LOUIS
0142
0150
contact
0136
Rear DDs
0227
RADFORD
RADFORD
RADFORD
0429
0240
0400
0413

NICHOLAS
O'BANNON
HONOLULU
HELENA
ST. LOUIS
JENKINS
RADFORD

JENKINS
O'BANNON
HONOLULU
ST. LOUIS

1/2 m. to Visivisu Pt.

**BATTLE OF KULA GULF**
6 July 1943

**MAIN ACTION**

For clarity, U.S. destroyer tracks are
shown only where differing radically from
cruiser tracks.

Torpedo fire
Smoke screen
Opened fire
Yards
0        2000        4000        6000
0          1          2          3
Nautical Miles

I. J. G.

destroyers. McInerney inquired whether that meant guns or torpedoes. "Gunfire first," replied the flagship, "but hold everything."

Ainsworth, noting that Yamashiro's "big ships" were 10,000 yards beyond the nearer group and fast opening range, wisely changed his decision and ordered the cruisers to blast the nearer group first, then "reach ahead, make a simultaneous turn and get the others on the reverse course." The time was now 0156, the range 7000 yards. It was time to shoot but *Helena* was slow getting on her target. Not until 0157, with Akiyama's ships broad on the port beam distant 6800 yards, did the first gun sing out. Flame streaked from the ships, particularly from *Helena*, which had no flashless powder; the other cruisers had enough of that kind for the first three or four salvos only.

Surprise had been lost — long lost in the tempo of modern naval battle. At 0106 *Niizuki's* radar detector had reported enemy ships. By 0146 the range had closed to a bare 12,000 yards. Admiral Akiyama, already suspicious, rang up 30 knots, came 40° left from course North and ordered Yamashiro, loaded down with troops as he was, to come along and fight.

When American gunfire flashed at 0157, Akiyama's torpedomen had a nice point of aim, but *Niizuki* never had a chance to use it. The first American salvo smothered this ship, knocking out her steering gear and tossing her out of formation. *Suzukaze* and *Tanikaze*, untouched by gunfire, had 16 "long lance" torpedoes hurtling toward the Americans at 49 knots within a minute of the opening gun.

Donald MacDonald, veteran skipper of veteran *O'Bannon*, remembered so well the Battle of Guadalcanal that his only thought was to fire torpedoes. Although his gunnery officer reported a perfect solution, he withheld gunfire until certain he had lost the chance for a torpedo attack. *Nicholas*, far in the lead, was in a similar quandary. Both ships fired their 5-inch guns tardily, while torpedoes lay idle in the tubes. Same condition with the two rear destroyers: *Jenkins* would not fire guns until she had a chance to launch torpedoes, which she did not have until 0201; and she so fouled *Radford's* range that Commander Romoser could fire nothing.

If sheer weight of metal had counted, as in the old days, Ainsworth's cruisers would have won the battle in the first five minutes. Over 2500 rounds of 6-inch poured at the enemy, whose guns replied only weakly. They accused us of having "6-inch machine guns"! Ainsworth was convinced that the Akiyama group was "practically obliterated," which was not true. Only *Niizuki* was heading toward the bottom; the other two were doing fairly well. *Suzukaze* had her searchlight knocked out, her forward gun mount disabled, a machine-gun ammunition locker aflame, a few punctures in the hull, but only three men hit. *Tanikaze* fared even better: a dud in the anchor-windlass compartment flooded the rice and barley stores. *Amagiri* took four hits which destroyed her forward radio room and electrical circuits; three duds damaged *Hatsuyuki.*

At 0203 Ainsworth ordered countermarch to course 112°. But before the signal could be executed, Akiyama's torpedoes arrived. "Happy *Helena*" was the unhappy victim. Between 0204 and 0207 three "long lances" made lethal hits; the first sheared off her bow between Nos. 1 and 2 turrets. She flooded rapidly and jackknifed. We shall leave her momentarily to follow the battle; for Ainsworth, intent on the countermarch which he executed at the time of the first hit, was unaware of her plight. Captain Colin Campbell of *St. Louis* cut hard right to avoid collision with *Helena,* coursed clear, and had just straightened out on course ESE when a dud torpedo clanged into *Helena's* hull aft.

While American gunfire slackened with the departure of *Suzukaze* and *Tanikaze* (*O'Bannon* and *Radford,* in clear water at last, sent nine torpedoes swimming in a futile stern chase of them), Yamashiro's transport-destroyers began to register on American radar screens. They were 13,000 yards distant, galloping north at 30 knots. At 0207 Ainsworth came right 30° to course 142° and seven minutes later left 60° to course 82°.

*Helena's* failure to answer signals tipped Ainsworth off that something was wrong, but this was no time to worry. At 0218 his first salvos started toward *Amagiri* bearing SSW distant 11,600 yards. Three minutes later the Admiral ordered "Turn 3" to course 112° again. By these maneuvers Ainsworth capped the "T" on *Yamashiro*. The Japanese column, pointed fair at American broadsides, was taking enfilade fire, with only the lead ship able to retaliate. American gunners, seeing flames and explosions at the target, fired faster than ever. They should have hit *Amagiri*, but she knuckled hard right, laid a smoke screen and escaped with minor damage. They did prevent her from launching torpedoes. *Hatsuyuki*, second in column, came under fire at the same time and three shots found her. None exploded; but even so they damaged the gun director, wrecked communications, knocked out steering from the bridge, pierced a boiler and a main feedline, twisted a torpedo mount, destroyed three spare torpedoes and killed five men. Pretty good for duds! *Hatsuyuki* then turned away left, replying gamely with gunfire, but failed to fire torpedoes. *Nagatsuki* and *Satsuki* in the rear, unable to see their foe, were glad enough to countermarch from these shell-pocked waters to Vila roadstead, there to get rid of their troop passengers. *Nagatsuki* had taken one 6-inch hit.

At 0227 Ainsworth made a sweeping 150-degree right turn back to course West; but found targets scarce. *Honolulu* fired sporadically while *St. Louis* pierced the darkness with star shell. Nothing was visible, and on the radar only friendly destroyers and a chunk of *Helena's* bow registered. At 0235, sailors heard the order which signals the end of a fight: "Unload All Guns Through Muzzle."

During the engagement with *Yamashiro's* transports, *Nicholas* and *O'Bannon* brought up the rear. On McInerney's orders *O'Bannon* sluiced off five torpedoes at 10,000 yards' range — long for us — which had no scoring chance when the enemy reversed course. *Nicholas* saw no targets in her radar and did not fire. *Radford* fired 5-inch shells in the direction of sinking *Niizuki*, maneuvered to avoid collision with a ship which proved to be a phantom, and ended up four miles astern of the formation. *Jenkins* carefully conformed to Ainsworth's tactical orders, but her guns stayed cold the entire night; her skipper was waiting to fire more torpedoes. He did so, at 0258, at an imagined target.

Reports reaching Ainsworth after 0230 indicated that the enemy was in full flight. He made a right dogleg up the Slot on course 292°, several of his ships whacking away at *Niizuki* wreckage (and probably at *Helena's* bow too) en route. *Nicholas* fired five torpedoes at the same target and then forged ahead, made a radar sweep of Vella Gulf and completed it at 0315. *Radford* slowed to 15 knots while her radar pried into the depths of Kula Gulf. They found nothing except what appeared to be a ship beached off Waugh Rock, which Romoser reported to Ainsworth, who radioed Admiral Mitscher (Comairsols) to deal with it in the morning. Actually no ship was there, but Ainsworth's request for an air strike proved to be very fortunate. The Admiral, who had just come to course ESE, directed McInerney to stay behind with *Nicholas* and *Radford* to rescue survivors. His cruisers' ammunition was down to a few rounds per gun. At 0330, certain that victory was his, the Admiral headed for Tulagi.

Now let us see what had happened to *Helena*. Nobody on board had any warning before the first torpedo exploded near the waterline between Nos. 1 and 2 turrets,[2] shearing off a good quarter of the ship's length. In the after engine room Lieutenant Commander Charles O. Cook, engineer officer, was standing by the gauges, his practised eyes shifting from one to another, his ears listening to the muffled *whoomf-whoomf* of 6-inch guns plugging away at Akiyama's ships. Suddenly the ship lurched with the torpedo hit. Cook's eyes skimmed the gauges: steam pressure normal. Wherever the damage, it was not in his B-section.[3] As his phone talkers were testing all stations there came a second blow, nearby and violent. This torpedo exploded deep under No. 2 stack. Steam pres-

[2] Buships *Summary of War Damage to U.S. Battleships . . .* , *8 Dec. 1942–7 Dec. 1943* p. 8.

[3] Ships are divided into three lettered sections for identification. The A-section forward of the engineering spaces; B-section the engineering spaces; C-section abaft the engineering spaces. It is possible to locate and identify a compartment by its number-letter designation. Thus A–210–L would be a space in the forward section second deck, port side, used for living quarters.

sure dropped fast on all indicators. Normal lighting faded, leaving only the foggy glow of emergency lamps. Engines aft testing. . . . Forward, no answer. Steam and shaft room, pressure down and dropping fast. . . . To Lieutenant Commander Cook, who had practised such casualties time and again, this meant just one thing — a hit between the forward engine room and No. 3 fireroom, the dividing line between forward and after plants. He knew that this meant that No. 4 fireroom would flood too. He called bridge; circuit dead. Better start the men out. He ordered the armored access hatch opened, and in the dim glow of emergency lights he sent his black gang topside, keeping only six men with him to try repairs. Then the third torpedo hit, very near the second, cracking the ship's bottom like a nutshell. Fuel oil spurted into the faces of Cook and his men. They heard the deep gurgle of water flooding in from below. Out on the double! Up access trunk to third deck! Hurry! Hurry! Sea water was at their heels. They tried to slam a door against it but the water pressure was too great. Get the lead out of your feet, scram! Up another ladder to second deck; the rising water swept Cook off his feet but he clung to the rungs and made it. There he ran into Lieutenant Robert E. Beisang USNR who, with no order to abandon ship, was holding his men on station. Beisang did not recognize his oil-soaked, capless chief until Cook identified himself. They conferred briefly. No communications, said Beisang. A sailor pointed to water squirting into the compartment at eye level. Was the main deck already under? Hurry again! Up that ladder, sailors! Main deck at last, tilted crazily with stern high. From up forward came a gnashing of fractured metal; the hull pulling apart. Men leaped into the oily water and thanked God it wasn't on fire.

As the after section of the ship rode stern-high, so what was left of the forward section rode bow-high. Captain Cecil shouted "Abandon Ship!" to all within earshot. The communications officer, twice knocked unconscious and badly injured, needlessly worried about the destruction of confidential documents and codes; his assistants in orderly fashion had lugged lead-weighted bags out on deck and tossed them over. The radar officer jettisoned secret radar parts. The C.I.C. officer[4] supervised the launching of life rafts and all hands went over the side, Captain Cecil last. He swam through sticky puddles of fuel oil to a nearby raft. Six minutes later *Helena* jackknifed and disappeared into a 300-fathom deep while the previously severed bow floated free.

*Helena* sailors were well prepared for this sort of thing. The chief engineer remembered to keep his shoes on lest he land barefoot on some coral-spiked beach. He had his pneumatic lifejacket too, but the unyielding oil made swimming like going through quicksand and his shoes had to go; but he could not get a grip on their slippery leather, nor could his fingers grasp the snaps to get his lifejacket into position for inflation. But he reached a raft. Others found the floating bow section and clustered hopefully about. A salvo of shells slapped into the water around them, whether from friend or foe they could not tell. Captain Cecil formed a convoy of three rafts, and men with watertight flashlights tested them against the time when rescue ships might approach. Officers led cheers amongst the men — "Hip, hip hooray!" in unison — not for joy but in hope of being heard by friends. Some blew bosun's whistles. At 0341, when *Radford* and *Nicholas* hove-to and commenced rescue by lowered boats, the survivors were still spirited but scattered, and the night was dark. Before many could be picked up, and just as eight bells struck, *Nicholas* made a radar contact to the west, distant eight miles and closing fast. Shortly after, *Radford* uncovered another to the south.[5] Time to renew battle! The two destroyers snaked their way through knots of survivors, passing the word, "Hang on! We'll be back for you!"

McInerney did well to knock off rescue. His radar contact was

---

[4] These three officers were Lt. V. W. Post USNR, Lt. R. W. Gash USNR and Lt. Cdr. John L. Chew. BuShips *War Damage Report No. 43* is devoted to *Helena*.

[5] There is confusion here. *Nicholas's* contact was far removed from *Radford's*. Yet the Japanese state that only *Suzukaze* and *Tanikaze*, traveling together, were in the vicinity.

destroyers *Suzukaze* and *Tanikaze* coming back for another try with the "long lances." Since breaking off action at 0159 they had been circling at a safe distance, reloading torpedoes. The Japanese destroyers carried a full load of spare torpedoes on deck, brought them to the torpedo tubes in a hand car running on rails, and reloaded the tubes by a simple device operated by the pneumatic motor used for training the tubes. Ordinarily this operation took only 20 to 25 minutes, but *Suzukaze* had received a hit in the machine-gun ammunition locker, and torpedomen working directly below that fiery spot lost their "presence of mind and calmness." It was difficult to handle these three-ton monsters on a vibrating deck, and so many accidents and distractions occurred that an hour and a quarter passed before Japanese torpedo officers reported their tubes ready for another try at Ainsworth. But the Admiral was gone when they approached the battle scene; he would find out about torpedo reloads the hard way, next week. And they saw neither *Nicholas* nor *Radford*. So the Japanese, shortly after appearing on American radarscopes, retired in the belief that both the enemy and *Niizuki* were gone. A bit of luck for the *Helena* men. *Radford* and *Nicholas* could start fishing again, and Ainsworth, who had come about to support McInerney, could resume his retirement.

While Ainsworth tacked across the top of the Gulf like a lashing whip, the Japanese transports delivered their goods and 1600 passengers at Vila. So far this mission had cost the enemy one destroyer; now the hazards of night navigation took another. *Nagatsuki*, piloting without radar, ran aground hard and fast off Bambari Harbor, five miles north of Vila. *Satsuki* passed lines and tugged in vain to haul her off, gave it up at 0400, and in company with damaged *Hatsuyuki* retired by way of Blackett Strait, preferring to risk mines rather than guns. Both made Buin handily.

Yamashiro's flagship *Amagiri* took the bolder course, steaming north along the east coast of Kolombangara. At 0515 shouts were heard from the water and *Niizuki* survivors were sighted, paddling in a pool of oil. *Amagiri* hove-to and commenced recovering them.

At the same time *Nicholas* and *Radford* were rescuing American survivors some 13,000 yards to the NNW. But this was no gentleman's war in which rescue squads of each side respected the other's. The two Americans had radar contacts on *Amagiri* even before she stopped, and they were seen by Japanese lookouts at 0518.

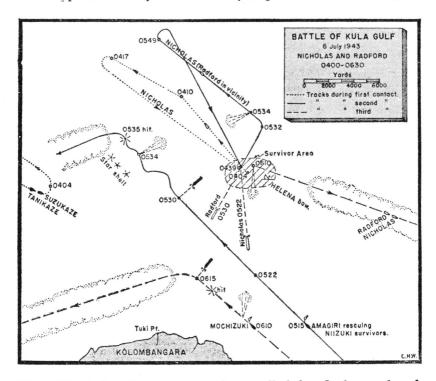

Yamashiro belayed rescue operations, called for flank speed and headed northwest. McInerney, two minutes earlier, had done the same and trained all weapons on the new target. *Nicholas* at 0522 launched a half salvo of torpedoes at 8000 yards' range. *Amagiri* at 0530 replied in kind. Each ship escaped by good luck; American fish passed *Amagiri* ahead and astern, and a Japanese "long lance" porpoised 15 feet astern of *Radford*.

At 0534 the antagonists opened gunfire. The Americans, aided by star shell illumination from *Nicholas*, scored a hit on *Amagiri* amidships which knocked out fire control circuits and blew up the radio room. Her skipper had no stomach for more fighting; he ordered firemen to put smoke tips in burners, and off he went in a cloud of smoke which *Radford* and *Nicholas* regarded as evidence of vast damage. Very few survivors had been recovered from *Niizuki;* three hundred men, including the captain and Admiral Akiyama, were lost.

*Mikazuki* and *Hamakaze* of the other transport unit, in the meantime, were unloading troops and supplies while apprehensively watching the northern sky flicker with gun flashes and explosions. They too retired through Blackett Strait. But *Mochizuki* took an hour more to unload and it was therefore 0600 before she commenced retirement. The squadron commander on board, Captain Orita, chose the Kula Gulf route, hugging the Kolombangara coast in hope of an unmolested passage. But his enemy's radar sniffed him out and presently daylight gave McInerney's sailors their first good look at their foe. "If the s.o.b. wants a fight we'll give him a fight" muttered Andy Hill of *Nicholas*. Again she and *Radford* shoved off survivors and boats, and their gunners went to work at 5-mile range. During the brief gunfire engagement that followed, there were plenty of close misses on both sides. *Mochizuki* launched a single torpedo at 0615 and then vanished in her own smoke, nursing hurts on a gun mount and a torpedo tube. The Americans likewise sought shelter in smoke.

McInerney wondered how many more of the enemy would be spewn out of Kula Gulf, but he knew that there would be an air attack if he stuck around; and he had 745 *Helena* survivors on board. Therefore at 0617, after leaving four boats with volunteer crews to continue human salvage, *Nicholas* and *Radford* turned southeast at top speed for Tulagi. We shall tell of their further salvage efforts in due course.

So the battle ended with destroyer *Nagatsuki* still stranded on the Kolombangara shore, her men in some respects worse off than the drifting *Helena* survivors, because certain to get an air bombing with morning light. They had some respite, however; the Kolombangara coastwatchers counted 14 boatloads leaving her before 0715,[6] but it was not until 1010 that American planes arrived — 11 SBDs and 10 TBFs covered by 18 fighters. Deprived of mobility, *Nagatsuki* had only flak and seven "Zekes" to protect her; the former never touched the American fliers as they bombed the ship, and four "Zekes" fell victims to the Corsairs. An afternoon flight of B-25s set the destroyer afire; her magazines blew up before dark. The crew stood gamely by their shapeless ship until next morning, when they made their way overland to Vila.

## 2. Jungle Interlude, 6–12 July

Guns were not yet cool in the Gulf when Colonel Liversedge's troops, whom we left sleeping in the jungle, shouldered their weapons, forded a river and hit the slimy trail toward Dragon's Peninsula. Off to the westward, they could hear the thud of bombs at Enogai Inlet from an air strike which was supposed to be coordinated with their own assault.

That morning, when he reached a fork in the trail, Liversedge ordered the 3rd Battalion 148th Infantry (Lieutenant Colonel Delbert E. Schultz USA) to take the south fork heading toward the Munda-Bairoko road while the raider battalion and two infantry companies took the north fork toward Enogai Inlet. Lieutenant Colonel Griffith remarked cheerily that it was less than a mile from the bivouac to the upper reaches of the Inlet "as the crow flies," to which a Marine retorted, "That may be, Colonel, but we ain't crows." [7] It took the raiders half a day to reach the river, and another half to cross its swollen waters by a slippery log to a swamp, where they spent the night of 6–7 July. At dawn everyone cleaned guns in expectation of meeting the enemy outposts. Scrambling up the slopes of sharp coral ridges, they crawled over

---

[6] Comairsopac Daily Intelligence Bulletin reported a DD beached at the mouth of the Okopo River 6 miles north of Bamberi Harbor, where *Nagatsuki* was beached, an obvious duplication.
    [7] Lt. Col. S. B. Griffith "Action at Enogai" *Marine Corps Gazette* XXVIII No. 3 (Mar. 1944) p. 15.

trees uprooted by air bombs the previous day, and at noon walked into a village and ambushed an enemy patrol. Captain Clay A. Boyd USMC then led the advance guard south of the Inlet to Triri and into another minor clash. In three days, Colonel Liversedge's force had advanced seven miles.

Out of Triri one trail led to Bairoko and another to Enogai. Before dawn 8 July, a company of Marines was sent down each. The Bairoko bunch walked into a fight which cost the enemy 50 dead; but the Enogai trail petered out in a bog and the disgusted raiders returned to Triri just in time to give the soldiers guarding it a hand in repelling an enemy raid. Since there was nothing to eat at Triri but maggot-filled Japanese rice, the raiders set out for Enogai next morning without breakfast. They broke through to the heights overlooking Kula Gulf and Enogai Point, but enemy resistance halted them short of the main garrison and its rice warehouse.

"Harry the Horse" Liversedge [8] awoke hungry and unhappy on the 10th. His wounded desperately needed hospitalization. His troops could not fight much longer without food. At any moment he expected a *Banzai* attack. He could not call for help, since during the night a falling tree had crushed his only radio. There seemed nothing to do but rout the enemy from Enogai Point. A flight of Marine Corps planes dropped supply-laden parachutes. Famished men rushed to open the first package — mortar shells! But K rations and chocolate bars came down next, and the mortar shells proved handy next day to cover a final bullet and bayonet charge by Griffith's men. By nightfall Liversedge owned Enogai. Among the prizes were those 150-mm guns which had given Ainsworth's destroyers a bad time. At the price of 51 dead and 76 wounded, Liversedge had a new beachhead and a springboard for Bairoko.

About eight miles across the western peninsula of New Georgia

[8] Col. Harry B. Liversedge, who stands about 6 ft. 4 in., won this nickname in the Marine Corps because he was always drawing tough assignments.

"as the crow flies," General Hester's main force, which was supposed to take Munda Field on 7 July, was badly bogged down. By that date the 169th Infantry had advanced only a mile and a half inland from Zanana Beach. Marine Corps and Army artillery bombarded enemy positions at daybreak 9 July, while as a diversion nearly a hundred planes bombed and four destroyers bombarded positions near Munda Point.

The soldiers then moved slowly forward along what they called the Munda Trail, under conditions similar to those met by Liversedge's men — swift and flooded rivers, impenetrable thickets and treacherous footing. Whole columns were held up by single snipers clad in green, hidden in mesh baskets and armed with flashless, long-barreled 7.7-mm rifles. The infantry advanced only half a mile that day.

General Hester, to shorten the supply route, now ordered a new beachhead to be secured at Laiana on the southeastern cape of Munda Peninsula, by sending the 172nd Infantry left to take it from the rear while the 169th continued along the Munda Trail. This was perhaps the worst blunder in the most unintelligently waged land campaign of the Pacific war (with the possible exception of Okinawa). Laiana should have been chosen as the initial beachhead; if it was now required, the 172nd should have been withdrawn from Zanana and landed at Laiana under naval gunfire and air support. Or Hester might have made the landing with his reserves then waiting at Rendova. As it was, General Sasaki interpreted the move correctly and by nightfall had brought both advances to a standstill.

That night, Turner sent Merrill's cruiser-destroyer task group to clear the jungle. The problem in this kind of bombardment was the ancient one that probably troubled the gunners at Agincourt: to spare one's own troops while hitting the enemy's. Army officers, distrusting the accuracy of ships' guns laid at night by radar ranges and bearings, asked Merrill to leave a mile-wide lane between his estimated fall of shot and their own front lines. Further, they asked that his ships shoot parallel to the front lines rather than perpendicular to them, so that "overs" would not hit friends. From our chart it can be seen that this gave Merrill no alternative to shooting from the confined waters of Blanche Channel, which meant that he would have to look out for Japanese submarines as well as nighthawk planes. His antidote being plenty of destroyers, he collected ten of them in addition to his usual four cruisers.

"Tip" Merrill was not the only one on the prowl that night (11–12 July). "Pug" Ainsworth's task force was out too, in order to cover a group of APDs bringing supplies from the Russells to Colonel Liversedge. This was Ainsworth's fourteenth combat mission up the Slot, less than a week after the one that had resulted in the Battle of Kula Gulf. The two task groups passed out of Ironbottom Sound together in the late afternoon of 11 July, exchanging blinker signals typical of the men. Tall, hearty Ainsworth with a sailor's light blue eyes, florid complexion and engaging smile, has his signalman snap out: —

Give 'em hell, Tip. I'll try to drive 'em through so you can take the forward pass! PUG.

Short, dark Merrill, with the poet's face and shy glance, returns a more formal: —

Admiral Ainsworth, I'm afraid you've spoiled the hunting by taking too much game on your last hunt. Good luck! MERRILL.

There was plenty of good hunting left for both, but not that night.

H.M.N.Z.S. *Leander*, sister ship to the famous *Achilles*, is now assigned to Ainsworth to replace *Helena*. A light cruiser of the same size but more powerful than our *Omaha* class, slower (28 knots) than *Honolulu* and *St. Louis* and of wider turning radius, she does have torpedo tubes; so Ainsworth puts her in the screen to help McInerney's five destroyers. She is a handsome ship, distinguished by a tall foremast unspoiled by radar grid. Her bronze-skinned men (the New Zealand Navy fights shirtless and in shorts) are in marked contrast to the American bluejackets, who wear long-legged dungarees for protection from burns, and blue-dyed caps so as to attract no strafing bullets. "Pug" gives *Leander* a hearty welcome, and she blinks back, "Hope to help you avenge the loss of *Helena* and *Strong*."

Ainsworth's run up the Slot that night (11–12 July) is uneventful; but *Taylor*, supporting the APDs in Kula Gulf, probably destroys *RO–107*. Merrill's mission to Munda is almost routine, too. After forty minutes' bombardment, throwing 3204 rounds of 6-inch and 5470 rounds of 5-inch shell at Munda, Merrill retires through the open sea south of Rendova. And what good did it do? Merrill himself remarked that the no man's land before our lines probably provided a neat refuge for Sasaki's people during the shelling; that "considering the accuracy of our modern fire control equipment, this margin of safety seems unnecessarily large." He was right. Hester's soldiers distrusted artillery, even their own; so a number of Japanese who might have been shelled survived to kill a good many Americans who should have stayed alive. The Marines, on the other hand, loved naval gunfire support and did not worry about getting hit themselves until the salvos threw dust in their eyes. They also recognized the limitations of bombardment: that it stunned the enemy only for the moment, and did not relieve the foot soldier of going in with rifle to clean up. Cincpac's staff analyst tried to drive this lesson home in his commentary on this month's operations,[9] and the assaults on islands like Tarawa and Kwajalein would put close gunfire support to the test. As the war in the Pacific progressed, naval gunfire was used more often in support of ground troops than in sea battles or bombardment raids.

Merrill's bombardment robbed Americans of sleep as well as the enemy; but, rested or not, the 172nd RCT had to march on the morning of 12 July. They made slow progress, and by nightfall, without food or water and subject to effective mortar fire, they still had a quarter-mile of swamp between them and Laiana beach. And the Japanese had closed in on their rear and cut communication with the 169th.

[9] Cincpac monthly report "Operations in Pacific Oceans Areas" July 1943 Annex D.

Now the campaign which had opened with such high hopes ground to a halt on all fronts. Colonel Liversedge to the north could advance no farther without reinforcement. General Hester on the south would be in a bad fix whenever the Japanese chose to assault his hungry, divided and disorganized troops. On the Japanese side General Sasaki's position was bolstered by the arrival of 16 troop-filled barges from Vila, and on the night of 12–13 July Japanese destroyer-transports were to bring in 1200 more troops. To stop that, Ainsworth was sent up the Slot a second night in succession, and the Battle of Kolombangara was fought.

Admiral Turner was right in requesting additional troops for this campaign,[10] and Halsey had been right in wishing to start it in April. Unless the Navy could break up the Shortlands–Vila–Munda barge-line, there was no limit to the reinforcements Sasaki might obtain.

## 3. *The Battle of Kolombangara, 12–13 July* [11]

"Once more upon the waters! Yet once more!" The Byronic quotation came forcibly to mind on board *Honolulu* at Tulagi the afternoon of 12 July 1943 when an order arrived from Admiral Halsey that she was to go up the Slot again that night. At the same time, Ainsworth was informed that he would have six more destroyers. "Must be something big coming down," he remarked. "Kelly Turner never lets go of anything if he can help it."

[10] On 12 June 1943 Turner asked Halsey for two additional reinforced infantry divisions, three Marine defense battalions, four Marine raider or parachute battalions and 14,000 other troops (Seabees, medical, boat pools, service, supply, etc.). The original plan called only for one reinforced infantry division, one Marine defense battalion, one Marine raider battalion, and some shore-based naval units. CTF 32 Memo to Comsopac 12 June 1943.

[11] In addition to the items in note 1 to this chapter, Cominch Information Bulletin No. 11 *Battle Experience, Naval Operations Solomon Islands Area 12 July–10 Aug. 1943;* writer's own notes on battle; Naval Secretary, Dominion of New Zealand, "R.N.Z.N. Operations in South Pacific" 7 Nov. 1946, prepared for this History; ATIS document No. 15685, translation of Japanese Action Report; additional information obtained in Tokyo through ATIS. There is a mixup about the name of this engagement. It is sometimes called the Second Battle of Kula Gulf, as fought in the same water as the action of 6 July. It has been confused with the later Battles of Vella Gulf and Vella Lavella, and the Japanese call it the Battle of Sumbi Point, Choiseul.

Halsey's precautions were justified. At 0530 that morning a formidable Tokyo Express departed Rabaul to land troops at Vila. The core of it was the famous Desron 2. Rear Admiral Tanaka was no longer on the bridge of his old flagship, light cruiser *Jintsu*. He had been "put on the beach" for talking up to his superior officers, and the composition of his squadron had been changed; but the old punch was there. *Jintsu* and five destroyers were covering four destroyer-transports that were carrying 1200 soldiers to Kolombangara. Their organization was as follows: —

SUPPORT GROUP,* Rear Admiral Shunji Izaki

Light Cruiser * JINTSU
Destroyers MIKAZUKI, Capt. T. Orita (Comdesdiv 30), YUKIKAZE, Capt. Yoshima Shimai (Comdesdiv 16), HAMAKAZE, KIYONAMI, YUGURE
Destroyer-Transports SATSUKI, MINAZUKI, YUNAGI, MATSUKAZE

* Lost in this action.

Ainsworth's reinforcement of six destroyers under Captain Ryan of Squadron 12 was welcome; but, belonging to three different squadrons, they had never operated before with the Admiral or with one another, and they joined only at the last minute — once more the setup of Tassafaronga. There was just time for Ainsworth and some of his captains to confer with Ryan, and enjoy a last drink with "Scrappy" Kessing ashore; most of Ryan's ships were unable to join until the formation was off Santa Isabel that evening.

The task organization, in its battle order, follows: —

TASK FORCE 18, Rear Admiral Walden L. Ainsworth in *Honolulu*

Destroyer Squadron 21, Capt. Francis X. McInerney
NICHOLAS          Lt. Cdr. Andrew J. Hill
O'BANNON          Lt. Cdr. Donald J. MacDonald
TAYLOR            Lt. Cdr. Benjamin Katz
JENKINS           Lt. Cdr. Madison Hall
RADFORD           Cdr. William K. Romoser

Cruiser Division 9, Rear Admiral Ainsworth
HONOLULU          Capt. Robert W. Hayler
H.M.N.Z.S. LEANDER    Capt. C. A. L. Mansergh RN
ST. LOUIS         Capt. Colin Campbell

Capt. Thomas J. Ryan (Comdesron 12)

| | |
|---|---|
| RALPH TALBOT | Cdr. Joseph W. Callahan |
| BUCHANAN | Lt. Cdr. Floyd B. T. Myhre |
| MAURY | Cdr. Gelzer L. Sims |
| WOODWORTH | Cdr. Virgil F. Gordinier |
| *GWIN | Cdr. John M. Higgins (Comdesdiv 23) |
| | Lt. Cdr. John B. Fellows |

* Sunk in this action.

The Admiral's battle plan is the same as for Kula Gulf: as soon as visual contact is made, send van destroyers to fire torpedoes, cruisers make simultaneous turns to parallel or converge on the enemy's column, get a solution before he sees us, smother him with rapid gunfire and turn away promptly to avoid torpedoes. It might have worked if the enemy had not seen us first.

At 1700 July 12 Ainsworth's group sorties from Tulagi for its 15th run up the Slot. A gallant sight at that hour, the cruisers so proud and handsome with their curling bow waves and frothy wakes, the destroyers thrusting and turning, now golden with the sun, now dark shadows against the sea; and this is a gorgeous afternoon, with bright cumulus clouds under a thin layer of cirrus and Ironbottom Sound blue as the Gulf of Maine. The coxcomb of Savo Island actually looks beautiful, and the westering sun makes the kunai-grass slopes of Cape Esperance shine warm and golden, while the wooded valleys are in deep shadow.

As the ships pass Savo Island, a cloud making up over the Cape glows fiery red, and then night closes in. A run up the Slot is never routine. One feels keen anticipation of a fight but apprehension too, and, in this instance, fatigue; there is always so much to do in port after a night run that nobody has had time to catch up with his sleep. Lucky ships are in this group — *Honolulu* and *O'Bannon* have been in fight after fight without the enemy's "laying a finger" on them — but their luck cannot last forever.

Now the sky clears, a light wind makes up from the southeast but the sea remains smooth. As a better than first-quarter moon is in the sky, Ainsworth hugs the Santa Isabel coast to avoid detection by Japanese reconnaissance planes. Several of these snoopers are out looking for him, but friendly fighters from the Russells are on the watch for them, and one is shot down. A bugle call announces General Quarters at 2300. The moon, bearing southwest, is much too bright for sailors' comfort; Arcturus glows dead ahead, the Southern Cross is already sloping toward the horizon, and in the northern sky is the familiar triangle of Vega, Altair and Deneb.

At midnight the ships cut diagonally across the Slot toward Visu Visu, and at 0036 July 13 a searching Black Cat reports one enemy cruiser and five destroyers standing down on course 128° at 30 knots, about 26 miles distant. It is Izaki's Support Group. Ainsworth forms his one-column battle disposition and increases speed to 28 knots, the best *Leander* can do.

At 0100 the flagship's radar makes contact; "I smell a skunk" goes out on voice radio. At 0103 *Nicholas* sights the enemy, and Ainsworth orders McInerney to bend on a few knots and get ahead. At 0106 the Admiral turns the cruisers simultaneously 30 degrees right to unmask main batteries and put the enemy on the starboard beam. At 0109 he telephones McInerney, commander of the van destroyers, "Attack with Torpedoes!" It has become an open-and-shut night; high visibility between rain squalls. Right now the southern sky has become overcast, hiding the moon; but the dark shape of Kolombangara, many miles distant, is visible, and over its summit Scorpio raises his tail and glares through his baleful eye, Antares.

Although Ainsworth had radar and the enemy none, he had no reason to expect to surprise them, nor did he do so. The Japanese task force is using a new and clever radar-detecting device. By receiving and plotting the electric impulses from the American radar Izaki has determined the presence of Ainsworth's force almost two hours before, and plotted his approach accurately for one hour before the battle joined. "We, who possess no radar," reads the Japanese treatise on Battle Lessons, "consider it good strategy to use torpedo power and carry out a concealed torpedo attack before the enemy opens fire." They had done it before and now they do it again, at 0108 July 13, immediately after Ainsworth's leading ships became visible to the naked eye.[12]

McInerney's van destroyers began firing torpedoes a few seconds after 0109, when the range from *Nicholas* to *Jintsu* was under 10,000 yards. *Jintsu* promptly turned on her searchlight, and replied with both gunfire and torpedoes. Ainsworth waited until *Honolulu* had closed to 10,000 yards, the maximum range at which his best combination of FC and SG radar could spot 6-inch salvos effectively at night. He then ordered the three cruisers to commence firing. After five salvos from *Honolulu*, the Black Cat spotter (Lieutenant Marvin E. Barnett) signaled "Up Two!" (200 yards short); Ainsworth ordered continuous rapid fire; and a minute or two later *Jintsu* appeared to explode near No. 3 stack. Barnett signaled, "You got the big one!" and the cheery voice of Captain Bob Hayler announced from the bridge, "We got the cruiser!" We had.

As usual in early days of radar-controlled gunfire, all ships concentrated on the plumpest pip on the radar screen. *Jintsu* was fairly smothered with 6-inch shellfire, and no wonder; for the three cruisers threw 2630 rounds her way.[13] Her steering gear was knocked out at 0117, her firerooms received what the Japanese conservatively described as "more than ten" hits, and she went dead in the water. Then one of McInerney's torpedoes exploded in her after engine room, and apparently at 0145 she took a second. One of these whipsawed her abaft No. 2 stack. The two halves drifted apart, burning and exploding furiously; the Admiral, the Captain, and 482 other officers and men — practically all hands — were lost.

The only scoring gunshot from *Jintsu* and her consorts cut the main radio aërial on *Leander*. But their torpedoes, fired between

[12] "Battle Lessons Learned in the G.E.A. War (Torpedoes) Vol VI" (Jicpoa Item No. 5782 pp. 6, 19, 20.) ATIS doc. 15685, "Battle of Kolombangara" says they sighted us visually at 0108 and opened fire immediately with guns and torpedoes.
[13] *Honolulu* expended 1110 rounds 6-inch common and 123 rounds 5-inch; *Leander*, 160 rounds 6-inch; *St. Louis*, 1360 6-inch and 230 5-inch, between 0112 and about 0130.

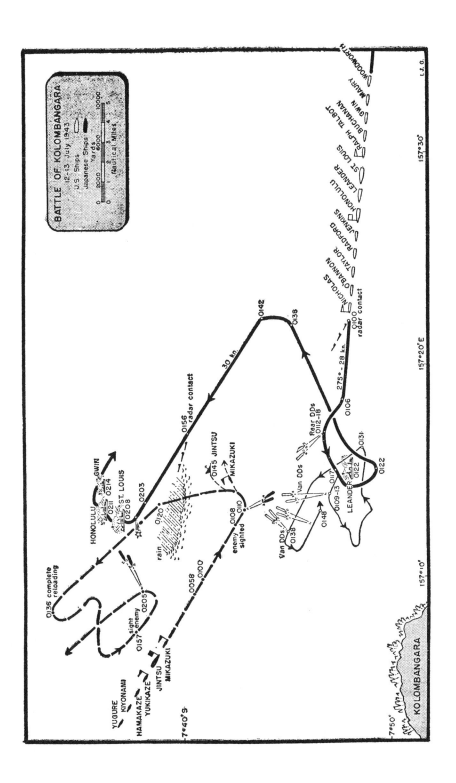

BATTLE OF KOLOMBANGARA
12-13 July 1943

U.S. Ships ⬜
Japanese Ships ▬

Nautical Miles
0 1 2 3 4 5

Yards
0 2000 4000 6000 8000 10000

0108 and 0114, told another story. Ainsworth, who had been steering almost due west when the action started, at 0117 ordered a simultaneous turn to due south when the range was around 9000 yards. *Honolulu's* voice radio chose this inopportune moment to grow faint; the cruisers and some of the destroyers did not get the word but did their best to follow their flagship's movements, through the dense smoke made by our own gunpowder. *Leander* turned very wide and at 0122 caught a torpedo which cost her 28 dead and put her out of the battle. Since Ainsworth had executed his turn in enemy torpedo water, his force was lucky to have but one fish strike home; *Radford* dodged two, and *Jenkins* one.

Captain Ryan, commanding the rear destroyers, had intended to close before firing torpedoes. Seeing the cruisers all jumbled on his radar screen, and the enemy column 2 ½ points on his starboard bow, range 7900 yards and closing, he commenced launching at about 0112, so he thought; probably it was a few minutes later. The actual range turned out to be 11,000 yards, but one of the torpedoes may have hit *Jintsu*.

The picture before Admiral Ainsworth in his flag plot was now somewhat confused. A report from the Black Cat at 0115 said that four enemy destroyers were headed north at high speed, so the Admiral ordered McInerney "Go get 'em – go get 'em!" *Radford* and *Jenkins* were detached to stand by *Leander*. McInerney with the other three destroyers at 0131 turned to course 325° for the chase; signaling to Ainsworth, "Don't throw anything at us!" to which the Admiral replied "Wouldn't do it for the world – go get the bastards – good luck!" Lookouts and radar alike gave optimistic estimates of from three to six enemy ships exploding and burning,[14] and the Black Cat modified her report by saying that only two were

---

[14] The writer was one of these lookouts. About 0131 he "saw with his own eyes" three ships burning and exploding. Two are accounted for by the whipsawed *Jintsu;* the third must have been merely the flash from another ship's guns, because no other was hit. And the radar screen in *Honolulu* after she had completed the turn, at around 0130, showed three distinct pips on the screen. What was the third? Probably *Mikazuki* standing by *Jintsu;* but she was not hit. Just before 0145 the writer observed an exchange of gunfire to port – that may have been *Jintsu's* last defiant salvo, or *Mikazuki* throwing stuff at "Mac" before retiring.

escaping, which gave the impression that four were dead in the water, sunk or sinking.

Nevertheless, all the "bastards" except *Jintsu* were doing very well. The destroyer-transports had retired unseen along the Kolombangara shore. *Mikazuki* seems to have stood by the cruiser for a few minutes and then tried to catch up with the other four destroyers of the Support Group.[15] These, under the command of Captain Shimai in *Yukikaze*, scampered up the Slot as soon as they had emptied their torpedo tubes. There, in a convenient rain squall, they reloaded their tubes in the remarkably fast time of 18 minutes. At Kula Gulf, as we have seen, their sister ships had taken over an hour to reload.

*Honolulu* and *St. Louis*, after turning very wide to clear damaged *Leander*, steered northeasterly until they were out of torpedo water, firing on the radar targets. These were *Jintsu*, and probably *Mikazuki*. At 0138–0142 Ainsworth altered course to northwest, followed by Ryan's destroyers which had countermarched with him but had become rather scattered in so doing. McInerney's destroyers, now over ten miles westward, were then achieving the destruction of *Jintsu* by torpedo and gunfire, but (owing to the inadequacy of TBS at that range) were completely out of touch with Ainsworth. The Admiral telephoned McInerney, "Work up to Skunk Hollow (Shortlands) and see what you can find," but the message did not get through. After *Jintsu* had disappeared, at 0148, these destroyers found no enemy ships on their radar screens.

"Mac," assuming that the entire enemy force was now sunk, bent on 30 knots and steered east to rejoin "Pug," in the belief that his task group commander had retired down the Slot.

If Ainsworth had then decided to call it a night, the score would have been all in his favor — one of the fightin'est ships in the Japanese Navy sunk with all hands, at the cost of *Leander* damaged. But the Admiral remembered the cripples which he supposed

---

[15] Some Japanese authorities say she steered northeast by herself; others, more probably correct, that she followed the other DDs north but failed to catch them.

had escaped at Kula Gulf and he was eager to clean up. So up the Slot he continued in pursuit of more game.

While on course 300° at 0156 *Honolulu's* radar picked up a group of ships sharp on her port bow, distant 23,000 yards. What ships were they — McInerney's or the enemy's; if enemy, were they the same ships already engaged or not; were they coming or going? Ainsworth's instinct was to open gunfire and sink them before they could close to torpedo range; but, uncertain of the whereabouts of McInerney's destroyers, which had had time enough to reach the position indicated by the radar pips, and mindful of his promise not to "throw anything," the Admiral decided to call each destroyer in order to check her position. As there were many destroyers and much chattering over the circuit, this inquiry lasted about seven minutes.

In flag plot under the chartroom, small, hot and crowded with 25 officers and men, the Admiral gazes at the radar screen as reports flow in from bridge, combat information center and other points; everyone waits tense and sweating for his verdict. This is one of the many, many moments in naval warfare when one's fate hangs by a hair. Some "wise guy" insists that the radar targets are *Nicholas* and *O'Bannon*. The Admiral remarks quietly that it is strange then that we, making only 28 knots, should be overhauling them. At 0203, still uncertain, he orders his two cruisers to illuminate the targets with star shell, but to withhold gunfire. Two minutes later, just after the first star shell bursts, and observing that the doubtful targets are now countermarching (for they had just fired their torpedoes), Ainsworth decides that they are enemy. He orders his ships to turn right 60° to unmask main batteries and gives "Commence Firing!" Alas, the two cruisers and destroyer *Gwin* turn right into the path of the deadly "long lances," fired by Captain Shimai's four destroyers. Immediately after Commence Firing goes out, *Honolulu's* bridge signals, "Torpedo just passed us!" Before either cruiser can open fire, *St. Louis*, at 0208,[16] is hit

[16] The Japanese report "Battle of Kolombangara" says at 0205, which may indicate that Japanese clocks were 3 minutes faster than ours. This assumption makes

by a torpedo well forward; *Honolulu* maneuvers violently to avoid others. Clever ship-handling by Bob Hayler dodges four or five, but one just catches her at the tip of her bow and a second, a dud, overtakes her aft. *Gwin*, ahead of *Honolulu*, receives one amidships in her engine room at 0214 and at once explodes, burning white-hot – a terrible sight. *Honolulu* just manages to avoid a collision with her.

The four Japanese destroyers had made a fine score with their 31 reloads. Captain Shimai waited for the calculated moment when Ainsworth would turn, fired all he had, and quickly retired. *Gwin* was done for. *Ralph Talbot*, who had fired torpedoes ineffectively at 0213 – the only offensive action by any American ship in this phase of the battle – took off *Gwin's* crew after their heroic damage control efforts had proved unavailing. She gradually settled and had to be scuttled around 0930. Two officers and 59 men were lost.

Fortunately the cruisers had been hit so far forward that there were no serious casualties. *St. Louis's* bow was twisted to one side; *Honolulu's* dipped down like a tapir's snout, with the anchor chains dragging. The second torpedo had hit her square stern right in the middle at the waterline, dangled there in the wake for a few moments, and then fallen out.[17] A damage control detail under Chief Carpenter's Mate Peter L. Vlasich did a quick, effective job shoring up bulkheads so that she was able to make 12 to 15 knots; *St. Louis* could too, and both cruisers shoved water ahead like square-bowed barges and made wakes as wide as Broadway. *Leander*, with a head start, was doing almost as well. Ainsworth signaled to Admiral Turner at Guadalcanal that he needed plenty

---

more credible the statement in the Action Report that Ainsworth was sighted visually from *Yukikaze* as early as 0157. She had been tracking him with her radar-detection device for some minutes earlier. The track chart in Jicpoa Item No. 5782 says *Yukikaze* fired at 0206; the other three, 1 to 2.5 minutes later.

[17] The gun captain of the aftermost machine gun requested permission of bridge to secure, saying there was a torpedo sticking in the stern immediately below his gun position. The bridge phone talker tried to laugh him off. The request was repeated, and this time conveyed to Capt. Hayler, who granted permission if the gunner was certain. He certainly was! Later that morning the aviators whose quarters were in the fantail sent a delegation to thank Chaplain Jack Sharkey for his effective prayers!

of fighter cover after daylight, and Turner saw that he got it. As day broke, with Orion riding gloriously above the dawn, about 18 "Vals" protected by 20 "Zekes" came roaring down the Slot to attack, but fighter planes from the Russells intercepted and drove them back off Visu Visu.

The Japanese destroyer-transports, whose presence had been detected but once during this action, by the radar of destroyer *Jenkins*, countermarched as soon as they heard the firing, steamed into Vella Gulf, called at Sandfly Harbor on the west coast of Kolombangara and discharged 1200 troops, finishing at 0340 July 13. They then searched the battle area for *Jintsu* survivors, unsuccessfully, and returned to Buin, where they joined the Support Group.

The Japanese thought they had sunk all three of the cruisers they had hit. None the less, Rear Admiral Izaki may be said to have lived up to the fine squadron traditions established by Tanaka. He had lost his flagship and his life, but had carried out his mission, sunk a destroyer and knocked out three cruisers — two for several months and one for the rest of the war.[18]

Ainsworth's force made Tulagi late in the afternoon of the 13th and received a warm and noisy welcome from the Marine band, the men of anchored ships, and, best of all, "Scrappy" Kessing. The Admiral felt as depressed as a football quarterback who has called the wrong play in a championship game. But his feeling, shared by all hands, that they had exacted a heavy price for their losses was confirmed three days later when a survivor of *Jintsu*, picked up off Kolombangara, declared that not only his ship but four destroyers had been sunk. The Black Cat spotter, too, was sure that he saw a destroyer go down. It is certain, however, that *Jintsu* was the only Japanese casualty of the battle.[19]

[18] *Honolulu* was fitted with a new bow at Pearl Harbor in the short time of ten days, but she and *St. Louis* were sent to Mare Island for main battery regunning and replacement of 1.1-inch machine guns by 40-mm. They were not in action again until November. H.M.N.Z.S. *Leander* made the long passage to Boston, where she spent the better part of a year being refitted.

[19] Three of the Japanese destroyers which escaped this action undamaged were sunk within two weeks. *Mikazuki* ran aground near Cape Gloucester 27 July and

"Looking over one's shoulder," wrote Ainsworth to Nimitz on
16 July, "one can always see how we should have done differently,
and no one knows the fallacy of chasing Jap destroyers with cruisers better than I." To which Cincpac replied "You have fought two
hard actions featured by aggressiveness and tactical skill."

## 4. Rescue Mission for HELENA, 6–17 July

*Helena's* crew were not unique in believing that, having fought
as a privilege, they could expect rescue as a right. But they also
believed in helping themselves. Most of the men still adrift on the
morning of 6 July gathered in two clusters. One group of 88, led
by Captain Cecil, formed a small-craft flotilla of three motor
whaleboats, each towing a life raft, labored all day bucking wind
and current, finally rounding up at nightfall at an island seven
miles from Rice Anchorage. Next morning Chief Signalman
Charles A. Flood blinked an S.O.S. to *Gwin* and *Woodworth*
who had been sent to hunt for them, and who picked them up
safe if not altogether sound.

The second group of nearly 200 officers and men had neither
boat nor raft. The riddled bow of *Helena*, pointing straight upward, acted as their precarious perch. One stout fellow retrieved
a provisions crate and with great difficulty hauled it on board the
bow, only to find spoiled tomatoes. Lieutenant Commander Chew
took charge of this band of unfortunates, half blinded by fuel oil.
What could they do? The bow was sinking. Kolombangara on the
southern horizon looked green and pleasant, but it was also distant
and hostile. Well after daylight, a Navy Liberator piloted by
Lieutenant James C. Nolan USNR swooped low, dropped all her
life jackets and four packaged rubber lifeboats. One boat failed to
open and sank, but the other three inflated.[20] Three rubber lifeboats

was blasted by Kenney's B–25s next day. *Yugure* and *Kiyonami*, when engaged in
convoy duty, were sunk south of Choiseul in the early hours of 20 July by Airsols
planes.

[20] Letters from Mr. Nolan 1 Jan. and 8 Feb. 1950; Gilbert Cant "They Live to
Fight Again" *Sea Power* Apr. 1944; conversations with survivors in 1944.

for close on 200 men! The able-bodied placed the wounded on board and then clustered around, using their legs for propulsion. For all they could do, the SE wind and set of current carried them up the Slot, farther into enemy waters. Chew thought they had better try for Kolombangara and they pushed and paddled hard; the sticky sludge of fuel oil stayed along too, making paddling difficult but at least discouraging sharks. "Zekes" passed close over and the men thought they saw the pilots grinning derisively; but since the pilots failed to strafe it is probable that they were unable to tell the nationality of these oil-blackened men. American search planes missed them altogether.

Kolombangara gradually faded away to leeward, a night passed miserably, and, as the wounded died and the crazed or impatient tried to swim, more places were found in the boats. On Wednesday morning, 7 July, Vella Lavella loomed ahead in the path of wind and current. Chew had read that the natives there were friendly; it was the last chance and the paddlers turned to again. At noon Major Bernard T. Kelly and five others of *Helena's* Marine detachment joined up, after swimming for 30 hours. A second night fell. The boats separated and more men gave up or swam away but those who held on saw Vella Lavella only a mile distant at dawn. One boat landed safely at Pareso Bay on the northeast coast. The others appeared to be drifting past Vella Lavella toward Shortlands. Several strong swimmers struck out for the shore. With the boats thus lightened, paddlers were able to beach them eight miles from the first.

On Vella Lavella, coastwatchers Henry Josselyn and Robert Firth controlled a loyal coterie of Melanesians who at once spotted the Americans, and Josselyn radioed the news to Guadalcanal. He and Firth strained their meager resources to arm, feed, clothe and medicate these guests. No large body of men could escape Japanese notice, so everyone took to the jungle. Major Kelly organized a Marine and bluejacket defense line armed with antique firearms. The natives guarded the trails and annihilated one enemy patrol which came dangerously close.

Josselyn had given Comsopac a real problem, to snatch so large a number of men from under Japanese noses. No Dumbo or submarine or PT could handle 165 men in one swoop, but it had to be done that way or not at all. And that meant ships. Could ships get within 60 miles of Japanese air bases and naval roadsteads? Perhaps, under cover of darkness.

Appropriately, Captain McInerney with his four destroyers which had fought both the Kula Gulf and the Kolombangara engagements, drew a part in this mission. In the late afternoon of 15 July, only two days after finishing the second battle, *Nicholas*, *Radford*, *Jenkins* and *O'Bannon* sailed out of Tulagi for the deepest penetration of the Slot yet attempted. Three hours ahead of them, shaping their course south of New Georgia, steamed Commander Sweeney's destroyer-transports *Dent* and *Waters*, escorted by Captain Ryan's destroyers *Taylor*, *Maury*, *Gridley* and *Ellet*.

A brilliant moon was out that night and so were the Japanese snoopers, ranging up and down the Slot. Naturally they found McInerney's ships and showed much interest as they continued on past Kolombangara and across Vella Gulf to a point ten miles north of Vella Lavella. But the transport group escaped notice as they passed Gizo Island and rounded up into Vella Gulf, hugging the Vella Lavella shoreline. Off Pareso Bay on the northeast coast *Maury*, *Ellet* and *Gridley* began a slow patrol while *Taylor* felt her way in with radar and leadline, followed by *Dent* and *Waters*. At 0200 July 16 a coastwatcher's signal blinked from the shore. Landing craft were lowered quickly and the 61 men at Pareso with one Japanese prisoner were brought on board. The APDs, piloted by another coastwatcher, then crept eight miles along the coast to Lambu Lambu, and the 104 men hiding there, together with 16 Chinese who were tired of being guests of the Japanese, were shuttled out to the ships. By 0450 both McInerney and Ryan were headed full-tilt down the Slot. En route they sighted a number of Japanese floating on boards; these were survivors of cruiser *Jintsu*, sunk in the Battle of Kolombangara; and two of them, who were sitting in a motor whaleboat of *Gwin* that they had picked up, submitted to being rescued and told the tale of four destroyers sunk that confirmed our exaggerated score.

When *Dent* and *Waters* reached Tulagi, the score of those rescued from *Helena* reached 739. Missing for all time were 168, most of them entombed in their ship.

Only those who have served in the Solomons know what fearful odds these rescuing sailors had accepted, and active imaginations magnified the odds many fold. The northeast coast of Vella Lavella, charted in dotted lines on available charts, was spiked with reefs. The Tokyo Express had been running almost constantly since July, and it might have included some heavy cruisers that night. I-boats, too, were known to be abroad. Yet all hands, even the destroyer sailors who had spent two nights in succession up the Slot, were eager to serve in this mission.

## 5. *Conclusion to Kula Gulf and Kolombangara*

The results of the Battles of Kula Gulf and Kolombangara, as nearly alike as two naval battles could be, should have raised doubts as to American battle efficiency in every mind; and doubtless would have done so in many minds if the results had been known. But as usual in night battles, each side found consolation for its own losses in imaginary damage inflicted on the enemy. Admiral Ainsworth, upon returning to Tulagi on the afternoon of 6 July, reported in all sincerity a score of seven to nine enemy ships sunk; eight days later he topped this claim with five more at Kolombangara. Even more misleading was his belief that at least some of his torpedo hits were from submarines and that in the second action he had fought two separate forces. There were none to say him nay until Intelligence found out which enemy ships had been present, and discovered that all except sunken *Jintsu* and *Niizuki* and beached and bombed *Nagatsuki* were still afloat and only slightly damaged.

This writer, who shared in one of these night actions, felt a dis-

# Illustrations

*Seated:* Franklin D. Roosevelt, Winston Churchill
*Standing, left to right:* General H. H. Arnold, Admiral King, General Marshall, Admiral Sir Dudley Pound, Air Chief Marshal Sir Charles Portal, General Sir Alan Brooke, Field Marshal Sir John Dill, Admiral Lord Louis Mountbatten, General B. B. Somervell

*Casablanca Conference, January 1943*

Air view taken in 1945 at period of greatest development. Facing north
*Lower Left:* 14th Naval District motor pool. The long building with the
dogleg is Service Force Pacific Fleet
*Left Center:* Cincpac Headquarters, the oblong building with the blast
walls. Admiral Nimitz's office was at north end of first deck. Next flat-
topped building to rear is Fleet Radio Unit, and the one farthest north is
Jicpoa (Joint Intelligence Center). The water to the right is Makalapa
Crater, the north shore of which was used as a dump
*Center:* The three-story building with wings is junior bachelor officers'
quarters; downhill from it are the open-air movie theater, tennis and handball
courts. The individual houses were used as senior officers' quarters, four
officers to a house; the admirals' quarters were along the edge of the crater,
off the picture
*Upper Left:* Beyond the canefields, Aiea Naval Hospital; upper right,
Red Hill Seabee Headquarters

## *Cincpac-Cincpoa Headquarters, Makalapa, Pearl Harbor*

Port Moresby

Milne Bay

*New Guinea Prizes*

Lieutenant General Robert L. Eichelberger and staff members at Buna

Native stretcher-bearers

*Buna-Gona Campaign*

Japanese destroyer under attack

*Battle of the Bismarck Sea*

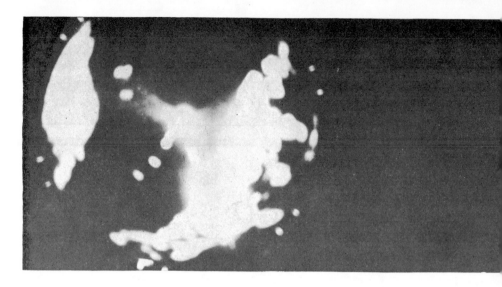

Radarscope (U.S.S. *Denver*) showing situation at 0110
Solid white areas are Kolombangara and New Georgia; the three spots between
them are the U.S. ships; the two spots above are *Murasame* and *Minegumo*

U.S.S. *Denver*

*Action off Vila, 6 March 1943*

*Cartoon by Corp. George Blinn, Engineer Section XIV Corps*

Air raid

LSTs loading

*Guadalcanal, 1943*

Admiral Mineichi Koga

*Japanese Photos*

Admiral Yamamoto: The Admiral is saluting pilots at Rabaul about to embark on "I" operation, 11 April 1943. Vice Admiral Kusaka is on his left

*Commanders in Chief Combined Fleet*

Munda Point under air attack — looking west
*Insert:* Vila airfield, Kolombangara

*Bombardment Targets*

U.S.S. *Nicholas* firing at Vila, 12 May 1943

U.S.S. *O'Bannon*

*Fighting Ships*

*Rear Admiral Daniel E. Barbey* USN

LCT at Kiriwina

PT and LCVP at Nassau Bay

*Landings in the Southwest Pacific*

Rendova. Plane over beach is a P-40

Viru Harbor

*Landings in the Central Solomons*

LSTs approaching Rendova

LCIs unloading at Rendova

*Amphibious Supply*

U.S.S. *Helena* firing her last salvo

*Photo by Lieutenant James C. Nolan*

*Helena's* bow floating next morning

## Battle of Kula Gulf

Swabbing out the guns — U.S.S. *Honolulu*

Transferring U.S.S. *Strong* survivors from U.S.S. *Nicholas* to U.S.S. *Honolulu*

*After Battle*

U.S.S. *Honolulu* with damaged bow

*Battle of Kolombangara*

*Three Cruiser Commanders Relax: Merrill, Hayler and Ainsworth*

*U.S.S.* Selfridge *and U.S.S.* O'Bannon *after the Battle of Vella Lavella*

Torokina, looking north. (Fighter strip at far left; "Piva Uncle" and "Piva Yoke" strips inland)

Marines disembarking from transport. War dog in sling at right

*Bougainville Landings*

Wrecked Japanese barge

PT sailors

*Barge Warfare, New Guinea*

LCI 339 damaged by bomb

Lae

Airfield, wrecked Japanese planes

*Rear Admiral A. Stanton Merrill* USN

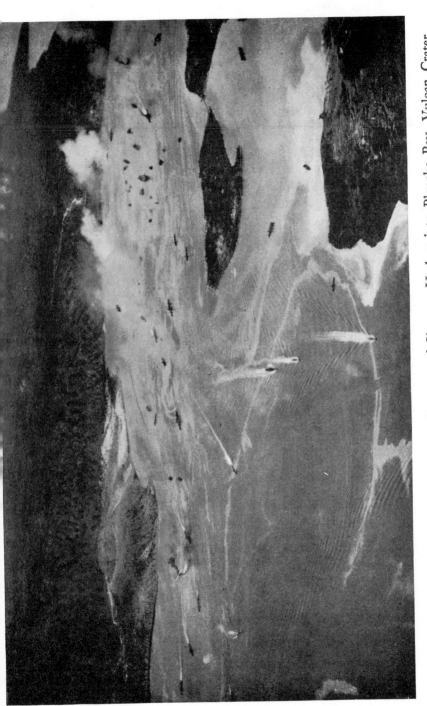

Looking west. Cruisers and destroyers standing out of Simpson Harbor into Blanche Bay. Vulcan Crater, upper left; Sulphur Point, lower right; Matupi Island, right center. Flak bursts above Matupi. Cruiser, right center, has been hit.

*Japanese Ships at Rabaul under Attack, 5 November 1943*

Hellcat

Liberator

Avenger

Corsair

*Navy Planes*

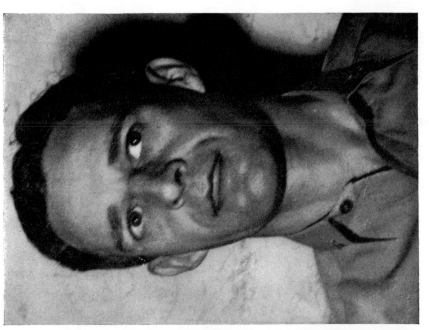

Commander Frederick Moosbrugger

Captain Arleigh A. Burke

*Photo from painting by Commander Albert K. Murray USNR*

*Destroyer Skippers*

Bougainville

Cape Gloucester

*Jungle Mud*

*Rear Admiral Frederick C. Sherman* USN
On flag bridge of U.S.S. *Saratoga*

U.S.S. *Bunker Hill*

Saluting the dead with S-turns in Ironbottom Sound: Destroyer Squadron
Twelve returning from Kavieng bombardment. Savo Island in background

*Kavieng Raiders*

General MacArthur and Admiral Kinkaid on board U.S.S. *Phoenix* during invasion of Admiralties

Troopers going ashore on Negros Island

*Beyond the Barrier*

may second only to that of his commanding officer when the truth came out, and has naturally been curious to know why things happened the way they did. It seems to him that the reasons for our overestimates simmer down to overconfidence in 6-inch gunfire, overconfidence in radar, and ignorance both of Japanese torpedo performance and of Japanese ability to track without radar.

Some U. S. Naval officers were gunfire- rather than torpedo-conscious, and light cruiser commanders were particularly proud of the 6-inch continuous rapid-fire technique which they had worked out before the war. They might have learned by mid-1943, from the experience of *Brooklyn* at Casablanca [21] and from sundry naval bombardments of Munda, that 6-inch continuous rapid fire, though impressive in volume, was inaccurate. Radar operators would select the fattest or nearest pip as target, gunners vied with each other in speed, and visual spotters were distracted by the shock and flash. Nevertheless we all believed in 1943 that, by closing the enemy to within 10,000 yards and using radar-controlled gunfire, one could register with the first salvo and sink or disable any target before it could launch torpedoes. It worked O.K. on *Jintsu.*

Overconfidence in radar was reflected not only in the belief that it could lay guns accurately and trace their salvos but in its presumed ability to give us the jump. We did not learn until long after that the Japanese in both these actions detected us before our radar found them, and had launched torpedoes almost as we opened fire. Equally incorrect was the belief that, if a pip on the SG screen, representing an enemy ship, disappeared, that ship was sunk. It usually meant that the foe had hauled out of range or blended into a land background.

Consider next the Japanese Model 93 or "long lance" torpedo that did all the damage to Allied ships in these two battles, besides sinking the *Strong* earlier, and winning the Battle of Tassafaronga in 1942. Invented [22] as early as 1933 and perfected in prewar years,

[21] See Vol. II of this History pp. 75–76, 100–112.
[22] It was 61 cm. (24 in.) in diameter, 9 m. (29½ ft.) long, and weighed 2770 kg. (6107 lb.).

this oxygen-fueled weapon packed 470 kilograms (1036 pounds) of high explosive, twice the charge of the contemporary 21-inch American torpedo. It could travel 20,000 meters — almost 11 miles — at 49 knots, or twice as far at 36 knots, outreaching even a battleship's guns.[23]

The question then arises, why was everyone in the South Pacific, from Admiral Halsey down, ignorant of this "long lance" and its performance? Japanese destroyers had employed it since the begin- ning of the war. One is said to have been picked up on Cape Esper- ance in January or February 1943 and taken apart, and the data sent to Pacific Fleet Intelligence, but nothing except rumor appears to have reached the Fleet — not even Halsey's staff knew about it. Captain Cecil of *Helena*, who had heard the rumor, warned Ad- miral Ainsworth, when discussing his battle plan before the Kula Gulf action, against closing to 10,000 yards; but Ainsworth, with no definite information, and believing that *Strong* had been sunk by a submarine's torpedo, felt he could dismiss the tale as "scuttle- butt." A radical change of night-battle tactics was called for by this enemy torpedo, and by the equally unknown device for re- loading which rendered Japanese destroyers doubly effective; but it took two battles to bring that about.

Perhaps it is inherent in American thinking to assume that our own gadgets and machinery, from plumbing to atomic bombs, must be the world's best. A dangerous way of thinking, indeed. As a Roman poet wrote at the beginning of the Christian era, "It is right to be taught even by an enemy."

There is some consolation in the fact that the Japanese exagger- ated the tactical results of these two battles even more than we did, reporting not only the two ships that were sunk, but claiming two more cruisers and a few destroyers. A more realistic assessment of damage, however, might not have deterred them from further

[23] U.S. Naval Technical Mission to Japan *Ordnance Targets, Japanese Torpe- does and Tubes* Apr. 1946 (Index No. 0–01–1). The standard American destroyer torpedo (Mark 15) could travel only 3 miles at 45 knots, 5 miles at 33.5 knots or 7.5 miles at 26.5 knots. It was 21 inches in diameter, and originally contained 789 lb. of explosive.

operations to reinforce Munda. A series of tactical successes such as these often obscures a faulty strategy.

The enemy continued to lose planes and ships which he could not replace, as well as men, to save Munda and Vila; then he continued to lose more planes, ships and men, to get them out of Munda and Vila. Both reinforcement and evacuation were very well done; but a string of such victories adds up to defeat.

# CHAPTER XII

# Conclusion of the New Georgia Campaign

## 13 July–20 September 1943

East Longitude dates; Zone minus 11 time.

### 1. *The Siege of Munda, 13 July–5 August*

WHILE SAILORS celebrated a victory that they thought they had won, the soldiers were properly skeptical. Kolombangara had not in the least bettered the situation for them. In the north, Liversedge would be unable to move until 20 July, after receiving reinforcements. In the south, Sasaki had almost got Hester's troops on the run. And the sea lanes via Bairoko and Diamond Narrows were still open for the Emperor's troops and supplies.

Admiral Halsey and his top Army commander, General Harmon, found it difficult to believe the desperate situation ashore until Major General Oscar W. Griswold, the XIV Corps commander, radioed that things were going badly on New Georgia and that at least one more division would be needed promptly. Halsey then sent Harmon north to straighten matters out. He took one look at the situation and gave the field command to General Griswold, in addition to his corps responsibility.

Griswold inherited a mess. Recall that on 12 July the enemy had cut communications between the 169th Infantry, on the Munda Trail, and the 172nd striking southward to Laiana. On the 13th, the 172nd reached Laiana intact; but Sasaki promptly interposed a full battalion between it and the 169th. Next day reinforcements from Rendova got ashore at Laiana despite enemy artillery and mortar barrages, but these soldiers now had to fight their way over the same route to bring help and supplies to the 169th. The folly of not taking Laiana first was now apparent.

The 169th Infantry was hungry, dispirited and completely fagged out. Supplies coming along the trail had to be carried by hand; parachute drops were infrequent. The troops were up against a solid line of Japanese pillboxes bristling with automatic weapons. Many men were suffering from dysentery. One battalion was completely isolated and the gap left by the departure of the 172nd was wide open. At this point, the Japanese put on a campaign of terror by night and relentless attack by day.

Darkness came to the jungle like the click of a camera shutter. Then the Japanese crept close to the American lines. They attacked with bloodcurdling screams, plastered bivouacs with artillery and mortar barrages, crawled silently into American foxholes and stabbed or strangled the occupants. Often they cursed loudly in English, rattled their equipment, named the American commanding officers and dared the Americans to fight, reminding them that they were "not in the Louisiana maneuvers now." For sick and hungry soldiers who had fought all day, this unholy shivaree was terrifying. They shot at everything in sight — fox fire on rotting stumps, land crabs clattering over rocks, even comrades. Yarns heard at Guadalcanal which they had been told to forget, about Japs signaling to each other by bird or insect calls, were now remembered; the creak of a beetle or cry of a nighthawk was enough to start aimless shooting. A mounting list of sick and wounded, supply shortage, the ease with which the enemy moved through their lines (even attacking the regimental command post) and his ability to ambush stretcher parties moving to the rear, added to the nightmare. Long lines of broken men staggered toward Zanana.

General Griswold needed ten days to bring in fresh troops from Guadalcanal and the Russells and to reorganize them for a coordinated offensive. In the meantime air, artillery and limited ground offensives tried to pin Sasaki down. Air assaults damaged his supply lines and kept him from receiving naval and air assistance. An artillery offensive on the southern front provided a useful softening. One enemy noncom, after mercilessly forcing his men to hold their dugout positions during a bombardment, confessed to his diary, "It is really more than I can bear."

American ground offensives east of Munda were confined to a modest westward push and to opening trails between Laiana, Zanana and the beleaguered 169th Infantry. On the day Griswold took over, six Marine Corps tanks waddled to the western outposts of the Laiana front, operating against coconut-log bunkers and clearing a hilltop for advancing soldiers. On 16 July three of them outdistanced their supporting infantry and entered a maze of sunken pillboxes so cleverly concealed by shadows, vines and leaves that they were "easier to smell than to see." The Japanese traveled like termites in shallow trenches from one pillbox to another, exposing themselves only when in a tank's "blind spot." They placed magnetic mines in the path of the tanks, damaging all three and forcing them to withdraw. That day the infantry suffered severely from "friendly" bombs and artillery shells as well as from enemy mortar barrages. On the third day, emboldened Japanese camouflaged with leaves planted a mine directly on one tank, sprayed another with a flame thrower and popped grenades all around them, again driving them off. This was no terrain for tanks.

Now came Sasaki's innings. Despite the battles in the Gulf and the loss of Enogai Inlet, significant reinforcements had reached him. With 3000 men defending Munda strip and 2000 more guarding the Vila rice line, Sasaki confidently ordered Colonel Tomonari "to seek out the flank and rear of the main body of the enemy who landed at Zanana and attack, annihilating them on the coast." To keep the enemy facing west, one Captain Kojima would make a simultaneous frontal attack.

First warning to the Americans came on 17 July when a Japanese party appeared at a watering hole on the Munda Trail between Zanana and the 169th Infantry. Patrols shortly discovered that we

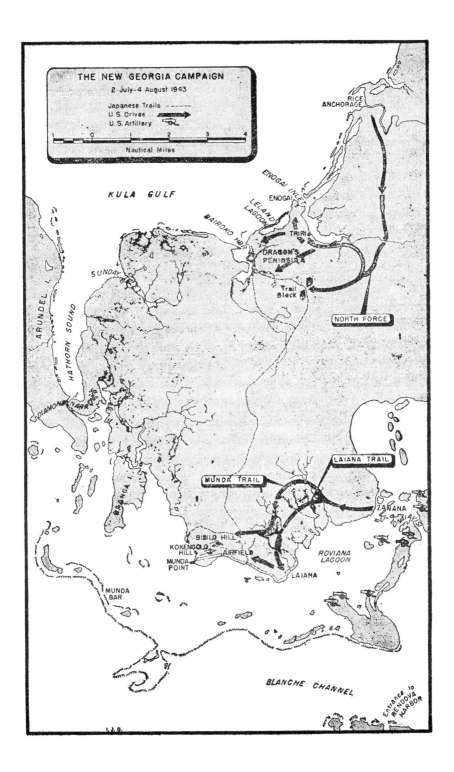

THE NEW GEORGIA CAMPAIGN
2 July-4 August 1943

Japanese Trails ------
U.S. Drives
U.S. Artillery

1    0         1         2         3         4

Nautical Miles

KULA GULF

RICE ANCHORAGE

ENOGAI INLET

LELAND LAGOON

ENOGAI

BAIROKO HBR.

TRIRI

DRAGON'S PENINSULA

Trail Block

NORTH FORCE

SUNDAY

HATHORN SOUND

ARUNDEL I.

DIAMOND NARR.

WANA WANA

LAIANA TRAIL

MUNDA TRAIL

ZANANA

ONAIAVISI

BIBILO HILL

KOKENGOLO HILL

AIRFIELD

MUNDA POINT

ROVIANA LAGOON

LAIANA

MUNDA BAR

BLANCHE CHANNEL

Entrance to RENDOVA HARBOR

I. J. G.

were flanked. That night the Japanese attacked the 43rd Division command post near Zanana. They wrecked the telephone switchboard, mauled the camp kitchen like hungry grizzlies and charged into an aid station, where two patients snapped out of war neurosis long enough to kill four Japs. Luckily the marauders overlooked one telephone wire running to an artillery post. Over this line went shouts for help, and directions for herding the enemy back with artillery. Captain Kojima smashed at the American front lines simultaneously, but mortar fire took the heart out of his attack.

The distress calls brought a part of the fresh 148th Infantry to Zanana with orders to open the Munda Trail and relieve the 169th Regiment. The enemy ambushed an advance patrol on the 18th, so next day a full battalion set forth on the Trail. At a river bridge another ambush met the Americans. This brought two more battalions into the relief forces. Finally, on the 20th, a battalion broke through to relieve the 169th which had been in an impossible situation for a hellish two weeks.

So far, the results of Sasaki's counteroffensive had been negative, and he was not pleased. He told Tomonari to deploy for a major onslaught on the 25th. There ensued a five-day relative calm while both sides sharpened weapons.

In the north Colonel Liversedge planned to take Bairoko on the 20th, with the aid of 700 Marines brought up 18 July. On paper he now had two Marine raider battalions and two Army battalions but, because of disease and battle casualties, his strength was actually no greater than it had been on his original landing at Rice Anchorage. He ordered a two-pronged drive across Dragon's Peninsula, Marines to follow the western shoreline, soldiers to strike inland.

Without artillery or naval gun assistance, without air support (owing to a gross blunder at Henderson Field), Liversedge was unable to penetrate the enemy's fixed positions and had to withdraw to Enogai, assisted by a 250-plane air raid by Guadalcanal planes trying to make amends for their absence the day before.

At dusk 21 July the last platoon of Marines filed into Enogai with news that the Japanese were evacuating wounded and key men from Bairoko. That was important, for it meant that the Munda-Bairoko line had been severed. The Marines had lost heavily — 48 killed and 190 wounded in one day — but their pressure on the Bairoko front had pinned down Japanese troops who would otherwise have reinforced Munda.

In order to replenish Liversedge's depleted supplies and to evacuate casualties, Admiral Wilkinson dispatched a convoy to Enogai on 23 July under Commander Arleigh A. Burke, who was to become famous in these waters, while Merrill's cruisers and destroyers covered up the Slot. At 0100 July 24, the convoy arrived off Enogai and, after a brief search, located a Marine signal light on the landing beach. At 0124 boats started ashore, and in an hour and a half they landed their supplies. The enemy woke up to what was happening as the APDs were taking on board the last of the American wounded. The only opposition was a tardy and haphazard bombardment from enemy shore batteries which were promptly silenced. At 0323 the transports reported "all buttoned up and standing out," and all returned safely to Purvis Bay. Both supplies and bombardment gave the troops at Enogai a needed morale boost, but lack of numbers still limited their offensive action to patrols and trail blocks.

General Griswold, with no troops to spare for Bairoko, concentrated on the main push toward Munda. His men were ready to jump off on the 25th. Realizing the immense value of support from planes, naval guns and artillery, he carefully scheduled the use of each arm.

At 0609 on the 25th, Commander Burke showed up with six destroyers to bombard Lambeti Plantation between Munda Field and Laiana. Shells flew down the lanes of coconut trees, 70 shells for each 1000-yard square, 4000 rounds all told. Minutes later, planes droned over and made the heaviest raid so far along the shoreline. Army artillery macerated the jungle with 105-mm and 155-mm fire. The destroyers flattered themselves that they had made the target area "extremely unhealthy for any living being"; [1] yet, as soon as the barrage ended and soldiers on the seaward side started west, the enemy, who had crept to comparative safety close to the American lines during the bombardment, remanned his pillboxes. And, as the Marine tanks could not climb such steep hills as were there, the sun set on a stalemate.

Next day was better. The troops stepped back so that the artillery could work over the no man's land where the Japanese waited. Then the barrage moved on westward while men and tanks followed, mopping up 74 pillboxes before nightfall. During the next few days, soldiers and tanks were busy ripping the tops off pillboxes which the enemy insisted on reoccupying every night.

Up on the Munda Trail the Army started its 25 July drive against Bibilo Hill, an eminence overlooking the airfield and the coast. But before the troops could reach it, they had to climb several others which were occupied by Sasaki's men. One of these infested hills stopped the first day's advance. On the second day, six Marine Corps tanks fresh from the Russells charged forward, surrounded by supporting infantrymen carrying flame throwers, automatic weapons and grenades. The Japanese wiped out the infantry and then went to work on the tanks, disabling two and sending the others back.

On the right flank of the Munda Trail American troops found little opposition and in two days advanced to within half a mile of Bibilo Hill. The enemy made the next few days hectic for all. The American center faced a series of ridges in which Japs, hiding like ants in a hill, reduced daily gains to feet instead of yards. Soldiers would walk over pillboxes without seeing them, and when the pillbox crew retired it always left behind one soldier in a steel vest who proved very hard to kill. On the northern flank the

[1] After the capture of Munda, Capt. Festus F. Foster of Buord and Cdr. David M. Tyree, Amphibious Force gunnery officer, inspected the bombarded areas, paying particular attention to Lambeti which had come under naval gunfire only once. They reported devastation everywhere from bombs and shells, yet some blockhouses and dugouts had withstood everything but a direct hit. Admiral Wilkinson thought that it needed for saturation 3 times the number of shells fired. O.N.I. Combat Narrative No. 10 *Operations in the New Georgia Area.*

troops, unhampered by such nuisances, outran their supplies so that 200 of Sasaki's men promptly surrounded the ration dump and separated the regiment from its friends to the south. It took four infantry companies to relieve the pressure on the dump, and this diversion cost numerous casualties including three company commanders killed on the 30th. To regain contact the northern regiment had to retire, destroying ammunition and heavy equipment en route. All this was bad enough but would have been much worse if Tomonari and Kojima had coöperated. Japanese lack of coördination may have stemmed from bad communications or from the disruption of their own offensive.

Jungle troubles again seeped up to the Halsey and Harmon level. Both officers had already projected their thinking to a Bougainville invasion. The delay and the large troop commitment at Munda naturally disturbed them. On 29 July General Harmon wrote, "We *have* to make this Munda-Bairoko business go — and as quickly as possible. . . . We have got to get it done before we go on to the next stop. . . . We have a bear by the tail — or perhaps a fighting badger in his hole."

On 1 August the fighting badger temporarily sheathed his claws and shifted his hole. For the first time in the campaign the 43rd Division headquarters could say, "The going is easy." The enemy decamped so hurriedly from the ridges blocking Munda Trail that he abandoned both dead and wounded. On the 2nd the American advance accelerated all along the front; the only opposition encountered was on Bibilo and Kokengolo Hills, both north of the airfield.

Sasaki was indeed yielding. His fighting strength was halved. His medical facilities, never good, were practically nonexistent. His communication link with Rabaul was gone. Kojima and many other leaders were dead. His men were nervous and disgruntled. One growled, "Everybody's pulling dirty tricks like hiding cigarettes or secretly eating canned goods." On the 3rd Sasaki ordered an evacuation; but where retreat was not possible each soldier was to fight until death and take at least ten Americans with him.

The American soldiers now brightened up. On 3 August troops converged on the eastern edge of the field while others swept around it to the north to straddle the Munda-Bairoko Trail. When, next day, a fast-marching column isolated the airfield, Harmon radioed Halsey, "Griswold's north flank dunked shoes in salt water north of Munda." But Sasaki's remnants were still able to charge admission to Munda Field by bitter resistance, particularly at the base of the two hills. Army infantrymen and Marine tanks harried the enemy all day. On 5 August the Americans inundated the hills with mortar and 37-mm fire until they literally made the top of Bibilo bounce. Japanese soldiers' guns and pillboxes flew as much as 15 feet into the air, while other unfortunates blown out of their holes "ran around in little circles like stunned chickens," to be mowed down by machine guns. When Kokengolo Hill, too, was riddled, the American tanks and infantry moved into Munda unopposed.

## 2. *Air-Surface Actions, 17 July–3 August*

By mid-July a plethora of shipping was reported in Tonolei Harbor, Bougainville. This called for a daytime strike by light bombers. On the 17th, Airsols dispatched 223 planes up the Slot. As 31 four-engined bombers made for Kahili airdrome, 50 interceptors scrambled aloft. Seven Army Liberators bombed merchantmen from a 4-mile altitude, doing them no harm but attracting "Zekes" as fat chickens draw hawks. A strong fighter cover of 114 planes was ample to protect them and while dogfights raged high up, the real business, 72 bomb-carrying SBDs and TBFs, dropped down fast and blasted Tonolei shipping. But the damage was even less than that of the mammoth Japanese raid on Guadalcanal in April. Out of 23 naval and auxiliary vessels present, destroyer *Hatsuyuki* was sunk, but no merchantman of over 500 tons, although some must have been damaged.

At 2230 on 19 July a Black Cat's radar whiskers sensed something in the Slot between Vella Lavella and Choiseul. The pilot circled and made out a whopping big Tokyo Express – eleven ships on course SSE. Actually there were three heavy cruisers, one light cruiser and nine destroyers commanded by Rear Admiral Shoji Nishimura. Admiral Kusaka at Rabaul had evidently determined to outgun the next American light cruiser raid and he must have expected Merrill since Ainsworth was supposed to have been "annihilated" at Kolombangara. At about midnight three destroyer-transports peeled off, heading into Vella Gulf, while the main force prowled the Slot to await whatever Halsey might send up; but that night he sent nothing. The Cat followed the transports and, shortly after midnight, made a low-level bombing or strafing run which netted slight damage. Meanwhile six Avengers, in reply to his warning, skimmed up the Slot from Henderson Field and dropped one-ton bombs on the combatant ships, from masthead level. Destroyer *Yugure* promptly sank; heavy cruiser *Kumano* took a bomb in her starboard side aft and slowed down. During the two hours before dawn, 20 July, five torpedo-carrying TBFs and eight skip-bombing B–25s lashed the enemy ships but made no hits. Admiral Nishimura now decided to retire. Destroyer *Kiyonami*, left behind to rescue survivors, then became daylight target of some skip-bombing B–25s, who sent her down to join *Yugure*. Two Mitchells and two Avengers were expended in these attacks.

Assuming that the Shortlands would next be invaded, Admiral Koga brought seaplane carrier *Nisshin* down from Truk and at Rabaul loaded her and three destroyers with reinforcements: one artillery battalion and three of infantry. This group skirted the north coast of Bougainville and by noon 22 July were in Bougainville Strait. There they were pounced on by a routine anti-shipping strike of 12 heavy (PB4Y) and 34 light (SBD and TBF) bombers with fighter escort. Sixteen defending "Zekes" found themselves heavily outnumbered by the American fighters. The Liberators missed, but the light bombers got six hits on *Nisshin* and she sank within half an hour. The destroyers called at Buin to debark their troops, then returned to rescue 189 of *Nisshin's* floating survivors.

Prohibitive losses of destroyers forced the Japanese to establish a barge line between the Shortlands and Kula Gulf. Their barges were of many sizes and types, but the kind they used most in the Solomons was Type A *Daihatsu,* a metal-hulled, diesel-powered craft, 41 to 49 feet long, weighing 8 tons, capable of making 8 knots and carrying 100 to 120 men or 10 to 15 tons of cargo. At least two machine guns were standard equipment for each *Daihatsu,* but in battle waters the Japanese added anything up to 37-mm field pieces, while troop passengers contributed automatic weapons. Both coxswain and the engine compartment were protected by makeshift armor. The *Daihatsu,* with nice lines like those of fishing sampans, was a very neat little craft for that kind of war.[2]

Barge trains traveled by night, and in daytime, snug in bosky inlets and draped with jungle greenery, they could rarely be seen by planes. Coastwatchers reported and aërial photographers snapped the hideouts, but they were so difficult to identify from the air that pilots too frequently missed, or even shot up a native village by mistake. Not until the Bougainville campaign did "barge-bopping" become a fine art.

General Kenney's bombers of the MacArthur command frequently helped the New Georgia campaign by striking shipping or raiding the Rabaul airfields. On 15 July a mine planted by Australian Catalinas damaged light cruiser *Nagara* in Kavieng Harbor. On 28 July, near Cape Gloucester, several skip-bombing B–25s sank destroyers *Ariake* and *Mikazuki.* On 3 August, south of Rabaul, Southwest Pacific fliers mashed the topsides of destroyer *Akikaze.* Kenney's raids on Rabaul, about every three days, further relieved pressure down the Slot.

[2] Sopac Combat Intelligence Center Bulletin "Japanese Barges" Jan. 1944. *Daihatsu* is an abbreviation of *Ogata Hatsudokitei* — "large-type landing barge."

# 3. *Motor Torpedo Boat Actions,*
## *23 July–2 August* [3]

The PTs suffered from great expectations. Americans had always relished a David and Goliath setup on the sea since Jeffersonian gunboat days; and Bulkeley's motor torpedo boats had produced so many mythical victories in the defense of the Philippines that many people expected them to perform miracles. In Central Solomons waters they found their proper employment as scourges to Japanese barges; and by the end of this campaign the bedeviled Japanese would be writing treatises on how to deal with this menace.

Four PT squadrons (5, 9, 10 and 11), comprising about 52 boats, operated in the New Georgia campaign from two bases: one in Rendova harbor, whence they could cover everything to the western entrance of Blackett Strait, and one at Lever Harbor [4] on the Slot side of New Georgia, within easy cruising of Kula Gulf. Rendova was the headquarters of Captain E. J. ("Mike") Moran, former skipper of cruiser *Boise*, who now had the resounding title of Commander Motor Torpedo Boat Squadrons South Pacific.

After the first indeterminate engagement west of Rendova on 3 July, business fell off for the PTs. Ainsworth and Merrill insisted that the Lever Harbor boats stay home during their frequent visits to Kula Gulf, lest they foul things up,[5] while on the Rendova side Japanese barge traffic was still slight. But on the night of 23–24 July three boats prowling Blackett Strait took on an equal number of barges, sank one and chased the others away. This set-to delayed a barge rendezvous with Japanese troop-carrying destroyers, which pulled out before unloading.

---

[3] Cdr. R. J. Bulkley usnr unpublished History of the PTs; Comairsopac Daily Intelligence Bulletins; PT Action Reports.

[4] The Japanese thought the "Lever Boats" were based at Enogai; hence frequent and heavy air raids there.

[5] Accidental encounters on 30 June and 17–18 July justified the cruiser commanders' apprehensions. In another between B-25s and PTs in Ferguson Passage on the 19th, two aviators were killed, one PT boat sunk and 11 sailors wounded.

On the night of 26–27 July three PTs entered a running gun fight with six barges. Their bullets bounced harmlessly off the *Daihatsus'* armored sides, and whenever the gunners paused to reload the barges closed range and fired. The Japanese bullets did little damage other than ventilating the plywood hulls; but the PTs learned to load guns alternately so as to keep barges continuously under fire, and to attack from astern, hitting their tender hindquarters. Torpedoes were useless in barge fighting, so 37-mm anti-tank guns and 40-mm machine guns were procured and mounted. The enemy replied by adding more armor and armament to the *Daihatsus.* Next American countermove was to attach to the PT formations large landing craft carrying 3-inch guns. Eventually, specially fitted SCs and LCIs were enlisted to keep the PTs company on the barge-blasting expeditions.

Admiral Samejima scheduled a destroyer run for the night of 1–2 August and sent 18 bombers ahead to raid the Rendova PT base. They wrecked two boats which were tied up. But that same night, when four destroyers slipped along the west coast of Kolombangara, 15 PTs, split four ways, were blockading the southern and western approaches to Blackett Strait. *PT–159* (Lieutenant Henry J. Brantingham), one of the few which had radar, picked up the enemy about midnight. Brantingham, followed by *PT–157*, closed to strafe what he believed were landing craft. The destroyers declared their identity with gunfire and the two PTs fired six torpedoes but made no hits. The Express continued until sighted by *PT–171* (Lieutenant Arthur H. Berndtson) which dashed in under fire and launched four non-scoring fish. Three boats keeping company with Berndtson did not see the destroyers until too late. *PT–107*, radar-equipped, also picked up the enemy and outran three companion boats to launch four torpedoes, all misses. A final hurdle, the Blackett Strait blockade, was also surmounted. Three PTs saw the fracas to the northwest and closed range. A strafing float plane and destroyer salvos failed to stop them from getting off twelve torpedoes, but the torpedoes failed to score, and the Japanese destroyers swept through to Vila and discharged their cargoes.

Even worse luck attended the PTs during the enemy's retirement. *PT-109* (Lieutenant John F. Kennedy USNR) teamed up with *PT-169* and *PT-162* and swept slowly southward. Suddenly a lookout in Kennedy's boat shouted, "Ship at two o'clock!" Everyone looked out on the starboard bow to see an enemy destroyer bearing down on them. Kennedy spun the wheel but the destroyer's bow slit his boat like a buzz saw. Skipper Kennedy landed topsides on his back, thinking that was how it felt to be killed. But destroyer *Amagiri* tore on without pause and Kennedy stayed alive on the forward half of the boat. When a fire that broke out on the PT died down, six survivors returned on board the bigger half of the hull and took a muster. Of thirteen crew members only two were missing, although five answered the roll call from the water. Able swimmers spent a tough three hours rescuing the others. One sailor complained that he could swim no farther; Kennedy, a fellow townsman, said, "For a guy from Boston, you're certainly putting up a great exhibition out here." He made it after that.[6] *PT-162* avoided a similar fate by yards. *PT-169* fired torpedoes at a range too close for the warheads to arm. Last shots of the battle were two torpedoes from *PT-157*, also misses. Thirty fish had been launched that night, yet the only damage to the enemy was a dent in *Amagiri's* bow.

Kennedy expected planes to come to his rescue in the morning but none showed up and by midafternoon, with the half-hull of *PT-109* sinking, he decided to swim for it. Kennedy clenched between his teeth the tie-ties of the lifejacket of his badly burned engineer, and towed him. The others made it unaided. Before dark they reached a small island east of Gizo. That night Kennedy donned a lifejacket, grabbed a salvaged battle lantern and swam into Ferguson Passage to intercept the nightly PT patrol, but none came. The current pulled him into Blackett Strait, but in the morning returned him to where he had started, and he crawled ashore exhausted. On 5 August friendly natives delivered a message scratched on a coconut shell to the coastwatcher on Wana Wana,

[6] John Hersey "Survival," *New Yorker* 17 June 1944.

who dispatched a war canoe to the rescue and sent the word to Rendova, where memorial services had already been held for the crew of *PT-109*. On 7 August, with Kennedy hidden under ferns in the bottom of the war canoe, natives paddled to Wana Wana waving gaily at unsuspecting Japanese planes. That night Kennedy boarded a rescue PT, piloted it to the camp and picked up his men. On the way home, one devout sailor sat on deck with his arms around two mission natives, all three singing "Yes, Jesus Loves Me!"

## 4. *The Battle of Vella Gulf, 6–7 August*[7]

For a full year, destroyer men had been banging fists on wardroom tables and bellowing, "When are they going to cut us loose from the cruisers' apron strings?" In one fight after another the admiral had kept destroyers in the van and rear of his column to protect the cruisers, instead of sending them on an independent torpedo attack. Not once since the savage battles of Bali and Balikpapan early in 1942 had United States destroyers had a chance to fight alone; they had been used for anti-submarine warfare, escort, jacks-of-all-trades, with so few opportunities for teamwork that task force commanders doubted their ability to fight independently. Moreover, the performance of American torpedoes so far had been miserable. But there was no use telling that to destroyer sailors, "Just give us a chance!" was their reply to every criticism. Now, Admiral Wilkinson was to accept this challenge from Commander Moosbrugger, who met it admirably.

The chance occurred because Wilkinson suspected on 5 August

[7] Action Reports of ships and commands involved; Letter of Capt. Moosbrugger to Cdr. Shaw 5 May 1950; Cincpac "Battle Experience – Naval Operations Solomon Islands Area 12 July–10 August 1943" (Information Bulletin No. 11, Dec. 6, 1943); USSBS *Campaigns of the Pacific War* and *Interrogations of Japanese Officials*; O.N.I. "Kolombangara and Vella Lavella," Combat Narrative XI; ATIS Doc. 15685 "The Night Battle of Vella Lavella"; Japanese Naval Torpedo School "Battle Lessons Learned in the Greater East Asia War (Torpedoes)" Vol. VI (Jicpoa Item No. 5782) Apr. 11, 1944; Lt. V. A. Sherman USNR "The Battle of Vella Gulf" *U.S. Naval Inst. Proceedings* LXXI (1945) No. 1 pp. 61–69.

that the Japanese would run a Tokyo Express to Kolombangara the following night, because Moosbrugger was Johnny-on-the-spot and because Wilkinson, an old destroyer man himself, allowed Moosbrugger to make his own battle plan. No cruisers were available: Merrill's force was then too far away to get there in time, and Ainsworth's had not been rebuilt since the July battles.

Commander Frederick Moosbrugger, newly arrived at Tulagi to be Comdesdiv 12, was more pleased than surprised to receive this dispatch from Rear Admiral Wilkinson on 5 August:

Comdesdiv 12 with Desdiv 15, minus *Gridley* and *Wilson*,[8] depart Tulagi 1230 August 6 proceed Vella Gulf S. of Russells and Rendova to arrive Gizo Strait 2200 and make sweep of Gulf. If no enemy contact made by 0200 return down the Slot. Kelly's PT boats will operate in southern Kula Gulf.[9] Comairsols to furnish Black Cat and fighter cover 6th and 7th at dawn.

This looked like destroyers going it alone at last. Moosbrugger lost no time in steaming across to Koli Point for a conference with the Admiral. Wilkinson gave him such intelligence as he had, and told what had happened in earlier actions up the Slot. Wilkinson (who at this late date had no exact knowledge of the "long lance") said that "in the opinion of others" the Japanese had better torpedoes than we, but that our gunnery was superior to theirs, so we should engage at long ranges. Moosbrugger observed that destroyer sailors were confident of their own superiority over the enemy in torpedo work; that he and Desdiv 12, in which he had served since May 1941, had trained and trained making radar-controlled night torpedo attacks until it had become second nature to them. Wilkinson seemed relieved to hear this, and said in effect, "You know your ships better than I do; it's up to you how to fight them." Thus, the Admiral dictated the course of Moosbrugger's approach, but left him complete freedom of action after passing through Gizo Strait.

[8] These DDs were engaged in escort duty.
[9] Wilkinson took rather a dim view of PTs, since they had been worsted in tangles with *Daihatsus*, and so judged it advisable for them to operate in a different gulf from the destroyers, in case the Japanese got through the Strait.

Moosbrugger accordingly planned his fight with the Tokyo Express just the way he always wanted to do it — forming his force with division guides on line of bearing about two miles apart, in order to give the enemy the "one-two" punch. Moosbrugger, in overall command, would strike first if the Express proved to be a destroyer outfit, as expected. Rodger Simpson, commanding three destroyers which had sacrificed half their torpedo power to mount 40-mm quads, would deal the initial blow if the Japanese appeared in barges. The task organization follows: —

TG 31.2, Commander Frederick Moosbrugger

Division A–1, Commander Moosbrugger (Comdesdiv 12)

| | | |
|---|---|---|
| DUNLAP | Lt. Cdr. Clifton Iverson | 12 torpedoes; 4 5-inch, 8 20-mm guns |
| CRAVEN | Lt. Cdr. F. T. Williamson | 16 torpedoes; 4 5-inch, 7 20-mm guns |
| MAURY | Cdr. Gelzer L. Sims | 16 torpedoes; 4 5-inch, 7 20-mm guns |

Division A–2, Commander Rodger W. Simpson (Comdesdiv 15)

| | | |
|---|---|---|
| LANG | Cdr. John L. Wilfong | 8 torpedoes; 4 5-inch, 4 40-mm, 4 20-mm guns |
| STERETT | Lt. Cdr. Frank G. Gould | 8 torpedoes; 4 5-inch, 4 40-mm, 4 20-mm guns |
| STACK | Lt. Cdr. Roy A. Newton | 8 torpedoes; 4 5-inch, 4 40-mm, 4 20-mm guns |

On the morning of 6 August the two division commanders breakfasted together, called in the skippers and went over the plan again until everyone understood what to do in every possible situation. Moosbrugger ordered them to get under way at 1130 and then pass the word to the crews.

About the time that the American ships were making their customary S-turn salute to the dead in Ironbottom Sound,[10] four Japanese destroyers north of Bougainville were heading southeast at high speed. *Hagikaze*, *Arashi* and *Kawakaze* carried 900 soldiers and 50 tons of supplies bound for Kolombangara; *Shigure* carried 250 troops. Captain Kaju Sugiura, commanding the group in *Hagikaze*, observed an American search plane spotting him. Bitterly he realized that his plan was exposed. Yet, like most Japanese destroyer men, he had courage and persistence. The Express had run the PT gauntlet four nights before; no reason why it should not do

[10] This custom, if not initiated by Rodger Simpson, was always followed by him: see the last illustration in this volume.

so again. So, he shaped a course and planned the speed to get his four destroyers to the entrance of Vella Gulf at 2330.

Moosbrugger's six destroyers steamed south of Savo, the Russells and Nev/ Georgia, aiming for Gizo Strait. Torpedomen puttered with their fish, hoping that tonight they would not be left to droop in the tubes. The search plane's report, arriving at suppertime, said that a "fast fleet" was north of Buka at noon, steering S by W. This was Sugiura's four destroyers; Simpson estimated correctly that they would be in Vella Gulf by midnight. Nightfall brought a stinging rain squall which completely blotted out the shore, but the circling wand of light on each SG radarscope showed friendly ships and islands as little luminous patches. At four bells in the evening watch, the destroyers changed course to 50° and slowed to 15 knots for a cautious transit of Gizo Strait. Sixteen minutes later they emerged into Vella Gulf and assumed their battle formation, *Dunlap* leading *Craven* and *Maury; Lang, Sterett* and *Stack* veering to starboard; Simpson's flagship bearing 150° from Moosbrugger's. At 2228 both columns came right simultaneously to course 124° in order to sweep the approaches to Blackett Strait. After that they steered due N with Simpson's division fairly close inshore, and at 2323 changed course to 30°, to follow the Kolombangara coast.

Ten minutes later *Dunlap's* radarscope showed a speck ten miles to the north, in the open waters of the Gulf and closing. Over TBS Moosbrugger informed his skippers, "Surface contact 351° true, range 19,700 yards." The pip promptly split three ways. *Dunlap's* skipper, "Swifty Clifty" Iverson, checked with *Craven's*. He had it too; so did *Maury's*. Radarman Savage in *Dunlap* sounded off: "Four in column — I see 'em! I see 'em!" Four ships were heading south at between 25 and 30 knots. A light breeze brushed the clouds aside, revealing a black moonless sky; on the surface of the Gulf there was scarcely a ripple.

Moosbrugger brought his three ships left to course 335° to engage the enemy's port side on reciprocal courses. Simpson trailed on the starboard quarter. Within Moosbrugger's ships, C.I.C. and gun plot piped target data to torpedo directors, which in turn ground out bearings to indicating dials in torpedo mounts. Petty officers cranked mounts to indicated bearings, struggling to keep pace with the rapid movement of the targets down the port side. The radarless enemy still could not see them at 2340, range 8000 yards, with two-mile visibility. Now another course change, 15 degrees right. At 2341 Moosbrugger signaled to *Dunlap, Craven* and *Maury:* "Fire torpedoes!" Eight from each ship went into the water with their peculiar *sshwoonk*. Conditions could not have been better. The firing range was about 6300 yards, yielding a torpedo run of about 4000 yards (4½ minutes at 26½ knots), and hits would be normal to target hulls. Knowing the caprice of the magnetic influence detonator, the destroyer people had disconnected the device completely. Flash hiders on the tubes prevented the enemy from seeing the burning impulse powder at the instant of firing. The TBS screeched another command, "Turn Nine," and each ship heeled in a right-angled turn to haul clear of possible enemy torpedoes.

On board the Japanese destroyers, everyone except the watch relaxed at battle stations, expecting that if any Yanks were out that night they would be riding PT boats near the entrance to Blackett Strait, still far away. On deck the shrill whine of the fireroom blowers, the swish of churning water and the whistle of air around the superstructure discouraged conversation. Soldiers weighted down with packs squatted on their haunches and dozed.

At 2342 a *Hagikaze* lookout searching to port made out a black form against the misty Kolombangara coast. Seconds later, an *Arashi* man reported a motor torpedo boat on the same bearing. *Shigure* chimed in to report a wake on the port bow. *Kawakaze* observers, not to be outdone, imagined a PT on the starboard bow, which drew attention to a harmless quarter at a crucial moment. A minute passed, and *Hagikaze* announced her sighting as four destroyers swinging rapidly to starboard. Her torpedomen struggled desperately to open torpedo valves. On board *Shigure* the captain shouted, "Torpedo Action to Port. Opposite Course! Gunnery Engagement to Port!" But *Shigure* was ill-prepared for action as the Americans had been at Savo Island, and with less excuse. The

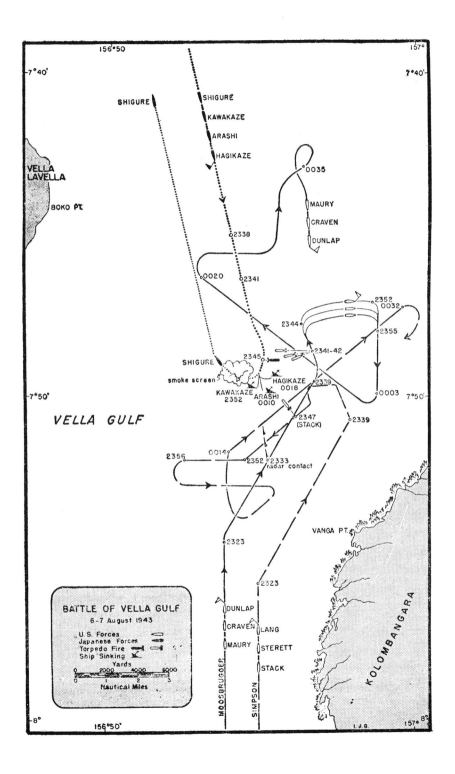

BATTLE OF VELLA GULF
6-7 August 1943

U.S. Forces
Japanese Forces
Torpedo Fire
Ship Sinking
Yards

2000  4000  6000
0        1         2        3
Nautical Miles

torpedo officer found the director operator asleep, his post manned by an assistant, and the torpedo crewmen away from their tubes on lookout duty. Black night, high speed, surprise and men off station brought "considerable confusion," said the skipper of *Shigure*.

That was nothing to what followed. Soon frothy torpedo wakes were sighted. *Hagikaze* and *Arashi* threw their helms hard-a-port too late; one or two torpedoes stabbed into a fireroom of the first. Two, maybe three, torpedoes burst in the other's firerooms. As *Kawakaze* wheeled to starboard, an American fish gouged her in a magazine below the bridge and her whole forward part burst skyward in a ball of ruddy flame. *Shigure* alone held her course and alone escaped destruction; torpedoes slid harmlessly under her hull. Her tardy crew got off an eight-torpedo salvo at 2345, not quick enough to catch Moosbrugger's ships retiring. *Shigure* then skidded into a hard right turn, laid down a dense smoke screen and scampered north to reload.

The four minutes following the launching of torpedoes had been eternity to the Americans. Moosbrugger, still concerned about retaliatory torpedoes, surged eastward, ships in line abreast. Simpson, itching to whack the Japanese, spun his column left to a southwest heading (230°), capping the enemy "T" and thus unwittingly steering clear of *Shigure* torpedoes. So far, not a gun had ripped the silence of the Gulf. At 2346 *Dunlap's* sound operator heard a torpedo explosion, yet unbroken darkness stretched along the horizon to the west. An explosion should have been seen before it was heard; what could be wrong? Doubts vanished when three brilliant flashes flowed over the horizon like molten metal from a bursting caldron; then four more in succession, from left to right.[11] When the slower course of sound brought explosion after explosion, officers and men shouted with joy and slapped each other's shoulders. Shapes of enemy destroyers stood up against the bright flames like paper cutouts.

---

[11] Flash from a deep torpedo hit may be obscured by the oil and water curtain which is thrown up; hence the possibility of hearing an explosion without sighting it.

Following doctrine, Simpson's ships now turned 5-inch guns on the enemy, concentrating first on *Kawakaze* less than three miles distant. *Stack* loosed four torpedoes. *Kawakaze* rolled over and went down, her gushing fuel tanks still feeding a circle of flame around the survivors.

At 2352 Moosbrugger, by a right angle turn to course South, formed his ships in an inverted column, *Maury* leading. Three minutes later, impatient gunners commenced salvo fire at a burning "cruiser," probably *Arashi*. Panic-stricken Japanese gunners in *Arashi* and *Hagikaze* fired raggedly in all directions; not only at the destroyers, but at what they supposed to be motor torpedo boats, aircraft and cruisers.

By midnight the guns of both cripples were silent. Simpson countermarched to course East, his guns firing steadily. Moosbrugger doubled back to the northwest, hoping to battle any supporting units that might be entering the Gulf. He almost had his wish. *Shigure*, having reloaded her torpedo tubes in 23 minutes, was charging back in at 0010 August 7 when *Arashi's* magazines exploded, fusing chunks of steel into a shower of fiery meteors. *Shigure's* captain, hearing a Black Cat overhead, took one look at *Arashi* and decided that since his sister ships "were being bombed by enemy planes" retreat was honorable. Besides, he believed one of the flaming hulks was an American destroyer suffering from his own torpedoes. He reversed course and got out. Awed PT sailors in Kula Gulf 28 miles away sighted the loom of flame and thought that the volcano on Kolombangara must have blown its top. *Hagikaze*, drifting through the radiance, invited fire from all six Americans and exploded at 0018. Four minutes later, Simpson pumped out six more torpedoes at the wreckage of *Arashi*. After that the radar screen showed clear.

Moosbrugger, finding no enemy to the north, doubled back and joined Simpson in a close inspection of the flame-swept, wreckage-littered water. Commander Wilfong of *Lang*, swinging his night glasses over waters dotted with bobbing heads, heard weird human noises and, thinking his crew had gathered to jeer, ordered them back to stations. But as *Lang* shoved deeper into the mass of men and flotsam he realized that the sound was a chant in unison from the water; it sounded like "*Kow-we, Kow-we*," [12] punctuated with shrieks of pain and terror. As Moosbrugger had asked Simpson's division to fish out some Japanese, the ships cruised slowly for half an hour, ready to toss lines to any willing enemy; but none were willing. Whenever they heard English spoken, someone blew a whistle, the chanting ceased and they swam away. So at 0200 Simpson gave up his attempts at rescue and followed Moosbrugger's wake out of the Gulf and down the Slot.

Two hours later, the crews secured from general quarters; but nobody slept, with spirits still "bouncing off the overhead." Men gathered in groups around coffeepots and chattered about the three destroyers and one cruiser which they believed they had sunk. They had suffered only one bit of damage – a broken-down feed pump in *Maury;* and one casualty – a gun loader's crushed hand in *Lang;* neither inflicted by the enemy.

Moosbrugger's victory received the tributes it deserved from all quarters. As Admiral Nimitz pointed out, it was due to good intelligence of the enemy's movements, wise planning, the utmost exploitation of surprise, the withholding of torpedo fire until salvos would course at right angles to the enemy, turning away before he could counterattack, and prompt follow-up with gunfire. To which one may add good training, and the commander's ability to make correct estimates and quick decisions.

On the other side, *Shigure* joined her squadron flagship *Sendai* at Buin with a tale guaranteeing that the Japanese Navy would at last respect American torpedo fire. Destroyer officers complained bitterly that they had parts of radar sets on board, but no complete units; that the bad weather which grounded their scheduled reconnaissance plane did not prevent the Americans from flying; that their vital communication circuits ran down one side of the

---

[12] Capt. Ohmae believes that this was *kowai*, "terrible"; i.e., terrible to let yourself be captured.

ship and could be severed by a single shell. Two complaints might have been lifted from an American action report: the enemy's gun flash was small, compared with their own; available charts were inaccurate and unsafe for inshore navigation. Finally, they griped at "senseless logistic operations" which diverted destroyers from their name-function. Fair enough. At Vella Gulf the three victims were modern, first-rate ships; *Hagikaze* and *Arashi* were only two years old. Their only consolation was the illusion that it had taken cruisers, seven destroyers, PTs and planes to beat them. "The enemy took the initiative from us and we drank the bitter dregs of defeat."[13]

Over 1500 soldiers and sailors perished under Moosbrugger's assault. About 300 Japanese swam or drifted nine miles to Vella Lavella. Some escaped to the Shortlands by barge, others died of disease or Allied bullets, and some were received hospitably by natives who turned them over to the Allies at first opportunity.

A disappointing anticlimax to the battle, from the torpedomen's viewpoint, occurred three nights later. Admiral Wilkinson, assuming that the Tokyo Express would enter Vella Gulf again on the night of 9–10 August, ordered Moosbrugger to conduct an encore. After consultation with Simpson he decided to use the same plan and organization as before. They scoured the waters for an hour but located nothing larger than barges. Moosbrugger then ordered Simpson's division to tackle a three-barge group west of Kolombangara. *Lang, Sterett* and *Wilson* (substituted for *Stack*) closed to half-mile range and opened fire with 5-inch guns. The barges, showing desperate effrontery, replied with .25-caliber machine guns which put some souvenir dents in *Lang's* superstructure, and pulled the old trick of running in tight circles to confuse American gun spotters. The destroyers kept hammering, but sank only one or two *Daihatsus*.

Moosbrugger in the meantime prowled the upper reaches of the Gulf, still hoping the Express might come. Convinced at last that it would not, he looped down the Vella Lavella coast, joining

[13] Japanese Naval Torpedo School "Battle Lessons."

Simpson in two more barge encounters. Altogether a frustrating experience, like shooting cockroaches with a pistol. The Americans churned about the Gulf for four hours and then opened throttles for an uneventful voyage back to Purvis Bay.

## 5. *Mopping Up after Munda, 6 August–20 September*

With Munda in hand, the high command checked off that campaign and looked to the Northern Solomons. But, only 1671 dead had yet been counted out of Sasaki's estimated strength of more than 5000; there had to be a mop-up. Until we controlled the troop and supply funnels from Vila, Sasaki could threaten the field. Contrariwise, American control of western New Georgia and the islands fringing Kula Gulf would effectively neutralize Vila. So, while Seabee battalions repaired and improved the battered Munda Field, ground forces vanished into the jungle for another six weeks' battling.

Major General J. Lawton Collins USA, the Guadalcanal veteran, set out to cleanse the southwest snout of New Georgia from Hathorn Sound to Bairoko; Colonel Liversedge's Marine raiders once more tackled Dragon's Peninsula. Schultz's soldiers by-passed Bairoko and trekked south to join Collins. It took the latter a fortnight to slosh through seven miles of muddy jungle to the hills overlooking Bairoko. Finally on 18 August he combined with the Marines in enveloping all land approaches to the harbor. The Japanese had time to destroy their equipment and evacuate soldiers by barge through our PT-boat blockade; 19 bargeloads of troops and critical supplies broke through to Vila. As at Guadalcanal, the last Japanese pulled out of Bairoko only a few hours before the Americans marched into Sasaki's empty encampment on 24 August.

Farther south the Japanese were not so accommodating. The American 27th Infantry Regiment, aiming to control Diamond Narrows between Arundel Island and New Georgia, trudged toward a spot on the map called Zieta, which a native guide offered to find. Before Joe could prove his knowledge, the soldiers bumped into last-ditch Japanese resistance which withstood infantry, artillery and tanks for a week. Finally, on 15 August, the 200 enemy holdouts retreated into a 25-man American ambush which wrought great execution while ammunition lasted. Next morning the troops discovered a river with an embarkation dock and several abandoned boats. Schultz's veteran battalion, reduced to 100 men, merged with troops outbound from Munda and on 23 August reached the coconut grove fringing Hathorn Sound. That ended ground fighting on New Georgia.

Concurrent with the New Georgia purge was a vicious little campaign for Baanga Island, a sentinel guarding the channel from Kula Gulf to Munda Point, garrisoned by Munda refugees and fresh troops from Vila. American soldiers of the well-blooded 43rd Division tackled this island on 10 August. The enemy continued to resist until the 20th, when he pulled the old vanishing trick and left the island to the Americans.

Arundel Island, the stopper in the bottom of Kula Gulf, still remained in enemy hands. Whoever owned it controlled the Blackett Strait route from the north, and the Diamond Narrows passage from the south. Long-range artillery properly emplaced on Arundel could register on Vila or Munda at choice.

The Americans hoped that one tired regiment (172nd Infantry, 43rd Division) could seize the island and, for a while, it looked as though the hope would be justified. Landing at dawn 27 August unopposed, they pushed northward, discovering no enemy for five days. But the 200 Japanese on the island seemed to multiply like rabbits as barges brought in reinforcements nightly from Vila. On 15 September an American attack fizzled and backfired under a strong Japanese counterthrust. General Griswold had to send in two more infantry battalions, an anti-tank company and 13 Marine Corps light tanks to get the enemy out by 20 September, when he retreated across Blackett Strait, leaving 500 dead on Arundel Island. The Americans lost 44 dead, 256 wounded.

**Peace now descended on Arundel and on New Georgia.**

The Central Solomons campaign ranks with Guadalcanal and Buna-Gona for intensity of human tribulation. At the end of 84 days' fighting, one reinforced battalion of the 172nd Infantry had lost 777 dead, wounded and sick out of an original strength of 1002. Total American losses in ground fighting were 1136.[14] A few hundred Allied sailors were lost in the Battles of Kula Gulf and Kolombangara, together with cruiser *Helena*, destroyers *Strong* and *Gwin*, and three cruisers damaged. The air took its toll too. We had Munda, and we needed it for the next move, toward Rabaul; but we certainly took it the hard way. The strategy and tactics of the New Georgia campaign were among the least successful of any Allied campaign in the Pacific.

[14] 189 Navy and Marine Corps, 947 Army killed; 494 Navy and Marine Corps, 3646 Army wounded; 23 captured and missing. Monthly Progress Report, Army Service Forces, *Health* 31 May 1945. These are for ground forces only; the airforce, surface Navy and submarine casualties have not yet been compiled. Capt. Ohmae estimates that total Japanese casualties in the Munda campaign were 12,000, but this seems excessive.

# CHAPTER XIII

# Vella Lavella

## 15 August–7 October 1943 [1]

East Longitude dates; Zone minus 11 time.

### 1. Leapfrog to Barakoma, 15 August

JULY of 1943 was the month of Allied victory in Sicily and on the Russian front, while in the Atlantic sea lanes the tide definitely turned against Germany. But the stubborn Japanese resistance at Munda threatened the entire Pacific timetable. So far, MacArthur's strategy in New Guinea, like Halsey's in the Solomons, called for a rung-by-rung climb, or an island-to-island hop, each hostile post on flank or rear being snuffed out as one went along. Sasaki's defiance made sense, provided the Allied pattern remained rigid. While he held out, Kolombangara could be reinforced; while Kolombangara fought, Bougainville could be strengthened. This was the old familiar defense in depth, the "fire and fall back" tactics of Civil War days; and it might have worked had not the Americans suddenly decided to leapfrog.

General Tojo shortly before his death told General MacArthur that our leapfrogging strategy was one of the three principal factors that defeated Japan; the other two being the depredations of United States submarines and the ability of fast carrier forces of the Pacific

[1] U.S. Army Historical Monograph "The Vella Lavella Campaign" (a ms. prepared during the war), U.S. Army Historical Section Translation "Southeast Area Operations" Part 2 (Navy); O.N.I. Combat Narrative XI *Kolombangara and Vella Lavella;* Cincpac "Operations in Pacific Ocean Areas, August 1943"; Action Report 13th Fighter Command 15 Aug. 1943; Comairsopac Daily Intelligence Bulletins; *Campaigns of the Pacific War;* Jicpoa Item No. 5782 Japanese Naval Torpedo School "Battle Lessons Learned in the Greater East Asia War (Torpedoes)" Vol. VI; Action Reports of ships and commands involved.

Fleet to operate for long periods away from their bases. In other words, the Japanese war leader believed that if we had continued to fight an island-hopping war, and if the Japanese merchant marine had been able to keep the sea, and if Mitscher's carriers had clung to their bases instead of roving all over the Pacific to shoot down planes, sink ships and beat up airfields, the Japanese strategy of contesting every island to the last man, and falling back to a shorter and stronger perimeter, would have wearied the American people of the war and obtained for Japan a negotiated peace. Be that as it may, the leapfrogging strategy was vital to Allied success in the Pacific.

There was nothing new about leapfrogging, by-passing or, as both General MacArthur and Admiral Wilkinson called it in baseball phraseology, "Hitting 'em where they ain't." [2] President Roosevelt and Admirals King and Nimitz recommended it in January 1943. A Naval War College staff study of about 1940 proposed that in case of war with Japan the Navy by-pass the Marshall Islands and concentrate on taking Truk. Rear Admiral Wilkinson, a student of naval strategy, had long been eager to take advantage of Pacific topography, by-pass the strongest Japanese garrisons, seal them off by air and sea and leave them to "wither on the vine." So were the top strategists of General MacArthur's staff.[3] Captain Thurber of Halsey's staff advocated the by-passing of Munda early in 1943 but, as we have seen, had to give it up for several cogent reasons. American forces in the Pacific were like a football team well practised in forward passes but unable to get one away because of an opponent's too powerful line.

The first demonstration of leapfrogging came about inadvertently in the Aleutians. Admiral Nimitz had planned to recapture Attu and Kiska simultaneously; but as he had insufficient forces for

---

[2] Baseball player "Wee Willie" Keeler's explanation for his high batting average in spite of his small stature. He hit .393 for the Baltimore Orioles during 1894–98. Keeler meant that he hit the ball into a part of the field where there were no opposing players, thus increasing his chances of a safe hit.

[3] MacArthur's command also "leapfrogged" at the first opportunity; the first instance was the landing at Lae 5 Sept. 1943, by-passing Salamaua.

more than one at a time, he first concentrated on the more important Attu. And, before he was ready to take Kiska, the enemy, rightly regarding that island as an expensive liability, secretly evacuated it.[4] Nimitz on 11 July 1943 suggested to Halsey that Kolombangara be given the Kiska treatment — land troops on Vella Lavella to the northwest and leave alone the island with the long name. Four days later, Wilkinson relieved Turner as Commander III 'Phib. Neither he nor Halsey's staff needed any further suggestion; a plan was promptly drafted to place Vila airfield under the fire of American artillery, to sever the enemy's supply lines to Kolombangara by air and surface power, and to seize the lightly held Vella Lavella for a fighter-plane base.

Neither side had as yet given much heed to Vella Lavella. The Japanese, possessing Munda and Vila 40 miles to the southeast and Ballale 60 miles to the northwest, saw no reason to secure a mountainous, jungle-covered island with no good harbor. They used it only as a barge stop en route to Kolombangara and New Georgia. The Americans ignored it because no Japanese were there. Survivors from U.S.S. *Helena,* as we have seen, lived unmolested on Vella Lavella for ten days; Japanese survivors of the Battle of Vella Gulf wandered across the island without meeting friend or foe. The 2000 natives concentrated at Mundi Mundi plantation and Biloa Mission had yet to feel the impact of modern war. But with the New Georgia invasion Vella Lavella began to interest staff planners on both sides. Fortunately, the American scheme to take it matured before the Japanese could transform it into another strong point to protect Bougainville.

Admiral Wilkinson needed fresh intelligence of this new objective so badly that on 21 July he sent up from Rendova a motor torpedo boat carrying a mixed Army, Navy and Marine Corps reconnaissance party. That night the scouts transferred to native canoes off the southeast coast of Vella Lavella and were paddled ashore. Accompanied by a missionary, a New Zealand coastwatcher and native guides, the men explored the island for six days without

---

[1] The Aleutians campaign will be covered in Volume VII of this History.

meeting a single Japanese, although they did pick up the crew of a wrecked Catalina; and on the 28th they made a safe return by PT. Acting on their recommendation, Admiral Wilkinson designated Barakoma, a shallow bay on the eastern foot of the island, as the invasion target. With Halsey's and Harmon's approval, he issued a plan calling for a landing on 15 August and the use of fast, handy APDs as transports. This small expeditionary force was organized as follows: —

### III AMPHIBIOUS FORCE
Rear Admiral Theodore S. Wilkinson in *Cony*

ADVANCE TRANSPORT GROUP, Captain Thomas J. Ryan

Transdiv 12, Cdr. John D. Sweeney

| | |
|---|---|
| STRINGHAM | Lt. Cdr. Ralph H. Moreau |
| WATERS | Lt. Cdr. Charles J. McWhinnie |
| DENT | Lt. Cdr. Ralph A. Wilhelm |
| TALBOT | Lt. Cdr. Charles C. Morgan |

Transdiv 22, Lt. Cdr. Robert H. Wilkinson

| | |
|---|---|
| KILTY | Lt. John W. Coolidge |
| WARD | Lt. Cdr. Frederick W. Lemly |
| MCKEAN | Lt. Cdr. Ralph L. Ramey |

Destroyer Screen, Captain Ryan (Comdesdiv 41)

| | |
|---|---|
| NICHOLAS | Lt. Cdr. Andrew J. Hill |
| O'BANNON | Lt. Cdr. Donald J. MacDonald |
| TAYLOR | Lt. Cdr. Benjamin Katz |
| CHEVALIER | Lt. Cdr. George R. Wilson |
| CONY | Cdr. Harry D. Johnston |
| PRINGLE | Cdr. Harold O. Larson |

SECOND TRANSPORT GROUP, Captain William R. Cooke
LCI Unit, Cdr. James M. Smith

LCIs *61, 23, 67, 68, 332, 334, 222, 330, 331, 333, 21, 22*

Destroyer Screen, Captain Cooke (Comdesdiv 43)

| | |
|---|---|
| WALLER | Cdr. Laurence H. Frost |
| SAUFLEY | Cdr. Bert F. Brown |
| PHILIP | Lt. Cdr. William H. Groverman |
| RENSHAW | Lt. Cdr. Jacob A. Lark |

THIRD TRANSPORT GROUP, Captain Grayson B. Carter

| | |
|---|---|
| LST-*354* | Lt. Bertram W. Robb USNR |
| LST-*395* | Lt. Alexander C. Forbes USNR |
| LST-*399* | Lt. (jg) Joseph M. Fabre USNR |

Screen, Commander James R. Pahl (Comdesdiv 44)
CONWAY                  Cdr. Nathaniel S. Prime
EATON                   Cdr. Edward L. Beck
SC-760, SC-761

LANDING FORCE, Brigadier General Robert B. McClure USA

35th RCT of 25th Division United States Army, 64th Field Artillery Battalion, 4th Marine Defense Battalion, 25th Cavalry Reconnaissance Troop, 58th Seabees, Naval Base Group, and various small units. Total, about 4600 officers and men.

The move to Vella Lavella tied in so closely with the drubbings that Airsols bombers were handing the enemy air bases anyway, that in the week before the landings Comairsols was able to step up his air effort without arousing enemy suspicion. But the increase in American radio traffic and the press of shipping around the lower Solomons inspired the Japanese to try an air raid on Guadalcanal. In this attack on 13 August transport *John Penn* was sunk, but the assembled invasion force was untouched. Admiral Koga's Combined Fleet traveled down to Truk from the Inland Sea in early August and all ships and planes of the Eighth Fleet were warned of an impending blow.

On the night of 12–13 August four American PTs sped up to Barakoma with a scouting party of 45 men to mark the beaches and select bivouacs. A "Pete" plane bombed and strafed them en route for almost two hours, planting a near-miss astern *PT-168* (Ensign William F. Griffin) which riddled the boat with shrapnel and wounded four men. The other three boats continued and landed their scouts, who ascertained that several score Japanese sailors, survivors of the Battle of Vella Gulf, were still at large, armed with clubs, grenades and nondescript firearms. So at daylight on the 14th four more PTs sailed into Barakoma with reinforcements.

Incredible as it seemed, the American objective was still secret. The Japanese on Vella Lavella either did not or could not sound a warning; snooping float planes never thought of the PTs as invasion craft. Wilkinson stole a 200-mile march on the enemy. His slowest wave, the LSTs, left Guadalcanal before dawn 14 August, followed by the faster LCIs in the forenoon and the speedy APDs in late afternoon, so that their order would later be inverted. All that day these nice targets sailed within striking range of enemy planes. taking the southern route via Blanche Channel and Gizo Strait. Finally, just before dawn 15 August, they were sighted by a Japanese plane. By daybreak the destroyer-transports were already sending boats ashore with no opposition in sight.

Admiral Wilkinson took a ringside seat in destroyer *Cony* while the landing craft chugged importantly from ship to shore, waggling white bustles of foam. Overhead P-40s darted in nervous flocks, tiny specks against a blue dome. In destroyer sonar rooms the questioning *ping-ping* got no echoes. Radar antennas revolved leisurely like vertical bedsprings, pausing as operators checked suspicious blips on the screen. At 0645 August 15 the destroyer-transports secured boat falls, hoisted cargo nets and hauled clear. First landing was completed.

Now the twelve LCIs, looking like a formation of surfaced submarines, advance to the beach and run into trouble. The narrow strand can accommodate but eight of them. Even with landing craft helping, that means delay. At 0741 a tardy strike of six "Vals" and 48 "Zekes" appears on radar screens. Seventeen minutes later, Airsols fighters mingle with the "Zekes" almost directly over the formation. The bombers circle eastward into the sun's rays, draw beads on the screening destroyers and plunge downward. Destroyer gunners cannot see them against the low sun, and all six get through. Three bombs drench *Cony* with water and spent shrapnel; others near-miss *Philip* and *LST-395*. Corsairs of VMF-123 and VMF-124 tear after retiring planes and splash three "Vals" and a half-dozen defending "Zekes"; the P-39s take care of others. Japanese aviators who get back to Kahili report that they have "repulsed fifty aircraft," and Admiral Kusaka prepares to exploit this "victory" with additional bombing raids.

At 0915 the LCIs back away and head south, escorted by six destroyers. Now Captain "Chick" Carter's LSTs of the third wave close the beach while their escort, destroyers *Conway* and *Eaton*, maneuvers off shore and two subchasers patrol the entrance to Gizo

Strait. Coral at the water's edge prevents the LSTs from making dry-ramp landings but their skippers are prepared for this. Bull-dozers wade ashore first and throw up piles of sand to support the ramps. As usual, the combat troops find stevedoring distasteful and unload so slowly that Carter doubts he will be able to finish before dark.

Shortly after noon, destroyers' radar registers bogey indications to the north and fighters intercept eleven dive-bombers and 48 "Zekes." On board the beached transports, sailors remember un-easily a recent boast by Tokyo Rose that no LST will be allowed to land its cargo. She may have known that the Navy Department had allotted only seven machine guns to each LST, but she did not know that, by begging and borrowing, the "Love-Sugar-Tares" had tripled their fighting equipment for this occasion and had trained their black gangs to boil up from below to double as gunners. When eight "Vals" pop up over the western mountains, LST bullets bring down three and ruin the aim of others. Two more, striking at *Conway*, are splashed; the others miss. Seven strafers then hedge-hop the hills and swarm over the landing beach, where LST and destroyer gunfire drives them off with two or three more losses.

Unloading continued during the afternoon of 15 August under a sky so clear that Venus could be seen with the naked eye. The enemy did not attack again until 1724, when eight planes got through for an ineffective try. Withdrawing to Kahili, they flew into eight Corsairs of VMF–214, up from the Russells on the first strafing mission ever attempted over that Bougainville airfield. The American planes had sneaked in around Choiseul and, in line abreast, skimmed the tree tops onto the field. In the words of four Marine pilots, this is what happened: —

Ovis D. Hunter: "A big black plane with a red stripe and a big meatball was just landing. He was caught in my fire and flopped over on his back."

James G. G. Taylor: "I shot down a 'Val' which was in the traffic circle. A 'Betty' on the runway with a big crowd around it came into my fire. I wiggled my tail a couple of times and really sprayed them."

DAVID W. RANKIN: "I was lined up on two gas trucks refueling two planes with a lot of Japs around and caught them all square. I almost hit the control tower."

EDWIN J. HERNAN: "I almost hit two 'Zekes' in the air. If I ever see those two pilots I'll recognize them. There was a 'Zeke' and a lot of people on the ground. I covered them plenty."

Other pilots told similar tales. They spent but a few seconds over the field and were off and away before the dumbfounded enemy was sufficiently alerted to shoot back.[5] Many a sailor in the Love-Sugar-Tares owed his life to this surprise raid of the Marines. It spoiled Japanese plans to attack them in the light of a full moon.

Only a handful of torpedo planes located the LCI group early in the evening watch. They attacked singly for an hour but were thwarted by rapid maneuver and repelling gunfire. "Pete" seaplanes found the LSTs at 2034 and worried them with bombs and flares until nearly midnight, guided by an assortment of dancing red, green and white float-lights. *Conway* and *Eaton* foxed every "Pete" with intermittent smoke screens and fired whenever the radar screen showed one to be within range. Not a single American ship was damaged and only two of their protecting planes were lost. *Conway's* skipper attributed her escape to "a perfectly phenomenal supply of good luck"; but besides luck there was a sound plan, fine shooting, well-laid smoke screens, smart ship handling, and plenty of plain courage.

The Japanese pilots made up in talk for their lack of performance, claiming the sinking of four large transports, a cruiser and a destroyer, damage to four more large transports and destruction of 29 planes. They admitted the loss of 17 planes; we claimed 44 shot down.

This story of our first day at Vella Lavella has been told in detail because it established a pattern for the future. In days that followed, the Vella Lavella run became an American version of the

[5] Action Report 13th Fighter Command 15 Aug. 1943.

old Tokyo Express, except that with 9-knot LSTs it was more like slow freight. Just as at Guadalcanal in 1942 Japanese ships had sailed in under the shadow of planes from Henderson Field, so now American ships ventured within a few minutes' flight of Ballale, Kahili and the Shortlands seaplane base.

## 2. *Securing the Island, August–September*

Brigadier General McClure's first task after landing on Vella Lavella on 15 August was to establish a base insulated from the rest of the island by a defensive perimeter. It looked easy. He had met no opposition except from Japanese planes, which had killed 12 and wounded 50 of his men on the beach; he commanded 4600 troops, each carrying three units of fire. Succeeding supply echelons would swell the ranks and Seabees would toil on roads, underground shelters, airstrip and LST ramp. Meanwhile, all Allied forces in the Solomons would remain alert to the possibility of an enemy counter-landing.

No such event occurred. Imperial Headquarters on 13 August forbade any further drain of the Emperor's troops down the Slot. Soldiers already in the Solomons were ordered to fight holding actions as long as possible and then withdraw by barge or destroyer-transport. Commanders Southeast Area Fleet and Army must continue strengthening the defensive posts around Rabaul, especially in Bougainville. Thus, when word of the Barakoma landing reached Rabaul, Admiral Kusaka and General Imamura regarded Vella Lavella not as an island to be won back but as a mere nuisance to the evacuation route from Kolombangara. The Army ruled out a one-brigade counter-landing against McClure as akin to "pouring water on a hot stone," and any force larger than a brigade would be too much for naval transportation to take care of. So the commanders at Rabaul decided to establish and defend a barge-staging point at Horaniu on the northeast shoulder of Vella Lavella.

That they did quickly. Two Army companies and a Navy platoon embarked near Buin on the morning of 17 August in 13 barges and three motor torpedo boats, protected by a light screen.[6] In addition, Rear Admiral Matsuji Ijuin steamed down from Rabaul with destroyers *Sazanami, Hamakaze, Shigure* and *Isokaze* to fend off surface interference. In the early afternoon an American air scout tipped off Admiral Wilkinson to what was going on. "Ping" promptly ordered his screen commander, Captain Thomas J. Ryan, to intercept with *Nicholas, O'Bannon, Taylor* and *Chevalier*, which had returned to Purvis Bay after covering the landing. They shoved off at 1527 August 17 for a 32-knot race up the Slot. When they were north of Kolombangara, half an hour before midnight, lookouts reported flak bursts in the sky ahead.

Ryan's lookouts were right. Eight Airsols Avengers dropping bombs at the enemy destroyers had provoked a spirited gunfire response, but neither side scored. The American planes informed Ryan that the enemy flotilla was still steaming toward Vella Lavella. In the meantime a "Pete," aided by the unclouded light of a full moon reflected on the calm waters, discovered Ryan and circled to attack. And at 0029 August 18, Ijuin's ships registered on Ryan's radarscopes, bearing 313°, distant 11½ miles. A few minutes later the barge group to the west of the destroyers also registered.

While "Pete" loosed bombs and flares over Ryan, his destroyers made flank speed toward the barges. Radar showed Ijuin's destroyers on the starboard bow, on a course almost parallel to his. At 0050 a 30-degree right turn put the barges dead ahead. Ryan, following Moosbrugger's successful precedent, held fire, came another 30 degrees right, and concentrated on catching the destroyers unawares. At 0056 he signaled "Emergency 6 Turn" (60 degrees to port) and his destroyers swung back into column headed toward Ijuin's, now five miles north of west. Simultaneously, Japanese salvos whistled overhead.

[6] Transport unit: 3 PT, 13 *Daihatsus*. Close screen: 1 PT, 2 SC, 2 armed *Daihatsus*, 1 armored boat.

Admiral Ijuin had broken formation when dodging the Avengers' bombs. At 0035, when he sighted the Americans over 9 miles distant, SE by E, Ijuin ordered long-range torpedo fire, held his westerly course and told *Shigure* and *Isokaze* to fall in behind *Sazanami* and *Hamakaze* in battle column. *Shigure* at 0045 got off

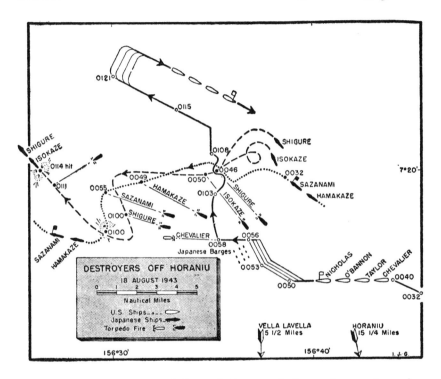

the first torpedo salvo, followed four and five minutes later by *Hamakaze* and *Isokaze*, and at 0055 by *Sazanami;* one minute later the Japanese opened gunfire at ranges between 12,000 and 17,000 yards. Thirty-one torpedoes had been fired, but the torpedomen's solutions were upset by Ryan's maneuvers to avoid the barges and bring his short-winded torpedoes within range. The few fish that reached the Americans were evaded by smart ship handling.

The relative positions of the opponents when gunfire opened at 0056 provided the enemy with a tactical advantage. Since Ryan's ships were in column on course West, Ijuin easily capped his "T" by coming to course South. And a bright full moon behind the Americans silhouetted them nicely. But neither advantage paid off. Initial Japanese salvos fell a quarter-mile over, and later became worse. After Ryan had erased the "T" by an 80-degree column right, at 0058, his three leading ships doled out 5-inch shells at ranges of four to six miles, and at 0100 drew first blood with a hit on *Hamakaze* which set that veteran destroyer badly afire. *Chevalier*, awaiting opportunity to shoot torpedoes, found an opening when *Shigure* cut sharply toward the American formation; she launched a four-torpedo spread at 0058 at a range of 9000 yards. But *Chevalier's* warheads had no chance to connect with a hull. At the very moment of launching, Admiral Ijuin retired from the fray — much to the disgust of Captain Ryan, who was just about to expend the rest of his torpedoes.

Gunfire petered out at 0103 as the fast-legged Japanese opened range. Ryan, wary of enemy torpedoes, zigzagged northward until 0111, when he came left to parallel Ijuin on a northwesterly heading. *Isokaze* then tried an 8-mile torpedo salvo. None scored, but American gunners landed a nice 5-inch shell on her. A cranky feed pump in *Chevalier* limited Ryan's top speed to 30 knots, and no hope remained of catching the 35-knot Nips. So Ryan grudgingly gave up the chase, looped back and overtook the small fry.

The barge skippers, every man for himself, had dispersed during the destroyer battle, and most of them escaped. Ryan did destroy two subchasers, two motor torpedo boats and one *Daihatsu*. He spent the last hour of the midwatch fending off "Pete" and vainly searching the Gulf for barges; then he returned to Tulagi.

The Japanese barges spent all that day, 18 August, hiding out on the north coast of Vella Lavella. Proceeding on the 19th, they found Horaniu and landed 390 men who, within a week, established a barge base.

Ijuin returned to Rabaul with a report that he had sunk one enemy ship and that his fighting strength was unimpaired — *Hamakaze* and *Isokaze* had sustained only minor damage. Why then had he run? Simply because men and barges could be replaced, while the Imperial Navy could not risk further depletion of its destroyer strength. Forty had been lost during the previous fourteen months; Japanese shipyards were unable to replace them.

The second American echelon for Barakoma, commanded by Captain William R. Cooke,[7] had arrived at 1625 August 17, planning to unload that night. When fighter-plane cover withdrew at dusk, a trio of "Vals" dropped bombs close aboard the LSTs, showering them with coral dust. General McClure decided to order the ships out to sea for the night. Enemy planes trailed and attacked them through anti-aircraft fire and destroyer smoke screens. Destroyer *Waller* sideswiped *Philip* while maneuvering radically at high speed, laying a smoke screen and engaging a "bandit." *Waller* had to return to Tulagi for repairs. Two hours later a gasoline vapor explosion in *LST-396* set off a fatal fire; the crew abandoned ship before a series of explosions tore the hull apart. At daybreak the remaining LSTs beached at Barakoma and continued unloading in spite of two more bombing attacks, one of which shoved *LST-339* bodily forward onto the beach. She was unable to retract until destroyers steaming at high speed close aboard had kicked up enough wash to refloat her. On the return trip, bogies stayed on the screen until 0200 August 19, when the men secured from a 36-hour session at general quarters.

The third echelon, second trip of Captain "Chick" Carter's LSTs, sailed for Vella Lavella on 20 August and in Gizo Strait ran into a dawn welcome from Kusaka's fliers in the shape of torpedoes, bombs and strafing bullets. All torpedoes missed; but destroyer *Pringle* suffered 27 casualties from a near-miss and strafing.[8] The LSTs calmly beached and commenced unloading.

[7] Composition: — transport unit (Lt. Cdr. Roy W. Lajeunesse), *LST-339, LST-396, LST-460*; screen, *Waller, Saufley, Philip, SC-1266*; landing force (Maj. Frank G. Umstead USMC), detachments from 35th RCT, 4th Marine Def. Bn. and 58th Seabees.

[8] Lt. Harvey F. Kruesburg USNR, the ship's doctor, ignoring his own painful wounds, saved the lives of several wounded while James F. Sigel, Chief Torpedoman, and Harold L. Still, Gunner's Mate, pawed through the 40-mm magazine until they came upon and jettisoned a burning ammunition case set afire by enemy bullets.

This time the destroyers retired to Rendova for the day. When a flight of "Vals," briefed to attack them, arrived at Barakoma in midmorning, they flew in bewildered circles, disregarded the LSTs and finally dumped bombs without effect over *SC-505*. Kusaka then sent down a score of planes to get the LSTs. Easier said than done! The big beaching craft had even more guns than a week earlier, and soldiers of the 35th Regimental Combat Team on board manned their own guns as well. Many of the "Vals" and "Kates" refused to enter the tracer-filled air over the LSTs, and the few who did so were punished; at least four were shot down and others crippled. Several bombs that landed on the beach and in the shallow water alongside the LSTs flung huge coral boulders onto their decks. This unusual rock bombardment knocked down all hands topside *LST-354* and put her guns out of action. While sailors and soldiers were still wondering what hit them, the 58th Seabees, described as "grayheaded veterans of the last war," marched on board, repaired the guns, cared for the wounded and resumed unloading. *LST-395* was lifted bodily by an explosion and *LST-398* caught fire, but her crew quenched it. All three withdrew on schedule, and for once "Pete" allowed them a peaceful return passage. Captain Carter justifiably glowed with pride over his homely craft and added praise for the Army and Seabee shore parties.

As the weather improved and the moon waned, succeeding echelons had less trouble. Fighter cover stayed overhead during daylight and dark nights foiled the enemy scouts. There were no more casualties.

In the fortnight following the invasion, Wilkinson's III 'Phib had delivered 6305 men and 8626 tons of cargo at Vella Lavella, had fought off planes in scores of battles, lost but one beaching craft, and proved that Tokyo Rose was not always a good prophet.

The Americans slowly pushed up both the east and the west coasts of the island. A skirmish on 4 September netted a dozen enemy dead, together with the defense plan for Horaniu and points north. As the Japanese scrupulously followed this plan, it was easy to counter, and American heavy artillery backing the infantry forced the enemy to the last pages of his plan sooner than he had expected. His barge depot at Horaniu fell on 14 September and the garrison retreated northwestward. On the 18th, Major General H. E. Barrowclough of the New Zealand Army brought in a part of his 3rd Division and relieved the American troops. Two New Zealand combat teams continued the amphibious pincer movement up both coasts and by 1 October cornered the enemy, still about 600 strong, on the northwest shore. And there he stayed for another week, when the effort to evacuate him brought about the most important naval battle between those of Vella Gulf and Empress Augusta Bay — the Battle of Vella Lavella.

## 3. The Blockade of Kolombangara, 25 August–3 October

The vault to Vella Lavella proved to be a poor example of leap-frog strategy, as compared with many later operations, because our sea power was still incapable of isolating Kolombangara. In the narrow seas of the Central Solomons, even nearer to Japanese bases up the Slot than Ironbottom Sound had been in 1942, control shifted every dawn and dusk. The Allies were improving their technique of night fighting by air and sea, but never could put a stop to the Tokyo Express runs of destroyers or to the *Daihatsu* barge line. Their utmost efforts to blockade Kolombangara never succeeded in sealing it off completely. The Japanese concentrated on withdrawing their garrison by late September, and most of it got out. In preparation they began hauling down the Rising Sun from outlying points: the seaplane base at Rekata Bay, Santa Isabel, at Gizo and Ganongga; only men enough to operate and protect barge depots were left on Choiseul.

This contraction allowed the Americans to concentrate their attention on Kolombangara. Airsols planes bombed Vila both by day and by night, strafed barges in daylight and intercepted them in darkness, besides maintaining pressure on Kahili, Ballale and the Shortlands. The enemy seldom accepted battle over his own airfields, Kahili and Ballale, which caught it so often that work was started on a second airfield at Kara, inland in southern Bougainville. But the Americans completed a new airstrip at Barakoma on

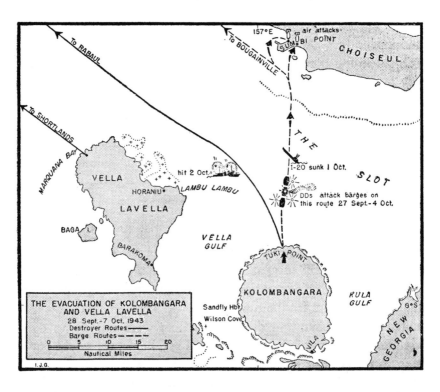

24 September. Allied fighter planes turned their guns on barges, getting a number of *Daihatsus;* on one day the Corsairs knocked off nine. Light and heavy bombers entered the game, seeking out barge hideaways and occasionally catching the craft at sea. Tokyo Express kept out of range during the early days of the blockade and suffered only a few near-misses. Allied bombers and heavy artillery based on New Georgia chiseled away at Kolombangara. Enemy air retaliation in the form of sporadic bombing of Barakoma, Munda, the Russells, Guadalcanal and Espiritu Santo pro-

vided more sport than it did damage. A long-range raid on Espiritu Santo scored only on a cow. Ships and air transport planes operating between the Solomons and the New Hebrides underwent a few bombing and strafing attacks but were never hit. We were getting on with the war, but the Slot was not yet suitable for moonlight picnics.

After the American capture of Horaniu, Japanese barges plying between Kolombangara and Bougainville had no alternative but to stage through Choiseul. Commencing 20 September the enemy dispatched over a hundred *Daihatsu* from Bougainville, due to reach the big round island on the moonless night of the 28th. Eleven destroyers were ordered to screen and help the transport job. The Vila garrison headed by foot and canoe for Tuki Point on Kolombangara's north shore.

Admiral Wilkinson guessed correctly that the enemy would attempt withdrawal during the dark of the moon. Beginning 22 September he sent Admiral Merrill nightly to inspect the Slot north of Vella Lavella with two cruisers and four destroyers, strengthened by a second cruiser group as the moon waned. Nothing happened until the night of 25–26 September when Japanese submarine torpedoes narrowly missed *Columbia*. With snoopy "Pete" broadcasting ship positions to submarines in the Slot, Wilkinson decided no longer to risk cruisers in those waters, but on the night of 27–28 September he sent Captain M. J. Gillan in command of destroyers *Ausburne, Claxton, Dyson, Spence* and *Foote* to patrol points designated "Hellsfire" and "Brimstone" astride the barge route. Barges cluttered the Slot but "Pete" belled the stalking destroyers with flares and floatlights so successfully that they got only four of them. And the following night, 28–29 September, there was a big movement north. Two torpedo boats and a PT, escorting eleven barges, took 1691 men to Sumbi Point, while four APDs escorted by no fewer than nine destroyers picked up 2115 sick and wounded at Tuki Point and rushed them all the way to Rabaul. Nobody was there that night to intercept them, but on the third night, 29–30 September, Captain Frank R. Walker was on hand with destroyers *Patterson, Foote, Ralph Talbot* and *McCalla*. They sank a few barges and exchanged long-range salvos with a group of enemy destroyers.

Two destroyer groups, Captain William D. Cooke's *Waller, Eaton* and *Cony* and Commander A. D. Chandler's *Radford, Saufley* and *Grayson*, operating independently on 1–2 October, found more targets than they could handle. Submarine *I-20*, which had joined the evacuation fleet, was caught on the surface by *Eaton* (Commander Edward L. Beck). Close-range gunfire disposed of the boat; under the glare of star shell she was seen to roll belly-up like a dead fish. Shortly after, a Black Cat reported to Cooke and Chandler that four enemy destroyers were operating to the north-west. The Americans, leaving waters full of floating bodies and sinking barges, hastened to the spot; the enemy refused surface combat. His float planes, however, braved soupy weather and flak to plant bombs close aboard *Saufley*, killing two men and wounding 18. On the following night (2–3 October), Captain Cooke's group was out again, with Commander Harold O. Larson's *Ralph Talbot, Taylor* and *Terry*. They had a long-range brush with four destroyers evacuating troops from Kolombangara and holed *Samidare* thrice above the waterline, but she and her consorts hauled clear after firing torpedoes. Cooke and Larson then broke up a barge, motorboat and canoe flotilla. *Terry* (Commander George R. Phelan), a new ship, inaugurated 40-mm machine-gun fire by radar control through the 5-inch director.

On the night of 3–4 October it was Commander Chandler's turn again, but his pickings were small because the enemy's evacuation of Kolombangara was finished. In five days Japanese barges had retrieved 5400 men and destroyers another four thousand, including General Sasaki. The utmost efforts of the Americans had succeeded in destroying only one third of the barge fleet and less than a thousand men. Japanese evacuation technique still had the United States Navy stymied. Admirals Halsey and Merrill at the time were well satisfied with their destroyers, but they did not know the score. We could hardly have dispensed with destroyers, since the enemy had them; but our "cans" should have done better since they had radar, and the Japanese, who moreover were tied to a definite evacuation route, had none.[9] The use of PTs stationed hard by Tuki Point might have worked better, and Airsols might have imitated the enemy float planes. Unfortunately the memory of tragic identification errors prevented use of planes, PTs and destroyers within gun range of one another.

Kolombangara – King of the Waters – belonged again to the Allies. But the evacuees lived to fight again.

## 4. *The Battle of Vella Lavella, 6–7 October* [10]

Retreat from Kolombangara left Japanese troops on only two islands in the Central Solomons: Choiseul and Vella Lavella. There was no hurry about evacuating Choiseul, but the advance of New Zealand troops on Vella Lavella required an immediate decision, either to leave the garrison to its fate or to risk ships in an evacuation effort. Since fewer than 600 men were involved, nobody would have been surprised if the easy alternative had been chosen. But the Japanese high command wished to keep up its pretense of a "voluntary" withdrawal after "pinning down" or "annihilating" the enemy, as it claimed to have done at Guadalcanal, New Georgia and Kolombangara; so it was decided to get the garrison out. Admiral Ijuin marshaled nine destroyers and a dozen small craft to extricate his Vella Lavella waifs on the night of 6–7 October, and organized them as follows: —

[9] Cdr. Halford Knoertzer, at that time C.O. of *McCalla*, tells us that the ineffectiveness of DD fire against barges was due to the AA fuzes on the 40-mm shells, which were so sensitive that they exploded upon impact, while the barges were too lively to be hit by 5-inch shells.

[10] "Naval Battle of Vella Lavella" (ATIS Doc. No. 15685) with track chart furnished Lt. Cdr. Salomon in Tokyo 1946; "Southeast Area Operations" Part 2 (Navy) and documents mentioned in note 1 to this chapter. James D. Horan *Action Tonight*, is a lively biography of *O'Bannon's* first year in the South Pacific.

## VELLA LAVELLA EVACUATION FORCE
Rear Admiral Matsuji Ijuin

SUPPORT GROUP, Rear Admiral Ijuin
AKIGUMO, ISOKAZE, KAZAGUMO, *YUGUMO, SHIGURE, SAMIDARE
DESTROYER TRANSPORT GROUP, Captain Yuzo Kanaoka
FUMIZUKI, MATSUKAZE, YUNAGI
SUBCHASER-TRANSPORT GROUP, Captain Shigoroku Nakayama
4 SC, 4 PT, 4 landing craft

Cautious Ijuin shoved off from Rabaul with the destroyers early
on the 6th, ignoring Airsols snoopers as he sailed along the outer
coast of Bougainville. Before nightfall he entered the Slot. At 1814
he detached *Shigure, Samidare* and the APDs to push on ahead to
the evacuation point at Marquana Bay on northwest Vella Lavella.
They overtook and passed the subchasers, which had left Buin at
1653.

Three of Captain Walker's destroyers patrolled the Slot on the
night of 5–6 October, retiring to the Choiseul coast during daylight. When on the afternoon of 6 October search planes reported
Ijuin's progress, Admiral Wilkinson found himself at a loss, since
all his destroyers except Walker's three were already committed
to convoy duty. However, he directed Walker to steam up the
Slot to a point 10 miles off northwestern Vella Lavella, and detached three of Captain Larson's destroyers from a convoy south
of New Georgia to join him by running full speed south of
Ganongga and thence west of Vella Lavella.

Thus, by 1900 October 6 these six destroyers were converging
toward Marquana Bay: —

Northern Group, Captain Frank R. Walker
SELFRIDGE        Lt. Cdr. George E. Peckham
*CHEVALIER       Lt. Cdr. George R. Wilson
O'BANNON         Lt. Cdr. Donald J. MacDonald

Southern Group, Captain Harold O. Larson
RALPH TALBOT     Lt. Cdr. Richard D. Shepard
TAYLOR           Lt. Cdr. Benjamin Katz
LAVALLETTE       Lt. Cdr. Robert L. Taylor

After sunset Walker's ships enjoyed the sight of friendly planes streaming down the Slot from a strike on Kahili, running lights aglow and navigational flares dropping. When the first bogeys appeared on his radar screens around 1940, Walker slipped into a rain squall and altered course and speed; but everywhere that Walker went, "Pete" was sure to go, supplementing the light of a first-quarter moon with flares and floatlights.

Wilkinson had warned Walker that Ijuin's strength was at least nine destroyers, and predicted that he would beat Larson to the rendezvous. Walker knew that "Pete" had deprived him of the sailorman's favorite advantage, surprise. He might have slowed down to wait for Larson but he chose the bolder course of pushing ahead to engage the enemy with gunfire at long range, hoping to toll him southward into Larson's arms.

Five bells struck in the evening watch. Walker could see down *Selfridge's* wake 500 yards to *Chevalier's* bow wave, and the loom of *O'Bannon* another 500 yards astern. He called Larson's group on the voice radio; no answer, as expected. So be it — three ships against nine. He followed the curve of Vella Lavella's northwest coast and at 2230 was steering course 210° toward the rendezvous. Marquana Bay bore SSE distant 10 miles. At 2231 TBS rasped. Two surface contacts 10 miles west — two groups swinging from an easterly to a westerly heading. Was Ijuin following his habit of fleeing, even when lightly opposed? Walker would soon find out. He eased his column right, toward the contacts. At 2236 the compass read 300°. Speed built up to 30 knots.

Walker's approach had actually caused the weaker portion of the Japanese force, Captain Kanaoka's destroyer-transports, to retire. As early as 2058, having seen Walker's three ships silhouetted by aircraft flares and having heard the snooper report them as a cruiser and four destroyers, the Kanaoka group had reversed course and headed for home; but their escort, *Shigure* and *Samidare*, joined the Admiral. And what both moon and radar saw at 2231 was these two groups of four and two destroyers, respectively, just before their rendezvous.

This time Ijuin intended to fight, as his superiors expected him to do.[11] Four minutes after the first American radar contact, Japanese lookouts sighted Walker's three destroyers bearing ESE distant 19,500 yards. Their location puzzled the Admiral. Could they be his subchaser-transport group, en route to Vella Lavella? He continued west until 2238, then swerved southward. If the unknown ships were American, he figured, they would follow him away from Marquana Bay, when he could "annihilate them at an opportune moment." *Samidare* and *Shigure*, which had not yet joined Ijuin, shaped a course roughly parallel to his. The subchaser-transports stolidly chugged along toward Marquana Bay.

In the American group, the minutes following contact were busy indeed. On board *O'Bannon*, especially, bluejackets who had seen one ship go after another wondered if their ship's luck would still hold out, because tomorrow would mark a full year since she had entered the South Pacific. Two brothers asked to be put side by side in the same fireroom. Others whispered to shipmates what to tell wife or sweetheart, just in case. Routine pre-battle checking of torpedoes, guns and engines was done. Lieutenant Carl F. Pfeifer was busy sorting and evaluating radar evidence in the combat information center. And, as in the days of sail the "chirurgeon" laid out knives and saws in the "cockpit" aft and below, so here Lieutenant Robert C. Manchester USNR spread his modern surgical instruments on the wardroom tables.

At the head of the little column Lieutenant Commander Peckham, who had taken command just four days before, conned *Selfridge* toward the foe according to Captain Walker's directions from C.I.C. At 2240½, course 280°; at 2247, column left to course 240°. A radioman tapped out a message to Admiral Wilkinson at Guadalcanal, "Eight enemy destroyers sighted." Another pled over voice radio to "Gay" (Larson's group), "Hello! Gay from Toby" (Walker). "Come in *any one* in Gay's group. Come

---

[11] He was a son of the famous Fleet Admiral Ijuin, Vice Chief of the Naval General Staff in the Russo-Japanese War, C. in C. Combined Fleet after Togo and founder of the "no holidays" system of fleet training — see Vol. III p. 24.

in *please!*" No answer; Larson's ships were 20 miles to the south, beyond TBS range.

*Selfridge's* radar plotted the large enemy group on southerly courses at 33 knots, and the smaller and farther one steering southwest. At 2251 Ijuin's larger group, bearing nearly dead ahead at six miles, veered sharp left, apparently to attack. Range closed at over 40 knots. Walker grasped this chance to strike the first blow by swinging right to course West. When the enemy bore SW, distant 7000 yards, he ordered Execute William (fire torpedoes). Fourteen fish swooshed overboard from the three ships. Twenty seconds later he gave Execute Dog (commence gunfire) and his fifteen 5-inchers began to talk. To keep them bearing, Walker deliberately maintained course West into enemy torpedo water.

Admiral Ijuin had missed his best opportunity. When sighting the Americans, at 2235, he should have headed southeast to cap the "T," but he meandered southward, opening range at 2248 by a simultaneous ships-right to course 207°, and four minutes later cutting left in line of bearing to course 115°. Thus when the first American salvos were ready to score, Ijuin's destroyers were staggered along the American line of fire, *Yugumo* at the close range of 3300 yards; the other three dared not fire torpedoes for fear of hitting friends. *Yugumo* further fouled the range by peeling off to charge at the enemy; at 2256 she fired eight torpedoes and opened gunfire. *Kazegumo* hurled shells over her at the American targets, but the other two destroyers continued on their course, torpedoes dormant and guns mute. *Yugumo* by reason of her nearness attracted a concentration of fire. While she rocked under the assault, Ijuin executed a ships-right into column, laid smoke and hauled his three leading ships to the south undamaged. *Yugumo* did not make it. At 2305 an American torpedo disemboweled her and presently she was drifting swathed in flame.[12]

Walker's men knew they had won the first round when they saw *Yugumo* crumple, but their exultation was brief. *Selfridge* shifted fire to *Shigure* and *Samidare*, bearing 258° distant 10,600

[12] WDC No. 160621, Tabular Records of Japanese destroyer movements.

yards, and eased right to keep her guns unmasked. *Chevalier's* captain was preparing to machine-gun some motor torpedo boats reported to starboard when at 2301 a torpedo from *Yugumo* clanged into her port bow opposite a magazine. Torpedo and magazine erupted together, tore off the bow as far aft as the bridge, blew the bridge crew into the air and slammed them, stunned, to the deck. The captain staggered to his feet and ordered Chief Signalman Crudele to warn *O'Bannon* by blinker. Crudele fainted before he could send the message. The propellers, still thrusting, threatened to submerge the ship "like a submarine." Ensign McQuilkin carried an order from the captain to the engine room, "Back Emergency Full." Seconds later came a shock as *O'Bannon* smashed into the starboard side of *Chevalier's* after engine room. The executive officer toured the ship and found her soaked in oil and littered with wounded from amidships forward. Where the wardroom had been, men struggled to haul shipmates through an emergency hatch from the interior communications room below. The two firerooms and the after engine room were taking water. But nobody would give *Chevalier* up. Skipper Wilson asked only that *O'Bannon* remove the wounded; later he would get a tow. He ordered topside weights jettisoned and among these were the remaining torpedoes, which he carefully fired at blazing *Yugumo*. Perhaps one of them hit her. At any rate, down she went.

In the first minutes of the gun battle, *O'Bannon* had galloped through a pall of her own gun smoke which dimmed skipper MacDonald's view both of the battle and of *Chevalier* ahead; the latter, swinging right uncontrollably as her engines balked, made collision unavoidable. Nobody in *O'Bannon* got hurt and she backed clear, but she was out of the chase.

Captain Walker in *Selfridge* continued full cry after *Shigure* and *Samidare*, guns baying wildly. The range was too great for American torpedoes but not for the Japanese "long lances." At 2306 a sixteen-fish spread fired five minutes earlier by *Shigure* and *Samidare* boiled viciously around *Selfridge*. She combed several wakes, but one torpedo caught her at frame 40, port side, thrust-

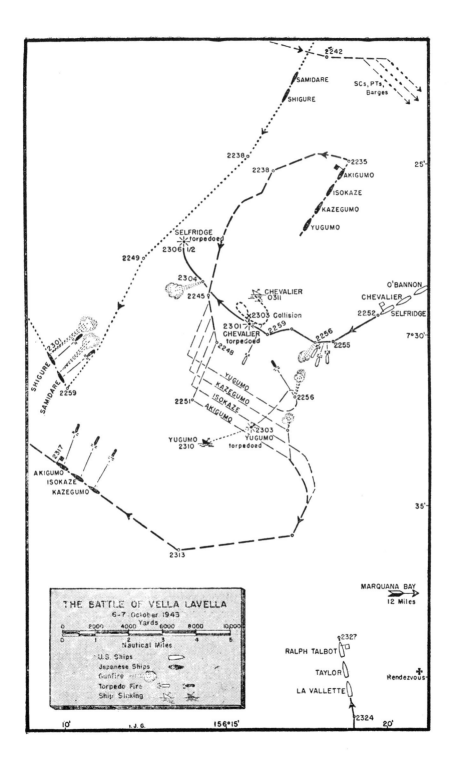

THE BATTLE OF VELLA LAVELLA
6-7 October 1943
Yards

Nautical Miles

U.S. Ships
Japanese Ships
Gunfire
Torpedo Fire
Ship Sinking

ing its explosive effort out through the narrow hull so that the crew thought they had been torpedoed from both sides at once. As usual in such cases, the forecastle became a tangled mess as far aft as the bridge, and decks below were flooded as far as the forward fireroom bulkhead. The ship shuddered and came to a stop. Fortunately no fires broke out and no magazines exploded. Walker discovered the TBS still perking, and called to Larson's group to take up the fight.

By this time snoopers had found Larson's three destroyers – the Southern Group – and reported them to Admiral Ijuin, who did not relish engaging more "cruisers." He ordered a retirement and by 2313 his destroyers were heading toward Rabaul. *Akigumo*, *Isokaze* and *Kazegumo* emptied their torpedo tubes – 24 shots – for a long and fruitless 16,000-yard run toward Walker's cripples. At 2340 Ijuin ordered the destroyer-transports waiting off Shortlands to join him in flight to Rabaul, but he did not recall the subchaser-transport group.

Larson's three destroyers missed Ijuin by a slim 15 minutes as he went snorting up the Vella Lavella coast. They had seen the flickering gunflashes tearing at the dark northern horizon, had picked up dying *Yugumo* on their radar screen and now, at 2335, had arrived in the battle waters. For half an hour they sniffed and pried from Marquana Bay to the west and north, but nought did they find save battered *Selfridge*, bruised *O'Bannon* and *Chevalier* minus a chunk of her bow. At 0020 October 7 they closed these damaged ships to help.

By this time Lieutenant Commander Wilson had to admit that *Chevalier* could not stay afloat. His crew gathered the wounded amidships and lowered an undamaged boat. Lieutenant Commander MacDonald sought to bring *O'Bannon* alongside for a deck-to-deck transfer but her warped bow resisted such delicate maneuvering. A bomb, compliments of "Pete," cracked ahead of *O'Bannon* but MacDonald ignored it and ordered two of his boats into the water to ferry wounded from *Chevalier*. Able-bodied survivors abandoned ship over the side, swimming to the boats or to

*O'Bannon,* helped by a Japanese float light. By 0125 October 7, MacDonald had recovered 250 out of the 301 in *Chevalier's* crew. Dr. Manchester treated the wounded, many of whom, including both the skipper and the "exec.," were suffering from broken bones.

*Selfridge,* with magazines and engines intact, had a better chance. Peckham backed her slowly eastward while damage-control parties shored forward bulkheads and topside crewmen jettisoned heavy weights. *Taylor* closed at 0051, took off Captain Walker and a majority of the crew. Lieutenant Commander Peckham then gingerly rang up 5 knots ahead. Bulkheads held, and he gradually increased to turns for 16 knots which gave 10 knots through the water.

American concentration on the cripples was so intense that neither eyes nor radar noted the quiet passage of Captain Nakayama's subchasers into Marquana Bay at 0110, an hour after moonset. These craft embarked the 589 waiting men and at 0305 sailed for Buin.

Four of the American destroyers departed at the same time, skirting Vella Lavella's west coast. *LaVallette* stayed behind to search for survivors on board *Chevalier* and in the water. Finding none, she fired a single torpedo from a range of one mile into *Chevalier's* after magazines. The ship went up in balls of fire and clouds of smoke so thick that they "furnished excellent cloud cover from Jap planes." *LaVallette* next inspected *Chevalier's* bow section and destroyed it with depth charges. When *LaVallette* turned to overtake her companions, the battle scene was empty except for *O'Bannon's* boats, left behind for any stray survivors. One of them was the means by which three officers and 22 men from *Yugumo* reached home. After break of day, a group of American PT boats picked up the remainder of that destroyer's survivors, 78 men. One of these struck a final blow for the Emperor by killing a sailor of *PT-163* who was giving him a cup of coffee.

At dawn the two American cripples, surrounded by Larson's trio, were still west of Vella Lavella with all hands anxiously scanning the skies. At 0717 radar picked up bogeys closing fast, but old friends saved the day. Nineteen fighter planes patrolling the upper reaches of the Slot heard the call for help and seven of them turned back 15 "Zekes." The enemy did not bother the ships again, and on 8 October they triumphantly entered Purvis Bay.

Captain Walker believed that he had sunk three destroyers and damaged several others. On the Japanese side, Admiral Ijuin claimed sinking two cruisers and three destroyers. Even as it was, Ijuin had won the Battle of Vella Lavella. His torpedoes had sunk one destroyer, damaged two others and permitted the transports to accomplish their mission, at a cost of but one of his own ships. Yet the courage displayed by Walker in taking the short end of three-to-one odds, and the tenacity with which damage control parties worked to save *Selfridge*, were admirable. And, as in the case of Kula Gulf and Kolombangara, the firm conviction of victory on the American side really nullified the actual victory of the Japanese. They knew that they were losing the last of the Central Solomons; we knew that we were winning the war, even if we lost an occasional ship.

In mid-October Lieutenant Commander MacDonald made a simple announcement to the crew of *O'Bannon:* "We are going home." That great little ship had been fighting constantly in the Solomons since the Battle of Guadalcanal eleven months earlier; her departure from those waters made a fitting end to the campaign, even to a way of warfare. The Central Solomons campaign had taken from February to July to plan and prepare, from July to October to execute. Although the Allies had extended their power 250 miles closer to Rabaul, it had cost the United States Navy six warships and had deprived the Imperial Japanese Navy of seventeen.[18] But Tokyo was still nearly 3000 miles away, and three months was too long to spend on a 250-mile advance which had scarcely touched either the Japanese Army or the Combined Fleet.

[18] U.S.N.: *Helena, Strong, Gwin, Chevalier, McCawley, John Penn;* Japanese Navy: *Jintsu, Nisshin,* 10 destroyers and 5 submarines.

Henceforth, the United States Navy would conduct the Pacific war with mass-production methods. There was plenty of bloody, desperate fighting ahead, but seldom would the issue be in doubt. Moreover, the Allies now had the strategic initiative; they would call the measure, selecting where and when to fight.

# CHAPTER XIV

# Lae and Salamaua

## 16 June–15 September 1943

East Longitude dates; Zone minus 10 time.

### 1. *Vitiaz and Dampier: the Vital Straits* [1]

D URING July and August 1943, while Halsey and Wilkinson slowly masticated the Central Solomons, MacArthur and Barbey had to be content with digesting their easily won gains in the Trobriand Islands and Nassau Bay. Nobody questioned their desire to get going on the New Guinea-Mindanao axis, but everyone wondered how they would start. Until the Bismarcks Barrier was broken, all roads must lead to Rabaul. Theoretically the most direct route would be an amphibious hop across the Solomon Sea to New Britain, there build a base, stock it with planes and make another coastwise jump, repeat until the volcanoes of Simpson Harbor are in sight; then get Halsey's help to subdue Rabaul. But any such plan required a rotation of front, so that instead of facing the Japanese on the Finschhafen Peninsula, MacArthur would expose his left flank. Since war is calculated risk, exposure of flank is often made deliberately; but in this instance enemy strength and a 50-mile expanse of sea between New Guinea and New Britain made the risk too great. Rooke Island split this body of water into Vitiaz Strait and the narrower Dampier Strait — both of which pro-

---

[1] Gen. HQ SWPac Area, Mil. Intell. Sec. Gen. Staff's Daily Summary of Enemy Intelligence; Com Seventh Fleet Op Plan 5–43 (19 Apr. 1943), Com VII Amphibious Force Op Plan 2–43 and writer's notes in New Guinea; USSBS "Employment of Forces under the Southwest Pacific Command"; *Gen. Kenney Reports;* sources mentioned in note 1 chap. ix, above. See chart in chap. ix above for places mentioned here.

vided ready access for enemy shipping to the Solomon Sea. These were the two principal entrances to the Bismarcks fish weir which must be secured before MacArthur could pass the Barrier.

The enemy realized this well enough, but New Guinea topography did not allow defense in depth and retreat from post to post, as in the Solomons. Lae and Salamaua and Finschhafen must be held and then reinforced to push back the Allies. Plans for such an offensive had already been drafted when the Allies landed at Nassau Bay on 30 June. The Japanese reacted to this small landing as if the Emperor's life were at stake. Their commander at Lae and Salamaua appealed to General Hatazo Adachi, Eighteenth Army commander at Rabaul, for more men, and set up a barge line to carry troops from New Britain to the threatened New Guinea bases.

At the same time, General MacArthur decided to take all three places. But his prerequisite for success was local air superiority. The Lae and Salamaua airstrips did not bother him; they had been of slight account since April,[2] but the New Britain and western New Guinea fields did, and Dobodura was too far from Lae and Salamaua to permit fighters based there to tangle with "Zekes" on equal terms. And the Seventh Fleet had no carriers to bring air power forward. So the General decided that new interior air bases must be built, close to the targets, and that troops and supplies must be advanced well along the coast.

Early in June an Allied reconnaissance party trekking northwest from Wau scouted a deserted gold miners' airstrip at Tsili Tsili near Marilinan, 40 miles inland from Lae. General Kenney accepted it as an advanced fighter-plane base, and on 16 June flew in troops to occupy and engineers to improve the field. By 26 July the new strip was nursing fighters. Meanwhile, a few miles to the northwest at a place called Bena Bena, natives under Allied orders scarred the landscape with a dummy strip calculated to distract the enemy from the main effort at Marilinan.

---

[2] Owing to inability to keep them supplied by sea. Capt. T. Miyazaki (senior staff officer 25th Air Flotilla, Rabaul) in *Inter. Jap. Off.* II 413.

General Sir Thomas Blamey, Allied commander of ground forces, selected two Australian divisions for a two-pronged advance against Lae. One division, seaborne, would land on 1 August to the east of the town, while the second, airborne to a point west of Lae, would strike from the opposite side. The enemy, caught in a giant vise, would be squeezed into the ocean or jungle. And by moving Australians from Wau and Americans from Nassau Bay against Salamaua, the enemy would be deceived into believing that Salamaua was the main objective. Finschhafen, 50 miles east of Lae, could be taken at leisure once Lae had fallen.

Preparations for Operation "Postern," as the Lae-Salamaua show was designated, went forward with little hindrance from the enemy, then thoroughly committed to defending Munda; but delays in receiving transport aircraft and in training troops pushed the invasion date into the first week of September. General Kenney's fliers occupied the interval by an air offensive to soften the enemy. They not only bombed Lae, Salamaua and Finschhafen but flew deep into the Japanese perimeter to maul Wewak and Madang in New Guinea.[3] At sea they hunted for barges. While so engaged on 28 July, they encountered bigger game. Destroyers *Ariake* and *Mikazuki* (the latter had escaped unhurt from the Kolombangara fight) were escorting a convoy from Rabaul to Cape Gloucester, on 27 July, when they ran on a reef close to their objective. Next day they were discovered by General Kenney's B-25s, which made sure, with skip-bombing, that they would never leave the reef.

By this time the superiority of Allied fighter planes – excepting the Spitfire [4] – over the Japanese was so marked that General Kenney went so far as to suggest to General Marshall in Washington that he supply him with "an old or a new boat fixed up with a painted wooden or other cheap deck and smokestack so that she looks like a carrier, put some dummy aircraft on deck, and let me have her." He proposed to maneuver this decoy in circles to at-

[3] Little attention was paid by the V Army Air Force to Rabaul at this time.

[4] Spitfire squadrons defending Darwin suffered serious losses from Japanese raiders, mainly because their fuel capacity was so small that when pursuing the raiders they often ran out of gas before returning to base.

tract Japanese planes, while V Air Force fighter planes, stacked high, waited to jump the attackers. Although the Navy was not consulted, presumably they would provide the suicide crews for the dummy. This scheme came to nought when General Marshall wired "Get the boats locally," for no "boats" that could be converted to mock-up carriers existed in Australia or anywhere else.

The motor torpedo boats with their forward base at Morobe took over barge hunting from the planes at sunset. A few examples will illustrate their work. On the evening of 27 July, *PT-151* and *PT-152* ambushed the Finschhafen-Lae supply line and sank four barges. Next night *PT-149* and *PT-142* in Vitiaz Strait sailed into a school of thirty barges making passage from New Britain to Finschhafen. Light signals from the barges alerted the boats, who opened up with everything they had. One barge attempted to ram, and a PT wriggled clear by inches. Six barges went down that night at a cost of one American wounded and a riddled engine room in *PT-149*. Engineers used surgical tape, raincoats, and galley pots and pans to effect repairs. On the night of the 29th three boats braved shore gunfire east of Lae to get three barges.

These motor torpedo boats became so expert at ferreting out barge trains that one Japanese diarist at Finschhafen wrote thankfully that on 29 August he had made the only trip "when barges were not attacked by torpedo boats." But they got his barge on its return passage. Skipper John Bulkeley of *PT-142* sent "Boarding Party Awa-ay!" in old Navy style to capture a barge that refused to sink. So devastating had been the PT's machine guns that only one Japanese out of a crew of 13 was alive. When barge traffic dwindled, the PTs made strafing runs on Japanese shore installations and bivouacs. The enemy retaliated by bringing in a type of twin-engined Army bomber that we called "Sally." But, unlike her pestiferous brother the New Georgia "Pete," "Sally" failed to score.

Between the Nassau Bay landings and the Lae invasion, the PT's fired not one torpedo. Seven enemy submarine transport missions escaped their vigilance during July, to land 195 men and 238 tons of supplies; and on 2 August and 5 August two destroyer-transports made unobserved runs to Cape Gloucester, a good springboard for New Guinea, with 1560 troops and 150 tons of supplies.[5]

While planes and PTs blockaded Huon Gulf and the Straits, the 3rd Australian Division tramped northeastward from Wau to join elements of the 41st Infantry Division U.S. Army. Supported closely by air and by artillery, these troops pushed the Japanese to Tambu, six miles from Salamaua. Late in July, Army amphibious engineers (2nd Engineer Special Brigade) ferried troops from Nassau to Tambu Bay where, in mid-August, they shattered enemy counterattacks and commenced an advance in true Papuan tradition — jungle mud and painful uprooting of enemy positions.[6] This move accomplished its purpose of focusing Japanese attention on Salamaua. By the end of July so many of their troops had been transferred from Lae to Salamaua that the latter place then had 8000 defenders, four times as many as Lae.

In mid-July Japanese aviators spotted the gash in the jungle at Bena Bena and at once attacked, with bombs and bullets, the dummy field. MacArthur's communiqués colored the deception by deadpan reporting of such items as "Seventeen enemy bombers attacked Bena Bena yesterday. No damage was reported."

Bena Bena, Salamaua and the blockade of Huon Gulf stimulated the Japanese to put on a counteroffensive. On 10 August the Japanese air forces in New Guinea, strengthened by 250 Army planes from Rabaul, were ordered to attack air bases, Allied convoys moving along the Papuan coast, and (on 1 September) to coöperate with the Army in a raid on Bena Bena. On four airstrips at Wewak, New Guinea, 310 miles northwest of Finschhafen,

---

[5] Japanese Naval War Diary and data from Capt. Ohmae.

[6] Office of the Chief Engineer GHQ Army *Engineers in Theater Operations* Vol. I. Engineer Special Brigades (earlier called Engineer Amphibian Brigades) manned the Army's small boat navy. Each brigade contained 8000 men with equipment to transport a full infantry division over short water distances, then to set up a beach supply, evacuation and defense system. Their "fleet" consisted of such craft as LCVP, LCM and dukws. Anything of LCT size or larger was manned by Navy men. It was most fortunate that these Army specialists were on tap in New Guinea in 1943 when the Navy had so little to offer.

the Japanese parked their reinforcements wing to wing, believing the distance from Dobodura would protect them from air attack. On 14 August a Japanese reconnaissance plane discovered the Marilinan field and their planes at once began attacking it. Good search radar and three dozen P-39s saved the field from serious damage. General Kenney decided to hit the menace at its source, which from air photographs he suspected to be Wewak.

On the morning of 17 August, just as the Japanese were servicing planes for a bigger raid on Marilinan, 48 of Kenney's bombers, 31 Mitchell strafers and 85 Lightnings droned up to Wewak and destroyed 70 planes. "Enemy air strength in New Guinea may have been halved overnight," was the estimate; actually, over one third of it was shattered, and a follow-up strike next day brought the score well into three digits. These strikes blasted all chance of a Japanese offensive. "The Allied air attack against Wewak this week," correctly stated General Willoughby, "is unquestionably a milestone in the Pacific war. This is the first major reversal suffered by the Japanese Army Air Service in the Pacific.[7]

Now it was the Navy's turn. On 20 August 1943 a dispatch from Admiral Carpender at Brisbane to Captain Jesse H. Carter at Milne Bay read: —

> Inasmuch as there is good reason to believe that the enemy is moving both supplies and troops from Finschhafen to Salamaua, you will select four destroyers and make a sweep of Huon Gulf — during darkness 22–23 August — and follow this with a bombardment of Finschhafen. Targets of opportunity are to be destroyed.

In the Southwest Pacific this dispatch, which would have been routine under Halsey, marked a significant turning point. It was the first time a naval bombardment had been scheduled in 18 months' ground fighting. We have already discussed the reasons for this tardiness — shortage of ships, apprehension of air attack and want of hydrographic information. Reluctance to pile into the Solomon Sea was understandable during the Buna-Gona campaign,

---

[7] Daily Intelligence Summary for 17/18 Aug.; Appendix A to Summary 22/23 Aug.

when naval resources were slim and the enemy air force mighty; but why should the Navy have hung back after the Solomon Sea had been surveyed and Dobodura airdrome established, and when destroyers equipped with SG radar and good sound gear were available? One reason was that the survey ships had not yet covered waters north of Morobe; another, the reluctance of General Kenney to promise fighter cover in advance for a naval operation in those waters; he had his own plans, which gave full employment to his fighter planes. Yet it was high time the Navy did something down there besides guard approaches and escort merchant ships. As one of Admiral Carpender's staff remarked, "It will be worth while to prove the Navy is willing to pitch in, even if we get nothing but coconuts."

Captain Carter, the squadron commander, flying his pennant in *Perkins*, led *Smith*, *Conyngham* and *Mahan* from Milne Bay for a night run to Buna. Calling there next morning, he went ashore to discuss air cover and take a look at photos of Finschhafen. At 1500, with an Australian Air Force liaison officer on board, the four destroyers headed northwest. Their sweep of the Gulf was uneventful. Near Cape Cretin their navigators were worried by uncharted reefs, but careful use of sonar kept them clear. Then, at 0121 August 23, they gave the Japanese on New Guinea their first dose of naval shells. The 540 rounds of 5-inch took but ten minutes to fire and produced, as predicted, nothing but coconuts. Seventeen hours later, the ships anchored in Milne Bay. It was a tricky feat of navigation both ways, but it did suggest that the destroyers might have been permitted to give gunfire support to Allied troop advances near Salamaua, as their fellows had done to good purpose off Guadalcanal.

During the last week of August, Allied fliers pummeled Japanese bases everywhere within reach and Allied soldiers massed for a final drive against Salamaua. On 30 August Imperial Headquarters, Tokyo, authorized a retreat to the strategic straits. But they ordered the defenses of Vitiaz and Dampier to be strengthened and the supply line kept open by "every means available, such as the use of submarines, boats and small craft." No mention was made of fleet support and none was intended. Both commanders at Rabaul, General Imamura and Admiral Kusaka, ordered the defenders of Lae and Salamaua to hold fast there and also to strengthen Finschhafen; but the only material support they offered was the promise — never kept — of sending two battalions of troops from Madang, 150 miles west of Finschhafen.

## 2. *Lae Punched Out, 4–15 September*

The little village of Lae, outlet for peacetime mineral and agricultural exports, had good anchorage and an airfield. It was the key to the valleys of the Ramu and Markham Rivers, where good sites for airfields were numerous and roads could be built. For months the Japanese had been sweating out a highway through these valleys which, if completed, would assure Lae a supply line from Madang independent of the coastwise barge route. Simultaneously the Allies were pressing construction of a road from southern Papua across the Owen Stanley Mountains which, if completed, would give them a short trucking line to Lae, and more airfield sites inland. General MacArthur was not content to leave the decision to the rival roadbuilders; Admiral Barbey's VII 'Phib could now float in enough soldiers to break up the battle of the bulldozers. That is why Lae was first objective in the conquest of Huon Peninsula.

Admiral Barbey undertook to ferry the Australian 9th Division from Milne Bay and Buna to landing beaches 15 to 17 miles east of Lae, near the eastern end of the narrow coastal plain on the rugged Huon Peninsula. His rough task organization follows: —

VII AMPHIBIOUS FORCE, Rear Admiral Daniel E. Barbey

Destroyers CONYNGHAM, FLUSSER
Destroyer-transports BROOKS, GILMER, SANDS, HUMPHREYS

LST Group, Capt. J. B. Mallard: 13 LST
LCI Group, Cdr. H. F. McGee: 20 LCI
LCT Group, Cdr. B. C. Allen: 14 LCT and *APc-4*

Cover Group, Capt. Jesse H. Carter: destroyers PERKINS, SMITH, MAHAN, LAMSON
Escort Group, Lt. Cdr. H. G. Corey: destroyers MUGFORD, DRAYTON
APc Group, Lt. Cdr. F. J. Leatherman: 13 APc, 9 LCT, 2 SC
Service Group, Capt. Roy Dudley: tender RIGEL, 3 LST, 10 SC, 5 YMS, 1 small oiler, tug SONOMA

Landing Craft Control Groups at Morobe, Buna and Oro Bay

Shore Regiment: 532nd Engineers, 10 LCM, 40 LCVP

There were big doings at Milne Bay on 1 September as the Australians completed loading APDs and amphibious craft for the passage to Lae. While winches ground and bosuns' pipes shrilled, Admiral Carpender discussed the plan for the last time with Admiral Barbey. Next day "Uncle Dan" and the Australian commander of the landing force boarded destroyer *Conyngham*. The boats and ships, in order inverse to their speed, doubled East Cape and steamed through Ward Hunt Strait up the Papuan coast to Buna and Morobe, where additional troops awaited their arrival to embark. Never before had the Solomon Sea witnessed such a fleet; few waters had ever seen one so strange to old seamen's eyes.

General Kenney's Air Force was now directing big bombing missions against Japanese bases: on 1 September, Madang; on the 2nd, Wewak. The now wary Japanese had left few targets on the battered Wewak field, so pilots turned to shipping in the harbor. Barrage balloons floated high over the ships, but the bomber pilots pushed through to sink a couple of *Marus* totaling 10,000 tons.[8] Then a bolt arrived from the blue — some 30 Navy-type "Zekes," the skill of whose pilots surpassed anything the Seventh Fleet had seen in a long time.

On 3 September nine "Bettys" made a high-altitude bombing run on LCTs and other craft loading at Morobe, but inflicted no damage. In the afternoon three audacious "Bettys" with six fighters got into the Lae airstrip despite a pulverizing Allied raid on that field a few hours before. American bombers over Cape Gloucester met determined opposition. Airplane photos of Rabaul showed nearly 200 planes nesting there. All this troubled the Allied high command. Had there been a leak somewhere?

[8] JANAC. General Kenney actually underestimated the destruction here.

Leak or not, Barbey's force steamed along that night. In view of his lack of information about the approaches and the beach, "Uncle Dan" insisted on a daylight landing. The Australians objected to losing tactical surprise, but the Americans consoled them with a pre-landing bombardment by Captain Carter's destroyers, and General Kenney sent fighter planes to follow the bombardment with beach strafing.

Morning twilight at 0600 September 4 disclosed the five destroyers with guns trained on the beach two and a half miles away. For ten minutes, 0618–28, orange flame flowed from gun muzzles and fire controllers marched shells along the coconut palm fringe. Destroyers then hauled clear to screen landing craft of the first wave. As soon as the bombardment ceased the first wave of assault troops in 16 rubber boats from destroyer-transports *Brooks, Gilmer, Sands* and *Humphreys* putt-putted through calm water and scraped the sand. Half of them landed at Beach Red, the other half at Beach Yellow, three miles farther east. The few enemy there abandoned defenses and fled. On Beach Red, which had been the target of the bombardment, nary a Jap was seen.

Fifteen minutes after the initial landing, the ungainly LCIs, charged with infantry, pushed shoreward. In the conning tower of *LCI–339* Ensign James M. Tidball USNR waited his turn. At 0704 he rang up one-third speed and headed in, dropping his stern anchor in the approved fashion some 250 yards off shore and veering chain. Suddenly six "Zekes" roared low over the formation; their spurting bullets killed several Australian soldiers. Right behind them came three "Bettys," disgorging bombs from 1500 feet elevation. The ship could not maneuver because of her stern cable and General Kenney's strafers had not yet arrived.[9] One bomb crashed into the deck of *LCI–339* just forward of the conning tower, and

[9] Of this incident General Kenney states, "As the Aussies were landing, a couple of Jap airplanes that had evidently been hidden away at Lae sneaked in under the haze and destroyed one of the small landing barges and damaged another. Our fighter cover, flying above the haze, did not see the Nips, who made just one fast pass at the beach and disappeared over the hills." Admiral Barbey, however, states, "The weather throughout the day was clear, ceiling and visibility unlimited."

two near misses bracketed her. Riddled by the strafing bullets and shrapnel, afire, sinking and with many wounded and 20 dead, she just made the beach. Tidball radioed to the flotilla commander who ordered him to abandon ship. The craft remained on the beach

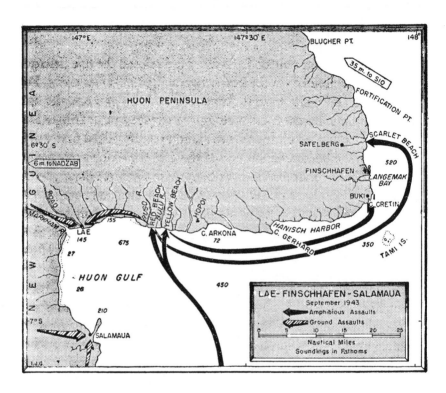

for a week, a nice target and landmark for the Japanese Air Force, and was then towed clear; but she drifted onto a reef and was lost.

Following the LCIs came the smaller LCTs and landing craft carrying Army engineers for roadbuilding and anti-aircraft gunners for defense; then six big LSTs and seven LCTs with vehicles, heavy guns and stores. By 1030 the last of 7800 troops had disembarked and by 1430 September 4, when the last LCT retracted, 1500 tons of stores had been beached.

Since the air raid there had been no sign of the enemy. His commander at Lae had called to Rabaul for help and began setting up defense positions along the river banks to the east of the village. Imamura sent 80 planes, but they were delayed by fog over New Britain and hampered by Allied fighters coached from destroyer *Reid*, stationed off Finschhafen with a fighter-director team on board. At 1300 *Reid's* radar picked up three large groups of planes flying down the spine of New Britain. She vectored 48 Lightnings to the scene, and in the ensuing brawl 23 of the enemy were splashed at a cost of but two Lightnings. *Reid* lay in the direct path of the enemy flight, three "Vals" peeled off over her, but she dodged their bombs and shot one down. Then came a coördinated torpedo- and dive-bomber attack on six LSTs escorted by three small minesweepers and two subchasers, 25 miles off Cape Ward Hunt. The puny armament of this "poor man's navy" could not reach out to the "Vals" before the peel-off point, and few guns were spared for the torpedo planes. A half-dozen "Vals" concentrated on *LST-473*, and at 1358 scored two hits and two near misses. The pilothouse crumpled and down went six Americans dead and 13 wounded, while 18 Aussies suffered wounds. Now twelve "Bettys" bored in from low altitude and launched torpedoes. Seaman Frederick Erickson, helmsman of *LST-473*, who had been blown clear of the pilothouse, crawled painfully back toward his station, as Seaman Johnnie D. Hutchins, mortally wounded, grasped the wheel and spun it full right so that one torpedo shaved the bow wave, another the wake. Then he died; shipmates had to pry his devoted fingers from the wheel. Other crewmen of *LST-473*, some hale, some wounded, but all in action for the first time, stuck to their guns or attacked gasoline fires in motor trucks below. The skipper, Lieutenant Rowland W. Dillard, expecting fire hazards, had provided his crew with the latest foam and fog equipment and had trained them in its use. Within ten minutes of the bomb hits, the fires were out.

*LST-471* was singled out by two "Bettys" who skimmed into half-mile range and dropped torpedoes. Both were splashed, but one torpedo banged into the LST's port side aft, wrecking the ship's stern, killing 51 crewmen and troops, and wounding 18,

Since no fires resulted and the starboard engine remained intact, Lieutenant George L. Cory usnr, the skipper, could hope to save his command. LSTs were tougher than anyone would have believed, but woefully undergunned in comparison with those then making the landings at Vella Lavella.

This amphibious assault on the enemy's east flank was the right jab. The left hook came next day, 5 September, with an airborne landing to the west. It was a wonderful show — one of Kenney's best. Over 300 planes from Moresby and Dobodura converged on the inland village of Nadzab where the Japanese had a dilapidated airstrip. There were fighters stacked to slash at "Zekes," B–25s sweeping the drop zone with strafing bullets, A–20s showering fragmentation bombs and making smoke, C–47s flying in paratroops of the 503rd United States Infantry Regiment, B–17s disgorging parachute supply packs, weather planes herding all flights around storms; and, high over it all, a trio of B–17s in which rode General MacArthur and some of his staff. In a little over a minute, 1700 men hit the silk. The Japanese were too astonished to offer much opposition. Within two hours the field was secured and American engineers, helped by Australian engineers who had rubber-boated across the Markham River, began improving the strip. Twenty-four hours after the initial landing, transport planes were landing on Nadzab Field. In the days that followed, several thousand troops of General Vasey's command were flown in and promptly marched down along the Markham River toward Lae. By 14 September these soldiers were drawing fire from Japanese batteries on the outskirts of the town.[10]

Meanwhile VII 'Phib operated a shuttle of troops and supplies between Buna and the Lae landing beaches. The Australian troops, marching west toward Lae, encountered swollen rivers and a flooded countryside which, coupled with Japanese delaying tactics, threatened to bog down the advance. The African desert had

---

[10] General MacArthur looks back with justified pride on this Nadzab operation as the first instance of "Hit 'em where they ain't" strategy in his command.

offered nothing like this to these veteran "Rats of Tobruk," who swam streams only to face enemy fire on the opposite banks with inadequate weapons. Obviously, the sea was the only possible route. Amphibious engineers furnished boats which snaked through coral-strewn passages and enemy fire, carrying troops and supplies from one tiny beachhead to another and cutting off small knots of Japanese troops. General Wootten's men arrived at the defensive perimeter around Lae on 14 September while Vasey's force was approaching from the west.

Enemy resistance diminished as the forces neared the town, and on 8 September four destroyers (*Perkins*, *Smith*, *Flusser* and *Mahan*) stood off Lae during the midwatch and laced the town with a vicious bombardment, an ordeal never imposed on Buna. On the 9th submarine *I-174* slipped into the harbor with Rear Admiral Mori to take charge. A bombardment next night by destroyer-transports *Brooks*, *Gilmer*, *Humphreys* and *Sands* underscored the garrison's isolation and Mori decided to head for Sio, 50 miles across the Huon Peninsula.

The march began in well-organized fashion with the non-seagoing sailors jumping off, followed by three other groups, the last pulling out on the 15th. On the first leg of the journey, the troops were harassed constantly by Australians whose lines they skirted. Their advance guard was surrounded and destroyed. On 20 September they entered the foothills, scrambling up cliffs, hacking through underbrush and shivering through dank nights in flimsy tropical uniforms. Admiral Mori, stricken with an infection, gave up and turned command over to his communications officer, Captain Ikeda. The sick men dropped by the wayside and the weak fell over cliffs. Yet 1500 of the 2000 men went on over the mountains and to the north coast, finally reaching Sio on 14 October; but of these only 400 were fit to bear arms. It was as bad as General Horii's retreat over the Owen Stanleys.

So it happened that on 16 September General Vasey's airborne troops marched into Lae standing up and joined hands with General Wootten's men hiking in from the east. The enemy admitted that by cutting off exit to the sea and the Markham Valley the Allies had "inflicted an annihilating blow on us without engaging in direct combat." What a contrast to Buna a little sea power had made!

Prior to the Lae and Nadzab landings, Salamaua's place in Allied strategic planning was that of a leech to bleed off the Lae garrison. Now it had no significance beyond the fact that it sheltered enemy troops behind Allied lines. The Australians and Americans set about to clean out the infestation with a renewed offensive which brought Salamaua and adjacent territory into Allied hands just one day before Lae fell.

# CHAPTER XV

# Finschhafen and Beyond

## 16 September–20 October 1943

*East Longitude dates; in early October the Southwest Pacific Command shifted time from Zone minus 10 to Zone minus 11.*

## 1. Finschhafen Falls, 2 October

ALTHOUGH Lae collapsed sooner than had been expected, General MacArthur had plans for pushing his advantage by capturing Finschhafen promptly. The question was, Where to land troops? From charts and conversations with old New Guinea hands, a 600-yard ribbon of sandy beach six miles north of the town looked good. General MacArthur on 17 September set D-day only five days ahead, and Admiral Barbey met the challenge. In Huon Gulf ports he collected 8 LSTs, 16 LCIs, 10 destroyers and 4 APDs.[1] The LSTs loaded bulk supplies at Buna; the task group assembled off Lae on the 21st. Brigadier Windeyer's 20th Australian Brigade embarked, and by midafternoon an echelon of small craft got under way for the landing. Near sunset, six "Sallys" flew over the Rawlinson range north of Lae on a high-level bombing mission against ground installations. The sight of ships in the Gulf proved too tempting and they released bombs over the water, missing by a quarter of a mile. To top it off, the United States Army fighter-director officer in *Reid* recalled a homebound combat air patrol which downed several "Zekes" and all but one of the bombers.

In spite of the promise of fighter cover and several pre-invasion

[1] The escorts were destroyers *Conyngham* and *Henley;* the APDs, *Brooks, Gilmer, Sands, Humphreys.*

air strikes at neutralized enemy fields, the Navy expected Finschhafen skies to be actively hostile during the landings. For this reason
Barbey suggested a midwatch landing under a bright quartering
moon. The Australians demurred and a compromise resulted —
H-hour to be in the darkness before dawn, ships to clear the beach
before daylight air attacks could develop. The Australians proved
to be right; "Uncle Dan's" outfit was not prepared for a neat night
landing. The usual snafu developed but the Japanese were unable to
profit by it. Major General Yamada, commanding at Finschhafen,
had expected that place to be next on the list; but, assuming that
his enemy would march overland, he stationed some 3000 men
south and west of Finschhafen, leaving less than a thousand in the
village and only a few hundred, who promptly retired inland, at
the landing beaches. He was completely surprised by the landings,
and several days passed before he could mount a counteroffensive.
Japanese air forces, too, had planned to act quickly, but the only
dangerous strike which broke through consisted of six "Bettys"
and 35 "Zekes" flying down from Rabaul. *Reid's* efficient radar
picked them up shortly after noon. Off Finschhafen they swerved
southeastward to attack the retiring convoy. Circling destroyers
splashed the leading three planes; three LSTs' gunners and tug
*Sonoma's* took on the rest. Fighter air patrol helped too. The Japanese boasted two cruisers, two destroyers and two transports sunk;
but no cruisers and no transports were there, and not a single ship
was even damaged. Actually this little action helped to dispel an
old Southwest Pacific bugaboo, the fear of land-based air attack
which had long kept ships out of the Solomon and Bismarck
Seas.

The rest of this 22nd of September was quiet enough. In midafternoon, three more LSTs sailed up from Morobe under escort of
destroyer *Flusser* which encountered and disposed of three enemy
barges en route. Arriving at the Finschhafen beach after dark, the
LSTs fumbled and fumed until the shore parties lighted the landing
points; but before the midwatch ran out at 0400 on the 23rd they
were empty and steaming south. Dan Barbey's men had certainly

learned how to load beaching craft for expeditious unloading. Captain Bern Anderson, his planning officer, says it was done by staking out a mock-up LST deck on the beach, where the Army could pile up their stuff just the way they wanted it to come off.

For a week, nothing much happened. On the night of 29–30 September three APDs brought up reinforcements and supplies which Brigadier Windeyer badly needed. General Yamada, spoiling for a fight after having been outwitted, had shifted his force to Satelberg Mountain, six miles inland from the beach, and was planning a counterattack with fresh troops coming down the New Guinea coast. Meanwhile, the Special Naval Landing Force south of the beach fought a rear guard action to protect Finschhafen. But that place was in Australian hands on 2 October.

No Tokyo Express interfered with this operation because Admiral Koga feared lest it run into another Battle of the Bismarck Sea. And Japan could no longer produce enough planes to defend all sides of the Bismarcks Barrier by air power alone.

## 2. Tucking in the Pennants, 1–20 October [2]

Just as no taut ship puts to sea with "Irish pennants" such as trailing lines and dangling fenders, so MacArthur's military machine, before sailing through Vitiaz Strait into the Bismarck Sea, had to scour the inland river valleys leading from the west, polish off the enemy on the Huon Peninsula and secure the smaller Dampier Strait. General Vasey's Australian division, after the fall of Lae, started tidying up the Markham and Ramu Valleys. His paratroops stormed Kaiaput, a Japanese garrison and airfield at the headwaters of these rivers, on 19 September; just in time to prevent a reinforcing regiment's getting in there from Madang. Another detachment

[2] SWPac Daily Intelligence Bulletins; Allied Land Force Headquarters, "Report on New Guinea Operations, July 1942–1944"; Operation Plans, War Diaries and Action Reports of units and commands involved: "Southeast Area Operations" Parts 2 and 3 (Navy).

of Aussies advanced into the Ramu Valley from Bena Bena. Brigadier Windeyer's men had already turned to on the second task, erasing the enemy troops at Satelberg. After dealing with them he would scrub out the jungle and coast to the west and north. As for New Britain, that would have to wait until troops, ships and planes were ready for another amphibious leap.

When Kaiaput airfield was captured, the 21st and 25th Australian Brigades flew in from Nadzab. Enemy strength dissipated like smoke in a gale. In early October the Red Ensign with the Southern Cross streamed out from the flagstaff at Dumpu. There General Vasey established his division headquarters, and thence patrols prodded northward along the trail to Bogadjim on the coast 20 miles south of Madang. After this quick capture of the river valleys, United States Army engineers moved in and commenced leveling ground for new airstrips.

On 3 October, the day after Finschhafen fell, the Japanese had yet to strike a telling blow against the invaders. Their air power had been brushed aside by fighters and anti-aircraft guns. Yamada's main force, now at Satelberg, had been left out completely by the flank landing. Four submarines stationed in the Gulf traffic lanes had failed to score so far, but soon they would. Captain Jesse Carter directed a destroyer sweep off Finschhafen for the night of 3–4 October, to get these subs. Destroyers *Reid*, *Smith* and *Henley*, then at Buna, drew this detail. In midafternoon they sailed into Huon Gulf northward at 20 knots, strung out in a loose column so that sonar would function despite thudding propellers and rumbling wakes. At sunset when the word went out to darken ship, there was nothing on the radar, and the monotonous ping of the sonar had aroused no echo, except from Mitre Rock. The I-boats were supposed to be much farther north, and since at 20 knots a ship is usually safe from submarines Commander Harry H. McIlhenny of *Reid*, the O.T.C., ordered a straight course without zigzag. *Henley's* old-fashioned, unstreamlined sound dome, useless at this speed, was secured. At 1818, when 25 miles north of Cape Ward Hunt, the gun control officer in the second destroyer,

*Smith,* sighted three torpedo wakes abaft the port beam. Signalman C. L. Davis saw them too and reacted in unorthodox but inspired fashion by shouting an order to the helm, "Right Full Rudder!" Skipper Theobald added "Emergency Full Speed Ahead!" His ship swung parallel to the fish and combed their wakes, but *Henley,* with rudder full left, could not dodge. A torpedo hit her amidships, and in about fifteen minutes this fine ship was a broken hulk on the bottom. Hold-down tactics by the other two destroyers kept the Japanese from exploiting the victory, and 241 men were rescued out of the 258 on the muster roll.

Now the heaviest burden of naval activity in New Guinea waters fell on the PTs. They turned guns on night-flying "Bettys" and knocked down a couple. They took soundings in channels and off possible beachheads. In company with heavily gunned Australian motor launches, they hunted barges and submarines. And they even had a fight with destroyers.

In Dampier Strait on the night of 8–9 October *PT–194* and *PT–128* lay-to at 0115 off the New Britain coast, looking for some target on which their passenger, Mr. Richard Patton of the Raytheon Corporation, could test their new SO radars. Suddenly the PT men saw a blob of black smoke rise into the clear night over the Strait. They decided to investigate and headed toward the smoke with muffled engines. Off Grass Point, New Britain, the radar showed pips moving seaward. Two separated and headed toward the boats. At 0220, still over three miles distant, the first identified itself as a hostile warship by plunking a 5-inch shell so close to *PT–194* that everyone on board was thrown flat. Then a searchlight caught the boat and more salvos straddled. The Americans turned south at high speed, grinding out a smoke screen which did not spoil the aim of the two enemy destroyers — for such they were. Both PTs were keen to fire torpedoes but every time they turned to increase target angle the enemy turned with them. *PT–194* knocked out an enemy searchlight with 40-mm fire as a near-miss lifted the boat's stern out of the water and sprayed her with shrapnel which killed the 40-mm gunner and wounded two other men. The civilian engineer [3] coolly rendered first aid. The boats finally escaped by doubling back through their own smoke screen and emerging from the northern end of the Strait. It was obvious that Japanese destroyers had acquired fire-control radar.

The amphibious craft too were busy transporting troops and supplies closer to action areas. No train dispatcher ever had a more difficult task than Admiral Barbey's staff in routing these many convoys. Big doings were in the offing; General Krueger's Sixth Army training, mounting and inching forward for future thrusts; the 1st Marine Division, up from Melbourne for the first time since Guadalcanal, training for Cape Gloucester; Seabees and Army engineers building docks, depots, airfields, roads and defenses.

The Australians fortunately captured General Yamada's operation order and learned that a land attack from Satelberg and an amphibious attack from seaward on our Finschhafen beachhead were imminent. By first light 16 October, the Aussies were prepared, and that day they repulsed repeated attacks from inland. Three barges which attempted a counter-landing were sighted by an American amphibious engineer who cut loose with his 37-mm gun. Two other engineers held fire until the barges were at 25 yards' range, when they slashed both barges and occupants like papier-maché. A few Japanese swam ashore with their weapons and were taken on by two gunners who fought bravely until all were dead.

On 17 October the Japanese 20th Division, newly arrived from Madang, joined Yamada in a major attack. Infiltration tactics forced Australians to withdraw toward the beach. But the 26th Australian Brigade with tanks was already sailing up from Lae in 13 LCTs and 3 LSTs, escorted by Captain Carter's destroyers and subchasers. En route they were attacked by an I-boat and from the air, but the convoy landed its troops successfully at Langemak Bay near Finschhafen, under a bright moon. Yamada's soldiers now

---

[3] Civilian war correspondents received a lot of publicity for entering zones of action and, moreover, had a monument dedicated to their memory; but we have yet to hear any public mention of the numerous civilian engineers like Mr. Patton who risked their lives in ships and planes to keep intricate machinery operating.

withdrew from their coastal salient and by 26 October, exhausted by battle and malaria, suspended the offensive. The Aussies buried 49 comrades and 679 Japanese and prepared to open an offensive of their own in mid-November. Thrice more during the latter half of October amphibious craft steamed into Finschhafen with reinforcements and each time enemy air interference diminished.

This happy situation in the skies derived from decisions and events little known to the soldier who took passage in the LST or to the sailor who manned her. The Japanese treasured Bougainville, last stop short of Rabaul, more than they did the Straits, and no longer would or could give New Guinea priority in air and sea support. On 12 October General Kenney had taken the first step in his part of the campaign to erase Rabaul. On that day, 349 planes, "everything that was in commission and could fly that far," took off against Rabaul for the biggest air attack to date in the Pacific. The planes blasted the airstrips, hacked at shipping and pummeled the supply dumps. The General's score, as usual, was considerably ahead of the actual damage inflicted, which was the 6000-ton transport *Keisho Maru* and two small craft sunk, two destroyers damaged by near misses and large fires in the storage areas.[4] Thenceforth, whenever the weather permitted, Rabaul would have no peace even after it had been reduced to impotence early in 1944.

Thus, beginning on Columbus Day 1943, the Japanese had three offensive campaigns to stave off: one in New Guinea, one in the Northern Solomons and one over Rabaul itself. Since the last two were the greater threats, they had to neglect New Guinea. So we may now leave this theater and examine the big doings being prepared for Bougainville.

[4] *General Kenney Reports* (1949) claims that the 87 B–24s in this raid sank "3 merchant vessels, between 5000 and 7500 tons each, 43 small merchant ships of 100- to 500-ton size and 70 smaller harbor craft. In addition direct hits were scored, badly damaging 5 more medium-sized cargo vessels, a destroyer tender, 3 destroyers and a tanker." All this with the loss of but 5 planes. Mathematically the General's claims require that 87 bombers score 126 hits! He also claimed 100 enemy planes destroyed on the ground or in the air, but our "Record of Allied Air Raids on Rabaul" compiled from data in "Southeast Area Air Operations" lists only 2 out of 34 interceptors shot down, 9 set afire or severely damaged on the ground, and 36 others receiving minor damage. This may well have been short of the truth.

*PART III*

# The Bougainville Campaign

*All dates in Part III are East Longitude, and the times, unless otherwise specified, are Zone minus 11.*

CHAPTER XVI

# The Seizure of Empress Augusta Bay

## 12 October–2 November 1943

### 1. Bougainville[1] in Pacific Strategy

**B**OUGAINVILLE ISLAND, about 130 miles long and 30 miles wide, was discovered by the Spaniards in the 16th century but named by the Sieur de Bougainville, who rediscovered it on his voyage around the world in 1767. A century and three quarters later, it was still undeveloped in the modern sense. The Emperor and Crown Prince mountain ranges which run down the center, rising to over 10,000 feet altitude, include two active volcanoes which are religiously avoided by the superstitious natives. The slopes of these mountains and their outlying spurs along the coast, are covered with a tropical rain forest even denser than the jungles of Guadalcanal. At the southern end of the island a gently undulating plain, 15 to 20 miles wide, fans out from the base of the Crown Prince Range. This is the most heavily populated section of Bougainville. Here were the big coconut plantations and here the

---

[1] The writer visited Empress Augusta Bay in May 1944, and Lt. Salomon subsequently spent two weeks there, gathering information at the Naval Advanced Base (Cdr. Earle H. Kincaid) and the XIV Army Corps Hdqrs. (Maj. Gen. O. W. Griswold) in June 1944. Additional information has been furnished by Rear Admiral Robert B. Carney, chief of staff to Admiral Halsey; Rear Admiral T. S. Wilkinson and Capt. O. O. Kessing, commander of the Naval Advanced Base 20 Nov. 1943 to 20 May 1944. For the most part this chapter is based on Action Reports and War Diaries. The Cincpac Monthly Summary written by the Analytical Section of Cincpac Staff (Capt. Ralph C. Parker commanding) has been of inestimable value, as have the various Sopac and Airsols Intelligence Summaries for air activities. The official Marine Corps history, Maj. John N. Rentz *Bougainville and the Northern Solomons* (1948), has not altogether superseded an earlier report by Capt. William G. Wendell USMCR on the ground operations, or one by Capt. Warren H. Goodman USMCR on Marine air activities.

enemy had convenient anchorages in Tonolei Harbor and nearby Moisuru Bay, from which roads ran to the Kahili and Kara airdromes.

Numerous rivers carry abundant rainfall down to the sea, together with silt which, in course of time, has built up a sort of dam along the western shore from Buka to Mutupina Point. Consequently that coast is lined with extensive swamps and brackish lagoons less than one hundred yards inland from the beach. This sodden coast, where we elected to establish a beachhead and build an airdrome, was thinly inhabited by natives and had never been developed or even surveyed by the white overlords. There was a network of trails over the island, but the only roads passable for wheeled vehicles were in the southern plain. White people generally went from place to place by boat, and the natives used their dugout canoes.

Owing to the fact that Bougainville belonged to Germany until World War I, it was never a part of the British Solomon Islands Colony. With the adjoining islands, Buka, Shortlands, and the Treasury Islands, it became the Kieta District of the Territory of New Guinea for which Australia obtained a mandate from the League of Nations in 1919. The total native population was estimated in 1940 at about 43,000, most of whom lived inland in villages of 50 to 200 people. Eighteen different languages were spoken. As in New Guinea, the Australians endeavored to secure the coöperation of the natives by good treatment and by making their headmen responsible for local areas; but they were less successful here than elsewhere — owing in part to the influence of German missionaries, who welcomed the Japanese invaders.

In the spring of 1943, after the enemy had been thrown out of Guadalcanal and was hard pressed in the Central Solomons, he began, with the aid of the natives, a systematic mopping up of coastwatchers and Australian Army patrols in Bougainville. The position of these men became untenable and, in March 1943, the United States Navy sent submarine *Gato* to Teop Harbor on the northeast coast to evacuate them. Nine women, 27 children and three nuns also were rescued.[2] Thereafter the Allies had no native sources of intelligence on Bougainville.

Some 40,000 Japanese troops and 20,000 naval personnel were on Bougainville and outlying islands by 1 November 1943; most of these were in the southern part, 6000 at Buka, 5000 or more in the Shortlands; while Empress Augusta Bay, the most weakly defended area of all, had only two to three thousand. For airfields, the Japanese had Kahili in the south and Buka in the north and also one on Ballale Island off Shortlands to start with; Kara, about seven miles northwest of Kahili, as well as Bonis on the east bank of Buka Passage, were completed in 1943. Another, at Kieta on the east coast, was never finished. These airfields, however, were not our objectives in Bougainville. Rabaul was what we had been after right along; Rabaul had been the *terminus ad quem* of old Operation "Watchtower" which opened with the landings at Guadalcanal. Rabaul was already well within bomber range of Allied fields in Papua, the Central Solomons and even Guadalcanal; but forward airdromes were necessary as bases for light bombers and for fighters to escort the heavies. That was the one and only reason why the J.C.S. authorized Halsey to seize a section of Bougainville: to establish forward airfields for strikes on Rabaul.

The Bougainville campaign, like the preceding one in the Central Solomons, was planned by the small staffs of Admiral Halsey at Nouméa, of Vice Admiral Aubrey W. Fitch at Espiritu Santo, and of Rear Admiral Theodore S. Wilkinson and Lieutenant General Alexander A. Vandegrift usmc at Guadalcanal. One

[2] Submarine Operational History World War II p. 860. The C.O., Lt. Cdr. R. J. Foley, said in his patrol report: "All were troupers and were quickly adopted by the ship's company. The adoption was reciprocal. Typical example: One 10-month-old child would sleep nowhere else but in the arms of a bearded torpedo-man who manned the telephone at the forward tubes. They made a weird picture on watch. Brief impressions of the *Gato's* incongruous family: The children — through a cycle of awe, apprehension, mischief, ravenousness and unwilling sleep. The mothers — distraught, then trustful. The nuns — benign and patient. The soldiers — 'Haven't you some dirty jobs we can help you with?' and 'Is there any beer in Brisbane?' The *Gato* crew — clumsy but enthusiastic volunteer nursemaids. The children on this trip discovered that the top of the rotating sound gear made an excellent merry-go-round, and accompanied by shouts of laughter, fought for a place on the turntable."

week before it started, Halsey's whole operational staff moved up to Koli Point, Guadalcanal, adjoining "Camp Crocodile" where Wilkinson maintained his headquarters and marshaled and trained the III 'Phib. "Ping" Wilkinson, who had planned and conducted the Vella Lavella operation, was the happiest choice in the world for planning and commanding the Bougainville operation. Exactly forty years earlier, he had won a school essay contest with an account of an amphibious operation by Alexander the Great. A scholarly, widely read officer with an excellent combat record, considerate of his staff and of everyone who worked with him, Wilkinson went into Bougainville as if he had been preparing for it all his life.[3]

General MacArthur, responsible for the overall strategy in this area, was frequently consulted and his approval was obtained for every major move, but he gave Admiral Halsey a completely free hand. Halsey insisted on exercising unity of command over all forces in the South Pacific and enforced this principle right on down, retaining personal direction of the covering forces only. Wilkinson ran the entire amphibious expedition afloat and ashore, whether Army, Navy, Marines or Air Forces; only when the beachhead was established on 13 November 1943 did he relinquish his powers to the commanding general of the ground forces, Major General Roy S. Geiger USMC.[4] General Geiger then took complete charge at Empress Augusta Bay of everything, including naval forces assigned to the defense of the perimeter.

[3] Born Annapolis 1888; St. Paul's School '05 where he won the top classical scholarship twice; Naval Academy '09, first in his class; head of landing company from *Florida* at Vera Cruz, 1914; in Bu. Ordnance during World War I; gunnery and fire control officer, *Kansas* and *Pennsylvania*, 1919–20; commanded four destroyers in succession, 1920–26; three years in Bu. Nav.; fleet gunnery officer Scouting Force, 1930–31; secretary to General Board until 1934; "exec." *Indianapolis* to 1936; head of planning division Bu. Nav. 1936–39; chief of staff to Commander Scouting Force to Jan. 1941; C.O. *Mississippi;* Director of Naval Intelligence 1941–42; Combatdiv 2; Deputy Comsopac Jan. 1943; Com. III 'Phib June 1943; Vice Adm. 1944; J.C.S. Strategy Committee Jan. 1946; died 21 Feb.

[4] Major General Barrett USMC, who was to have commanded the ground forces, died before the expedition started; and General Vandegrift, then on his way to Washington, was recalled and given the command. General Geiger was his deputy commander until 9 Nov., when he relieved General Vandegrift.

When this campaign was first discussed by Admiral Halsey's staff, the plan was to take possession of Choiseul and the Shortlands, perhaps to establish a small beachhead near Kahili. This strategy was reconsidered for two reasons. First, our experience at Munda proved that the Japanese would defend their airdromes with terrific energy; any direct assault on Shortland or Kahili would take too many lives and consume too much time. Second, the first success of leapfrogging strategy, by-passing Kolombangara and landing on Vella Lavella, proved that it could be done. So, before the end of August, Admiral Halsey with General MacArthur's consent and approval decided to by-pass the Shortlands and Kahili and boldly to throw a landing force into a section of Bougainville where an airdrome could be established and from which Rabaul might be beaten down.

Once it was decided to seize a section of Bougainville where the enemy had no airdrome and was not present in force, the choice boiled down to Kieta Harbor, on the northeast coast, and Cape Torokina, Empress Augusta Bay, on the southwest coast. Each was about the right distance for basing fighters to join bomber strikes from Munda on Rabaul. Kieta had a protected harbor, while Empress Augusta Bay would be on the exposed side of the island during the approaching monsoon season. Kieta seemed to be better placed to ward off air attacks launched from Rabaul; but to take it we would have to move up by the longer outside passage and secure Choiseul first. Empress Augusta Bay was on the inside and shorter route to Rabaul; and although the Treasury Islands must first be secured they were an easier preliminary than Choiseul. Cape Torokina, moreover, was so inaccessible to the enemy's main positions on Bougainville that it was rightly calculated he would require weeks and months to prepare a counterattack.

During the last week of September, an examination of each locality was made by reconnaissance teams boated up in submarines. The Kieta party, commanded by Captain Bertram S. Behrens usmc, went up in *Gato*, whose crew already knew this coast. They reported on 30 September that the harbor was mostly foul ground and that the Japanese had given up trying to make Kieta airstrip work. The southwest coast party under Captain Harry B. Barker USMC, sent up in submarine *Guardfish*, turned in a somewhat more favorable report than Empress Augusta Bay merited, because they had landed about ten or fifteen miles north of Cape Torokina where there were no swamps behind the beach; but one of the scouts made soil tests which showed the ground to be suitable for an airfield, and fortunately the soil at Torokina was similar. There was also a low-level aërial reconnaissance of Cape Torokina by a Catalina on 1 October, which spotted the small coconut grove where the first airstrip was built.[5]

If the west side of Bougainville was decided on, Cape Torokina must be the spot because no other part of the coast had even a partially protected anchorage. So, largely because it had fewer disadvantages than any other place, the bay named after old Kaiser Wilhelm's chaste consort was selected as the site of the landings and the future airdrome. On 12 October Admiral Halsey designated 1 November as D-day. On the 14th Admiral Wilkinson's operation plan was distributed.

Although the defense of Rabaul was key to the "New Operational Policy" adopted by Imperial Headquarters on 30 September 1943,[6] the Japanese could not imagine any such bold move as Wilkinson's leap to Empress Augusta Bay. But they knew that something was afoot — probably a move into the Shortlands or Kahili — and wished to break it up. Admiral Koga, Commander in Chief Combined Fleet, flew his flag in battleship *Musashi* at Truk. In early October he decided to reinforce Rabaul with the entire plane strength of his Third or Carrier Fleet, where they would combine with the land-based planes of the Eleventh Air Fleet to raid the Allied supply routes and crush the forthcoming offensive. This Operation "RO," as it was called, a repetition of Yamamoto's ill-fated "I" of April, was delayed by a curious series of alarums

[5] Rentz *Bougainville and the Northern Solomons* (1948) p. 17; information from Admiral Wilkinson's staff.
[6] See ch. i sec. 5; other details in "Southeast Area Operations" Part 3 (Navy).

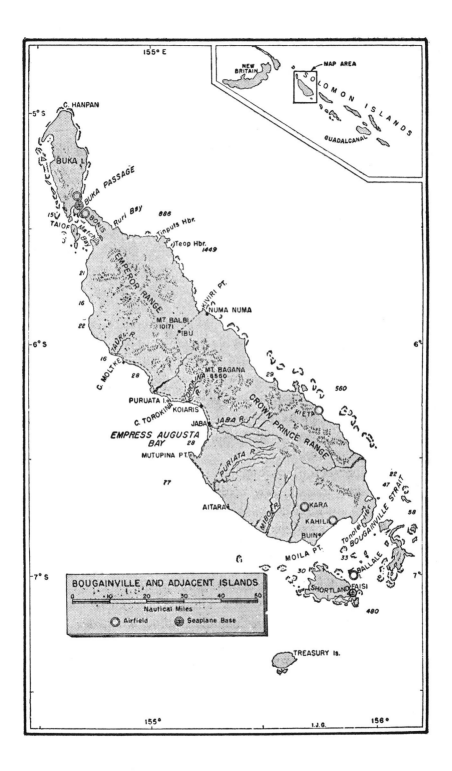

155° E

NEW
BRITAIN

MAP AREA

SOLOMON ISLANDS

GUADALCANAL

5° S

C. HANPAN

BUKA I.

BUKA PASSAGE

Ruri Bay

886

BONIS

TAIOF

Matchin
Bay

Tinputs Hbr.

Teop Hbr.
1449

15

EMPEROR RANGE

21

16

22

MT. BALBI
10171

IBU

KIVIRI PT.

NUMA NUMA

LARUMA R.

6° S

16

C. MOLTKE

28

MT. BAGANA
8650

29

560

KIETA

6°

PURUATA I.

KOIARIS

C. TOROKINA

JABA    JABA R.

CROWN PRINCE RANGE

EMPRESS AUGUSTA
BAY          28

MUTUPINA PT.

PURIATA R.

77

AITARA

MIBO R.

KARA

KAHILI

BUIN

22

47

BOUGAINVILLE STRAIT

58

Tonole Hbr.

33

BALLALE

7° S

MOILA PT.

G

30

480

BOUGAINVILLE AND ADJACENT ISLANDS

0    10    20    30    40    50

Nautical Miles

○ Airfield        ⊕ Seaplane Base

SHORTLAND    FAISI

7°

TREASURY Is.

155°

I.J.G.

156°

and excursions. A raid by the recently reinforced Fast Carrier Forces Pacific Fleet on Wake Island, 5–6 October, which was intended by Admiral Nimitz as a mere warm-up and practice for his air groups, was interpreted by Koga as a prelude to an attempt to reconquer Wake. Koga hoped this would afford him the big fleet action which he, like Yamamoto, believed Japan must win promptly, or lose the war. Plane-carrying submarine *I–36* was accordingly sent to reconnoiter Pearl Harbor. Its tiny scout plane was sighted from Barber's Point on 17 October, creating a tremendous hullabaloo; but it sent in a report that four carriers, four battleships and 17 destroyers were in the harbor. Koga, who appears to have known pretty well the strength of the Pacific Fleet, interpreted this as meaning that the bulk of the Fleet was on the warpath — actually it was engaged in training exercises. So the entire Combined Fleet steamed from Truk to Eniwetok, which Koga considered to be a good advance position from which to sortie and "annihilate" Nimitz. After a week's uncomfortable stay in that lonely lagoon, the Admiral decided that the Pacific Fleet was not coming out, and on 24 October led his Combined Fleet back to Truk. Four days later he executed "RO" by ordering most of the carrier planes to Rabaul.

These formidable reinforcements, the air groups of *Zuikaku, Shokaku* and *Zuiho,* comprised 82 "Zekes," 45 dive-bombing "Vals," 40 torpedo-carrying "Kates" and 6 reconnaissance planes: a total of 173. All had arrived by 1 November. Koga also alerted the Twelfth Air Fleet, then in Japan, to prepare to head for Rabaul.

In the meantime General Kenney's air forces of the MacArthur command had been "taking out Rabaul," as the General calls it in his book, for almost two weeks. The great 349-plane raid of 12 October on the shipping in Simpson Harbor, which we have already related, was widely publicized as having "knocked out" Rabaul; but the Bismarcks base was not even leaning on the ropes. On 18 October an equally big raid from Dobodura was so hampered by foul weather that only 54 B–25s got through. General Kenney claimed 60 planes shot down or destroyed on the ground, and one destroyer and a merchantman sunk. In reality very few planes were eliminated, and no ships larger than 500 tons were sunk.[7] General Kenney had predicted to a member of Admiral Halsey's staff that Rabaul would be "dead" about 20 October; but on that date the Japanese still had some 200 planes operational. On 23, 24 and 25 October the Southwest Pacific air forces made daylight raids on the Rabaul airfields with 45 B–24s, 62 B–25s and 61 B–24s respectively, covered by 47, 54 and 50 P–38s respectively. At the time, General Kenney claimed to have disposed of 175 Japanese planes in these three raids, but stepped the figure up to 181 in his book. From Japanese records the score was only 9 shot down, 25 destroyed on the ground, and 27 damaged; this may however be short of the truth.

On 29 October, 37 to 41 Liberators covered by 53 to 75 P–38s [8] dropped 115 tons of bombs on Vunakanau airdrome, Rabaul, claiming 45 planes shot down and destroyed. The actual score from Japanese records was 7 shot down and 3 destroyed on the ground.

On 1 November, the 173 Japanese carrier planes arrived from Truk to reinforce the "about 200" planes of the Eleventh Air Fleet still operational at Rabaul.[9] Kenney did not attack Rabaul that day (or the preceding) because of foul weather. On the 2nd, when he made a sizable raid of 75 B–25s covered by 80 P–38s, the newly arrived carrier planes "put up the toughest fight the V Air Force encountered in the whole war," shooting down 9 of our

[7] The claims quoted here are from the SW Pacific Daily Intelligence Summaries or from *General Kenney Reports* chap. xiii; the actual scores are from the "Summary of Enemy Air Raids on Rabaul," prepared by Lt. Pineau from ATIS "Southeast Area Operations" augmented and corrected by various Japanese documents. Ships' scores are from JANAC, but it must be remembered that JANAC does not list ships damaged, or those of under 500 tons sunk. The Japanese "Summary" and Rabaul War Diary are not completely accurate; but the score that they give us checks up pretty well with the observed number of planes operational at Rabaul at various times. JANAC lists a 100-ton SC sunk at Rabaul by Army aircraft on 16 Oct., perhaps a mistake for 18th. *General Kenney Reports* p. 316 steps up claims to a freighter and corvette. He claims having "practically ruined" Tobera airdrome. The Japanese went right on using it, although many of the installations were destroyed.

[8] The discrepancy is between the Daily Intelligence Summaries and *General Kenney Reports*.

[9] "Southeast Area Operations" Part 3 (Navy).

bombers and 10 fighters. General Kenney claimed "85 planes definitely destroyed and 23 probables," and that in 12 minutes his air attack had "destroyed or damaged 114,000 tons of shipping." The actual score was 20 planes destroyed, two small *Marus* totaling 4600 tons and a 500-ton minesweeper sunk; doubtless some others damaged. Yet General Kenney could still write of this raid in 1949, "Never in the long history of warfare had so much destruction been wrought upon the forces of a belligerent nation so swiftly and at such little cost." [10] Never, indeed, have such exorbitant claims been made with so little basis in fact — except by some of the Army Air Forces in Europe, and by the same Japanese air force which General Kenney believed he had wiped out. Even on that day the Japanese out-Kenneyed Kenney by claiming 22 B–25s and 79 P–38s as "sure kills."

Notwithstanding the exaggeration, the V Army Air Force in the Rabaul raids of 12 October–2nd November contributed greatly to the success of the Bougainville campaign: it diverted the enemy's attention from Bougainville — particularly useful on 2 November — and it did destroy enough planes to render Operation "RO" less effective. It beat up both harbor and airdrome installations. Fortunately, however, Admiral Halsey did not count on General Kenney's fliers' knocking out Rabaul, and in planning the assault on Bougainville he had air forces of his own — the famous Airsols command. [11]

## 2. Forces and Preparation, 12 October–2 November

In South Pacific staff conferences in Nouméa and Guadalcanal there was much grumbling about Bougainville being "Operation 'Shoestring' No. 2." Admiral Nimitz, preparing the spearhead of his

[10] *General Kenney Reports* pp. 319–21.
[11] The reasons for the comparative ineffectiveness of the V Army Air Force against Rabaul in contrast to its remarkable work in New Guinea waters were (1) Japanese interception of high quality, as over their most important base; (2) the harbor was too narrow for much skip-bombing; (3) too much of the bombing was from such high levels that targets were not hit; (4) excellent AA defense.

great Central Pacific offensive, with target date 20 November, was accused of giving Halsey only the leavings, just as Operation "Torch" had robbed "Watchtower." Nimitz, however, estimating correctly that Koga would not risk the heaviest ships of his Combined Fleet in the Solomons, thought Halsey could do with what he had; he feared lest ships lent to the Third Fleet would not get back in time for the Gilberts invasion. At the start of the operation Halsey had only one carrier group and Merrill's Crudiv 12. Nimitz did send Rear Admiral Laurance DuBose's new Crudiv 13 to replace Ainsworth's battered warriors, and a second carrier group, but they could not arrive on the scene before 7 November. South Pacific Force still had Captain Arleigh Burke's "Little Beavers" and about two more destroyer squadrons for amphibious escort duty and fire support.

The ground force allotted to Admiral Wilkinson was the I Marine Amphibious Corps (reinforced) commanded by Lieutenant General Alexander A. Vandegrift, the hero of Guadalcanal.[12]

As the Gilbert Islands operation required an enormous number of assault transports and cargo ships, Admiral Wilkinson was allotted only twelve APAs and AKAs, all but two of them veterans of the Guadacanal landing in August 1942. These were just enough to float the attack echelon with its equipment. The South Pacific Force was lucky to get that many, as several members of Cincpac Staff argued that, in view of the comparatively short distance of Bougainville from Guadalcanal, Wilkinson could get along with the beaching ships and craft just as Barbey did. But Wilkinson had correctly estimated that conditions at Torokina would require speed, and he was allowed to keep the big ships. LSTs and the like would have been fatally vulnerable during the violent air attacks of the assault phase.

\* \* \*

[12] Comprising (1) 3rd Marine Division, reinforced, Maj. Gen. A. H. Turnage; (2) 8th Brigade Group of 3rd New Zealand Division, Brigadier R. A. Row (for the Treasuries); (3) 37th Infantry Division U.S. Army, Maj. Gen. Robert S. Beightler; (4) Advance Naval Base Unit No. 7. All these units were then at Guadalcanal or the Russell Islands.

Amphibious forces engaged in the Bougainville operation were given excellent air and naval preparation and support. The first phase, the strikes on Rabaul from New Guinea, we have already examined. The second phase was the preventive bombing of Bougainville airfields. Wilkinson certainly needed all of that he could get; for the planned beachhead lay only 210 miles from Rabaul and much nearer the Bougainville airfields. To neutralize these he depended on "Airsols," the Solomon Islands force, subordinate to Vice Admiral Fitch's South Pacific Air Command. Command of Airsols rotated between the United States Army, Navy and Marine Corps. On 21 October 1943, when its headquarters shifted from Henderson Field to Munda, the commander was Major General Nathan F. Twining USA. By that time the new fighter strip at Barakoma, Vella Lavella, had been operational for almost a month, and three Marine fighter squadrons comprising 64 Corsairs and 108 pilots were flown in as a nucleus of the force to be based there for covering the Bougainville operation.

Airsols, despite a heterogeneous composition (planes of U.S. Army, Navy, Marine Corps, and Royal New Zealand Air Force), was one of the world's finest, with a matchless *esprit de corps*. Its fighter planes kept guard over every convoy running north of Espiritu Santo; its "Black Cats" scoured the darkness; its "Dumbo" rescue planes picked up shipwrecked mariners and bailed-out aviators, delivered rations to beleaguered coastwatchers, and rushed spare parts to the fighting front. Its photographic planes performed hydrographic services inestimable in that neck of the Pacific where German and British chartmakers alike had been content with 18th Century surveys by Bougainville and D'Entrecasteaux. For, as Admiral Merrill once observed, "The possibility of viewing the sunrise from the sloping deck of a ship stranded on an uncharted shoal is a thought not pleasant to contemplate, especially if said shoal is under the guns of the enemy's coast defense batteries."

In view of the enemy's fondness for night air attacks, one of the most important constituents of Airsols was two squadrons of night fighter planes; one consisting of six Corsairs (F4U–2) under

Commander William J. Widhelm, the famous "Gus" Widhelm of the Battle of Santa Cruz,[13] one of six twin-engined Vega Venturas (PV-1) commanded by Lieutenant Colonel Frank H. Schwable USMC. Both squadrons had been specially converted for night fighting, a process that required about six weeks and doubled the cost of the planes. Their pilots had been trained for night protection of an airdrome or beachhead with the aid of a mobile Ground Communication Information (GCI) radar unit to act as director. "GCI Moon" was set up 25 October on the northwest coast of Vella Lavella, an ideal location to pick up bogeys approaching from the north to bomb the Barakoma and Munda fields, and near enough to cover the Treasury Islands. These night fighter squadrons were also used to protect convoys and covering forces, to spot night bombardments and to hunt barges in partnership with PTs. At first they were not very effective, because fighter-director officers in ships were untrained in vectoring night fighters onto enemy planes, and slow to appreciate the necessity for that instantaneous and continuous flow of "bogey information" required for night interceptions.[14]

In October 1943, Airsols rendered vital support for the coming amphibious operation by neutralizing enemy airfields in and near Bougainville. General Twining's tactics were to do something every day, and the results may best be presented by a summary. A total of 158 flights comprising 3259 sorties were made by Airsols in October 1943, against land and ship targets at Kahili, Kara, Ballale, Buka and Bonis, and a few on Choiseul. A number of enemy planes — many fewer of course than the 139 claimed — were destroyed, at a cost of 26. Toward the end of the month the tempo of these strikes was accelerated and the force of each increased. The net result was to keep five Japanese airfields pulverized so

---

[13] See Vol. V of this History p. 213.
[14] Lt. Col. F. H. Schwable's Report of VMF-531 Operations 25 Aug.–25 Nov. 1943, attached to Comairsopac's Report "Air Coöperation with Surface Forces" 21 Dec. 1943; South Pacific Force Intelligence Section "The F4U-2(N) in the Solomons," 1 Mar. 1944 and "Combat Experiences of VMF(N)-531, Apr. 1944. These planes are properly called Night Fighters, *not* Black Cats, which are Catalinas equipped for scouting and night-bombing.

that the enemy could make no use of them. But for these initial poundings Empress Augusta Bay would have been straddled by planes from four airfields and one float-plane base, rendering the amphibious operation even more vulnerable to enemy air attack than was the landing at Guadalcanal in 1942. Rabaul and Kavieng, the remaining threats, were still intact after General Kenney's series of massive raids from New Guinea, but Airsols had built up to such strength (489 planes operational on 1 November) and provided such good coverage and interception over Empress Augusta Bay that the progress of our arms in Bougainville was never seriously hampered by enemy air power.

Naval gunfire also contributed to the discomfiture of the Japanese airfields within striking distance of Bougainville, and to the concealment of the true objective. Admiral Halsey assigned two bombardment missions to Rear Admiral Merrill's Task Force 39, comprising light cruisers *Montpelier, Cleveland, Columbia* and *Denver*, and Destroyer Squadron 23 (Captain Arleigh A. Burke, who by his actions in the next few days was to be awarded the nickname "31-knot Burke"). Merrill's force stood out of Purvis Bay at 0230 October 31, bound for Buka Passage. After steaming 537 miles it commenced bombarding the Buka and Bonis airfields at 0021 November 1. The task force had the benefit of spotting by two specially equipped Airsols planes; and well did it plaster the airfields. Enemy planes struck back, illuminating the ships with parachute flares and harassing the force with their familiar night tactics until the third hour of 1 November. But they scored never a hit. The only casualty was the Admiral's favorite typewriter, wrecked by a near-miss that exploded abreast the flag office. Making a "dignified retirement at 30 knots" (to quote Merrill), before dawn 1 November, Task Force 39 steamed almost 200 miles to perform its second mission, the bombardment of the Shortlands.

Carrier planes became available on D-day, when one of the fast carrier groups of Task Force 38 came down to help; this was Rear Admiral Frederick C. Sherman's group, consisting of the veteran *Saratoga* and the new light carrier *Princeton*, screened by two anti-aircraft light cruisers and ten destroyers. They steamed up the northeast coast of the Solomons and launched strikes on the two Buka Passage airfields on 1 and 2 November. There were few Japanese planes left there to retaliate, after these strikes.

Altogether these strikes ensured that the enemy would have no more use of his fields, at least during the first critical week.

## 3. *Treasuries and Choiseul, 27 October–6 November*

Choiseul, the great island which the Sieur de Bougainville had named after the foreign minister of Louis XV, and the small Treasury Islands south of Shortland, which Lieutenant Shortland RN had named after the source of his pay, were still in Japanese hands on 1 October 1943. South Pacific planners figured out that simultaneous landings on them would deceive the enemy and take his mind off Bougainville. Choiseul we did not propose to occupy, since it had no immediate military value; but possession of the Treasuries with their excellent Blanche Harbor[15] would provide a base for radar search, motor torpedo boat patrols and staging small craft to Bougainville.

As occupation of the Treasuries was early anticipated by Admiral Wilkinson, he sent up a party of Marine raiders in submarine *Greenling* on the night of 22–23 August. They located the best landing beach, selected a site for the radar station, and promptly withdrew. Two months later, on the night of 21–22 October, a second reconnaissance party from a motor torpedo boat landed on Mono Island, brought back accurate information on enemy positions, and estimated the enemy force to number only 225 men. Another PT boat brought an advance party which cut the wires between the Japanese observation post at the entrance to Blanche Harbor, and the main position.

[15] This harbor is the channel between Mono and Stirling, the two islands that make up the Treasuries. The historian wishes that the exploring captains of H.M.S. *Blanche*, *Renard* and *Gazelle* had not been so fond of their ships as to name several harbors, channels and sounds after each one.

To occupy the Treasuries, three echelons of APDs and beaching craft, mounted in Guadalcanal and the Russells, brought up about 6300 troops (mostly New Zealanders) and 3870 tons of equipment. Rear Admiral George H. Fort commanded the first echelon,

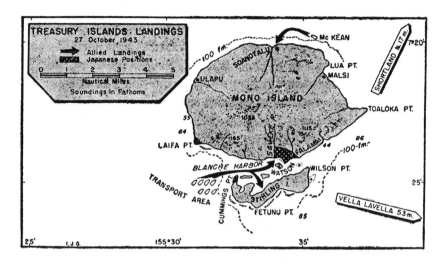

arriving 27 October. After a short preliminary bombardment of the enemy positions by destroyers and aircraft at break of day, the troops were landed on both sides of Blanche Harbor. Despite mortar fire few casualties were incurred; all transports were unloaded and clear by 2000. Destroyer-transport *McKean* put a radar party ashore at Soanatalu on the north shore of Mono Island; in four days' time it had a search radar installed.

A new feature of this operation was the use of light-draft improvised gunboats for close fire support of the landing craft, an invention of the ingenious Captain Roy T. ("Slim") Cowdrey, ship repair officer on Halsey's staff. Two Landing Craft Infantry, *LCI–24* and *LCI–68*, were given additional armament, consisting of two 20-mm, three 40-mm and five .50-caliber machine guns.[16] This required much larger crews and sacrificed most of their troop-

[16] Information from Admiral Wilkinson and members of the first two LCI(G)s; also from Com LCI(L) Flotilla 5 (Lt. Cdr. J. M. Smith) War Diary Nov. 1943.

carrying function, but the LCI(G)s (as they were designated) proved to be the answer to prayer for fire support of assault troops delivered close to shore. Further developments were made after a beachhead was secured at Bougainville, and the "Elsie Item Gunboats," as they were nicknamed, proved their worth in every later operation of the Pacific war.

The most spectacular incident of this landing was provided by the indefatigable Seabees. As one LST let down her ramp and flung open her gates to discharge, an enemy pillbox that had escaped damage in the bombardment began hurling machine-gun bullets into her open maw. A Seabee bulldozer, all poised to land, elevated its blade as an armored shield, charged the pillbox, lowered the blade at the moment of contact and buried guns and gunners in coral sand.

The Japanese were caught flatfooted at the Treasuries. Although they had an important seaplane and naval base only 25 miles away at Shortlands, they did not catch on to what was happening until our troops were ashore. At 1530 October 27, destroyers *Cony* and *Philip* took the brunt of their first air attack, delivered by 25 "Vals." They and the Airsols fighter patrol shot down twelve, but *Cony* received two hits aft, flooding her port engine room, killing eight men and wounding ten; she retired to Tulagi, towed by *Apache*.

By 6 November, when the third echelon landed, mopping-up operations in the Treasury Islands were complete. A motor torpedo boat base was promptly established on Stirling Island. Seabees began work on an airfield there before the end of the month, and Blanche Harbor became a valuable staging point for Bougainville.

In order to encourage the enemy's belief that we were planning a two-pronged attack on the Shortlands instead of a single one on Bougainville, a landing was effected on Choiseul almost simultaneously with that of the first Treasuries echelon. APDs *Kilty, Ward, Crosby* and *McKean*, on the very evening of the day when they had landed troops at Blanche Harbor, put in at Vella Lavella and embarked the 2nd Parachute Battalion, 725 strong, of the First Marine Amphibious Corps, commanded by Lieutenant Colonel Victor H. ("Brute") Krulak. These, guided by coastwatcher C. W. Seton, landed at Voza on the Slot side of Choiseul Island shortly before midnight 27 October; the transports then withdrew, leaving a fleet of rubber boats, manned by Navy crews, with the Marines. They raided an enemy outpost after daybreak, then ran into strong opposition near Sangigai, 25 miles from West Cape, where over a thousand evacuees from Kolombangara were encamped. Air support came from Munda but embarrassed the Marines by taking their rubber boats for enemy; nevertheless on the afternoon of the 30th the Marines drove the enemy out of Sangigai and destroyed his base for troop barges. Two platoons, staged northwest along the coast by boat, raised havoc in the Japanese supply base on an island just south of West Cape, making good their retirement with the aid of a PT boat. General Vandegrift, learning that the Japanese were moving up reinforcements from southern Choiseul, now ordered Krulak to retire, and sent up three LCIs to take the Marines out on 4 November.

What good this raid accomplished will probably never be known; the coastwatchers, however, were annoyed because the Choiseul natives believed that the Japanese had run the Marines out. Captured documents later revealed that the possibility of an Allied landing in Empress Augusta Bay was anticipated at Rabaul, but that Japanese headquarters at Kahili believed that the Shortlands and Choiseul were the major targets and took dispositions accordingly.

## 4. Cape Torokina Landing, 1 November [17]

The initial landing force for Empress Augusta Bay was the 3rd Marine Division reinforced,[18] commanded by Major General A. H.

[17] Rear Admiral Wilkinson's Action Report, War Diary Naval Advanced Base Torokina 29 Dec. 1943; Commo. Reifsnider's Report of Landing Operations Empress Augusta Bay 1–2 Nov., 22 Dec. 1943.
[18] Less 21st RCT and a few other components reserved for later echelons, plus certain corps troops and part of Naval Base Unit No. 7.

Turnage usmc. Many subsequent echelons were floated in LSTs but the 3rd Marines went up in style in twelve lightly combat-loaded transports and cargo ships. Task Force 31, as it was designated, was composed as follows: --

### III AMPHIBIOUS FORCE
Rear Admiral T. S. Wilkinson in *George Clymer*

Transports, Commodore L. F. Reifsnider in *Hunter Liggett*

Transdiv "A" Captain A. B. Anderson

| | | |
|---|---|---|
| APA | PRESIDENT JACKSON | Capt. E. P. Abernethy |
| APA | PRESIDENT ADAMS | Capt. Felix Johnson |
| APA | PRESIDENT HAYES | Capt. H. C. Flanagan |
| APA | GEORGE CLYMER | Capt. F. R. Talbot |

Transdiv "B" Captain G. B. Ashe

| | | |
|---|---|---|
| APA | AMERICAN LEGION | Cdr. R. C. Welles |
| APA | HUNTER LIGGETT | Capt. R. S. Patch uscg |
| APA | FULLER | Capt. M. E. Eaton |
| APA | CRESCENT CITY | Cdr. L. L. Rowe |

Transdiv "C" Captain H. E. Thornhill

| | | |
|---|---|---|
| AKA | ALCHIBA | Cdr. H. R. Shaw |
| AKA | ALHENA | Cdr. H. W. Bradbury |
| AKA | LIBRA | Cdr. F. F. Ferris |
| AKA | TITANIA | Capt. H. E. Berger |

Total of 14,321 troops carried in the transports.

Screen, Commander Ralph Earle (Comdesron 45)

Destroyers FULLAM, GUEST, BENNETT, HUDSON, ANTHONY, WADSWORTH, TERRY, BRAINE, SIGOURNEY, CONWAY, RENSHAW

Minecraft Group, Commander Wayne R. Loud

Destroyer-Minesweepers HOPKINS, HOVEY, DORSEY, SOUTHARD          Cdr. Loud
Minelayers ADROIT, CONFLICT, DARING, ADVENT          Lt. Cdr. A. D. Curtis usnr
Four small minesweepers (YMS)

Special Minelaying Group, Lt. Cdr. J. A. Lark (C.O. *Renshaw*)
BREESE, SICARD, GAMBLE

Salvage Group
Fleet Tugs APACHE and SIOUX

The separate detachments proceeded by different routes to the final rendezvous, in the vain hope of preventing Japanese air snoopers from appreciating the size and importance of the movement.

Transdiv "A" left Espiritu Santo 28 October and embarked Rear Admiral Wilkinson and Lieutenant General Vandegrift at "Camp Crocodile," Guadalcanal, on the evening of 30 October. Transdiv "C" embarked troops at Guadalcanal and departed, with the four minesweepers escorting, that forenoon. Transdiv "B," with General Turnage and Commodore Reifsnider, sailed from Efate 28 October. All three met on the morning of the 31st. The Commodore then assumed the duties of O.T.C., which he retained throughout the landing and unloading.

Thus united, well provided with air cover by day and night, the task force approached Bougainville along the southwest coast of the Solomons. The moon was three days old.

That coast of Bougainville had been very imperfectly charted by the German Admiralty about 1890, and nobody had troubled to correct it before the war. The principal chart, with which most of the transports were furnished, placed the positions of Cape Torokina and Mutupina Point, the two extremities of Empress Augusta Bay, respectively eight and a half and nine miles southwest of their actual locations. Fortunately, the reconnaissance planes and submarine *Guardfish* had supplied some major corrections to the latitude of the Bay, although even they did not get the longitude right.[19] Near the end of the approach, when the navigating

---

[19] The correct position of Cape Torokina established 18 Nov. by the Naval Advanced Base was lat. 6°15′20″ S, long. 155°02′30″ E. (N.A.B. War Diary). Commo. Reifsnider says in his Report that the best charts which he had were H.O. Misc. 10219–3, a photostatic reproduction of a German chart of 1919 (*Salomon Inseln, Bougainville, Nordwestlicher Teil*) and H.O. 2896; but there were Army Air Force charts based on submarine reconnaissance which were substan-

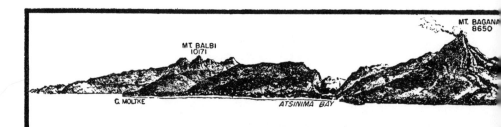

officer of a transport was asked by the captain for his ship's position, he replied, "About three miles inland, sir!"

The minesweepers who led the van found no mines but plenty of uncharted shoals, and even more were subsequently discovered by the time-honored method of hitting them with a ship's bottom. Fortunately the transport area, 4000 to 5000 yards from the beaches, proved to be clear of obstruction.

To the forces, as they approached, Empress Augusta Bay presented a magnificent but somewhat terrifying spectacle. Behind the curved sweep of the shore line, a heavy, dark green jungle, with an occasional giant tree showing a gray trunk, swept up over foothills and crumpled ridges to the cordillera which was crowned by a smoking volcano, Mount Bagana, 8650 feet above sea level. Wreaths of cloud and mist floated halfway between the beach and the crest, over which the sun rose at about 0630. It was wilder and more majestic scenery than anyone had yet witnessed in the South Pacific, and the thought that these thick, dank jungles and mountain fastnesses were full of Japanese pleased only the most hardened hunters.

---

tially accurate. The position of Cape Torokina, as laid down on a number of successive charts, is as follows: —

| Date | Chart | Latitude S. | Longitude E. |
|---|---|---|---|
| | Correct Position | 6°15'20" | 155°02'30" |
| 1881 | Imlay, Western Pacific No. 2 | 6°23'00" | 155°02'00" |
| 1919 | H.O. Misc. 10219–3 | 6°22'25" | 155°00'55" |
| 1940 | H.O. Misc. 2896 | 6°23'00" | 155°01'00" |
| Sept. 1943 | AAF overlay No. 7 | 6°15'02" | 155°02'25" |
| Oct. 1943 | AAF Chart No. 7, 3rd ed. | 6°15'00" | 155°05'35" |
| Nov. 1943 | AAF Chart No. 51, 2nd ed. | 6°15'20" | 155°05'35" |

BOUGAINVILLE ISLAND
Viewed from point three miles SW of Cape Torokina.
Adapted from Hydrographic Office Chart

RUATA I.    C. TOROKINA    PIVA R.    MAGINE IS.    MUTUPINA PT.
EMPRESS    AUGUSTA    BAY

Although between two and three thousand Japanese troops were deployed along the shores of Empress Augusta Bay, the actual area of the landings was defended by only 270 men, with a single 75-mm gun on Cape Torokina. But, never before in the Pacific, had a major landing been made so close to a major enemy air base as Torokina was to Rabaul. Everyone remembered what Rabaul-based ships and planes had done to Turner's amphibious force at Guadalcanal, 562 miles away; what might they not do to a landing only 210 miles away? Hence the meticulous care with which Wilkinson had planned this operation to ensure a quick getaway before the enemy could counterattack.

To a veteran of the landings in Morocco less than a year earlier, or of those in Guadalcanal in August 1942, the speed and smoothness of this unloading was astonishing. Initial troop waves in several transports were rail-loaded in LCVPs instead of crawling down into them by cargo nets, and the boats shoved off right away. There was no confusion among boat waves, no landing craft milling about for hours and making the troops seasick. *Clymer* had all her boats in the water in 19 minutes, and her assault waves were loaded 37 minutes after the order was given. *Jackson's* first wave hit the beach at 0726, forty-one minutes after the transports anchored, and four minutes ahead of H-hour. Seven to eight thousand troops were taken ashore in the first wave. A light southwesterly wind was blowing. Although the ground swell was not enough to embarrass landing craft when alongside the transports, a moderate surf was breaking on the shore. Of the twelve beaches assigned, covering a front of about four miles, those east of Cape Torokina were difficult and the three northerly ones were completely unusable. Sixty-four LCVPs and 22 LCMs were stranded, partly through the inability of the crews to handle them in surf, but mostly because the beaches were so steep that landing craft could not ground for a sufficient proportion of their length to prevent broaching and swamping. The only good beaches were those behind Puruata Island; but our preliminary bombardment had not knocked out the enemy's well-con-

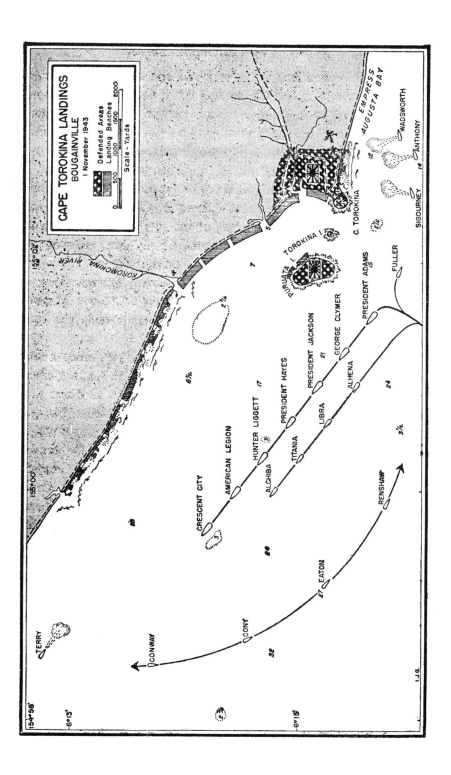

cealed machine-gun nests on that island and on Cape Torokina.

Shore gunfire harassed the landing craft, sinking four of them and hitting ten others, with a loss of 70 men. Most of this damage was inflicted by the 75-mm gun on Cape Torokina which enfiladed the west beaches. It was well emplaced in a log and sand bunker, the approaches protected by two smaller bunkers and a series of trenches manned by a score of Japanese. Calling on four Marines to assist him, Sergeant Robert A. Owens USMC placed them so as to cover the fire ports of the two small bunkers, and then charged directly into the mouth of the gun, entering its emplacement through the fire port and driving the gun crew out of the rear door, where they were shot down. Japanese in surrounding trenches concentrated their fire on this brave Marine, and his body was found riddled with bullets outside the rear entrance.

From the beach two narrow corridors of dry land, raised a few feet above ground-water level, led inland; there the Marines killed or drove away the small Japanese force that resisted. This area was densely wooded, giving a great advantage to the defense; but the 2nd Marine Raider Battalion had a new auxiliary for jungle work, the 1st Marine Dog Platoon. These 24 dogs, mostly Doberman pinschers, which had been training in New Caledonia and Guadalcanal since the summer, went forward with their handlers along the jungle trails. They proved invaluable in "pointing" snipers, concealed in the underbrush and among the roots of banyan trees, who otherwise would have waited to cut loose along prepared lanes of fire when the main column came along.[20] By nightfall the last enemy pillbox was reduced and the initial beachhead secured.

A unique feature of the landing was derived from a happy thought of Admiral Wilkinson, to let his transports bombard Cape Torokina. When they got the word, the crews burst out cheering. Nobody had any gridded maps and most of the shots fell

[20] Lt. Clyde Henderson "Battle Dogs of the Devil Dogs" *American Magazine* Aug. 1944 p. 24.

in the water, but it was good clean fun that boosted morale no end.

The first counterattack from Rabaul came in at 0735 on D-day; 9 "Vals" and 44 "Zekes" looked like a hundred to the Marines. Last boats of the assault waves were then clearing the ships. Admiral Wilkinson ordered all transports to get under way. Commodore Reifsnider maneuvered them in the offing for two hours. The fine work of 16 planes from Munda and Vella Lavella (8 Kittyhawks, 8 P-38s) prevented all but 12 planes from getting through, and their one exploit was a near-miss on *Wadsworth* which killed two men and wounded five. At 0930 unloading was resumed, to be again interrupted for two hours after 1300 when a second flight of about one hundred carrier planes swooped down from New Britain. They too were frustrated by 34 savagely aggressive Airsols fighter planes which were beautifully conned and vectored out by Lieutenant Reginald F. Dupuy's fighter-director team in *Conway*. Transport *American Legion,* aground on an uncharted shoal with *Apache* and *Sioux* attempting to haul her off, could not retire; but she was not hit and the tugs got her clear shortly.

In order to ensure fast unloading and quick getaway, Admiral Wilkinson had seen to it that the assault transports were loaded only to one-half and the assault cargo ships only to one-quarter capacity; and most of the matériel was handled in cargo nets which were not broken between the loading port and the beach. This method of light combat loading made for balance in unloading time between all holds and for easy handling, and allowed a proportionate discharge of rations, fuel and ammunition.[21] Moreover, a good 30 per cent of the ground troops were employed in unloading at the beach. So, in spite of the two interruptions and the loss of landing craft in the surf, eight of the twelve ships were completely unloaded by 1730 the same day — a record performance, accomplished (said Admiral Halsey) "in a most brilliant man-

[21] *Crescent City* carried only 440 tons cargo and the others from 520 to 550 tons each.

ner." [22] Some 14,000 men and 6200 tons of supplies had been put ashore in eight hours' working time.

With night coming on, our fighter cover withdrew and the ships, juiciest targets the enemy had ever seen so near to his main base, lay open to air attack. In addition, strong Japanese surface forces known to be in Rabaul might attack under cover of darkness. It was imperative that all ships withdraw for the night. Accordingly, at 1800, Admiral Wilkinson ordered all twelve transports under way, and Commodore Reifsnider led them safely out through the difficult channel by which he had approached. The four partially unladen ships contained vital stores. Wilkinson, convinced by General Vandegrift that the immediate need justified their exposure to air attack next day, detached them from the main force at midnight and sent them back to Empress Augusta Bay under the Commodore in *Hunter Liggett*.

A scout plane then reported the sortie of Admiral Omori's cruiser force from Rabaul. Wilkinson therefore ordered Reifsnider to reverse course and resume retirement until further orders. Soon the glad news came over the radio, first of Merrill's interception of the enemy, and then of his victory. Reifsnider could return to Torokina.

The Marines ashore, after a supper of K rations, passed a damp, uncomfortable and uneasy night, watching flashes of light over the western horizon which told them that a naval battle was in progress.

[22] Endorsement on Commo. Reifsnider's Report. The air score, in comparison with that of the landing at Rendova 5 months before, was equally impressive. The Japanese made 5 major attacks on that occasion and 4 on this. They destroyed 28 of our fighter planes and sank *McCawley* at Rendova, destroyed 4 fighter planes and scored a near miss on *Wadsworth* this time.

# CHAPTER XVII

# The Battle of Empress Augusta Bay[1]

## 2 November 1943

SUCCESSFUL as the landings were, everyone expected the Japanese Navy to attempt another Savo Island. And they were not disappointed. The principal enemy bid to break up the landings developed in the early hours of 2 November.

Admiral Koga preferred to keep Combined Fleet and most of the Eighth Fleet at Truk, beyond Allied bombing range, but Vice Admiral Sentaro Omori, Comcrudiv 5, happened to be at Rabaul on 30 October after bringing in a convoy. Admiral Samejima, Commander Eighth Fleet, more embarrassed than happy at this sudden increase of strength, wanted to send Omori back to Truk, but Koga felt that the opportunity was too good to be missed, and overruled him. So at 1000 October 31, Samejima ordered Omori to get under way with all Eighth Fleet ships present — his own heavy cruiser division (*Myoko* and *Haguro*), two light cruisers and two destroyers — to intercept an American task force reported to be steaming up the Slot. This was Merrill's bombardment mission. As we know, Merrill left the Slot to bombard the Buka Passage airfields, and so Omori, steaming along toward

[1] Rear Admiral Merrill's Action Report 3 Nov. 1943 includes the best track chart; Capt. Burke's Action Report 4 Nov. 1943 also is valuable, but those of other units involved add little. Capt. Ralph Parker's comments in his "Cincpac Monthly Analysis" for Nov., Annexes A and F, have been useful; Admiral W. S. Pye's comments on the battle (Naval War College, 13 Jan. 1944) brought out several points. Japanese sources now available are the Nov. 1945 interrogation of Vice Admiral Omori (*Inter. Jap. Off.* II 337); I discussed the battle with him and his flag captain in 1950; a valuable track chart obtained by Mr. Salomon in Japan; "Southeast Area Operations" Part 3 (Navy), and the following ATIS documents: 15685, a formal action report; 16269–C, critique by Cdr. Yamada of Omori's staff and Capt. Ohmae of Eighth Fleet Staff; 16648–A, answers to my questions presented by Mr. Salomon in 1946.

the Treasuries, missed him. When the Japanese received word at 0230 November 1 that Merrill was off Buka, Omori returned to Rabaul.

Upon his arrival, at 1100, Admiral Samejima, who had got word of the landings that morning at Torokina, ordered him to escort a counter-landing force of a thousand soldiers embarked in five APDs, and also to break up the American amphibious forces. And he gave him four more destroyers which (in Omori's words) "had just come in on that tide." No chance for a conference or a battle plan; just a pick-up job as we had assembled at Tassafaronga and Kolombangara. But Ijuin, the victor at Vella Lavella, was somebody worth picking up.

With this augmented force Omori sortied at 1700 November 1. After reaching St. George Channel, where the transports should have joined, he was told that they were not ready; he had to wait for them until 2030, and when they did join he found they could do no better than 26 knots. To add to Omori's discomfiture, his force sighted a United States submarine, and lost more time evading it. Then, at 2120, a plane dropped a bomb close aboard cruiser *Sendai*.[2] Assuming that he had been sighted, and in view of the several delays, the Admiral decided he could not make the counter-landing that night. He radioed Samejima recommending that it be called off, but that he be allowed to attack the American transports, which he assumed were still in Empress Augusta Bay. In other words he proposed to do what Mikawa had failed to do on 9 August 1942. Samejima agreed; the five troop-laden APDs returned to Rabaul, Omori bent on 32 knots and continued south. Here is his task organization: —

TOROKINA INTERCEPTION FORCE, Rear Admiral Sentaro Omori
Cruiser Division 5, Rear Admiral Omori
MYOKO, HAGURO
Screen, left flank, Rear Admiral Matsuji Ijuin
Light cruiser *SENDAI, destroyers SHIGURE, SAMIDARE, SHIRATSUYU
Screen, right flank, Rear Admiral Morikazu Osugi
Light cruiser AGANO, destroyers NAGANAMI, *HATSUKAZE, WAKATSUKI
* Sunk in this action.

[2] We have been unable to discover what plane this was.

While Omori was rushing south, Rear Admiral Merrill's cruisers and Commander B. L. ("Count") Austin's Desdiv 46 were passing a quiet day at sea near Vella Lavella, cleaning up and resting [3] after their two bombardment missions of 1 November. Captain Arleigh Burke, whose Destroyer Division 45 was low on fuel owing to some fast stepping during the second bombardment, had been sent to refuel from a barge in Hathorn Sound at the head of Kula Gulf. Burke finished this job at 1630 and made best speed to rejoin Merrill, which he did at 2315. Merrill was already steaming north to intercept Omori, of whose movements he had been accurately informed by reconnaissance planes.[4] But Omori did not expect to encounter anything but transports.

Merrill selected a meeting point well to the west of Empress Augusta Bay, and set course and speed accordingly. He deployed his force on a north and south line of bearing of unit guides, the leading destroyer three miles ahead of flagship *Montpelier*. The cruisers were spaced 1000 yards, and there was a 3000-yard interval between the rear cruiser and the flagship of Destroyer Division 46. Although this was the classic formation for such a force when going into night action, it differed in one essential respect from the tight column used a year earlier. "The destroyers were not tied in close to the main battle line, and held there within gun range. They were loose, well removed from the cruisers, with flexibility and freedom of action. They were used offensively instead of defensively, and were sent in to fire their torpedoes before opening gunfire." [5]

Merrill's force was composed as follows; the ships are listed in order of battle: —

[3] Since the terrible example afforded by the Savo Island battle of what fatigue can do to fighting men, the ships' internal organization had been rearranged in order to give personnel a certain amount of rest even during periods of continuous activity; and our battle-hardened bluejackets had learned the soldier's trick of relaxing completely when not working.

[4] "That the two reconnaissance planes which tracked and accurately reported the position, course and speed of the Japanese task force were piloted by Army officers is further evidence of the coöperation which exists between the several services in the South Pacific Area." (CTF 39 Action Report p. 41.) Admiral Merrill describes the reports of these pilots as "phenomenally accurate."

[5] Admiral Pye's comments, sec. 10.

TF 39, Rear Admiral A. Stanton Merrill in *Montpelier*

Van Destroyers (Desdiv 45), Captain Arleigh A. Burke (Comdesron **23**)

| | |
|---|---|
| CHARLES AUSBURNE | Commander L. K. Reynolds |
| DYSON | Commander R. A. Gano |
| STANLY | Commander R. W. Cavenagh |
| CLAXTON | Commander H. F. Stout |

Main Body (Crudiv 12), Rear Admiral Merrill

| | |
|---|---|
| MONTPELIER | Captain R. G. Tobin |
| CLEVELAND | Captain A. G. Shepard |
| COLUMBIA | Captain F. A. Beatty |
| DENVER | Captain R. P. Briscoe |

Rear Destroyers (Desdiv 46), Commander B. L. Austin

| | |
|---|---|
| SPENCE | Commander H. J. Armstrong |
| THATCHER | Commander. L. R. Lampman |
| CONVERSE | Commander DeW. C. E. Hamberger |
| FOOTE | Commander Alston Ramsay |

The four days' moon set early, leaving the night very dark with stars showing through patches in the overcast, except when a rain squall made up. The sea was calm, light airs were blowing from the southwest, and flashes of lightning were observed to the south.

At 0130 November 2 an American plane flew in out of the darkness and dropped a bomb on heavy cruiser *Haguro* which opened up some side plating and slowed the Japanese formation to 30 knots. Ten minutes later, a float plane from *Haguro* reported "one cruiser and three destroyers" about 50 miles off shore. This was Merrill's force, badly underestimated. Omori altered course to engage, but just after doing so, at 0200, he got word that another scout plane had dropped flares over Empress Augusta Bay and discovered "many transports unloading troops." Since no transports were then in the Bay, the plane must have seen the American minelayers, *Breese, Gamble* and *Sicard* escorted by destroyer *Renshaw,* which had just laid a protective mine field north of Cape Torokina and were retiring. Lieutenant Commander Lark, who led them, reported to Admiral Merrill at 0222 that he was retiring and "bringing the snooper along too." The minecraft passed Merrill's cruisers on reverse course, and had a front-row seat for the opening phase of the battle.

❉    ❉    ❉

Task Force 39 approached the rendezvous that was bound to be fatal for somebody at a speed of 20 knots, so that the wakes of the ships would not attract snooper planes. The situation was now similar to that of the fateful 9 August 1942 off Guadalcanal; but Merrill had exact knowledge of Omori's movements, and he knew

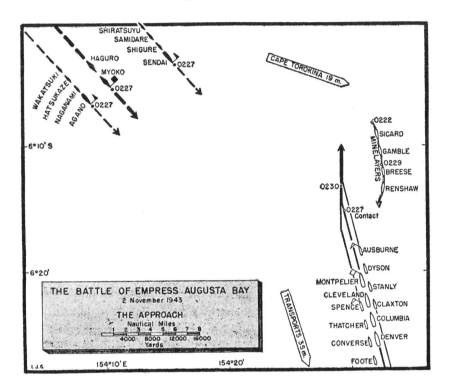

that the best defense for the transports was to drive him away. Merrill's battle plan was "to maintain the cruisers in a position across the entrance to Empress Augusta Bay and to prevent the entry therein of a single enemy ship." He proposed to push the enemy westward in order to gain sea room and to fight at ranges close to the maximum effective range of Japanese torpedoes, say 16,000 to 20,000 yards, in order to protect his cruisers from the fate of *Helena*. He planned to detach the two destroyer divisions for an initial torpedo attack, to hold his cruisers' gunfire until the fish struck home, and to give his destroyer commanders complete freedom of action once they were detached. Both plan and doctrine were well known to Burke but imperfectly so to Austin, who had just joined.

Omori, after receiving the false report of transports unloading troops, changed course at 0200 toward Empress Augusta Bay. He was in cruising disposition, in three columns: Ijuin's screen on the left; Omori's two heavies in the center; Osugi's screen on the right, 5000 meters or more between columns. Some of his ships had radar, but the operators were poor and Omori relied wholly on visual sighting. This time, Japanese eyes and binoculars were not so good as American radar.

At 0227 November 2, when Task Force 39 was steaming course 345° on line of bearing, speed 28 knots, about 20 miles W by S of Cape Torokina, "apple gadgets" (surface pips) began to appear on the flag radar screen, range 35,900 yards. "Believe this is what we want!" reported *Montpelier's* combat information center. It was the left enemy column; the other two showed up on the screen presently. Immediately after radar contact, Merrill changed course to due north, putting his ships in three columns; at 0231 Burke's four van destroyers shoved off, according to plan, to deliver a torpedo attack on the enemy's flank. At 0239 Merrill reversed his cruisers by a simultaneous 180° turn, instructing the rear destroyers to countermarch and become the van, and then to attack on the enemy's southerly flank with torpedoes as soon as they could get on the target. The battle now broke up into three distinct actions from our point of view; one by the cruisers, and one by each destroyer division. But from Omori's point of view it was all the same.

The Japanese admiral, at or about 0245, received two reports of the American position. A reconnaissance aircraft dropped a flare over Merrill's force, and light cruiser *Sendai* sighted it. Omori then ordered simultaneous turns right, to a southwesterly course, both in order to get into battle formation, and to close. While making this loop, between 0250 and 0252, the *Sendai* column fired about eight torpedoes. Thirty seconds before they launched, Merrill, who had been tensely waiting for Captain Burke's torpedoes (launched at 0246) to strike home, received a report from his C.I.C. of the enemy's movement and ordered his cruisers to commence gunfire.

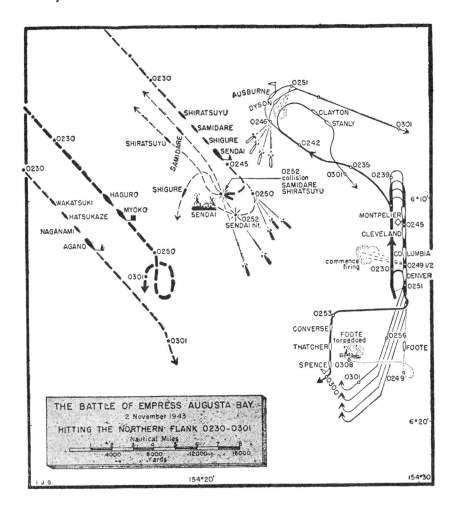

Omori said he saw "fierce shellfire" coming from the enemy, and it was *Sendai* that caught all of it — the typical concentration of night radar-controlled gunfire. *Sendai* had her rudder jammed. She appeared to be burning and exploding. Destroyers *Samidare* and

*Shiratsuyu*, in her column, collided while trying to avoid the 6-inch salvos, and hauled out from the battle. A pretty good initial score for Merrill — one cruiser and two destroyers eliminated when his guns were scarcely warm. Owing, however, to Omori's right turn, none of the 25 torpedoes fired by Burke's four destroyers found a target. The Japanese opening salvos, in the usual compact patterns that they favored, were short and ahead; but their star shell illumination was brilliant. To counteract this, Merrill's cruisers made smoke and, at about 0251, turned simultaneously to course 200° in order to maintain their range, which was then about 19,000 yards. As a result of these countermeasures, "and perhaps because we lead purer lives" (as Admiral Merrill remarked), his cruisers received not one hit during the first half hour.

Omori's two heavies, *Myoko* and *Haguro* in the center column, turned south at 0250. Next, failing to locate their enemy, they completed a 360-degree loop. The southern column, the *Agano* group under Rear Admiral Osugi (whose tactics in this action the Japanese regarded as deplorable), followed the center in a vague and uncertain manner. At this time Merrill's 6-inch shells were falling all around the ships of both the *Myoko* and the *Agano* columns. American gunnery was good — the third salvo "walked right into the target." [6] *Hatsukaze*, third ship of Osugi's column, was doing her best to dodge when she cut between cruisers *Myoko* and *Haguro* and collided with the former, at 0307. *Myoko* sheared off two of the destroyer's tubes and carried a chunk of her starboard bow back to Rabaul; Omori thought he had sunk her.

Merrill in the meantime was doing some radical maneuvering, as may be seen on our charts. At 0301, after steering south for some 20 minutes, he started the first loop of a colossal figure 8. The purpose of this maneuver was partly to shake off Desdiv 46, which was slow in clearing the cruisers' line of fire, and partly to hold an advantageous range; but mostly to make the torpedo-and-gun solution more difficult for the enemy. Merrill maneuvered his cruisers

[6] So Omori told the writer in 1950; he added that Merrill's fourth salvo was over, and he maneuvered to keep the rest over.

so smartly and kept them at such a range that no enemy torpedoes could hit, no matter how accurate a solution the Japanese might work out; for by the time their torpedoes had completed their runs the intended victims were somewhere else.

All this time the American cruisers were dishing out 6-inch gunfire from long range as they zigzagged violently at 30 knots. Admiral Merrill gave high praise to his captains for maintaining formation "during more than an hour of very violent maneuvering by voice radio amidst the deafening din, and for a portion of the time under a heavy cloud of chemical or funnel smoke." Very little damage, however, was inflicted on the enemy during this phase. *Haguro* took six hits but four of them were duds; she slowed down about 0315 but quickly picked up speed. Omori had only just sighted his enemy (at 0313); he then turned from course 180° to 160° in order to close, and both his heavy cruisers fired torpedoes. At the same time his 8-inch fire improved, straddling Merrill's three leading cruisers in salvo after salvo. Between 0320 and 0325 *Denver*, the leading cruiser, received three 8-inch hits forward, which fortunately failed to detonate but let in so much water that she had to cut corners to keep up, although her sister ships slowed to 25 knots. In the meantime, the *Myoko* group and the *Agano* group, with two destroyers, were steaming in a general SSE direction, converging with the course, due south, that Admiral Merrill held until 0326. At that time, since the range had closed to 13,000 yards, which put his cruisers within enemy torpedo water, Merrill executed a 180-degree turn counter-clockwise in order to open range, completing the lower loop of his figure 8.

Enemy planes now approached Merrill's force and dropped both white and colored flares.[7] At that point in the battle there was a cloud ceiling over the cruisers which acted as a silver reflector to the flares and star shell. These brilliantly lighted up the four grace-

---

[7] Commodore Reifsnider in his Action Report states that he sighted the running lights of planes at 0337 approaching the transports from the direction of Admiral Merrill. "While still at a considerable distance they orbited and headed back toward TF 39." These were undoubtedly the planes that dropped the flares but they could not be seen from the cruisers.

ful cruisers spouting flame as their prows hissed through the black waters, in which their salvos were reflected as broken splashes of orange light. Geysers from the enemy's 8-inch misses rose deliberately from the sea like fountains in some princely garden, flashed red, green and golden as they reflected the flares and the cruisers'

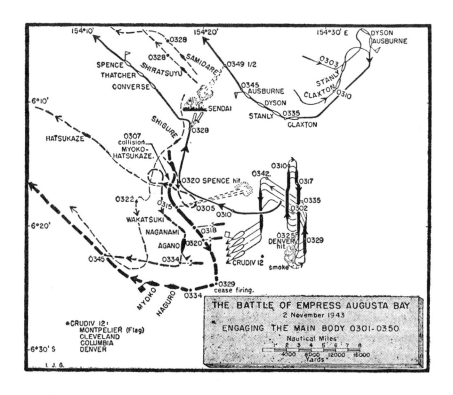

THE BATTLE OF EMPRESS AUGUSTA BAY
2 November 1943
ENGAGING THE MAIN BODY 0301-0350
Nautical Miles

gunfire, poised immobile for a split second, and tumbled back in a sparkle and glitter of phosphorescent spume. It was one of those rare moments of awful beauty that naval warfare occasionally vouchsafes to those who occupy their business in great waters.

Omori, nevertheless, was much disappointed at the performance of his star shell. Some fizzled out, others fell short, and he had only ten for each 8-inch gun. Such visual effect as he got was completely deceptive; he saw two high geysers arise on the engaged side of each of Merrill's three cruisers, and assumed that these near-misses were torpedo hits; the cruisers then disappeared — probably in their own smoke — and he thought he had sunk them. This happened at 0327. The Japanese admiral greatly overestimated both the number and the types of ships that were opposing him.[8] Three of his destroyers were out of action and *Sendai* was going down. So, believing he had done a good night's work and should tempt luck no further, he ordered a general retirement at 0337.

While Merrill's cruisers were tracing intricate patterns on the pathless deep, Destroyer Division 45 went off on a cruise by itself and Division 46 was in trouble. Burke's ships, after launching torpedoes at 0246, became separated in the darkness. It required a full hour for the Captain to reform his "Little Beavers" and come full circle to his former firing position. There at 0349 he encountered a target, the sinking *Sendai*, made several gunfire hits and observed her to be settling in the water as he roared by at 32 knots. *Samidare* and *Shiratsuyu* were observed ahead on the radar screen, so Burke went in hot pursuit of them. Presently he made radar contact with *Spence*, Commander Austin's flagship. Observing a ship ahead turning northward and apparently in a bad way, Burke called over voice radio to Austin, "We have a target smoking badly at 7000 yards and are going to open up," to which *Spence* replied, "Oh-oh, don't do it — that's us!"

Sadly enough, it was not *Spence* but *Samidare* or *Shiratsuyu* who thus obtained grace. Division 45 was then heading a little south of west. At 0457, out of touch with his Admiral, Burke executed a right 180° turn, at the end of which his radar screen showed another target to the southeast. *Spence* was already working over this ship, the damaged *Hatsukaze*, at point-blank range, and had her afire from stem to stern. Austin requested Burke to help finish her off; so the squadron commander turned again, opened fire at 0518 and, at 0539, had the satisfaction of seeing *Hatsukaze* sink. There were no survivors. Day was breaking as Division 45 hastened to rejoin the cruisers.

---

[8] Omori believed, until informed otherwise by the writer in 1950, that he had been opposed by 7 heavy cruisers and 12 destroyers.

The four destroyers of Division 46 had already accumulated all
the bad luck on the American side. Owing to their distance to the
rear, their radar contact on the enemy was delayed, and so they
lost the opportunity to deliver a torpedo attack before gunfire
opened. *Foote* misunderstood the Admiral's signal to counter-

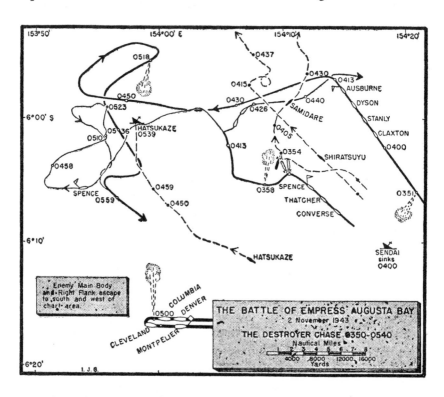

march, and, instead of following her leader in column, turned 180°
immediately, so that she was out of formation at 0245 when Austin,
having made radar contact, turned another 90° to course W in
search of a good torpedoing position. *Foote* soon discovered her
error and endeavored to rejoin, but while hot-footing it in Austin's
direction she ran smack into a Japanese torpedo that was intended
for the cruisers. Her stern was blown off by the explosion and she
went dead in the water right in the cruisers' path; *Cleveland* had to
use full rudder to miss her by 100 yards. *Spence,* turning right

angles in a frantic effort to avoid a more disastrous collision, sideswiped *Thatcher* but without impairing the speed of either destroyer.[9] *Spence* at 0320 received a shell hit at the waterline in such a manner that salt water entered a fuel tank and later slowed her down by contaminating fuel. Thus Austin lost the use of one ship and had two annoying mishaps before his division was able to fire a shot. On top of all that, he missed an excellent opportunity to fire torpedoes at 4000 to 6000 yards' range toward Omori's heavy cruisers, because his combat information officer insisted that the large pips on the radar screen were "friendly."[10]

Austin now turned north in search of other targets and encountered light cruiser *Sendai* making circles in the same locality where she had been hit, and still hitting back. *Spence* and *Converse* fired eight torpedoes at her at 0328. Two explosions were heard, but they did not sink her; Burke, as we have seen, fired the *coup de grâce* eleven minutes later. *Spence*, *Thatcher* and *Converse* then headed northwest, overhauling *Samidare* and *Shiratsuyu*. They had been standing by *Sendai* but started away upon Austin's approach. A brisk little torpedo and gunfire action ensued, but neither side appeared able to hit the other, although range at one time was only 3000 yards and Division 46 fired 19 torpedoes at 0352. *Spence*, with little fuel left, alternately lost and gained suction as salt water diluted her fuel tanks, so Austin designated Commander Lampman of *Thatcher* as O.T.C., sheered out of column at 0413 and steered a wide circle to the west and south which put *Spence* on the other side of the destroyer at which Burke was then firing. That target was probably *Shiratsuyu;* either she or Burke opened up on *Spence*

---

[9] This collision gave rise to a typical piece of CPO humor. After the battle, when *Spence* was going alongside another ship, Commander Armstrong passed the word to put a second fender out. A veteran potbellied chief boatswain's mate was heard to mutter, "If the captain can go alongside at 30 knots with no fender, he don't need two now!"

[10] Cdr. Austin had left the C.I.C. for the bridge on account of the collision; his bridge P.P.I. (Position Plotting Indicator) scope went black, and the C.I.C. personnel became disoriented without the division commander to direct them; hence this expensive error.

at 0425. Austin promptly voice-radioed to Burke, "We have just had another bad close miss. Hope you are not shooting at us," to which Burke replied, "Sorry but you'll have to excuse the next four salvos as they are already on their way!" *Spence*, as one might expect, took very radical evasive action.

At 0454 Austin heard the Admiral's order for all destroyers to join the flagship. As a target still showed on the radar screen he closed it to 4000 yards and opened fire. *Spence's* ammunition was running so low that Austin had to request Burke to take over and finish the job, a commission joyfully executed. That target was *Hatsukaze*, and as day was breaking both Burke and Austin saw her roll over and sink. *Spence* was now ready to call it a night, and fell in with Division 45 as it retired. *Thatcher* and *Converse*, which had turned eastward at 0415, also retired.

Merrill's cruisers, in the meantime, were off on a 20-mile jaunt to the west in search of more targets. Wounded *Hatsukaze*, the only one that they encountered, was fired at a few minutes before 0500, at a range of 17,500 yards, but apparently the cruisers did not hasten her demise. Burke, around 0500, asked permission to pursue fugitives and search for survivors, but the Admiral expected a heavy air attack at dawn and wished to gather his chickens near, if not under his wings; Reifsnider's transports, too, were on his mind. So he instructed Burke to collect all destroyers and rendez-vous at the position where *Foote* had been torpedoed. At 0505, when the flagship had reached a point about 10½ miles west of that position, it was light enough to see several of the destroyers closing in. An enemy scout plane sighted him and reported him a few minutes later. Eighteen "Vals" and 80 "Zekes" promptly took off from Rabaul to get him.

Merrill found *Foote* disabled but afloat. *Claxton* took her in tow with *Ausburne* and *Thatcher* as escorts; the Admiral with the cruisers commenced retiring southward. There were so many Jap-anese planes in sight or on the screen that a bluejacket wise-cracked, "Pipe to breakfast; how do you want your eggs?" Fighter direction in a destroyer still in Empress Augusta Bay was requested to vector every available plane to intercept the Nips and protect *Foote*. Flying weather was bad that morning and most of the scheduled Airsols fighter cover did not get up in time from Vella Lavella; but eight Hellcats, one Marine Corsair, three Army Lightnings and four New Zealand Warhawks were vectored out and shot down eight enemy planes before they reached the cruisers.[11]

The Japanese air strike of over 100 planes, all carrier planes that had arrived at Rabaul the day before, began to close Merrill's formation a few minutes before 0800. The air group commander brought his formation right over *Foote* without releasing a bomb; *Foote* shot at him and claimed splashing at least one. As the Japanese closed the remaining ten miles to the cruisers, Task Force 39, already in circular anti-aircraft formation, executed an emergency 90-degree turn in order to bring batteries to bear. At about 0805 the 5-inch guns began to talk at a range of 14,000 yards, causing deep concern among the American planes overhead who imagined the fire to be directed at them. Admiral Merrill recounts the ensuing action: —

With the 5-inch battery firing like overgrown machine guns, the first three planes seemed incredibly slow in reaching their release point. Soon the 40-mm guns were in action, and then the 20-mm joined in. The scene was of an organized hell in which it was impossible to speak, hear or even think. . . . The air seemed completely filled with bursting shrapnel and, to our great glee, enemy planes in a severe state of disrepair. The *Montpelier's* main battery got one sure 6-inch hit that tore the plane to pieces. Other planes were in flames as they passed over the flagship, exploding inside the destroyer screen. In a few minutes' time, while the guns were still firing at maximum rate, three Nips descended in parachutes, landing almost in the center of the formation. . . . Ten planes were counted in the water at one time, and seven additional were seen to crash well outside the formation.[12]

[11] Capt. Goodman's Report "Rôle of Aviation in Bougainville Operation" Historical Div. Marine Corps. p. 35.

[12] Action Report p. 30. Seventeen planes is also the claim recorded in Airsols Weekly Summary and Review 5 Nov. 1943. We have been unable to find any Japanese records to check this.

At 0807 Merrill ordered an emergency 360-degree turn in order to keep his formation spinning clockwise. The dive-bombers attacked in groups of three, well spaced, which allowed ships' anti-aircraft batteries to concentrate on each wave; and the combination of brisk gunfire and tight circling rattled the aviators as they corkscrewed down. Some broke off, others were shot down before reaching the releasing point, others bombed wildly, a few came in below masthead height without release and then crashed, their pilots killed during the dive. Only two hits were made on the entire force, both on *Montpelier's* starboard catapult, wounding one man seriously. The attack ended at 0812 and, although the surviving enemy planes reformed, a group of Airsols fighters vectored out from the Bay broke them up, shot down eight planes and chased the rest away.

Considering what the task force had been through the previous night, its success in beating off a major air attack without much air support was phenomenal. It was the pay-off for Admiral Halsey's insistence on frequent anti-aircraft practice. Task Force 39, however, owes a vote of thanks to General Kenney. By the time the air attackers had returned to Rabaul, a big V Army Air Force raid was on, and Admiral Kusaka was unable to send out more planes, as he had planned to do, to chase ships.

Merrill now hoped to retire to Purvis Bay for much-needed rest, fueling and replenishment of supplies and ammunition. But at 1310, when he was already 30 miles southeast of the Treasuries, the inexorable Halsey ordered him to return to Empress Augusta Bay to cover the retirement of Commodore Reifsnider's four transports that were still unloading. Three hours later, he received the welcome news that these ships were already on their way south; so he shaped a course for rendezvous and stayed with the transports through a dark and lowery night. At 0900 November 3, off Rendova, Merrill gladly handed them over to cruiser *Nashville* and destroyer *Pringle*, dispatched from Guadalcanal for that purpose, and turned up sufficient speed to make anchorage in

Purvis Bay at 1745. These fighting seamen, who had been on the go continuously, had fought two bombardments and one night action and had beaten off a major air attack since leaving the same port 63 hours before, now had to turn to, refueling and taking ammunition on board. *Foote*, minus her stern, towed by tug *Sioux* and escorted by *Claxton*, arrived safely next morning, 4 November, "amidst loud cheers, incongruously punctuated by yawns," as Admiral Merrill records.

A vast amount of ammunition had been expended by the cruisers of Task Force 39 during its two and a half days of bombarding and fighting. Here are the figures, not counting anything smaller than 5-inch for the night action.

| | *Buka Bombardment* | | *Shortlands Bombardment* | | *Battle of Empress Augusta Bay* | | | | | |
|---|---|---|---|---|---|---|---|---|---|---|
| | | | | | *Night* | | *Day Air Action* | | | |
| | 6″ | 5″ | 6″ | 5″ | 6″ | 5″ | 6″ | 5″ | 40-mm | 20-mm |
| MONTPELIER | 721 | 589 | 259 | 598 | 1489 | 0 | 47 | 305 | 1250 | 4662 |
| CLEVELAND | 750 | 400 | 176 | 577 | 840 | 0 | 0 | 230 | 794 | 942 |
| COLUMBIA | 750 | 599 | 0 | 740 | 1219 | 680 | 0 | 329 | 1974 | 2013 |
| DENVER | 730 | 487 | 0 | 509 | 1043 | 25 | 0 | 140 | 745 | 1044 |
| *Total* | 2951 | 2075 | 435 | 2424 | 4591 | 705 | 47 | 1004 | 4763 | 8661 |

The results, in terms of hits, show that the accuracy of 6-inch cruiser fire had not improved since the battles up the Slot. It is not known how many hits *Sendai* took at the start of the action, probably not more than five, since her fighting ability was not greatly impaired and only the fact that her rudder was jammed allowed the destroyers to sink her with gunfire and torpedoes. *Myoko* took but one or two 6-inch shell hits and *Haguro* six, of which at least four were duds. Possibly *Agano* and some of the destroyers in Osugi's column were hit, but not seriously. Let us allow 20 possible 6-inch hits obtained by Merrill's cruisers that night; not much for almost 4600 rounds fired. However, the effect of the cruiser gunfire was not limited to hits. By having forced rapid maneuvering on Omori's scratch task force, Merrill may claim credit for the two collisions. And of the 52 torpedoes launched by our destroyers, we can claim only two hits, both on *Sendai*. The destroyers also expended 2596 rounds of 5-inch shell during the night action.

Victory, however, is attained by relative, not absolute results. Omori had twenty 8-inch and six 6-inch guns to Merrill's forty-eight 6-inch. His ships mounted eighty-eight 24-inch torpedo tubes against Merrill's eighty 21-inch tubes. Yet all he accomplished was five shell hits on *Denver*, one on *Spence* and one torpedo hit on *Foote*. Although Omori reported nonexistent heavy cruisers and other ships sunk, his superiors were not pleased that he had failed to get at the American transports, and relieved him of command.[13]

Merrill deserved every bit of his victory. He made a good beginning by releasing destroyers to fulfill their primary function of torpedo attack; and if the results were disappointing that was to be expected of a lusty child just released from leading strings. He was bold when boldness was needed and cautious when caution was required; in the face of a constantly changing tactical situation he kept his poise, confidence and power of quick decision. His swift simultaneous turns to avoid enemy torpedoes, while he was pouring out continuous rapid fire, were masterpieces of maneuver.

Of his task force the Admiral said, "It functioned as a well-drilled team. Each officer and each man did his job as he had been trained to do it. . . . Officers and men alike were brave and calm and confident. They were confident in their superiors, in their subordinates, and in themselves. Though our losses might well have been greater, the final outcome of the battle was never in doubt."

Doubt, however, still hung over the final outcome of the Bougainville operation. The enemy had six to eight heavy cruisers at Truk, from whom a serious threat of surface attack developed within forty-eight hours. This time it was carriers to the rescue.

---

[13] Omori on returning to Rabaul sent a submarine south to rescue survivors. It got none from *Hatsukaze*, but many from *Sendai* including the C.O. and Admiral Ijuin; others reached Bougainville on rafts, but 320 were lost. The casualties in Merrill's force were limited to 19 killed and 17 wounded in *Foote*, 9 wounded in air attack on *Montpelier*.

# CHAPTER XVIII

# Carrier Strikes on Rabaul[1]

## 5–18 November 1943

### 1. Action of 5 November

A S SOON AS Admiral Koga heard of the landings at Empress Augusta Bay, he decided to reinforce Samejima's naval forces at Rabaul. Happily this decision came too late to augment Omori's forces on 2 November, but it promised trouble for someone later. The very formidable group that he sent south consisted of seven heavy cruisers of the Second Fleet, the battle-scarred veterans *Takao, Maya, Atago, Suzuya, Mogami, Chikuma* and *Chokai,* commanded by Vice Admiral Takeo Kurita; light cruiser *Noshiro* and four destroyers; and a suitable fleet train. These got through safely, but later increments were not so fortunate. At dawn 4 November, tankers *Nichiei Maru* and *Nissho Maru,* Rabaul-bound with two destroyers escorting, were crippled by bombs dropped from Airsols patrol planes. Kurita, whose force was in their vicinity, detached cruiser *Chokai* and a destroyer to tow them back to Truk. Three troop-laden transports, escorted by light cruiser *Isuzu* and two destroyers, also were caught by South Pacific Liberators in broad daylight 60 miles north of Kavieng on the 4th. Although this force was protected by fighter cover from Kavieng, two trans-

---

[1] At this point in our story the USSBS publication *The Allied Campaign Against Rabaul* (1946), compiled by a team headed by Brig. Gen. Lewis G. Merritt USMC, becomes useful. "Carrier Battle Notes 2–43" in Comairpac (Rear Admiral J. H. Towers) Air Operation Memorandum 17–43; Comairpac "Summary Account of Carrier Actions 1 Sept. 1943–1 Mar. 1944"; Rear Admiral F. C. Sherman to Cincpac 8 Dec. 1943; C.O. *Saratoga* (Capt. J. H. Cassady) to Cominch 15 Nov. 1943 with enclosures from squadron commanders. The Japanese sources are ATIS Doc. No. 16648–B, answers to questions from this writer about Rabaul, Lt. Cdr. Salomon's Tokyo Notes, and "Southeast Area Operations" Part 2 (Navy).

ports were hit and one had to be towed into Rabaul. And around noon that day another B-24 sighted Kurita's force, 19 ships all told, off the Admiralties and heading toward the western entrance of St. George Channel.

Admiral Halsey had barely digested the news of Merrill's victory when he received this word. Not so good! Obviously another threat to our amphibious forces at Empress Augusta Bay. Halsey had not one heavy cruiser to oppose them; every capital ship in the Pacific Fleet was warming up for the Gilberts. But Rear Admiral Frederick C. Sherman's fast carrier force (Task Force 38) built around *Saratoga* and *Princeton*, which had been assigned for the Buka-Bonis bombardment, was still under his command. At the moment when news of the Japanese "heavies" arrived, these carriers were fueling from tanker *Kankakee* south of Guadalcanal at a point near Rennell Island, whither they had been sent by Admiral Halsey in order to be "in readiness for anything that might develop." Carriers were not then supposed to be used against powerful bases such as Rabaul, but there was nothing else to send.

South Pacific staff hastily prepared a plan for rushing *Saratoga* and *Princeton* to launching position for a surprise attack on the ships assembled in Simpson Harbor. The enemy was believed to have at least 150 planes at Rabaul, and actually had more; there was a big risk that they might wipe out the carrier air groups. But when the plan with all its disagreeable implications was placed before Admiral Halsey it took him only a moment to order, "Go to it!"

"Ted" Sherman was just completing his fueling northwest of the Rennells on the evening of 4 November when he received the following dispatch from Halsey, dated 1638 local time. It was addressed also to CTF 33 (General Twining, Air Solomons) and to General MacArthur: —

Task Force 38 proceed maximum formation speed . . . to vicinity lat. 7° S, long. 154° 30' E. About 0900 Love November 5th launch all-out strike on shipping in Rabaul and north thereof (order of targets: cruisers, destroyers). Retire thereafter . . . Task Force 33 provide air cover from Barakoma over Task Force 38 during its daylight approach and retirement. Commander in Chief Southwest Pacific requested to strike Rabaul shipping about 1200.

Sherman's flagship was stately old *Saratoga*, Captain John H. ("Hopalong") Cassady. She carried Air Group 12, Commander Henry H. Caldwell, which had been training since June for just such a fight. The new light carrier *Princeton*, Captain George Henderson, had Air Group 23 under Commander Henry Miller; the screen consisted of anti-aircraft light cruisers *San Diego* (flying the flag of Rear Admiral Wiltse) and *San Juan* and nine destroyers, commanded by Captain Rodger W. Simpson in *Farenholt*.

In order to reach the designated launching point shortly after daylight next morning, this formation had to make a speed of 27 knots. Fortunately the weather was exactly what they wanted, smooth sea and overcast; for if the sea had been rough the destroyers could never have kept up that speed, and without cloud cover they would probably have been snooped.[2] The formation ran through a moderate front in the night, and after day broke encountered welcome rain squalls and what Admiral Sherman describes as "a comfortable wind of five to seven knots to facilitate launching." It arrived at the launching point, about 57 miles southwest of Cape Torokina and 230 miles southeast of Rabaul, at 0900 November 5. Promptly the carriers commenced launching every available plane. *Saratoga* put into the air 33 Hellcat fighters, 16 Avenger torpedo-bombers and 22 Dauntless dive-bombers; *Princeton* sent up 19 Hellcats and 7 Avengers. This total of 97 planes[3] left decks and hangars bare of everything but cripples. For, as we have seen from Halsey's operation order, the ships were furnished combat air patrol by the Airsols command.

Two hours after launching commenced, the birds were flying into the lion's mouth. They had one of the most rugged tasks ever

---

[2] Actually they were snooped after dawn, but the Japanese pilot reported them as 5 CAs, 2 APs and 7 DDs, so the contact was worse than useless.

[3] The commander of *Saratoga*'s fighters was Cdr. Joseph C. ("Jumping Joe") Clifton; of the TBFs, Lt. Cdr. Robert Farrington; of the dive-bombers, Lt. Cdr. James Newell.

handed to pilots in the South Pacific. Staff officers had been up all night, figuring out approach, attack and retiring plans, but they had no exact knowledge of where the Japanese cruisers were anchored. The configuration of Simpson, the inner harbor of Rabaul, and of Blanche Bay, the outer roadstead, is such that an almost circular curtain of flak could be thrown up at the planes. But Sherman had insisted on rigorously training his pilots to bomb moving ships, and he and his air group commander, Caldwell, had worked out the tactics. So short was the time for preparation that assignment of targets and detailed planning were largely accomplished in the air, after the planes had flown from the carriers, by group and squadron commanders over voice radio.

The weather gave them a wonderful break: rainy and overcast at the launching point, yet so clear over the land that Rabaul could be seen by the pilots from fifty miles away. It was easy to distinguish forty or fifty sail of shipping anchored in the harbor, including eight of the much-desired heavy cruisers and about twenty light cruisers and destroyers.

As the carrier planes swung into St. George Channel about 1110, Rabaul headquarters had a short warning from its 70 fighter planes airborne, but the ships in harbor were caught flatfooted; one heavy cruiser was fueling. Japanese fighter pilots were fooled by Caldwell's tactics. Expecting his force to split up into small groups as it neared the targets, they held off in order to gang up on them; but the American pilots held formation right through the flak and broke into small groups only at the last moment before diving or launching torpedoes. As the Japanese fighter pilots dared not fly into their own flak, this left them on the outside looking in, waiting to intercept the retiring bombers, and the Hellcat escorts, led by Clifton, were right on the job to get them.

The southeast trade wind drew right into Simpson Harbor; hence it was certain that the ships would be either at anchor heading into it or under way in the same direction. Dive-bombing, for full efficiency, has to be done fore-and-aft and preferably in the direction of the ship's movement. Torpedo-bombers come in parallel to their targets and then make quick right-angled turns to launch fish. So Caldwell led his strike of 22 dive-bombers and 23 torpedo-bombers with Hellcat escorts right across the Crater Peninsula through a curtain of flak, in order to sweep upwind parallel to the Japanese ships from the head of the harbor.

As the dive-bombers deployed for the approach, the torpedo planes broke off and came down low, taking advantage of some small clouds that afforded temporary cover, in order to attack immediately after the SBDs. Both sets of planes dove through the shore-based curtain into a blast of machine-gun fire coming from almost every ship in the harbor. Now thoroughly alarmed, the ships were "running every which way, like a flock of skittering cockroaches in a suddenly lighted dirty kitchen."[4] One heavy cruiser opened fire on the TBFs with her main battery. The pilots, after pulling out of their dives or runs, had to dodge over, around and between ships for four or five miles, skidding, jinking and climbing desperately to evade. It seemed a miracle even to them that they got through. Yet, after the action only 5 fighters and 5 bombers were missing out of the 97 that attacked; only 7 pilots and 8 crewmen were killed or missing.

Commander Caldwell, who had remained topside directing the dive-bombers, found himself, in company with one of *Princeton's* Hellcats, being chased by eight "Zekes." With his turret out of commission, the gunner wounded and photographer Barnett killed, his forward guns managed to drive one "Zeke" after another away. The Hellcat received more than 200 bullet holes (including a few in the pilot, Lieutenant H. M. Crockett), yet landed on board *Princeton* without flaps; Caldwell landed his Avenger on *Saratoga* "with one wheel, no flaps, no aileron and no radio."[5]

Although not one Japanese ship was sunk, the damage inflicted

[4] Eugene Burns "We Avenge Pearl Harbor" *Sat. Eve. Post* 22 July 1944 p. 19, vivid though inaccurate story based on reports of the returned pilots. Burns was on board *Saratoga*. This History almost lost its most prolific source of data from Japan that day; Capt. Ohmae, then on the staff of Admiral Kusaka, was in a small boat in the harbor delivering a message to Admiral Kurita when the strike came in; one of the planes strafed his boat and wounded one of the crew.

[5] Comairgroup 12, Report to C.O. *Saratoga* 13 Nov. (Enc. F in latter's report).

knocked out Kurita's Second Fleet for the time being. One of Lieutenant Newell's bombs dropped down the stack of *Maya*, the heavy cruiser that was fueling, and exploded in her engine room. It took five months to repair her. *Takao* took two hits which opened a large hole at the waterline. *Atago* suffered from three near-misses. *Mogami*, who had just returned after the damage suffered at Midway, was now sent back to Kure to repair bad bomb damage. Light cruisers *Agano* and *Noshiro* were hit, the latter by a torpedo; destroyer *Fujinami* took a dud torpedo [6] and *Wakatsuki* was holed by near-misses. All these ships except *Maya* were able to retire under their own power; but this strike ended the use of heavy ships in those waters. No heavy cruisers ever bothered Bougainville again.

General Kenney delivered the follow-up strike on Rabaul as requested, and on time, but it was then too late to do much good. Twenty-seven B–24s starting from Dobodura picked up 67 P–38s at Woodlark and arrived over Rabaul shortly after noon. Disappointed to find no planes on the ground, as all were hunting for Sherman, they bombed the town and wharves.

The American carriers, after recovering all planes about 1300, made a quick getaway and escaped unscathed. Japanese searchers located Sherman's ships at 1445 and 18 "Kates" were sent out by Admiral Kusaka to get them. At 1915 in late twilight they found their quarry — as they thought — and attacked. The result, as reported by their pilots at Rabaul and broadcast by Radio Tokyo next day, was "One large carrier blown up and sunk, one medium carrier set ablaze and later sunk, and two heavy cruisers and one cruiser and destroyer sunk." What a victory! Imperial Headquarters commended the Rabaul air forces and named this action "The First Air Battle of Bougainville."

---

[6] American aërial torpedo performance was still poor: only 2 hits out of 23 dropped and one a dud. "Drag rings," wooden frames that disintegrated when the torpedoes struck the water, first attached before the February 1944 strike on Truk, enabled TBF pilots to make high-speed attacks at 1000 feet altitude. Until that time our torpedo-plane performance was still markedly inferior to the Japanese. For instance, on 11 Oct. 1943 two torpedo-toting "Bettys" from Rabaul got into Ironbottom Sound at dark and torpedoed two Liberty ships, one of which, *John H. Couch*, sank.

There was no need, however, for Halsey to notify the families of Sherman's crews, or to write *Saratoga, Princeton, San Diego* and *San Juan* off the books. Here is what happened: That evening *LCI–70*, an "Elsie Item gunboat," and *PT–167*, a zebra-striped motor torpedo boat, were escorting *LCT–68* back from the Torokina beachhead to the Treasuries. At 1915, when about 28 miles SW of Cape Torokina, they sighted a flight of "Kates" against the fading twilight. The wing of the leading bomber struck the PT's radio antenna and the plane splashed; but its torpedo, without hitting the water or exploding, passed through the bow of the boat, leaving its entire tail assembly in the crew's head as a souvenir. A few minutes later the PT's 20-mm fire hit one of the second wave of attacking bombers and it fell in flames, so close to her port quarter that men on the stern were drenched by the splash. In the meantime *LCI–70* was having the toughest fight that any of her type had experienced. In 14 minutes she was subjected to four low-altitude torpedo attacks and one strafing run. Owing to her shoal draft, all the torpedoes aimed at her passed harmlessly below her keel, except one that porpoised into the engine room, killing one man but not exploding; the warhead slid off into the bread locker.[7] Fearing an explosion of the murderous torpedo, which was still smoking, the skipper, Lieutenant (jg) H. W. Frey, ordered Abandon Ship. After a decent interval had passed with no explosion, a damage-control party went on board the Elsie Item. *LCT–68* passed her a line and towed her back to Torokina, while *PT–167* went ahead with the wounded. Such was the reality of what the Japanese called "Air Battle of Bougainville," probably the biggest feat of lying in the entire Pacific war. Ensign Theodore Berlin USNR, skipper of the PT, for her part in the action, received a congratulatory message from Admiral Wilkinson which closed with, "Fireplug Sprinkles Dog."

Admiral Halsey, fearing the worst from his gamble with the two carriers, was delighted with the results. "It is real music to me," he radioed Sherman, "and opens the stops for a funeral dirge

[7] Gunnery Officer *LCI(L)–70* Report on AA Action 5 Nov. 1943.

for Tojo's Rabaul." That funeral procession lasted three more months and needed a lot more encouragement. Rabaul was still very formidable and its communications with Truk were intact, but the elimination of Kurita's heavy cruiser force enabled the Bougainville operation to proceed without another surface attack. That indeed was something; for with the Gilbert Islands operation coming up Nimitz could spare no heavy cruisers to protect shipping en route to Empress Augusta Bay.

## 2. *Action of 11 November*

It is a pity that Rabaul could not have been struck again in a day or two, for a one-two punch in air warfare is far more effective than two punches of the same strength a week apart. Halsey had asked for two carrier groups to cover the Bougainville landings and Nimitz planned to give him only one; but ten days before the operation started he relented and sent another, the new *Essex* and *Bunker Hill* and light carrier *Independence*, under Rear Admiral Montgomery. Unfortunately all the cruisers in the screen (Rear Admiral DuBose's division) and all but two of the destroyers were detached to support Wilkinson at Torokina after delivering the flattops at Espiritu Santo on 5 November, and days were lost while Halsey's operations officer frantically scoured the Pacific to find more destroyers for the screen. So Montgomery could not leave Segond Channel until 8 November, and his strike on Rabaul was scheduled for the 11th.

Admiral Kusaka's air force at Rabaul was now down to 270 planes, of which 100 belonged to the carriers. Third Fleet had expended 39 planes in the preceding week; Eleventh Air Fleet had lost 44. Sixteen fighters and 12 torpedo bombers were expected from Truk, but it is not certain whether they arrived in time for this fight.

"Ted" Sherman's *Saratoga* and *Princeton* group, which had delivered the 5 November punch, got in on this too. It approached north of the Solomons and launched from a point near the Green Islands, 225 miles E by S of Rabaul. Sherman's planes hit the target first, in soupy weather. They took a crack at a light cruiser and four destroyers dodging into squalls, returned on board, and that was that. Foul weather prevented launching a second strike, but by the same token no Japanese snoopers ever located them.

Montgomery's larger group won the honors this day. As finally constituted at Espiritu Santo, it was organized in this wise: —

TG 50.3, Rear Admiral Alfred E. Montgomery

ESSEX             Captain Ralph A. Ofstie

Air Group 9, Commander Paul E. Emrick

| | | |
|---|---|---|
| VF–9 | 36 F6F–3 (Hellcat) | Lt. Cdr. Philip H. Torrey |
| VB–9 | 36 SBD–4 (Dauntless) | Lt. Cdr. Arthur T. Decker |
| VT–9 | 19 TBF–1 (Avenger) | Cdr. Emrick |

BUNKER HILL             Captain John J. Ballentine

Air Group 17, Commander Michael P. Bagdanovich

| | | |
|---|---|---|
| *VF–17 | 24 F4U–4 (Corsair) | Lt. Cdr. John T. Blackburn |
| VF–18 | 24 F6F–3 | Lt. Cdr. S. L. Silber |
| VB–17 | 33 SB2C (Helldiver) | Lt. Cdr. James E. Vose |
| VT–17 | 18 TBF–1 | Lt. Cdr. F. M. Whitaker |

INDEPENDENCE             Captain Roy L. Johnson

Air Group 22, Commander James M. Peters

| | | |
|---|---|---|
| VF–22 | 12 F6F–3 | Lt. L. L. Johnson |
| VC–22 | 9 TBF–1 | Cdr. Peters |
| VF–6 | 12 F6F–3 | Lt. Cdr. Harry W. Harrison |
| *VF–33 | 12 F6F–3 | Lt. John C. Kelly |

Destroyer Screen, Commander C. J. Stuart

| | |
|---|---|
| STERETT | Lt. Cdr. Frank G. Gould |
| BULLARD | Lieut. Cdr. Bernard W. Freund |
| MURRAY | Cdr. Paul R. Anderson |
| MCKEE | Cdr. J. J. Greytak |
| STACK | Lt. Cdr. Philip K. Sherman |
| WILSON | Lt. Cdr. C. K. Duncan |
| EDWARDS | Lt. Cdr. Paul G. Osler |
| KIDD | Cdr. Allan B. Roby |
| CHAUNCEY | Lt. Cdr. Lester C. Conwell |

* These squadrons flew out from Ondonga and Segi Point to reinforce Combat Air Patrol.

The story of Montgomery's strike is here told in the words of my collaborator, Commander James C. Shaw, who was then assistant gunnery officer in *Bunker Hill* and has since examined all available Japanese as well as American records: —

We were 160 miles southeast of Rabaul when we launched, after an all-night, high-speed approach, the big carriers, putting up about 80 planes apiece including C.A.P. while *Independence* contributed 25. *Bunker Hill's* strike contained 23 SB2C dive-bombers — the new Hell-diver, alias "The Beast." Led by "Moe" Vose (who had spearheaded the crippling attack on *Shokaku* at the Battle of Santa Cruz), these planes were entering action for the first time and everyone wondered how they would compare with the veteran Dauntless.

It took an hour for the strikes to rendezvous and during that time we congratulated ourselves on having sneaked through the enemy air-search web. But we were wrong. At 0645 an early-bird scout had re-ported us to Kusaka and the attack by *"Sara"* and *Princeton* had alarmed him further. Unfortunately, neutralizing air strikes requested of Ken-ney's bombers had been cut to a handful of planes by weather on the 9th and 10th and completely aborted on the 11th. Consequently when at 0830 our planes roared past Cape St. George they collided with 68 "Zekes." Dodging fighters and flak, the Americans struck through a film of rain at what they could see in harbor and channel, *Essex* planes at 0905 followed by those of *Bunker Hill* and *Independence*.

Air group commanders flew TBFs, which "Zekes" loved to chase and, even with fighter protection, became involved in air battles to the detriment of strike coördination. Certainly neither they nor any other American could tell who hit what during the attack; but after the smoke cleared, the Japanese tallied the following damage: —

Light cruiser *Agano*, one torpedo hit.
Destroyer *Naganami*, heavily damaged by torpedo. Towed into port by *Makinami*.
Destroyer *Suzunami*, dive-bombed while loading torpedoes. Ex-plosions split hull. Sunk near entrance to Rabaul Harbor.
Light cruiser *Yubari* and destroyers *Urakaze* and *Umikaze*, slight damage from strafing.

Our torpedoes performed badly but perhaps it wasn't all the fault of that weapon. For example, *Independence* pilots had practised no "live-drop" torpedo runs since April.

Back in *Bunker Hill* it was Old Home Week. Twenty-four Corsairs of "Tommy" Blackburn's VF-17, which had trained in *Bunker Hill*, flew out from Ondonga, New Georgia, to bolster combat air patrol.

These planes, with their macabre skull-and-crossbones insignia, landed on board to refuel and give the pilots a shot of coffee. A dozen Hellcats of VF–33 also flew up from Segi Point, New Georgia. A squadron of Army Warhawks, supposed to beef up our C.A.P. at 1100, never showed up — another argument for Navy air supporting Navy ships.

Halsey, with his usual aggressiveness, had directed two strikes against the enemy, so when our planes returned before noon, Montgomery ordered rearming. A good idea, but Kusaka now voiced some convincing objections. During the morning his scouts had successively reported our carriers, Merrill's cruisers and Wilkinson's amphibs and only the matter of protecting the home base had kept his planes from executing counterattacks. But he had us "boresighted" underneath a scout "Zeke" which circled at tremendous altitude — where our radars couldn't track or guns shoot. With this pilot's information, Kusaka mounted a strike at noon sharp: 67 "Zekes," 27 "Vals" and 14 "Kates," followed shortly by a flight of "Bettys" — one of the largest anti-carrier strikes since the start of the war.

At 1313 American SK radars "glommed" onto bogeys, 119 miles distant and closing. Except for sending interceptors, Montgomery disregarded this warning and at 1325 planes of his second strike started aloft. At 1351 fighters tally-hoed the foe 40 miles away. Fighter directors asked "How many?" and one pilot shouted over voice radio "Jesus Christ! There are millions of them. Let's go to work!" They did too, herding seven "Vals" and several "Bettys" back up St. George Channel and continuing dogfights with others right to the fringe of our task group.

The weather may have been bad elsewhere but it was superb for us. A nine-knot breeze kicked up little white curls on the water. About a third of the sky was covered with high cirrus clouds against which planes stood out in vivid silhouette. In the distance Bougainville's mountains glowered gray-green — too far to shield the foe from searching radar. We steamed in a superior new AA formation, with carriers grouped together rather than separated — *Essex, Bunker Hill* and *Independence* forming a triangle on the 2000-yard circle with the nine destroyers spaced evenly on the 4000-yard circle.

Yeoman John Mroski's far-sighted eyes picked up the "Vals" at 20,000 yards, 22,000 feet up, flying in a beautiful flat V unopposed by fighters. At 1354 we opened fire at the bat-wings before they'd gone into their dives. Two fell smoking. Others pushed over.

Thereafter, the sky rained airplanes and bombs. Near-misses hammered alongside each carrier. I recall one "Val" pointed "right at me," motionless overhead like a planet but growing and growing until he released his bomb. "Looks like he's let go his belly tank," said a sailor from Arkansas. The "belly tank" exploded close aboard, splashing grimy water on our bomb-laden planes. Other "Vals" strafed and I cursed those winking gun flashes that looked so much like friendly signals.

While we were engaging the first "Vals," momentarily dead ahead, another group struck from the starboard quarter. From 1354 until 1430 "Vals" and "Zekes" dove in clusters or alone. Anti-aircraft gunfire and fighter opposition shattered enemy coördination and several "Vals" turned away in the face of flak. Two of our dive-bomber gunners climbed into parked planes and fired machine guns vigorously. Pilots jumped out of planes to pass ammunition on the ship's guns. An incredible shot from an *Independence* 40-mm detonated a bomb falling over that ship. At 1412 — eighteen minutes after the action started — the Admiral remembered history long enough to shout over the TBS: "Man your guns and shoot those bastards out of the sky!" He reluctantly canceled the second strike on Rabaul.

Our fighter planes, eager to get the Japs, swarmed in and out of the AA bursts and tracer streams. Some of them used unorthodox fighter-direction, heading for the heaviest AA where there would surely be game. Once *Bunker Hill* was shooting at a diving "Val" pursued by a Corsair, who in turn had a "Zeke" on his tail.

At 1430 the "Kates" arrived and gave us ten busy minutes. They did get off some fish, but maneuver saved our hulls. Captain Ballentine, *Bunker Hill's* skipper, was a magnificent shiphandler, one of the few aviators I know who loved ships more than he did airplanes, though he loved them too. His conning kept the ship clear of torpedo water. During the attack I saw a "Kate" about twenty feet off the water dart by the formation with a Corsair closing fast. Like a cowboy roping a wild steer the Corsair sent tracers licking out and the "Kate" went in with an awesome splash. Even the Helldivers and Avengers sought enemy scalps. The sea flowered with smoke blossoms from burning Jap planes.

Destroyer *Kidd* had a private war, having left the formation before the shooting to pick up a downed flier. Two "Kates," thinking her easier game than the task force, tried to torpedo her but were knocked down with no success.

The action lasted 46 minutes which seemed like 46 years and its intensity is illustrated by the ammunition expenditures of the carriers.

Rounds Fired

| Ship | 5"-38 | 40-mm | 20-mm |
|------|-------|-------|-------|
| BUNKER HILL | 532 | 4878 | 22,790 |
| ESSEX | 216 | 2302 | 8,891 |
| INDEPENDENCE | — | 1294 | 1,871 |

*Bunker Hill*, by chance the favorite Japanese target, fired over twice as many shots as *Essex* and probably more than went off in the entire battle for which she was named.[8]

After the battle, a grizzled gunner's mate of the Old Nyvee griped: "Ships fightin' ships is right and so's planes fightin' planes, but ships fightin' planes just ain't natural." Green sailors didn't share this view and their battle fears vanished with the last Jap plane, replaced by an amazing nonchalance. To them it had been so easy, and nobody got killed — only 10 sailors hurt in the task group. Guadalcanal veterans, on the other hand, *really* took fright now that it was over, imagining from experience what those bombs might have done.

We gathered in our planes — 11 were missing — and hauled away furiously from a scene certain to be visited by night-riding "Bettys." We weren't terrified of individual torpedo planes but dreaded the consequences of a lucky fish disabling us close to the den of flying jackals. After nightfall a round moon gilded sea and ships, and on the radar screen we watched the pips of approaching snoopers. One flew up our wake to within 20 miles, then turned away. Clear screen at last!

Admiral Kusaka at Rabaul, hearing that his afternoon strike had blown up a cruiser and damaged two carriers and three other ships, reacted with fear rather than joy. He ordered *Maya*, *Chokai* and three destroyers to clear for Truk and sent "Bettys" to "crush the enemy." Eleven of these planes, after missing us, found and tackled Merrill's cruisers. With the return of this flight Kusaka could take stock of the day's air losses: Six "Zekes" over Rabaul; 14 "Kates" (all that attacked), 17 "Vals," 2 "Zekes" and several "Bettys" over our task force. Only 3 out of 20 attacking "Vals" had escaped our flak and fighters, and though

[8] *Essex*-class carriers at that time mounted twelve 5-inch-38-cal., forty 40-mm barrels and fifty-five 20-mm, numbers which increased as the war went on. *Independence* mounted twenty-six 40-mm barrels and fifty 20-mm. When *Bunker Hill* was commissioning, Lieutenant Commander W. R. D. Nickelson (our gunnery officer) and I bitterly demanded more guns. "Nick," at Buord's request, flew up from Trinidad where we were shaking down, and met an armchair officer in Washington who was supposed to discuss armament. Nick was wearing the Purple Heart acquired in *Atlanta*, but when he asked for more guns was told: "Why don't you quit stalling and get that ship out and do some fighting?"

Kusaka didn't know it, the return on this heavy investment was nought.

Despite the small damage inflicted on Japanese shipping, this was a significant battle. It hacked up Japanese carrier air strength just before Tarawa, bled enemy air pressure from Bougainville and caused Koga to withdraw the remnants of his carrier planes from Rabaul the very next day, replacing them with a handful of inferior planes and pilots from the Marshalls (also a break for Nimitz). The Japs, counting wings at Truk, found that the carriers had lost 50 per cent of their "Zekes," 85 per cent of their "Vals" and 90 per cent of their "Kates" in less than a fortnight at Rabaul.

On the American side, Montgomery's carriers had successfully withstood the fury of all-out attack from land bases. If the flattops had suffered any serious damage there would have been reluctance in Pacific Fleet Headquarters to advance them as brashly as we later did. The vast improvement in a year's span in our fighters and ship anti-aircraft, as demonstrated that day, was a warning to the enemy and a happy portent to us.

Men who fought the flower of Japan's air strength 11 November 1943 won't forget. Every Armistice Day, *Bunker Hill* alumni meet to commemorate the event.

# CHAPTER XIX

# Securing the Beachhead[1]

## 2–13 November 1943

### 1. LSTs and Second Echelon, 2–7 November

W E LEFT the assault elements of the 3rd Marine Division along a very narrow beachhead on the night of 1–2 November. The next few days were devoted to sending out patrols, improving beach defenses, and rooting out a small but determined band of Japanese who were harassing the beaches with machine-gun fire from tiny Torokina Island. By the end of 5 November the beachhead had been extended about 2000 yards inland, at a cost to the landing forces of 78 men killed or missing and 104 wounded.

In the meantime the second echelon of the landing and occupation force, loaded at Guadalcanal, had sailed from Purvis Bay, in the early morning 4 November. This consisted of eight LSTs commanded by Captain G. B. ("Chick") Carter, the genial "Admiral of the Love-Sugar-Tares," and eight APDs, each carrying 200 to 250 Marines, escorted by six destroyers of Squadron 22 (Captain J. E. Hurff), *Waller*, *Saufley*, *Philip*, *Renshaw*, *Eaton* and *Sigourney*.

The inexhaustible Task Force 39 covered this echelon. Admiral Merrill's cruisers and destroyers, excepting damaged *Denver* and

---

[1] Add to authorities listed in note 1, chap. xvi, the following: War Diary Naval Advanced Base, Torokina; CTF 39 (Rear Admiral Merrill) Action Report period 5–8 Nov. 1943; LST Flotilla Five (Capt. G. B. Carter) Action Report 2nd Echelon Northern Force Empress Augusta Bay 4–8 Nov., 9 Dec. 1943; conversations at the time with Capt. Carter and Cdr. Roger Cutler USNR; Report of British Liaison Officer Pacific Fleet (Cdr. Harold S. Hopkins RN) to British Naval Attaché, Washington, 8 Nov. 1943; Maj. Gen. A. H. Turnage USMC Combat Report Bougainville Operations 1 Nov.–28 Dec. 1943.

*Foote*, sortied from Purvis Bay at twilight on the 4th after a "rest" of 48 hours, most of which had been spent in fueling and taking on supplies and ammunition. The night run northward was lively, with bogeys and "apple-gadgets" seldom absent from the radar screens, float lights blinking in the water, at least two bombing attacks by snoopers, near-misses, anti-aircraft guns crackling and tracer bullets spouting heavenward. Nobody got much sleep, but nobody was hit.

Off Simbo Island at dawn 6 November, Merrill made contact with Captain Carter's force, which arrived off Empress Augusta Bay at 0700.

As this was the first amphibious operation in the South Pacific that used any large number of LSTs, their performance and their new equipment, ordered in the light of only four months' experience, were watched with great interest. LST means Landing Ship, Tank; but actually these 325-foot floating garages were used in the Pacific for almost everything but tanks: as personnel transports, cargo carriers, ammunition lighters, repair ships, sea ambulances.[2] They proved to be the most useful all-around craft invented by the Navy. LSTs had never been intended to spend more than an hour unloading, for the tanks or trucks they were supposed to carry were designed to roll ashore as soon as the doors were open and the ramp was down. But in the South Pacific LSTs were wanted to handle supplies, not tanks; and if all supplies were preloaded in trucks the pay load of each LST became very small. The usual method was to stack up bulk cargo (such as oil drums, ammunition boxes, provision crates, lumber, marston mat, barbed wire) on the tank deck from the after bulkhead to a point well forward, leaving space for a few preloaded trucks which, after discharging initial loads, backed into the LST for more, while much of the bulk cargo was manhandled ashore. This method allowed an LST to carry about four times as much pay load as if everything had been

---

[2] They were used for tanks to some extent in the early days, but after the arrival of the LSDs it was found more convenient to preload tanks in LCMs which could be floated in and out of an LSD's dock. But LSTs were extensively employed to transport tanks across the Atlantic and to landing beaches in Europe.

placed on trucks. But eight hours more or less were required to discharge an LST loaded in that manner.

Accordingly Captain Carter and Captain Festus F. Foster of the Bureau of Ordnance put their heads together with various members of Sopac staff and decided that preloading the cargo on trailers that could be parked close and hauled ashore by tractors was the answer. Pending the procurement of the perfect trailer, Commander Cutler obtained from the United States Army depot at Nouméa, and brought up to Guadalcanal 22 October, some 85 vehicles that would fit into LSTs without too many "holidays." One LST would take in 33 of these jury-rigged trailers, as Carter called them, and that gave the LST a relatively large pay load. Trailers made for quick turn-around as well, for they could be parked ashore until the soldiers got around to unloading them, and could be picked up empty later. Trailer loading was first tried in this second echelon to Torokina, with limited success; but after much practice, and with an improved model designed for such work, it became doctrine for sending LSTs into beaches where air attack was expected.

Experience in the New Georgia campaign showed that an LST needed more armament than her original complement to repel air attack, and Carter's flotilla went up to Bougainville loaded for bear, with three to five 40-mm, eleven to eighteen 20-mm, four to eighteen .50-caliber machine guns and one three-inch 50-caliber gun apiece. Barrage balloons for LSTs, which had been used in the Sicilian landings that summer, were introduced to the Pacific by the second echelon. This device snared one Nip plane in early November and proved baffling to the pilots; but the balloons were finally discarded in 1944 because they gave away a task force's position to enemy search planes.

The first part of the second echelon arrived off Cape Torokina at 0700 November 6 and was safely piloted in by officers of the Naval Advanced Base who had given themselves an intensive course in Empress Augusta hydrography. What followed proved that all the answers to Love-Sugar-Tare questions had not yet been found, and furnished another illustration for Admiral Wilkinson's maxim, "Unloading is the world-wide difficulty of amphibious forces." [3]

Engineers of the 3rd Marine Division who had made the initial landing had been instructed by the Admiral to prepare eight suitable beaches for the eight LSTs. But only God Almighty can provide the sort of beach on which an LST can lie comfortably, discharge her cargo dry-ramp, and retract under her own power. Their bottoms are designed to fit a beach with a gradient of about 1 in 50. On such a beach the LST will ground her entire length and her ramp will fall on dry land. If the beach gradient is much steeper, the LST will not ground properly and is liable to broach; if it is more gradual, she will ground far out and require some sort of bridge between ramp and shore.

The only beach at Cape Torokina that fitted LST bottoms was one on Puruata Island that had room for only three. Here the trailer-loaded *LST-354* discharged 750 tons of cargo in 2 hours 10 minutes, but trouble met the other five LSTs as soon as they hit the beaches east of Cape Torokina. The gradient here was so gradual that they grounded about 60 feet from the shore line, with a two- to three-foot depth of water at the lip of the ramp; and a moderate sea was running. The motors of vehicles drowned out and they had to be hauled ashore by the Seabees' dozers and tractors. Thus, the LSTs discovered a new difficulty to be overcome, the gap between ramp and shore. Improvised coconut-log runways cracked up under the strain. But the answer to this problem was the steel interlocking pontoon units which had already been used for this purpose in Sicily.

Echelon Two squared away from the beach shortly after midnight 6 November, just in time to escape an enemy air attack which killed two men and wounded twelve ashore. Task Force 39 was maneuvering outside the Bay to cover their retirement. The next afternoon it was relieved as covering force for the Empress Augusta echelons, by Rear Admiral Laurance T. DuBose's Crudiv

[3] Quoted in Capt. Carter's Action Report p. 31.

13 — light cruisers *Santa Fe, Birmingham, Mobile* and *Biloxi* — with Desdiv 49 (Captain E. M. Thompson) escorting.

## 2. *Counter-landing and Koromokina, 7–8 November*

When Admiral Omori had first started for Empress Augusta Bay on 31 October he was supposed to cover a landing force; but on his advice the transports had been recalled to Rabaul. Twice more this counter-landing group was held up, but it finally took off on the afternoon of 6 November. The Japanese had failed in their second Savo Island; now they were to try a Tenaru River.

Elements of the 53rd and 54th infantry regiments, to the number of 475 officers and men, were embarked in four destroyers, destined for Torokina, while 700 troops were embarked in a light cruiser and destroyers to reinforce Buka Airfield. The covering force for both, commanded by the same Rear Admiral Osugi who had played an inactive part in the Battle of Empress Augusta Bay, comprised light cruiser *Agano*, with destroyers *Naganami, Wakatsuki, Shigure, Samidare, Shiratsuyu* and *Amagiri*. The Buka Passage force landed at 0125 November 7, and there we may leave them. The Torokina force, too, landed virtually unopposed, causing many red faces on the American side.

Eight American PTs from the Treasuries had already established a new advanced base on Puruata Island off Cape Torokina. Yet none of them discovered the Japanese landing force. The 475 men got ashore in 21 landing barges on the beaches between the Laruma and Koromokina Rivers, establishing a right flank only 4000 yards from Puruata Island, between 0400 and 0600 November 7. The destroyers then quietly withdrew, leaving the barges behind. So near did the Japanese land to the Marines' beachhead that one company cut off an outpost of 65 Marines.[4] The landing

---

[4] These were rescued next day by two landing craft from the Torokina boat pool, commanded by Lt. F. H. Hollander USNR. One LCM loaded the Marines while the other covered with machine-gun fire.

craft were seen by a Marine anti-tank platoon on the beach but not fired upon as they were presumed to be American. Surprise was complete.

The Japanese company on the right flank found some foxholes abandoned by the Marines when regrouping a day or two earlier, and, reinforced by more troops staged along the beach in barges, held off for some time an attack by two Marine battalions along the line of the Koromokina River. Then, early in the morning of 8 November, the Marines opened an attack along the Koromokina front, with five batteries of artillery, assisted by mortars, machine guns and anti-tank weapons. When artillery preparation ceased there was silence; for only a few punch-drunk survivors were left where the guns had played; the rest had taken to the jungle. Next day a dive-bomber strike in the area between the two rivers cleaned up sundry groups of Japanese who were creeping back to the beach from their jungle hideouts. This finished off the Koromokina landing force; the counted enemy dead numbered 377; the cost was 17 Marines killed and missing, 30 wounded.

Captured documents indicate that General Imamura intended to send up some 3000 troops from Rabaul in cruisers and destroyers, but was compelled to abandon these plans because the United States Navy and Airsols had won command of the sea and air approaches to Bougainville.

## 3. Three *"Air Battles of Bougainville,"* 8–13 November

Life was far from restful in waters contiguous to Bougainville.

During the early hours of 8 November there took place an accidental fight between two motor torpedo boats and destroyers *Hudson* and *Anthony*, amusing in retrospect because bloodless. Communications failure was the cause of this "Second Battle of Empress Augusta Bay." The destroyers had been told that all friendly PTs were at home, and Cape Torokina did not know that any destroyers were coming up.

*PT–163* was on night patrol, *PT–170* and *PT–169* were lying-to off the Magine Islands in the Bay, when *Hudson* and *Anthony* started to throw hardware in their direction. Assuming that their assailants were Japanese, the PTs took violent evasive action and endeavored to get in position for a torpedo attack. The destroyers hotly pursued, still firing. Skipper of *PT–170*, hoping to have his trail crossed by a fresh fox, informed *PT–163* by radio that he was leading "three Nip cans" his way, and wouldn't he like to take a whack at them? *PT–163* obliged with a long-range torpedo shot, which missed the hounds and failed to draw them off. After 45 minutes of this running fight, just as both motor torpedo boats reversed course to make a torpedo run on the "enemy," they received a message from *Anthony*, "Humblest apologies, we are friendly vessels." [5]

Just before this belated though welcome apology arrived, a mysterious incident occurred. *PT–170's* radar showed a new, large pip 10,000 yards dead ahead; and a moment later her crew observed projectiles that "looked like large ashcans" flying overhead, parallel to her keel. Nobody on our side admitted having done it, and the identity of ghost ship and flying ashcans has never been established.

After *Anthony* and *Hudson* had joined the transport echelon to which they were attached, they came under heavy air attack by "Vals" and "Bettys" at noon on 8 November. *Anthony's* gunners, their appetite apparently whetted by the PT foxes they had lost, "were steady, confident and bloodthirsty," according to their "exec."; possibly more confident than steady in their claim of shooting down eleven planes.

These assailants were really after bigger game. At 0800 that morning the second part of the second Torokina echelon, commanded by Captain A. B. Anderson, stood into Empress Augusta Bay. This group was composed of the three amphibious transports and three AKAs that had participated in the initial landings, escorted by Commander Ralph Earle's destroyer squadron and Com-

[5] Information from participants, especially Lt. Cdr. Edward Macauley of *PT–170* in 1945; *Anthony* Action Report 15 Nov. 1943.

mander Loud's minesweepers. They brought up the 148th Regimental Combat Team of the 37th Infantry Division and a battery of much-needed anti-aircraft artillery. During that day, the Japanese air forces put on two good shows. Twenty-six carrier dive-bombers, 71 "Zekes," and a few torpedo-toting "Bettys" attacked the formation at noon, when the transports were anchored and unloading. A few of them managed to get through the umbrella of 28 Airsols fighters, to make two hits on U.S.S. *Fuller*. But the transport's crew, while collecting their 5 dead and 20 wounded, fighting fires in two holds, making emergency repairs and plugging holes in the hull, continued to unload with such energy that their ship was one of the first to be emptied. And all transports departed at 1837 in a heavy rainstorm.

Although they missed the transports, thirty or forty of the Japanese planes sighted Admiral DuBose's covering force at dusk about 25 miles southwest of Mutupina Point, through a rift in the clouds, and delivered three attacks between 1911 and 0100, November 8–9. This task force, consisting of light cruisers *Santa Fe* (Captain Russell S. Berkey), *Mobile* (Captain C. J. Wheeler), and *Birmingham* (Captain Thomas B. Inglis), and four destroyers (Captain Edward M. Thompson), was arranged in anti-aircraft disposition, cruisers in the center and destroyers in a circle around them. Moonlight peering through breaks in the clouds helped the usual Japanese display of float lights. At 1917 the bomb from a "Val" that *Birmingham's* gunners shot down bounced into that ship's starboard counter just above the waterline and blew the hatch off her airplane hangar. Nine minutes later a "Betty" got a torpedo into her port bow, opening a 30-foot hole just abaft the chain locker. And at 1942 another bomb from a dead "Val" exploded on the face plate of turret No. 4. A second wave of planes attacked at 2000 and a third at 0054, without making a single hit; altogether about four of each were shot down. Thus, *Birmingham* opened her career of notable bad luck by collecting the only three hits made; but it took more than that to stop the "Mighty B," or discourage her tough skipper, Tom Inglis. She could still "float, move and shoot" and keep up with the formation at 30 knots.[6] "Thanks for taking on those bastards that were laying for us," radioed the retiring transports of the second echelon. If the Japanese pilots were disappointed they did not admit it. Both the Eleventh Air Fleet and the temporarily land-based carrier planes were represented in this attack, and their claims were fantastic. The former "sank one battleship (*King George* class) and two battleships (*Renown* class) with torpedoes and set others afire"; the latter "sank one battleship, blew up and sank two cruisers, set afire four cruisers or destroyers."[7] DuBose's ships were flattered. Imperial Headquarters sent more compliments to Rabaul and named this action, in which the correct score was the three hits on *Birmingham*, the "Second Air Battle of Bougainville."

A "Third" and "Fourth" followed close on the heels of the "Second." A few hours after DuBose's task force entered Purvis Bay, on 9 November, Merrill's TF 39 sallied forth again, to cover the third reinforcement echelon to Torokina, consisting of eight LSTs and eight APDs. On their way north, the bluejackets topside in destroyer *Spence* were goggle-eyed at an exhibition of Japanese *bushido*. Ordered to investigate a life raft, they observed what appeared to be seven bodies in it. The seven bodies suddenly sat up and started talking. One of them, apparently the officer, broke out a 7.7-mm machine gun, which each man in succession placed in his mouth, while the officer fired a round which shot the back of the man's head off. After six had been bumped off, the officer stood up, addressed a short speech in Japanese to *Spence's* commanding officer on the bridge, and then shot himself.

There followed what Merrill called an "uneventful" though exhausting night, with snoopers around as "annoying as flies in the

[6] South Pacific Force Intelligence Section, Air Battle Notes No. 29 "Japanese Night Torpedo Plane Attacks" 18 Dec. 1943 p. 5; Capt. T. B. Inglis "The Mighty 'B'" *Shipmate* June 1945 p. 124. On the passage home for repairs *Birmingham's* assistant damage control officer, Lt. Cdr. Van O. Perkins, devised a trunk leading up to the main deck from compartments open to the sea, so that water could vent and relieve pressure from the shored-up bulkheads. Geysers spouted from the trunk whenever the cruiser pitched, earning her the nickname "Old Faithful."
[7] "Southeast Area Operations" Part 3 (Navy) p. 21.

rainy season." Then, on the night of 11–12 November, Task Force 39 came in for the tail end of what the Japanese called the "Third Air Battle of Bougainville," the *Essex, Bunker Hill* and *Independence* carrier fight that we have already discussed. Eleven "Bettys" that were looking for Montgomery's carriers missed them but picked on Merrill, treating his ships to a shivaree all through the evening watch, with full pyrotechnical accompaniment. No hits were made, but the pilots claimed hitting one of three battleships, one of two heavy cruisers, and "virtually sinking" one of four destroyers. Anyway, they accorded Merrill's task force the same complimentary step-up that they had given DuBose's.

On Merrill's fourth night out, 12–13 November, when he was maneuvering off Empress Augusta Bay waiting to take the ships of the third echelon home, occurred a successful interception by an Airsols night fighter. The fighter-director in cruiser *Columbia* vectored a Ventura night fighter piloted by Captain Duane R. Jenkins USMCR, to a "Betty," which fell in flames at 0420. Three other "Bettys" maneuvering to attack then sheered off and could not be found. But four more came in low on the task force at 0455, boxed cruiser *Denver* with torpedoes and got one into her after engine room. It killed 20 men, wounded 11, and stopped the ship dead. She listed 12 degrees. Damage controllers quickly reduced list by counterflooding and, with the one remaining shaft, engineers coaxed out a speed of 4.5 knots. Two destroyers stood by; at dawn, fighter planes arrived, tug *Sioux* closed, and *Denver* "with an angel on her yardarm" was safely towed back to Purvis without a single air attack.[8] The Japanese called that night's encounter the "Fourth Air Battle of Bougainville" and claimed that they "blew up two cruisers" and hit one cruiser and a battleship.

More than a slow-down in the lie factory had happened in Rabaul. Operation "RO" was at an end. Everyone pretended it had been a brilliant success, as certainly it would have been if the

---

[8] Merrill to Halsey 13 Nov. 1943; conversations with *Denver's* former Gunnery Officer; Sopac Force Air Battle Notes No. 29 "Japanese Night Torpedo Plane Attacks" p. 4; "Combat Experiences of VMF(N)-531" p. 3.

official tabulation of 5 battleships, 10 carriers, 19 cruisers, 7 destroy-ers and 9 transports sunk, and 24 of all types damaged, had been even 10 per cent correct.[9] An Imperial Rescript commended all hands in glowing terms; but Kusaka knew, and Koga must have suspected, that the whole thing was a costly failure. Seventy per cent of the Third Fleet carrier planes flown into Rabaul on 1 No-vember — 121 out of 173 — had been expended; 45 per cent of the pilots and crewmen — 86 out of 192 — were killed or missing. The Eleventh Air Fleet had lost in the same proportion. So, on 13 No-vember, Koga withdrew the 52 remaining carrier planes to Truk, and he could collect only half that number as replacements to send back to Rabaul.

## 4. *Beachhead Secured*

Even before the Koromokina fight started, elements of two Marine raider battalions had been fighting, about a mile behind the beachhead, with elements of the 23rd Japanese Infantry who had come in by footpaths from other parts of Empress Augusta Bay and were blocking the Piva branch of the Numa Numa trail. Two battalions of this regiment were supposed to coöperate with the counter-landing in putting the bite on the Marines. Fortunately their timing was very crude, and the Marines had disposed of the Koromokina boys before the jungle Japs really got going on 9 November. Next day the Marines under Colonel Edward A. Craig moved forward, aided by their own artillery and Avenger planes, and by 1100 they had entered the small native village of Piva, which the Japanese had abandoned together with much equip-ment and heaps of supplies. Shortly after this, Commander William Painter USNR, a venturesome soul given to pre-invasion patrols and scouting, moved up the Piva Trail and selected airfield sites out-side the Marines' perimeter; a fighter strip just behind the beach

[9] So stated the telegram from the German ambassador in Tokyo to Hitler, 10 Dec. 1943, *Fuehrer Conferences German Navy 1943* pp. 152–54.

was already under construction. To clear the trail to these new sites, General Turnage sent the 21st Regiment up the Numa Numa Trail on 13 November. It ran into a Japanese ambush just short of one of the rare coconut groves of that region, and a two-day fight, which the Marines called the Battle of the Coconut Grove, cost them 20 killed and 30 wounded; but by the night of the 14th they controlled the junction of the Numa Numa and East West Trails.

Major General Roy S. Geiger, who had already relieved General Vandegrift as Commander I Marine Amphibious Corps, took over the command of all Allied forces in and around Bougainville from Rear Admiral Wilkinson on 13 November. On that day the fourth echelon, bringing the rest of the 129th RCT of the 37th Infantry Division, arrived. This shift of command from ship to shore marked the securing of the beachhead and the close of the first phase of the Bougainville campaign.

By 14 November, 33,861 men and 23,137 tons of supplies and equipment had been landed at Empress Augusta Bay.[10] The beachhead, which henceforth we shall refer to as the Perimeter, as yet had a circumference of only 16,000 yards, including 7000 yards of beach frontage, together with Puruata Island; but that was enough for the time being. Never, in the modern history of amphibious warfare, had there been such quick unloading and prompt getaway as by the transports and beaching craft of "Ping" Wilkinson's amphibious force; seldom has there been such effective coverage of an invasion as that afforded by Merrill's and DuBose's cruiser task forces, and by the Airsols and carrier planes. The enemy was not only surprised, he stayed surprised. General Imamura stub-

[10] The following summary is from Capt. Wendell's Bougainville Report.

| Echelon number | Day of November | | Men landed | Tons equipment and supplies landed |
| | Arrival | Completed unloading | | |
|---|---|---|---|---|
| 1 | 1 | 2 | 14,321 | 6,177 |
| 2 | 6 | 7 | 3,548 | 5,080 |
| 2A | 8 | 8 | 5,715 | 3,160 |
| 3 | 11 | 11 | 3,599 | 5,785 |
| 4 | 13 | 13 | 6,678 | 2,935 |

bornly insisted that we were only fooling at Torokina, and would presently attempt to transfer the entire force to Buka; so, instead of expediting a counterattack on the Perimeter by the 15,000 or more Japanese soldiers in southern Bougainville, he reinforced the region up north and there awaited an attack that never came.[11]

[11] "SE Area Operations" Part 3 (Navy) p. 30. Venturas and Avengers of Airsols planted 42 mines off Buka Passage on 16 and 17 November, but even that did not give Imamura the tip that we did not intend to move in there.

CHAPTER XX

# Busy Thanksgiving

### 15-25 November 1943

## 1. Activities in and around the Perimeter

WHILE the Seabees worked nobly to get the Torokina fighter strip operational, and even started work on the bomber strip, Airsols, whose nearest field was in the Treasuries, kept busy every day and most nights. Frequent bombing missions had to be flown over the Bougainville and Buka airfields to keep them inoperative. Echelons and task forces had to be covered. Bombing and strafing missions against Japanese troops in the jungle were constantly in demand by the Marines. Beginning mid-November, the big B–24s were sent every few days against Rabaul, where an air reconnaissance on the 26th spotted 59 bombers and 145 fighters on four airfields.[1] Munda and Barakoma airfields still had to be protected, although the last enemy air attack on Munda had been on the night of 6–7 November. "The scale of air activity alone may be judged by the fact that on 10 November, for the 13-hour dawn-to-dusk period, a takeoff or landing occurred on the average of one every 65 seconds – 712 in all."[2] Night fighters based at Barakoma took over the protection of the Torokina Perimeter and nearby shipping after dark, but there were too few of them to cope with the enemy bombers from Rabaul, a few of which managed to harass the Perimeter almost every night. On 17 November, Airsols fighters intercepted a flight of 35 Torokina-bound enemy planes and claimed shooting down 16, losing two Corsairs.

[1] General MacArthur's communiqué of 27 Nov. 1943.
[2] Airsols Intelligence Weekly Summary and Review 12 Nov. 1943. On 20 Nov. Maj. Gen. Ralph J. Mitchell USMC relieved Gen. Twining USA as Comairsols.

Rabaul got the word on 16 November that the fifth echelon was moving up to Torokina. Captain G. B. Carter in *Renshaw* commanded eight LSTs and eight APDs carrying Marines, with six escorting destroyers. A Japanese snooper reported them flatteringly as three aircraft carriers with 20 cruisers and destroyers. At 0350 November 17, when this echelon was only 22 miles from its destination, destroyer-transport *McKean* was struck by an air torpedo. She shot down the plane (one of five destroyed that night) but the explosion set off her after magazine and depth-charge storage, and ruptured three fuel tanks which splashed flaming oil over the after part of the ship. All light and power failed; debris falling on the siren whistle-cord added a weird blast to the confusion. Troops began jumping overboard, and almost everyone who did so before Abandon Ship had been ordered, burned to death in floating oil. In ten minutes' time *McKean* began to sink by the stern. Her skipper, Lieutenant Commander Ralph L. Ramey, after a final inspection to see that nobody alive was left on board, went over the side at 0412. All hands coöperated in pulling the burned and other injured onto life rafts; destroyers *Talbot*, *Sigourney* and *Waller* stood by to rescue survivors, although under constant attack by torpedo planes. Of 185 Marines embarked, 52 were lost; of 12 officers and 141 crew members, 3 officers and 61 men were lost.[3] The Rabaul lie factory inflated *McKean* to three carriers, two cruisers and one "unidentified ship" sunk, and glorified this action with the title "Fifth Air Battle of Bougainville."

We left the Japanese and Marines glaring at each other, as it were, through the swampy jungle a mile or two back of the beach. The enemy was trying to develop a good defensive position for counterattack; the Marines were feeling him out in preparation for

[3] *McKean* was the fourth of the converted "four-pipers," the others being *Little*, *Gregory* and *Colhoun*, to be lost in Solomon Islands waters. Old, weak and brittle, any explosion made them "fold up like an old shoe box"; but for lack of better ships they had to be used. One notable case of heroism was that of Marine Gunnery Sgt. Russell Scott who carried a man up from sick bay, eased him over the side and tended him in the water. (Story in *Honolulu Advertiser* 8 Dec. 1943.)

thwarting his plans. On the morning of 20 November a battalion of the 3rd Marine Regiment, accompanied by light tanks, by-passed a roadblock on the Numa Numa Trail and took a commanding hill, named Cibik after the platoon commander. The Japanese counterattacked three days running and were repulsed. By this time General Geiger had a plan to get rid of them altogether. Enfilading fire delivered by no less than 14 battalions of artillery opened at daybreak 24 November; and in 20 minutes 5760 rounds had been dropped into an area 800 yards square. When the assault troops advanced, they found this area completely pulverized; but outside it the enemy rallied, counterattacked, defended himself desperately and used 90-mm mortars and 75-mm field guns effectively. By the end of Thanksgiving Day the 25th, after tough hand-to-hand and tree-to-tree fighting, the 23rd Infantry Regiment of the Japanese Imperial Army was virtually wiped out, leaving over 1100 dead, including its colonel, on the field.

This Battle of Piva Forks, as the Marines named it, was the last serious ground resistance for a long time. During this battle the 6th Echelon, an LST outfit with six LCIs carrying troops, was unloading at Torokina. Enemy guns sighted on the beaches opened up on the LSTs and inflicted several casualties. This shelling continued all day, to the great discomfiture of the LST crews, but the guns were located next day and silenced by Marine artillery.

The second night after Thanksgiving, 26–27 November, was the first since the initial landing when there was no air alert at Cape Torokina.

## 2. The Battle of Cape St. George, 25 November [4]

About the beginning of the last week of November, South Pacific Intelligence suspected that Admiral Kusaka was about to

[4] Burke's Action Report 26 Nov. 1943 and conversations with him and with Cdr. Austin. The Japanese action report is ATIS Doc. No. 15685; the interrogation of Capt. Ohmae, at that time Kusaka's chief of staff, in *Inter. Jap. Off.* II 473 "Southeast Area Operations" Part 3 (Navy) is valuable for cause and effect.

send a Tokyo Express to Buka. They were right. Although the Japanese naval command rightly guessed that the Americans were in Empress Augusta to stay, the stubborn Army still insisted that they were merely building a fighter strip and would shortly move up to Buka Passage. So, as the Buka-Bonis airfields had been inoperative for three weeks, and as no soldiers had been landed there since 7 November, the Army, as usual obtaining its way, ordered the Navy to move up 920 troops in destroyers and pull 700 useless personnel out. This little operation was organized as follows: —

Buka Reinforcement Echelon, * Captain Kiyoto Kagawa

Transports, Captain Katsumori Yamashiro
Destroyers AMAGIRI, * YUGIRI, UZUKI

Screen, Captain Kagawa
Destroyers * ONAMI, * MAKINAMI [5]

* Lost or sunk in this action.

Halsey's staff at once made dispositions to intercept with destroyers, because enemy destroyers had recently been sighted in Simpson Harbor.

Destroyer Squadron 23, then taking on oil at Hathorn Sound, was ordered at noon 24 November to expedite fueling and make directly for a point off Empress Augusta Bay. En route, Captain Burke received his orders, brief and to the point as Halsey's commands always were: —

Thirty-One-Knot Burke, get this. Put your squadron athwart the Buka-Rabaul evacuation line about 35 miles west of Buka. If no enemy contacts by early morning, come south to refuel same place. If enemy contacted you know what to do. HALSEY.

For the benefit of Comairsols he added: —

CTF 33, get this word to your B–24s and Black Cats. Add a night fighter for Burke from 0330 to sunrise and give him day cover.

[5] Capt. Burke insisted that there was a third DD in the screen, but Japanese records make it certain there was not. After the battle a submarine, *I–177* from Rabaul, rescued 278 survivors of *Yugiri*, but all hands were lost in the other two except for a few who managed to reach shore on rafts.

The composition of the force that night was as follows: —

Destroyer Squadron 23, Captain Arleigh A. Burke

Desdiv 45, Captain Burke
| | |
|---|---|
| CHARLES AUSBURNE | Cdr. L. K. Reynolds |
| CLAXTON | Cdr. H. F. Stout |
| DYSON | Cdr. R. A. Gano |

Desdiv 46, Cdr. B. L. Austin
| | |
|---|---|
| CONVERSE | Cdr. DeW. C. E. Hamberger |
| SPENCE | Lt. Cdr. H. J. Armstrong |

By 1730 Burke had completed fueling and was steaming north near Vella Lavella at 30 knots. In the meantime, nine PTs under Commander Henry Farrow had been stationed near Buka Passage to get the enemy if Burke missed him. Around midnight three of the PTs made a radar contact on what appeared to be four friendly ships, and headed inshore to get out of their way. The two larger ships altered course to close; one of them at 0030 November 25 attempted to ram *PT–318* and both fired several 5-inch salvos which passed safely overhead. The PT skippers, persisting in their belief that these were mistaken friends, scattered and sought cover in a rain squall. *PT–64* fired a torpedo nevertheless, because her torpedoman misunderstood orders, but it did not hit.[6] The two ships encountered were Kagawa's *Onami* and *Makinami*.

Captain Burke, with true instinct for the chase, had already figured out that he would be more likely to intercept the enemy by patrolling across the western rather than the eastern half of his direct route to St. George Channel. This PT contact confirmed his estimate. Accordingly he proceeded as far west on the Buka-St. George line as he could get by 0130 November 25, then slowed to 23 knots so that his wakes would be less conspicuous from the air, and ten minutes later changed course to due north. The night was dark, with low-hanging clouds and occasional rain squalls. The waning moon would not rise until 0425 and day would not break before 0600. The sea was smooth, the wind force 2 from the ESE.

[6] Information from Commo. Moran's files at Bougainville.

Division 46 now took position 225 degrees from Division 45, distant 5000 yards. Only one minute later, at 0141, three of Burke's destroyers made radar contact eleven miles to the east. This was Kagawa's screen, which Yamashiro's transport destroyers, having finished their mission at 0045, were about to join.

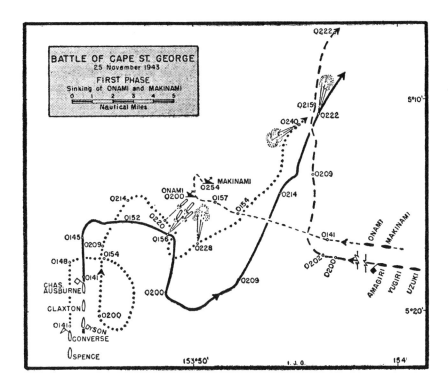

At 0145, Burke ordered his division to head directly for the enemy, who was steaming at 25 knots on a westerly course. According to battle plan, Austin would cover Burke in the torpedo attack, after which the two divisions would change places, Austin attack and Burke cover – strategy recently used by Moosbrugger and anciently by Scipio Africanus.

At 0156 the three leading United States destroyers reached the desired firing point 50 degrees on the enemy's port bow, distant 6000 yards for a run of 4500 yards; they launched 15 torpedoes and promptly turned 90° right in order to avoid any fish the enemy might offer. Austin then proposed to take his two destroyers around to fire on the enemy's opposite bow, but Burke greeted this suggestion with the laconic monosyllable, "Nuts!"

Captain Kagawa was taken by surprise. His lookouts sighted Burke after fish had been swimming four minutes, which gave him only 30 seconds to change course, and he steamed right into the torpedoes' tracks. Three explosions were heard. *Onami* appeared to disintegrate into a ball of fire 300 feet high; *Makinami* exploded and apparently broke in two; but she wanted some of "Count" Austin's courtly attention before she went down. Both were big, 2000-ton destroyers less than a year old. Enough bag for one night; but there was more to come.

Just before the torpedoes hit, *Ausburne* made a radar contact on the three transport destroyers in column 13,000 yards astern of Kagawa. Burke promptly went after them, ordering Austin to finish off the first lot.

Yamashiro, however, refused to coöperate; he wanted to land his troops at Rabaul. *Amagiri*, *Yugiri* and *Uzuki* fled northward, Burke in hot pursuit. By turning up 33 knots he managed to close the range to 8000 yards. At 0215, acting simply on a hunch, Burke zigged his division 45° right, and, after one minute on that course, zagged back to his previous one, N by E. At that moment three heavy explosions were heard by all hands. These were torpedoes from *Yugiri* detonating in the American wakes. *Yugiri* had done well to launch fish with some 300 soldiers cluttering her deck.

In a running fight the pursuer needs much more speed than the pursued, so that he can weave about and bring his broadside to bear. But Captain Burke sacrificed fire power for speed and at 0222 opened fire with the two forward gun mounts of each ship. On board *Ausburne*, this resulted in the blast from No. 2 blowing the hatch off No. 1 gun mount; but the No. 1 gun crew carried on gamely despite the smoke, fire and gas that poured down on their devoted heads, knocking some of them unconscious. When the enemy began returning fire, Burke fish-tailed to bring after batteries to bear. He thought he was hitting; he was, but not on all targets; only one, a dud, on *Uzuki*, none on *Amagiri* but plenty on *Yugiri*. The Japanese made no hits but consistently near-missed. At 0225 the three enemy destroyers fanned out in courses about 45 degrees apart. Burke chose to pursue *Yugiri*, as she looked the big-

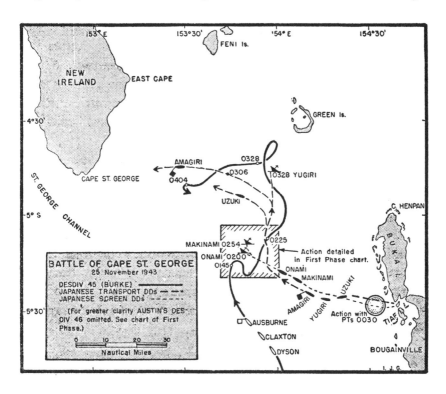

gest. At 0305 he observed large explosions in the unhappy target; she started circling, fired remaining torpedoes without effect and, as a result of gunfire poured into her by the three pursuers, sank. The battle had now reached a point about 60 miles east of the nearest land, Cape St. George.

*Converse* and *Spence* in the meantime were going after *Maki-nami*, the remaining destroyer afloat of the first division; they sank her by gunfire at 0254 and radioed to Burke, "One more rising sun has set." Austin never received his squadron commander's order to pursue the escaping destroyer transports; but he was now too far behind to catch up.

Burke turned westward about 0330 in the hope of catching *Amagiri* and *Uzuki* making off in that general direction. This search, however, was fruitless; and at a few minutes after 0404, with Cape St. George bearing W ½ N distant 33 miles, he broke off. For it was vital to open distance from Rabaul before dawn. That base was then but a few minutes' flight from his ships. Just before he reversed course Austin, whose flagship had only two boilers on the line, called over TBS, "Don't think we can go on much longer." "Unless we can get fuel in Rabaul!" retorted Burke. "We might have trouble with the fuel hose connections!" cracked Lieutenant Commander Armstrong of *Spence*.

All our destroyers expected furious retaliation from the air as soon as day broke, but the first and only planes they saw were the Airsols fighter cover that had flown all the way from Munda. "Never has the white star on a wing meant so much to tired sailors as those on these Lightnings," said Burke.

During the chase the squadron commander, who hails from Colorado, informed Admiral Halsey that he was "riding herd on the Japs" and emitted an occasional "Come a Ki-Yi-Yippee!" Now, realizing that the Admiral would like a little more information at his morning conference, he radioed: —

I almost omitted to inform you that I picked up 6 Nips, probably DDs, in two groups of three. Two exploded and sunk by torpedoes; another sunk by gunfire and torpedoes. After a long chase, one sunk by gunfire and one damaged.

And he concluded by reminding the Admiral that it was Thanksgiving Day.

Three sunk, without a single casualty to us, not even a hit; this Battle of Cape St. George was another cleanup like Moosbrugger's at Vella Gulf. "An almost perfect action," commented Admiral Pye, President of the Naval War College; one "that may be considered a classic." The squadron commander modestly attributed this glorious result to something more than the skill and valor of his officers and men. As he wrote: —

If this battle brings out no other points, it should clearly demonstrate that fortune of war is a fickle wench and that results hang by a narrow thread. There are many things which would have prevented this battle from being fought, and the Squadron Commander would much prefer to say that these matters were foreseen and steps taken to insure doing the proper thing. But they were not foreseen. The time of 0145 for reaching the Rabaul-Buka line was chosen merely at random. The desire to reach as far westward as possible was not based on abstruse reasoning. A fifteen-minute delay in time of fueling . . . would have prevented the battle from being fought. We reached the enemy by the narrowest of margins. The Squadron was so spontaneously grateful . . . that Thanksgiving services were held upon its return to port. The Squadron is proud of its accomplishments, but it is also humbly aware that these accomplishments were made possible by a Force beyond its control.

CHAPTER XXI

# Perimeter Defense and Development

## 26 November–27 December 1943

AFTER the Marines' Thanksgiving Day victory at Piva Forks,
General Turnage initiated an advance to the east, taking up
strong positions on hills along the west bank of Torokina River.
These new positions were separated from the Perimeter by a
dense swamp. The men plowed through muck often waist-deep
and sometimes up to their armpits, their advance barred by thorny
creepers that tore their clothes and flesh; at night machine guns
were lashed to tree trunks and men slept sitting in mud and water.
An advance of 300 yards a day was good going. Supplying these
troops even with the crudest rations would have been impossible
but for a battalion of 124 amphibious tractors, better known as
LVTs. These strange vehicles performed a service similar to the
rescue work in the Florida everglades for which they had originally been designed, wallowing through the slimy vegetation,
crushing rotten jungle growth with their tracked treads, bringing
in food, water and ammunition, and evacuating the wounded. A
few days earlier the fellows to these modern brontosauri were sav-
ing the day at Tarawa.

On the night of 3–4 December the ninth echelon to Cape Torokina, embarked in 8 LSTs and 5 LCIs and escorted by Captain
Ralph Earle's destroyers, *Fullam, Guest, Bennett, Terry, Braine*
and *Renshaw*, was off Empress Augusta Bay, with four of Captain Burke's destroyers covering. Nineteen Rabaul-based planes
attacked for 45 minutes, and were beaten off without scoring a hit;
but Burke called this "the most persistent, prolonged and confus-

ing attack by well-trained, experienced Japanese pilots we have observed." Rabaul called it the "Sixth Air Battle of Bougainville," claiming the sinking of a battleship, two carriers and two cruisers. Next day (4 December), after the ninth echelon had reached the beach, *Braine* and *Guest* bombarded Japanese positions outside the

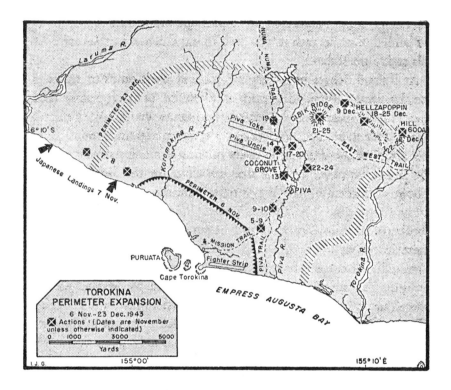

Perimeter. That sort of thing became routine with escorting destroyers, but there were too many Japs in too extensive a jungle for them to accomplish much.

The most important work within the Perimeter was done on the airstrips by eight Seabee battalions and a New Zealand engineer brigade, coördinated by a tiny staff of Marine Corps engineers. Terrain conditions were exceptionally bad. The swamps were like quicksand, and on more than one occasion a bulldozer completely disappeared. Since the fighter strip being constructed just behind the beach was the only dry spot in the Perimeter, everyone not on the front lines moved in, interfering with the engineers and Seabees; but Japanese artillery, by lobbing a few shells in and around the strip, cleared the "squatters" out on the double. On 24 November a Marine Corps SBD, damaged by flak, managed to land on Torokina fighter strip, but it was not officially opened until 10 December when a squadron of Airsols fighters and six light bombers landed. On the 17th it was used to stage planes in the first Airsols strike on Rabaul.

At Rabaul debate in the high command went on as to whether the Americans intended to stay at Torokina or move somewhere else. The Japanese Army were so sure that we would take the latter course that they even built up a defensive perimeter around Buin and also sent hundreds of soldiers hoofing it along native trails up the northeast coast to reinforce positions on the Buka Passage. About 15 December the Navy persuaded the Army to do something about the Torokina perimeter. In a halfhearted way, the Southern Bougainville command began trying to send troops up there in barges. Some got lost, others were sunk by PTs, Black Cats and Elsie Items, a few units landed at various points in southern Empress Augusta Bay, only to be rubbed out by Marine patrols boated up in landing craft. One group was dumped on the Magine Islands right in the Bay; LCI gunboats shelled them out of these on 20 December. In short, the whole small boat movement north was a "dismal failure."[1]

Admiral Kusaka, hopeful that these driblet counter-landings would accomplish something, renewed night bombing activity on 15 December and continued it with 10- to 15-plane strikes for ten days. On the night of the 18th, when the Airsols night fighter that was supposed to patrol developed engine trouble and could not take off, 40 to 50 bombs were dropped and four landing craft of the boat pool were sunk and others damaged, with a loss of 11 men. Total Allied casualties from ten days of air bombing were 38 killed and missing, 136 wounded.

[1] Capt. Ohmae, in Lt. Cdr. Salomon's Notes taken in 1946.

More serious than the counter-landings and air bombings was the work of enemy artillery, moved up from other parts of the Bay and emplaced on a ridge which the Marines nicknamed "Hellza-poppin." Marine Corps TBFs undertook to bomb the Japanese out. On 14–15 December, the ridge was the target of 34 Avenger sorties, each carrying twelve 100-pound bombs; but the enemy held on because the bombs were fitted with instantaneous fuzes, causing them to detonate on the branches of trees, which did not bother well dug-in troops. Six TBFs then attacked the ridge with delay fuzes which did the job. The 21st Marine Regiment advanced immediately and by Christmas Day had "Hellzapoppin."

Partly because Task Force 39 was getting bored with a long rest in Purvis Bay,[2] and also in the hope that Admiral Koga would send down a few heavy cruisers for him to sport with, Admiral Merrill obtained permission to deliver a pre-Christmas bombardment on Buka and Bonis. Indefatigable Captain Burke, who never gave his destroyers a chance to grow barnacles, went along too. Shortly after this, Airsols planes observed enemy activity on the northeast coast of Bougainville, arousing the suspicion that Kieta was being used as a supply and evacuation point. Rear Admiral Ainsworth, who had just got light cruisers *Honolulu* and *St. Louis* back from West Coast yards, took care of that. "Blue Goose" was now able to vary her 6-inch honk, long familiar up the Slot, with the pom-pom of new 40-mm quads; "Louie" too was newly gunned and equipped. Task Force 38 proceeded through Manning Strait off Choiseul, recently charted by U.S.S. *Pathfinder*, picked up an eight-plane Airsols fighter cover and two Black Cat spotters at 1535 December 27, and for 45 minutes bombarded Kieta; then

---

[2] In a "revue" put on by the sailors of *Montpelier*, the following was sung: –

Oh, we don't know how long we will be here;
Perhaps till we're old and we're gray,
But not as old as the movies we see here,
In Purvis Bay.

Oh, they say we're going to Button
For recreation and play,
But in Button we'll stock up on mutton
To eat in Purvis Bay!

repeated the performance at Numa Numa. There was no opposition. Returning at night, Admiral Ainsworth made the first Allied cruiser sweep around Bougainville and Buka, accompanied by night searching PBYs, and returned to Purvis Bay. Captain Rodger W. Simpson, who commanded Ainsworth's screen in this mission, found Blackett Strait a convenient short cut from Hathorn Sound to the west. He used it so frequently and at such high speed that the United States Army garrison on Arundel Island complained that their Japanese-style privies, extending out over the waters of the Strait, were being swept away. Captain Simpson accordingly sent the following order to his ships on 21 January: —

> Unless urgency demands, vessels of this Squadron will not use speeds in excess of 25 knots in Blackett Strait. It has been observed that wake from this speed gives Army privies a good flushing without damaging them. Practice of painting a hash mark under picture of privy on the bridge for each one knocked out will be discontinued.

Up to 15 December the entire work of defending and enlarging the Perimeter had been done by the I Marine Amphibious Corps, the core of which was the 3rd Marine Division (Major General Turnage) and the 37th Infantry Division United States Army (Major General Beightler). Admiral Halsey and General Harmon now planned to pull the Marines out and to relieve them by the Americal Division (Major General John R. Hodge), while the 37th Division, which by good luck had had little fighting in its own sector, stayed. The 37th and Americal Divisions formed the XIV Army Corps, commanded by Major General Oscar W. Griswold USA, who on 15 December 1943 relieved Major General Roy S. Geiger USMC as Allied commander in Bougainville. General Griswold, a calm, slow-speaking officer of basic simplicity and Spartan habits who had fought through the Munda campaign, was admirably fitted for this responsibility. He also had command of the "Bougainville Navy," which included all destroyers temporarily assigned for fire support, the boat pool, LCI and SC gunboats, landing craft and the PT squadron based at Puruata Island. Captain

O. O. Kessing, Commander Naval Advanced Base Torokina, was virtually the General's chief of staff for naval affairs, and the two became fast friends.

Christmas 1943 was a great day in Bougainville history. The thirteenth reinforcement echelon arrived, bringing turkey for all hands and, as passengers, the 164th RCT, Americal Division, which promptly relieved the 9th Marine Regiment.[3] But the biggest Christmas gift to the Perimeter was completion of the big bomber strip above the forks of the Piva, known as "Piva Uncle." Halsey punned to Griswold, "In smashing Jungle and Japs to build that strip there has been neither bull nor dozing at Torokina. Well done and Merry Christmas to all!"

The main objective of the entire operation was now attained. On Christmas Day, 1943, the doom of Rabaul was sealed.

[3] General Hodge relieved General Turnage in command of the eastern sector 28 Dec. The other two RCTs of the Americal Division, the 182nd and 132nd, took over on 1 and 9 January 1944 respectively, and by the 16th the 3rd Marine Division had been withdrawn altogether. Certain Marine units, such as the 3rd Defense Battalion, stayed. Rentz *Bougainville and the Northern Solomons* pp. 91, 144.

## PART IV

# Rings around Rabaul

*East Longitude dates; Zone minus 11 time.*

# CHAPTER XXII

# Moving into New Britain

*December 1943–January 1944*

## 1. Problem, Objective and Strategy

THE CONQUEST, defense and development of the Bougainville Perimeter had been a mighty effort, giving command of the entire Solomon Sea to the Navy and a final springboard for Rabaul to Airsols. Now it was time to throw a military chain around the entire Bismarck Archipelago.

General MacArthur wanted only a major breach in the Bismarcks Barrier to push westward by a series of bold leaps along the New Guinea-Mindanao axis. Finschhafen on Huon Peninsula had been in his hands since October, but not yet Rooke Island across Vitiaz Strait. Dampier Strait, a dangerous waterway for large ships but very convenient for barge traffic, was still in enemy hands. New Guinea topography was too tangled and complicated to permit a westward advance by land only; Admiral Barbey's VII Amphibious Force was indispensable for boating troops along the coast. The General believed that in order to get going toward the Philippines, he must gain control of the Vitiaz-Dampier bottleneck. And it might be inconvenient for these forces, to say the least, if nothing were done about Kavieng and the Admiralties. Local air superiority was the General's *sine qua non;* he could not leapfrog Wewak and strike down-west near the New Guinea bird's neck with enemy airplanes from Kavieng and the Admiralties on *his* neck. Consequently, this was the plan for the turn of the year: —

1. Amphibious landings in western New Britain, in order to control Vitiaz and Dampier Straits.

2. All-out, continuous assaults by Airsols on Rabaul.

3. Seizure of Nissan (Green Islands) and construction of an airfield there.

4. Seizure of the Admiralty Islands and construction of naval and air bases on Manus (Seeadler Harbor).

5. Seizure of Kavieng, New Ireland.

All but the last were carried out, as planned, between 15 December 1943 and 20 March 1944 (when Emirau was taken instead of Kavieng). By April, amphibious forces of the South and Southwest Pacific could sail right through the old Bismarcks fish weir and never sight an enemy plane or ship. By May, Rabaul and Kavieng were surrounded by a close-meshed net of sea and air blockade. By June the Admiralties were being used as a springboard for the Marianas, and as build-up for the Philippines.

New Britain is a mountainous island 250 miles long, of the same general character as Bougainville. Heavily wooded with a tropical rain forest, it was very slightly developed except on the Gazelle Peninsula where Rabaul is located. The only roads on the island were there. Although the Japanese had a garrison of 80,000 to 90,000 men in and around Rabaul, they could reinforce other parts of New Britain only by air, sea or footpath.

At Cape Gloucester, the northwestern point of New Britain commanding Dampier Strait, the enemy had about 7500 troops to defend a growing airdrome and other points on the west end of the island. General MacArthur believed that Cape Gloucester must be taken and used by us, in order to protect the passage of naval vessels through the Straits; Commander Seventh Fleet agreed and the Joint Chiefs of Staff authorized the operation. The wisdom of hindsight makes it seem superfluous. It was not necessary, in order to make use of Vitiaz Strait, to secure both sides of it and Dampier Strait too. The Japanese had no big artillery on the west end of New Britain to command the channel, and no way to get it there. Their only means of interference with Allied use of the Strait were motor torpedo boats, of which they had very few, and planes based on New Britain; Commander Mumma's PTs and the V Army Air

Force could have taken care of them. Certainly the United States and Royal Navies managed to make very good use of the English Channel when the Germans controlled its southern shore, and both sides of the Straits of Gibraltar were never secured during the war. But this is not to say that the high command was unwise to under-

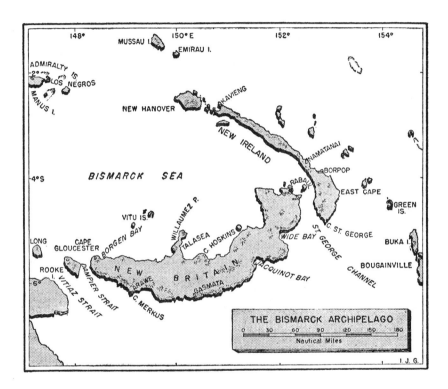

THE BISMARCK ARCHIPELAGO

take the operation. In the fall of 1943 the Bismarcks Barrier was still intact, and all waters north and west of it were under Japanese control. The possibility of the Combined Fleet's striking in force on the flank of the New Guinea-Mindanao axis had to be considered. From what it then knew of enemy installations and guessed of enemy capabilities, the Southwest Pacific command was justified in securing the Straits before commencing operations to the west. The operation might have started in November, but General MacArthur wanted the new airfields in the Markham and Ramu

Valleys to be completed first, in order to furnish close air support to the amphibious operation.

The plan provided for a staggered attack, first on Arawe outside, and second on Cape Gloucester inside. The first part was illconceived, a substitute for an earlier plan to take Gasmata, much farther east on the southern coast of New Britain. That was given up because the Japanese, anticipating attack, had moved in so many troops during the fall that the Seventh Fleet could not float up enough attack forces to take care of Gasmata as well as Cape Gloucester. As an inducement to General MacArthur to cancel this operation, on which he had set his heart, Admirals Carpender and Barbey put their heads together, looked over the charts and hit on Arawe as a place not difficult to take and so near existing bases that the assault shipping could be used over again for the Cape Gloucester landings.[1]

About 23 November General MacArthur directed that Arawe be substituted for Gasmata, with target date 15 December — ten days before Cape Gloucester. The official object of this was declared to be "the establishment of light naval forces" — motor torpedo boats — "to protect the southeastern flank of our forces in the impending seizure of the Gloucester Peninsula." But Morton C. Mumma, who commanded the motor torpedo boats in the Southwest Pacific, would have none of Arawe. He had all the bases he could use, and the Japanese barges used mostly the north coast of New Britain. He is said to have spent days "camping on Seventh Fleet's doorstep" to protest against setting up a PT base at Arawe; and to have departed only when assured by the Admirals that he need not have one if he did not want it.

---

[1] *General Kenney Reports* p. 327 also claims the paternity for the Arawe operation; he did support it well for a day or two.

# 2. *Arawe*

Arawe is the name of a harbor, an island and a plantation on the south coast of New Britain about 60 miles cross-country from Cape Gloucester. The harbor, suitable only for shoal-draft vessels, is formed by a number of islands clustering about Cape Merkus, site of a coconut plantation. The Japanese had moved in a few hundred troops and set up coast-defense guns and beach defenses; but they were using the harbor only for barge traffic. Close to the shore, about five miles to the east, there was an abandoned landing strip grown up with brush. Here, for once, an airfield was not the reason for an amphibious operation; the harbor that nobody wanted was the objective.

Planning for this operation, decided on only three weeks before D-day, was inadequate because of the difficulty of obtaining good air photographs, and because of the wide separation of the various headquarters involved. The troops allocated, the 112th Cavalry Regiment (Brigadier General J. W. Cunningham USA) were garrisoning Woodlark Island, and could not be concentrated at the staging area on Goodenough until 1 December.

The V Army Air Force dosed Arawe with 433 tons of bombs on 14 December and provided air cover on D-day; but General Kenney made it clear that the landing force could expect no help from him thereafter. His strategic missions, such as bombing Wewak, required all available planes.

Somewhat belatedly the 112th Cavalry Regiment, who hitherto had had no more training in amphibious warfare than Captain Jinks and his Horse Marines, were now given ten days to practise the art

---

2 CTF 76 (Rear Admiral D. E. Barbey) Operation Plan 10 Dec. 1943, Report of Arawe Operation, and Letter to Capt. Dudley W. Knox 17 Dec. 1944; Historical Report 112th Cavalry 24 Nov. 1943–10 Feb. 1944; Action Reports of Com LCT Flotilla 7 and of SC-743; "Southeast Area Operations" Part 3 (Navy); Japanese Army Air Force "Record of Southeast Pacific Operations." Frank L. Kluckhohn "Zero Hour on a South Sea Island" *N.Y. Times Magazine* 2 Jan. 1944 describes this operation and there are some colorful sketches of it by David Fredenthal in *Life* 21 Aug. 1944.

at Goodenough Island before embarking in LSD *Carter Hall,*
H.M.A.S. *Westralia,* and APDs *Humphreys* and *Sands.* General
MacArthur and Lieutenant General Walter Krueger, Commander
Sixth Army, inspected the troops as they embarked. It is a sad
business for old cavalrymen to part with their horses, boots and
saddles; they must have felt much as our naval forebears did when
"progress" robbed them of their beautiful sailing ships.

Most of the escorting destroyers joined at Buna on the Papuan
coast. The task force kept fairly close alongshore, and at 1800
December 14 passed close aboard Mitre Rock. That conspicuous
feature of the coast, rising 25 feet from the sea off Cape Ward Hunt
and cleft like a bishop's mitre, had so long been the jumping-off
place for enemy waters that one felt like tossing a penny on it for
good luck, as the Marblehead fishermen used to on Halfway Rock
before they squared away for the Grand Bank. At 2030 the ships
changed course for Arawe and reached the transport area at 0330
December 15. Black Cats covered them all the way. It was a bright,
clear night and the moon, four days past full, was near upper transit. H-hour for the main landing was set for 0630, about ten minutes before sunrise. The day broke fair, with a calm sea, and light
northerly winds averaging about five knots.

*Westralia* at once commenced lowering landing craft while
amphtracs boiled out of the dock in *Carter Hall's* belly. The two
APDs stood by, as they carried the raiders who were to land first.
*Humphreys* at 0505 launched 15 rubber boats with small outboard
motors, laden with 152 troopers. This landing on Pilelo Island,
which covered the main passage to the harbor, was entirely successful. The small enemy force on Pilelo retreated to caves where they
were promptly exterminated by flame throwers and hand grenades.

The other rubber-boat landing, from *Sands,* was a complete
failure. Its objective was a small beach situated at the head of a
cove and dominated by steep cliffs. The cavalry raiders were supposed to establish a beachhead and advance westward along the
Amalut Peninsula, to bottle up enemy forces there. Unfortunately
an American party of amphibious scouts in looking over that beach

on 10 December had caused the Japanese to suspect that a landing would take place right there, and they were ready for it with machine guns so sited as to enfilade the approaches. And the Cavalry Commander refused to allow the Navy to bombard the beach, hoping to achieve surprise in bright moonlight.

*Sands* had her rubber landing craft loaded, with 152 troopers and two war correspondents, by 0510. She then backed away while destroyer *Shaw* stood by to render fire support. Twelve minutes later, when the moonlight-silhouetted rubber boats were about a hundred yards from the beach, the enemy opened fire with rifles and heavy machine guns. Commander R. H. Phillips, *Shaw's* commanding officer, could not see whether the boats were afloat or ashore and dared not open fire on the beach lest he hit the troopers. Twelve of the 15 rubber boats were punctured and down they went, but most of the men escaped by striking out seaward; only 16 were killed or went missing. *SC-699*, the "Shootin' 699 of the Splinter Fleet," rescued 71 from the water under fire.

By this time forces destined for the main landing on what the Australians called Night Fireman Beach, were well under way. Ten of the newer armored amphtracs (LVT-2, "Buffalo") were used for the initial wave. Later waves were composed of the older (LVT-1, "Alligator"); all were manned by the First Marine Tractor Battalion. Behavior of amphtracs was little understood, and the line of departure was set too far out, five miles from the beach. All were successfully launched in nine minutes from *Carter Hall*, but they promptly became disorganized. When they were finally straightened out, the "Buffaloes" did pretty well but the "Alligators" kept stalling, with the result that the landing force was strung along in a disorderly column for a couple of miles. Once through Pilelo Passage, the control boat, *SC-742*, straightened them out while her sister subchasers launched 4½-inch rocket projectiles into the one machine gun that was firing on them, and silenced it. Two dukws, the rubber-tired amphibious trucks commonly used to run supplies ashore, also had been equipped with rocket guns for close fire support, and did their part well. At 0710 a squadron of B–25s from Dobodura bombed and strafed Night Fireman Beach; and at 0723 the first wave got ashore. They had no trouble securing a beachhead, since enemy forces were few and weak. Objectives were taken on schedule, and when the 2nd Squadron advanced up the peninsula in the afternoon it used two amphtracs with their machine guns in support.

More troopers landed in LCVPs and LCMs manned by Army Engineers. These boats followed the amphtracs in, but were unable to land until after 0800, owing to beach congestion. By that time the first supply echelon of 5 LCTs and 14 LCMs, handled by Army engineers' "webfeet," arrived from Cape Cretin escorted by *APc–4*, *SC–699* and *YMS–70*. While this convoy was awaiting a chance to land, word came that enemy planes were on their way from Rabaul. A scout had warned Admiral Kusaka of the Arawe landing at 0400, and he sent 8 "Vals" covered by 56 "Zekes" to break it up. About 16 P–38 fighters of the V Army Air Force, which had flown up as combat air patrol, went out to intercept; but they were not enough. The strike got through, but Admiral Barbey's flagship *Conyngham* evaded the bombs by quick maneuvering, as did the LCMs, LCTs and others of the supply echelon.

A total of 1904 troops was landed on D-day. A second supply echelon arriving December 16 was under almost continuous attack until its departure at 0830 next morning, when the Japanese planes chased it part way back to Cape Cretin. These beaching craft had to depend on their own anti-aircraft fire for protection; V Army Air Force was busy elsewhere. *APc–21* was sunk;[8] *SC–743*, who fired 2915 rounds during her 17-hour stay at Arawe, was damaged, as were *YMS–50* and four LCTs; about 42 men were killed or seriously wounded.[4] Another echelon, unloading on 21 December,

[8] The C.O. of *APc–21* turned in an Action Report that is a classic for brevity: "Under way to leave Arawe. About 15 Vals made surprise attack. Ship machine guns opened fire. Vals scored 1 direct hit, 1 near-miss, and strafed ship. *APc–21* sunk. Two planes damaged. (Signed) S. A. VAN EVERY."

[4] As a matter of comparison, only 35 ground troops were killed during the first two weeks of the occupation.

was subjected to three dive-bombing attacks from Rabaul and there was one each on the 26th and 27th, when *APc-15* lost 2 killed and 16 wounded. On the last day of the year, the eleventh supply echelon was attacked by 14 "Vals" and "Zekes" right in Arawe Harbor. "The attack was most determined, but was repelled by the combined fire of both LCTs and escorts," who shot down four planes. Rabaul was decidedly not dead!

Airsols, however, was doing its best to hasten the demise, and after the New Year only feeble and spasmodic air raids were made on Arawe. The LCT echelons which shuttled back and forth from New Guinea were more troubled by high wind and sea than by enemy aircraft. Foul weather played the devil with the LCTs and from half to three quarters of them needed repairs after every trip. Yet they brought up 6287 tons of supplies and 451 guns and vehicles in three weeks. It was a fine record that these beaching craft and their escorts made.

The troopers had little trouble, once they were ashore; a Japanese supporting unit, in order to avoid interception at sea and by-pass our troops, landed six miles short of Cape Merkus, took until Christmas Day to get into position and then attacked with no great vigor. The heroes of the Arawe operation were the little fellows of the "spitkits" and the "splinter fleet," faithfully landing their cargoes despite vicious air attacks and lack of protection from their own air force.

Arawe was of small value. The harbor was never used by us; the occupation served only to pin down some of our forces that could have been better used elsewhere, but it did divert a morning attack by the Japanese Air Force from hitting Cape Gloucester on D-day of that operation.

## 3. Cape Gloucester [5]

The capture of Cape Gloucester was an even greater waste of time and effort than Arawe. With the Huon Peninsula in our possession a big hole had been breached in the Bismarcks Barrier and there was nothing on Cape Gloucester to prevent General MacArthur from roaring through Vitiaz Strait to the Admiralties, Hollandia and Leyte. Be that as it may, the Cape Gloucester operation was well planned, well led and superbly executed by the VII Amphibious Force (Rear Admiral Barbey) and the 1st Marine Division (Major General Rupertus). And, as we have seen, General MacArthur, in the light of the intelligence which he then had, was justified in undertaking it. He had not the benefit of the historian's hindsight.

Cape Gloucester, New Britain, extends from Borgen Bay in the east along a roughly semicircular coastline to Lagoon Point. Along the chord that subtends this 180-degree arc rises a series of high mountains, the most conspicuous being a 6000-foot active volcano, Mount Talawe. From seaward the Cape unpleasantly resembles Guadalcanal; the slopes are clothed with a heavy rain forest, the bushy treetops making a stippled pattern except where a few rocky areas are covered with the deceptively soft-looking kunai grass. Target Hill near the edge of Borgen Bay and a hill overlooking the airdrome have sharp, kunai-covered ridges running right to the tops. At the end of the Cape, where the ground was fairly level, the Japanese had built a 3900-foot airstrip, to replace the inadequate prewar airfield. Borgen Bay was an important staging

[5] Rear Admiral Barbey Operation Plan 3B-43 and Report on Cape Gloucester Operation 3 Feb. 1944; Report 1st Marine Division on Cape Gloucester Operation; Rear Admiral Crutchley Letter of 13 Jan. 1944 covering Action Report Comcrudiv 15 (Rear Admiral R. S. Berkey); Capt. Frank O. Hough "The Cape Gloucester Campaign" Marine Corps *Gazette* Apr. 1944 is a good short account of the terrain and the ground fighting. But George McMillan *The Old Breed, A History of the First Marine Division in World War II* (1949) is one of the best unit histories of the entire war. An excellent overall view is Maj. R. M. Little's "Report on Operation at Cape Gloucester to 31 January 1944," issued by General Headquarters SW Pacific. Action Reports of all ships mentioned have been consulted.

place for barge traffic between Rabaul and enemy positions on New Guinea west of the Straits. Rooke and several smaller islands made convenient steppingstones across the Straits.

Along the Cape Gloucester shore there are very few beaches. As the rise and fall of tide is slight and the coast is protected by reefs, big jungle trees overhang the water's edge, except where mangrove swamps push out their roots "through which not even a cat could land," as Christopher Columbus said. The reefs are so complicated that a landing would have been impossible without good air photographs to reveal the reefs and boilers. Unfortunately, air cameras could not penetrate the jungle growth; hence we never knew until we got ashore that there was a waist-deep swamp extending from Borgen Bay and the airdrome. About 7500 Japanese troops were bivouacked in the vicinity of the airdrome and at Borgen Bay; and in both areas they had fixed defenses of dual-purpose guns. There were no roads on the Cape except a track running along the coast that was jeepable in dry weather. Normal communication was by footpath or boat.

Before the landings three separate reconnaissances of Cape Gloucester were made by an organization called the Alamo Scouts, accompanied by Marine officers and a former coastwatcher who knew the country. Three motor torpedo boats, *PT–327, PT–325* and *PT–110,* took them there and back safely, although on the third trip (21 December) they had a fight with Japanese armed barges.

After a careful study of all available intelligence, two small beaches — designated Yellow 1 and 2 — on the west side of Silimati Point and about five miles from the airdrome, were selected for the main landing. A clear channel to them could be charted through the coral reef that extended some two miles off shore, and at that point the enemy had few fixed shore defenses. A diversionary landing also was planned at a place called Tauali (Green Beach) on the Dampier Strait side of the promontory, six and one half miles southwest of Cape Gloucester. D-day was set for the day after Christmas, in the dark of the moon, so that the approach would be undetected; and H-hour was placed at 0745 in order to provide for a preliminary daylight air bombardment, and give time for buoying and sweeping the channel through the reefs.

Admiral Barbey's VII Amphibious Force conducted the operation with Admiral Crutchley's mixed Australian and United States cruiser division covering and contributing fire support. The ground

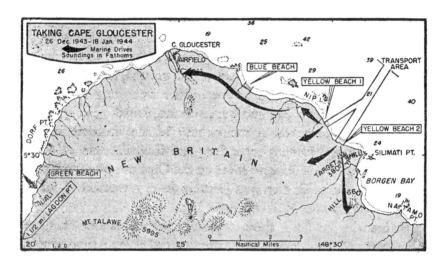

troops selected were the famous 1st Marine Division, beefed up by two battalions of aviation engineers, artillery and various corps units. This "crotchety, cantankerous, prideful and intolerant, but wise and fearless" division [6] had borne the heat and burden of Guadalcanal. After a long rest period near Melbourne the division had been moved in September 1943 to Oro Bay, Milne Bay and Goodenough Island, where climatic and terrain conditions were sufficiently nasty to give them the proper training and preparation for capturing a strong position only five degrees below the Line.

Planning for this operation had begun in June at General Mac-Arthur's headquarters in Brisbane. As General Krueger, commander of the Sixth Army, was ahead of the Marines in the chain of command, and as the Army Air Force also was involved,

[6] McMillan *The Old Breed* p. 1.

Krueger's and Kenney's staffs at Goodenough and Dobodura, as well as Barbey's on board *Rigel* at Milne Bay, participated in the planning. Continuous joint planning, such as the Central Pacific enjoyed in the close quarters of Pearl Harbor, was impossible. The Marines had a vital interest in the matter but their views were overridden until 14 December when Lieutenant Colonel E. A. Pollock USMC was able to express to General MacArthur the Division's strong objections to the original plan, handed them by General Krueger. It was then radically revised to meet their views.

Although the 1st Marine Division was a veteran outfit, amphibious warfare had developed so rapidly during the months since they had left the 'Canal that they needed training in the new technique that used APDs, LSTs, LCIs and amphtracs. A training group of these craft was formed and plenty of practice in landing from them was given to all hands. A full-dress rehearsal with all ships participating was held at Cape Sudest three days before the final embarkation.

The amphibious expedition was organized as follows: —

CTF 76, Rear Admiral D. E. Barbey in destroyer *Conyngham*

First Echelon
APD Task Group for Beach Yellow 1, Cdr. J. D. Sweeney

APDs STRINGHAM, CROSBY, KILTY, DENT, WARD, carrying 3rd Battalion Landing Team 7th Marine Regiment, 720 men.

APD Task Group for Beach Yellow 2, Cdr. J. S. Willis

APDs BROOKS, GILMER, SANDS, HUMPHREYS, NOA, carrying 1st Battalion Landing Team 7th Marine Regiment, 720 men.

Second Echelon
LCI Task Unit for Beach Yellow 1, Lt. Cdr. J. P. Hurndall USNR

LCIs *71, 72, 74, 338, 30, 226,* carrying 2nd Battalion Landing Team, 7th Marine Regiment.

LCI Task Unit for Beach Yellow 2, Lieut. (jg) R. O. Taylor USNR

LCIs *343, 337, 344, 73,* carrying 3rd Battalion Landing Team, 1st Marine Regiment.

The 1st and 2nd Echelons sailed together, escorted by destroyers SHAW, CONYNGHAM, FLUSSER, MAHAN, REID. SMITH (Captain J. H. Carter), and the following group: —

Beach Yellow Harbor Control Unit
SC–*981*, SC–*742*, YMS–*51*, –*52*, –*70*, Captain N. D. Brantly

Cruiser Bombardment Unit, Rear Admiral V. Crutchley RN

Airdrome Section: H.M.A.S. AUSTRALIA, SHROPSHIRE.

Yellow Beach Section: NASHVILLE, PHOENIX (Rear Admiral R. S. Berkey).

This cruiser group, which accompanied Echelons 1 and 2, was escorted by eight destroyers under Captain H. A. Spanagel in *Nashville*, including Desdiv 48, BUSH, AMMEN, BACHE, MULLANY, Captain W. F. Petersen.

Third Echelon

LSTs *466, 18, 66, 67, 68, 204, 202*, Cdr. C. H. Peterson USCG, each carrying 500 troops and 150 tons bulk stores, plus guns and vehicles. This also departed with the 1st and 2nd Echelons except one LST which loaded at Cape Cretin and joined at sea. This echelon was escorted by destroyers DRAYTON, LAMSON, MUGFORD, BAGLEY.

Fourth Echelon – Beach Green
Western Assault Group, Cdr. C. D. Reynolds in *Reid*

14 LCM, 12 LCT, 2 rocket dukws, SC–*637*, –*699*, PC–*479*, Cdr. B. C. Allen Jr. LCIs *25, 26, 27, 29, 224*, Lieut. C. E. Weyll Jr. USNR; carrying 1500 troops, vehicles, guns and 575 tons bulk stores of Battalion Landing Team 21. Escorted by DDs REID and SMITH.

(The LCIs joined the 2nd Echelon off Cape Cretin at 1800 25 December, peeled off at 0500 D-day and rendezvoused with rest of 4th Echelon.)

This Echelon proceeded to destination by Dampier Strait; all others followed the same route between Rooke and Tolokiwa Islands.

Fifth Echelon

LSTs *452, 454, 456, 457, 465, 22, 26*, Captain R. M. Scruggs, each carrying 480 troops of Combat Teams B and C, and 150 tons bulk stores, vehicles and guns; escorted by DDs HUTCHINS, BEALE, DALY, BROWNSON, Cdr. K. M. McManes.

This Echelon sailed from Cape Sudest ahead of the others and beached the afternoon of D-day.

Sixth Echelon

LSTs *459, 458, 168, 170, 171*, Lt. Cdr. D. M. Baker USNR, each carrying 240 troops of 12th Marines Defense Battalion and medical detachment, 250 tons bulk stores, vehicles and guns; escorted by PC *1119, 1120, 1122*, and, along last leg of route, by DDs FLUSSER and MAHAN. Tug SONOMA, Lieut. Nelson, joined the echelon, which was due at Cape Gloucester beaches at 0730 December 27.

Seventh Echelon

LSTs *474, 467, 468, 470, 475*, Cdr. T. C. Green, each carrying 250 Marine Engineers, 250 tons bulk stores, vehicles and guns. Joined en route by H.M.A.S. RESERVE, salvage tug. Escorted by SCs *703, 734, 738*; and along last leg of route, by DDs DRAYTON, LAMSON, MUGFORD, BAGLEY.

Reserve Group, Commander A. V. Knight RANR(s)
H.M.A.S. WESTRALIA, LSD CARTER HALL, AK ETAMIN

By way of diversion, during the three days before the Cape Gloucester landing Airsols planes struck airfields at Rabaul, a carrier group bombarded Kavieng, and the V Army Air Force delivered several heavy bombing attacks on Cape Gloucester and on Cape Hoskins to the east. Over 4000 tons of bombs were dropped at Cape Gloucester during the four weeks preceding D-day, and a little almost every day. General Kenney wanted to see the Marines go ashore standing up, and thought that air bombs could do it. Other Southwest Pacific planes struck Madang and Wewak on the 25th and 26th, to prevent air attack from those bases. Motor torpedo boats patrolled both Dampier Strait and the south coast of New Britain lest the enemy sneak up on us with light naval forces.

At sunset Christmas Eve, the troops embarked in their APDs and LCTs at Cape Sudest and proceeded to the nearby rendezvous in Buna Roads. It was neither a Silent nor a Holy Night for the Marines. The heat was intense, the little ships were overcrowded, and only those who secured a soft plank topside or a seat in a vehicle obtained much sleep. At 0300 Christmas Day "Uncle Dan" Barbey formed up his task force. The heavy cruiser group, commanded by Rear Admiral Crutchley of the Royal Navy, was there to give support and assurance. Speed of advance was only 12 knots, to accommodate the LCIs.

At 1030 the formation passed Mitre Rock. A Japanese coast-watcher in the jungle behind Cape Ward Hunt sighted the force and reported it to Rabaul. Even earlier, a snooper plane had reported the convoy. But Admiral Kusaka guessed that this task force was intended to reinforce Arawe, and so directed a major air attack on that place instead of on Cape Gloucester.

Major General Matsuda, a shipping specialist posted there to keep the barges running, commanded about 10,000 troops in the western end of New Britain, deployed from the Cape eastward about 50 miles to Iboki. They were a hodgepodge of all sorts of units. Two battalions of Colonel Sumiya's 53rd Infantry were posted near the beachhead. With no sea lanes open to him and only foot trails extending inland, he was ill-prepared to oppose a landing. The airfield, though in course of improvement, had never been anything but an emergency strip, and only about 20 planes were based there. If these elements and factors had been all, the Cape Gloucester assault should have been a walkover. But the Japanese had two formidable allies — the weather and the jungle.

The amphibious force passed Rooke Island and turned eastward. Break of day 26 December revealed Cape Gloucester with Mount Talawe's forbidding cone rising over the land. Light airs were blowing from the ENE, sea calm, visibility excellent as soon as the morning mist was scoffed up by the sun. Fire support cruisers and destroyers took position for the preliminary bombardment, incommoded by the LSTs and other transports which pressed too eagerly on their heels. Bombardment of the airdrome, the landing beaches and Target Hill commenced according to plan at 0600. The Aussies turned in a better radar performance than our ships. H.M.A.S. *Shropshire* had a radar with a tilting antenna and two "hot" operators who could pick up planes against a land background. A new feature of this bombardment was use of white phosphorus smoke bombs dropped from airplanes to smother observation posts and gun positions overlooking the beaches. The faint land breeze rolled the smoke slowly down into the landing area, and by H-hour (0730) both beaches were completely covered with the smoke, which then blew out over the boat lanes.

This smoke cover helped Captain Brantly's harbor-control unit to operate without let or hindrance. That unique little operation involved destroyers *Mahan* and *Flusser* and motor minesweepers *49* and *52*. The destroyers came in during darkness, navigating by radar and using the wrecked Japanese destroyer *Mikazuki* which bounced back a handsome echo. Once in through the reef, the destroyers used sound gear to find the shoals to be buoyed and pointed them out to the YMSs which went after them like "a dog for a bone." *Flusser's* motor whaleboat set out buoys improvised from powder cans.

The 7th Marine Regiment commanded by Colonel Julian W. Frisbie spearheaded the assault. Its 1st and 3rd BLTs debarked from APDs into LCVPs in the transport area, 9000 yards off shore. Leading waves hit Beach Yellow only a couple of minutes late; and the 2nd Battalion in LCIs was ashore by 0805. There was quite a surf on the beach, but the landing craft were well handled by their Navy coxswains. Admiral Kinkaid, Commander Seventh Fleet, credited rocket fire from dukws and LCIs for the lack of beach opposition.

Two companies of the 3rd Battalion 1st Marines landed at 0830 and immediately began marching toward the airdrome; General Rupertus established his command post between the two beaches by 1030. The first enemy resistance, encountered on the slopes of Target Hill, was quickly overcome and by noon that eastern anchor of the beachhead was secured. In the meantime, the other landing teams were making slow progress through the wet jungle to the west and southwest.

On this first day of the operation, no fewer than 13,000 troops and 7600 tons of equipment were landed on both sides of Cape Gloucester. These figures include the 1500 men of the 2nd Battalion 1st Marines who landed at Beach Green on the Dampier Strait side. These Marines set up a small coastal perimeter and dug in. Their mission — to cut off an enemy retreat or reinforcement effort — served no purpose. They rejoined the division on 13 January.

A large flight of bogeys appeared on the radar screens at 0900 D-day, but before getting within sight of Cape Gloucester or of our fighter interceptors they swung across New Britain and hit Arawe. By the afternoon Admiral Kusaka had learned his error, and the big blitz came at 1430: 20 "Val" dive-bombers escorted by 50 to 60 fighters. Bright sun, few clouds in the sky, sea smooth, light northeast wind. Destroyers picked up the planes by radar, 60 miles away. Four squadrons of P-38s and other V Air Force fighter planes failed to intercept but bravely followed on the tails of the bombers right down to the water. The enemy planes attacked destroyers *Hutchins, Shaw* and *Brownson*, which were steaming in column and maneuvering violently, eight miles north of Cape Gloucester. Two surprised the new *Brownson* from astern when she was preparing to fire on a third plane forward of her beam. The bombs hit alongside her after stack, shearing off everything above the main deck between her forward stack and after 5-inch gun mount. She began taking water fast, and it was soon apparent that the damage was mortal. Commander J. B. Maher ordered Abandon Ship and at 1459 *Brownson* went down. Fourteen officers and 215 enlisted men were rescued by *Daly* and *Lamson;* one officer and 107 men were lost.

*Lamson* in the meantime had beaten off an attack of five "Vals" with her main battery, got one of them, and escaped the bombs by radical maneuvering. *Shaw* shot down one "Val," which was followed hard by a second which released three bombs. All near-missed but plastered the ship with shrapnel which killed 4 and wounded 31 officers and men. *Shaw's* guns got the "Val," but Commander R. H. Phillips and his crew were barely able to keep her afloat on the return passage. *Mugford* received the attention of three bombers and suffered two near-misses which killed one man and wounded several.

During the next two days the ships discharging and approaching were subjected to small bombing attacks, but very slight damage was inflicted. The spell of foul weather that set in on 29 December ended enemy air activity over Cape Gloucester for the time being; and by the time flyable weather returned Airsols was keeping Rabaul so busy that nothing could be spared for offense.

After D-day no further gunfire support from the Navy was needed by the Marines, and the story of ground operations is largely one of rainstorms that never let up, of vehicles bogging down, of dirty fighting and general wretchedness. As at Bougainville, amphtracs were used in keeping front-line units supplied with ammunition and rations, and evacuating the wounded. As the units ordered to capture the airdrome pushed westward, another beach suitable for landing was discovered, and many supplies were transshipped thither by landing craft from the Yellow beaches. The Marines' engineers, commanded by Colonel H. E. Rosecrans USMC, with the 19th Battalion Seabees, worked untiringly to build and maintain the required roads and construct bridges over the many streams which crossed the troops' line of advance. The terrain was more hopelessly soggy than that of Torokina.

By 1630 December 28 the Marines had reached the nearer airstrip. But next day the weather broke, a northwest monsoon set in with torrential rain (as much as 16 inches in one day), and the coastal track became impassable. On slogged the Marines, defying the wet and the mud, took a hill behind the airdrome after desperate resistance, and overran Cape Gloucester airdrome on the 30th. At noon on the last day of 1943 the American flag was raised over Cape Gloucester. But the roughest fighting lay ahead.

Although the major objective had been taken it was believed necessary to establish a big enough perimeter so that the airdrome would be protected from artillery that the enemy might stage in from other parts of New Britain. That had happened at Bougainville. Japanese troops were still entrenched along the western shore of Borgen Bay, in possession of two strongly fortified hills, and their commander, Major General Matsuda, was wise enough to await our attack in areas over which the Marines must advance, instead of expending his men in futile charges.

The reduction of these hills by the 5th and 7th Marine Regiments was an exceedingly slow and tough operation, conducted partly under torrential rain, in swampy jungle, in high sharp kunai grass or on heavily wooded ridges. After two solid weeks of slogging through the spongy forested morass, the attack on Hill 660 was begun on 13 January 1944, preceded by a heavy artillery concentration. The enemy then yielded only the first of two deep ravines located on the slope. From that point the tanks could not proceed, and Lieutenant Colonel H. W. Buse, commanding the 3rd Battalion 7th Marines, had to withdraw his troops for the night, since the last 200 feet of the hill was almost sheer cliff, verdure-covered but slimy with rain. Next day the troops had to crawl up on their hands and knees with weapons slung. The enemy on top, not believing that human beings could come that way, was taken by surprise and all but exterminated. This happened on 14 January 1944.

Remnants of Japanese reformed in the jungle and made suicide attacks with the bayonet, but to no avail. In 16 days' fighting the enemy had been driven out of one strong point after another, his main supply route cut and his barge staging point captured, and 3100 of his troops were known to have been killed. General Matsuda's luxurious command post, well up in the ridges behind the bay, was captured intact, but the General managed to escape with about 1100 men.

Allied control of Cape Gloucester and the Straits was secured, but at a heavy cost. Between 26 December and 16 January the Marines lost 248 killed (25 of them by huge falling trees) and 772 wounded. Every veteran in the 1st Division swore that Cape Gloucester was worse than Guadalcanal, for the rain never let up.

This was one operation in which nature proved to be a worse enemy than the Japanese.

If a man hoped to keep his valued wallet, filled with pictures of family and girl friend, he had to resign himself to taking it out of his pocket at least once a day to scrape off the blue mold. Even with this care, the stitches might rot and the wallet fall apart, spilling out wrinkled and yellowed snapshots. . . .

Sturdy boondockers, the comfortable reverse calf Marine field shoes, the only type footwear ever issued in the Division while it was overseas, had to be scraped each morning — not for mud, but for vivid blue-green mold. Socks rotted faster than the quartermaster could replenish them, and many men recall the clammy feeling of bare wet feet in wet shoes. The laced issue leggings seemed only to hold the water in, and were soon thrown away. The rain made slop of the food, the at best unappetizing Cs and Ks, unless it was quickly eaten, for if the clouds above for once hung dry there was always a downfall from the dripping trees. Nothing suited quite so much in this climate as "a cuppa hot joe." Men seemed to live on coffee. But to make coffee you had to have fire, and almost nothing at Gloucester was dry enough to burn, nothing except the waxed paper and the cardboard that covered the K ration. These were hoarded against that time at dusk when only a cup of joe could make the long, wet night ahead bearable.

As these Leathernecks used to say, "Nothing was ever too bad for the 1st Marine Division." [7]

## 4. *Saidor and Sio* [8]

VII 'Phib was now so familiar with the technique of short amphibious hops that it was able to put one on at a moment's notice. On the day before Christmas, Admiral Barbey received a directive from Headquarters to land the 126th Regimental Combat Team of the 32nd Infantry Division at Saidor, on the second day of the New Year. There, at the western entrance to Vitiaz Strait and close by the eastern entrance of Astrolabe Bay, the Japanese had a landing strip which would help V Army Air Force planes to patrol the Strait and support Cape Gloucester. There was another reason, too, for taking Saidor. The Australian Army, which we left in October after the capture of Finschhafen pursuing the Japanese on the Satelberg, was now pushing them along westward by the coastal trail, which was studded with abandoned supplies and equipment and dead Japanese. At Saidor there were no Japanese, but at Sio (which the Aussies had by-passed inland) on the coast about 75 miles to the east, there were 12,000 enemy troops. So, this operation was not only good "leapfrog" strategy, it also "hit 'em where they ain't."

Three landing beaches at Saidor were selected by the study of photographs taken by reconnaissance planes, but proved to be narrow, rocky and exposed to heavy seas. The planning took place at Goodenough Island, whither 300 vehicles, 1800 tons of stores and the 7200 troops of the 126th RCT were boated in nine APDs,[9] several LCIs and two LSTs on 1 January 1944. Brigadier

[7] McMillan *The Old Breed* pp. 181, 162.
[8] Adm. Barbey's Report of Saidor Operation 3 Feb. 1944; "SE Area Operations" Part 3 (Navy); TU 76.1.4 Report 7 Jan. 1944.
[9] The same that were used at Cape Gloucester, less *Dent*.

General Clarence D. Martin usa had been training this regimental combat team at Milne Bay. The landing force was escorted and supported by destroyers *Beale, Mahan, Flusser, Reid, Lamson, Drayton, Hutchins* and *Smith*, commanded by Captain J. H. Carter; Admiral Barbey took command of the expedition in his flag destroyer *Conyngham*. Admiral Crutchley's cruisers as usual were hovering off shore to intercept any play by the Japanese Navy. But Admiral Koga could send nothing, because he had detected the presence of a United States fast carrier group that was about to hit Kavieng.

Landing 2400 troops at Saidor took place as scheduled, between 0700 and 0815 on 2 January 1944. The only casualty was Ensign Leo Leary, hit in the head by a radio transmitter blown off a bulkhead of *Mahan* by her own gunfire.

"It is most regrettable that our planes are inactive," wrote a Japanese general in his Rabaul diary when he heard of the landing.[10] The Japanese Army air force at Wewak was active enough, but weak from repeated bombings. They had only 39 fighter planes, 17 light and 7 heavy bombers; and these, after flying a dawn patrol over Madang, the other side of Astrolabe Bay from Saidor, had to refuel there before hitting Saidor. By the time of their first attack at 1600 D-day, all ships and beaching craft were out at sea, not a boat was on the beach, and all stores were well dispersed. Such expeditious unloading warmed "Uncle Dan" Barbey's heart and put VII 'Phib in the big league with "Ping" Wilkinson's boys.

By 3 January the Saidor area with its landing strip was in Allied possession and successive echelons of men and supplies were brought up without enemy interference.

The Japanese troops at Sio were still a problem, but mostly for their own officers. On 3 January General Hatazo Adachi, commanding the Eighteenth Army, tried to reach Sio from Madang, in order to superintend a retreat. Every time he tried to pass the

[10] General Kimihara, Cincpac-Cincpoa *Weekly Intelligence* I 17 (3 Nov. 1944) p. 38.

trail behind Saidor, American troops got in his way; so he had to give up the land route and ride a submarine, *I–177*. She tried to slip into Sio on the night of 7–8 January, but four motor torpedo boats were there on patrol. *PT–146*, after picking up some floating supplies in rubber bags, indicating the presence of a transport submarine, got a radar contact on *I–177* and depth-charged her without success. The submarine finally made Sio on 8 January. Two of our PTs were then busy breaking up a fleet of barges bringing food to the hungry troops in Sio. A coast defense 3-inch gun opened up on *PT–320* and *PT–323;* but their skippers imitated Admiral Foote's old Civil War gunboat tactic, charging right at the gun with everything firing. They then returned to the barges and destroyed ten that night. By this time the PTs were operating by day as well as night, and as far as Madang, from an advanced base in Dreger Harbor.

Word reached Headquarters that the Sio garrison was assembling at Gali, a coastal point 37 miles to the west, in the hope of being evacuated by sea. So on 8 January they were treated to two destroyer bombardments, one by *Reid* and *Mahan*, the other by *Beale* and *Mugford*. On 15 January Sio fell to the Australian troops, and the entire Japanese garrison at Gali was promptly bombarded by destroyers *Bush*, *Ammen* and *Mullany*. These unhappy soldiers finally started their hike to Madang on 23 January. Some two thousand fell by the wayside; the rest straggled in, weak and dispirited, in mid-February.

The outstanding success of this leapfrog operation, small as it was, encouraged the Southwest Pacific command to try the same thing on a larger scale, at Hollandia.

# CHAPTER XXIII

# Airsols' Assault on Rabaul

## 17 December 1943–1 May 1944 [1]

## 1. "Festung Rabaul"

R ABAUL has well been called a town of tragedies, but the
harbor is one of the most beautiful in the world. In 1782
Captain Simpson RN named the inner harbor after himself and the
outer one for his ship *Blanche*. The town that grew up on its
northern edge became the capital of New Guinea under both
German and Australian rule. Here, surrounded by active volcanoes
— the Mother, the two Daughters and Vulcan Crater — lived about
a thousand Europeans, government officials, traders, missionaries
and planters; and several thousand Chinese and natives. In 1941
the earth began grumbling again and the government decided to
move to Lae, but Rabaul had been only partly evacuated when
the Japanese erupted into the town (22 January 1942) and took
over.

[1] USSBS Naval Analysis Division *The Allied Campaign against Rabaul* (1946);
South Pacific Force Intelligence Section "The Air Assault on Rabaul 17 Dec. 1943–
19 Feb. 1944," "Fighters over Rabaul" (Air Battle Notes No. 30, 6 Jan. 1944), and
"Escort Tactics of South Pacific Fighters," 1 June 1944. Capt. Warren H. Good-
man USMCR "The Reduction of Rabaul," *Marine Corps Gazette* XXVIII No. 8
(Aug. 1944) pp. 10–17. Comairsols Intelligence Section "Reduction of Rabaul"
30 May 1944 and Daily Intelligence Summaries; Royal New Zealand Air Force
"The R.N.Z.A.F. and the Assault on Rabaul." John DeChant *Devilbirds* (1947);
*General Kenney Reports* (1949); interrogations of Cdr. Y. Doi and Capt. T.
Miyazaki in *Inter. Jap. Off.* I 209, II 413–18, 421; ATIS docs. No. 16948 and 17151
(answers to Lt. Cdr. Salomon's questions 1946). WDC No. 160303 "Records of
25th Naval Air Flotilla 1 Dec. 1943–5 May 1944"; "Record of Allied Air Raids
on Rabaul," compiled from data in "Southeast Area Air Operations"; I use the
latter for Japanese plane losses, although far from satisfied that it is complete,
and JANAC for ship losses; *The Allied Campaign against Rabaul* claims ships
sunk in this campaign which JANAC shows were sunk later if at all. For our own
plane losses I depend on Comairsols and Comairsopac Daily Intelligence Summaries
and Sopac Air Combat Intelligence.

At that time Rabaul had two airstrips, the commercial field at Lakunai on Crater Peninsula and the R.A.A.F. field at Vunakanau nine miles south of Rabaul. The Japanese improved these and soon built three others: Rapopo on Lesson Point 14 miles southeast of Rabaul, completed in December 1942; Tobera, 11 miles west of

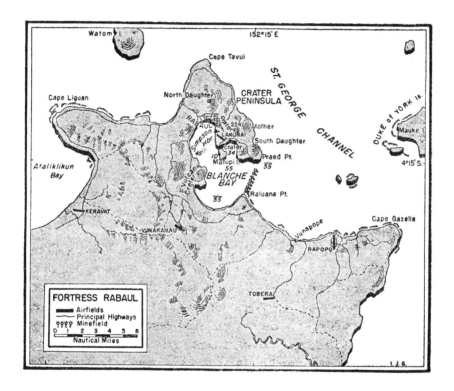

Cape Gazelle, in August 1943; and Keravat, 13 miles to the southwest of Rabaul, which was never more than an emergency and parking field because of inadequate drainage.

Each of these, except Keravat, had a concrete landing strip, revetments for 80 to 120 planes, miles of taxiways and ample installations. All in all, "Fortress Rabaul" had not only a harbor but an airdrome which any nation would have been glad to possess.

The bombing of Rabaul, begun by General Kenney's air force 12 October and continued through 2 November, destroyed many installations; and by the end of November, when Airsols planes were through with it, most of the buildings at Rapopo had been knocked down. The Japanese then began to burrow out underground hangars, repair shops and even barracks in the loose volcanic soil. They then had plenty of labor: 97,870 Japanese troops (including 21,570 Navy) in New Britain – all but a few thousand of these at Rabaul; 1457 Chinese (puppet régime troops and coolies) and 6000 Indians captured at Singapore. Earlier stockpiling of provisions, stores and equipment for the invasions of Port Moresby, New Caledonia and Fiji, for which Rabaul was to have been the springboard, assured the Army commander, General Hitoshi Imamura, that he could withstand a long siege. The airfields and harbor were well protected with 43 coast defense guns, 367 anti-aircraft guns, plenty of tanks and artillery. The local road system, too, was ample. Rabaul had an efficient search radar net which could pick up a coming air attack 90 miles away, and three quarters or more of the planes at Rabaul were fighters; but there was no fighter-direction unit.

The naval commander at Rabaul, Vice Admiral Kusaka, Commander Southeast Area Fleet, was not under Imamura, but there was no lack of coöperation between them. All planes except occasional visitors were Navy, and although Kusaka's fleet consisted largely of small craft – over a thousand barges – he had a large and efficient stevedore and transportation group to run these around the Bismarcks and handle supplies. Ship repair facilities were badly knocked about in one of General Kenney's October air raids.

Rabaul lay 391 miles from Munda and 349 miles from Barakoma Field on Vella Lavella, the two nearest Allied bases in the South Pacific before the Torokina strips were ready for use. When the first squadrons of Airsols fighters arrived and settled on the Torokina strip on 10 December 1943, Rabaul was brought within 210 miles of their striking power. One week later the campaign began. Seabees and Army engineers were still sweating over the "Piva Uncle" bomber strip, three and one-half miles inland from

Cape Torokina, which became operational on Christmas Day. A
fighter strip on Stirling Island, Treasuries, was ready 15 January;
and a second fighter strip at Torokina, "Piva Yoke," was in operation a week later. Now that a complete airdrome was established in
the Perimeter, Comairsols (General Mitchell) moved his headquarters thither from Munda.

The balance of forces is indicated in the following tables: —[2]

*Estimated Enemy Air Strength in the Bismarcks, 17 December 1943*

| | Fighters | Bombers | | Float | Total |
|---|---|---|---|---|---|
| | | 2-eng. | 1-eng. | Planes | |
| New Britain | | | | | |
| (Rabaul fields and Gasmata) | 100 | 50 | 25 | 26 | 201 |
| New Ireland and Admiralties | 40 | 10 | 25 | 16 | 91 |
| | 140 | 60 | 50 | 42 | 292 |

This was less than half the operational strength of Airsols, whose
planes were distributed among different types as follows: —

*Air Solomons Strength 17 December 1943*

| Type | Desig-nation | Arm | Avail-able | Opera-tional |
|---|---|---|---|---|
| Fighters: | | | | |
| Corsair | F4U | USMC, USN | 71 | 47 |
| Hellcat | F6F | USN | 58 | 53 |
| Lightning (2-engine) | P-38 | USA | 31 | 12 |
| Airacobra | P-39 | USA | 69 | 51 |
| Warhawk | P-40 | RNZAF, USA | 39 | 36 |
| Total | | | 268 | 199 |
| Bombers, Light and Medium: | | | | |
| Dauntless | SBD | USMC, USN | 102 | 88 |
| Avenger | TBF | USMC, USN | 55 [3] | 40 [3] |
| Mitchell | B-25 | USA | 47 | 39 |
| Ventura [3] | PV | USN, RNZAF | 48 | 33 |
| Total | | | 252 | 200 |
| Bombers, Heavy: | | | | |
| Liberator | B-24 | USA | 74 | 68 |
| Liberator [3] | PB4Y | USN | 29 | 24 |
| Liberator | PB4Y | USMC | 8 | 7 |
| Total | | | 111 | 99 |
| GRAND TOTAL | | | 631 | 498 |

[2] Tables from "The Air Assault on Rabaul" pp. 4, 5, with later corrections. The
Navy and Marine Corps night fighters and Black Cats which were not used against
Rabaul are not included.

[3] Approximate number.

At the outset of the campaign, Airsols planes were dispersed in fields stretching almost the whole length of the Solomon Isles, from Guadalcanal to Bougainville. Only a dozen fighters were based initially at Empress Augusta Bay; but all other fighters used in the assault, as well as light and medium bombers, were staged through the Torokina strip for fuel and briefing. Air strength based there was augmented as fast as the two Piva strips and their revetments were completed. Later, when the Stirling Island strip became operational, Lightnings, Mitchells and a Marine B–25 squadron were based there, 279 miles from Rabaul. Barakoma on Vella Lavella (349 miles from Rabaul) and Ondonga at the head of Hathorn Sound in Kula Gulf (385 miles) were used as fighter bases; Munda (391 miles) as a bomber base. Most of the four-engined Liberators continued to make their home at Henderson Field (562 miles), but were staged through Munda where an advanced echelon was located. This air force was adequate to deal with Rabaul, but the margin of fighter planes, the most vulnerable on strikes against strongly defended bases, was small.

Airsols was ready to go. Carrier pilots, who had taken part in the early November strikes, were flown over to tell them all about Rabaul; they made the eyes of Airsols pilots bulge with stories of a "big city with real streets"; a harbor "full of cruisers, cans, big fat AKs and hundreds and hundreds of barges"; ack-ack "so thick you could walk on it"; Zeros "all over the sky and more of them taking off from five airfields"; and finally, "no kidding, cement runways!"

The first strike of this campaign was a fighter sweep on 17 December, in which Navy, Marine and New Zealand pilots participated, with Major Gregory Boyington, the Marine ace, in tactical command. About 35 Japanese fighters intercepted but as many more refused to rise and fight. Each side was feeling the other out, as shown by the low score: two planes to each, including Wing Commander T. O. Freeman, an R.A.F. veteran who commanded the New Zealand contingent. The first bomber mission was flown on 19 December. With the big Liberators as bait, enemy pilots showed a greater willingness to tangle; but only five of them were shot down, and we lost four fighters; the B-24s sank one ship in the harbor and set fire to another. The enemy pilots proved to be greatly superior to any that Airsols had encountered for several months. Their group tactics and evasive maneuvers had considerably improved. Rabaul ack-ack was "heavy and intense, more accurate than any observed by our pilots over Jap Solomons positions."[4] But this was "something," at last, and the eyewitnesses brought back wonderful stories of dogfights, of a Japanese ace in a jet-black Zero with American flags painted on his fuselage, and of Boyington's mounting score of victories. Shortly after this, an Airsols pilot composed the following ditty: —

> If the engine conks out now,
> We'll come down from forty thou'
> And we'll end up in a rowboat at Rabaul,
> *In a rowboat at Rabaul.*
>
> We'll be throwing in the towel,
> 'Cause they'll never send a Dumbo 'way out here.
> We'll be prisoners of war
> And we'll stay through 'forty-four
> Getting drunk on *sake* and New Britain beer.[5]

The last line was much too optimistic; Allied aviators who bailed out or splashed, and were taken prisoner, suffered cruel, hard usage from their captors at Rabaul.[6]

On 21 December the Munda-based Liberators and Torokina-based fighters paid a return visit, bagging several planes and losing seven fighters. Dumbo did come to the rescue of the fallen, despite the doleful prediction, and recovered one pilot from the "drink" some 30 miles inside St. George Channel.[7]

[4] Air Operation, Barakoma, Weekly Intelligence Summary 25 Dec. 1943 and 1 Jan. 1944.
[5] Goodman pp. 11, 13.
[6] Major Boyington's experiences are told in DeChant *Devilbirds.*
[7] Rabaul records are puzzling, as the dates often do not agree with ours; but specific attacks can generally be identified by the numbers and types of planes. This 21 December raid, for instance, appears on the Rabaul records as one of 27 B-25s and 50 fighters on 23 December; the Japanese claimed 20 kills and admitted a loss of 6 shot down and 3 destroyed on the ground.

"Piva Uncle" was dedicated by launching a fighter strike on 27 December. As the planes flew up St. George Channel, stacked from 18,000 up to 30,000 feet, they sighted 30 to 40 of the enemy orbiting over Simpson Harbor at 16,000 feet. They swept around, enclosing the Japanese in a lufberry five to six miles across and tilted from 20,000 to 14,000 feet, made passes singly and in pairs, then climbed back into the circle. Thus the formation retained its altitude advantage and kept the Japanese "bottled up." Six were shot down. The same tactics were repeated next day, but on the last three days of 1943 the weather was too foul for flying.

The score for 17–28 December was 40 Japanese planes destroyed at the cost of 24 Airsols. The total weight of bombs dropped amounted to only 192 tons, and although these were concentrated on the Lakunai airfield they did not do much damage. Obviously all this was but a start, and good only because a start.

## 2. New Year's Intensification

During the last days of the old year, Rabaul received 40 more fighter planes from carriers that were escorting convoys to Kavieng. This raised the total on New Year's Day 1944 to over 200. But two unhappy months lay ahead.

Comairsols well knew, from results of the V Army Air Force bombing in October, that Rabaul could not be killed by high-level bombing. He was using the Liberators merely as a stop-gap until Torokina was ready to base dive- and glide-bombers. When a photographic reconnaissance made on 3 January 1944 showed six destroyers, four submarines, thirty cargo ships and hundreds of barges in Simpson Harbor, and nearly 300 planes on four of the Rabaul airfields; and when news arrived that on that same mission Major Gregory Boyington had been shot down after making his 26th kill, together with his wing man Captain G. M. Ashmun USMC,[8]

[8] Air Operations Vella Lavella Weekly Intelligence Summary 8 Jan. 1944. Gaither Littrell "Pappy's Blacksheep" *Flying* Dec. 1944 p. 25. "Pappy" Boyington was made prisoner and survived.

Airsols Dauntless and Avenger pilots felt like turning-to and helping the Seabees at Torokina.

The "Piva Uncle" bomber strip with revetments was ready to stage the SBDs and TBFs on 5 January, but was not yet provided with sufficient repair, refueling and housing facilities to be their base; so a strike of the light bombers was organized, the planes taking off from Munda at dawn and fueling at Torokina going and coming. This meant they could not reach Rabaul before noon, when at that season it is generally protected by a heavy cloud cover that piles up during the morning hours. So it happened that day, and again on the 7th when the same tactics were repeated. "The damage caused by these successive raids was small," says General Kimihara in his Rabaul diary, "but the enemy's fighting spirit must not be underestimated." The 7 January strike knocked down only two out of 70 Japanese planes that intercepted, together with five on the ground. On their way home the planes dive-bombed the Cape St. George lighthouse. But this flight returned five planes short.

On 14 January, 36 SBDs and 16 TBFs, fighting their way through 70 interceptors who came out to meet them over New Ireland, dove down after shipping in Simpson Harbor. Interception began as the B–25s flew over New Ireland toward the target, and the Nip fighters pursued them after their pull-out for 30 miles beyond the rallying point. No bombers were lost, but four fighter planes with two of their pilots went missing, and only three enemy planes were shot down, according to the Rabaul records. Hits were claimed on seven freighters and a destroyer, but none were sunk. That day the enemy made one of his few and feeble counterattacks, dropping four bombs harmlessly three miles from the field at Barakoma.[9] These Dauntless and Avenger attacks on shipping were repeated every few days; the second, on the 17th, brought the first pay-off, four *Marus* for a total of 13,500 tons and a 5000-ton salvage vessel.

The next good bag was on the 24th: one 5000-ton freighter, a

[9] Barakoma Weekly Intelligence Summary 16 Jan. 1944.

6500-ton oil tanker, and the 5000-ton army transport *Yamayuri Maru* with ten planes and a number of trucks on board. "Great damage" was noted, according to General Kimihara; Rabaul's sea communications were becoming more difficult and expensive. But the air was still open, and on the 25th no fewer than 133 Navy planes (70 fighters, 36 dive-bombers, 27 torpedo planes) were flown in from Truk, which built up the total again to about 300. The quality and quantity of Japanese anti-aircraft fire, especially from ships in the harbor, improved during these attacks; in one week, 16–22 January, it helped the interceptors to shoot down 33 of our planes; we claimed 72 of his, but the Rabaul air records for that week are blank and we have no other means to check. "The Japanese are putting up a strong defense over Rabaul," reported Air Intelligence, "much stronger than they have shown elsewhere. They are exacting heavier losses than we have yet suffered." [10] Moreover, the ground forces were still repairing, expanding and improving Rabaul airfields faster than we could damage them.

Around 21 January the weather improved and the Dauntless and Avenger light bombers had by now been moved up to Bougainville. Rabaul was struck at least once daily from 23 to 30 January inclusive. The Rabaul records admit the loss of 37 planes in that one week, including the first of the new and much heralded "Tojos" to be shot down, and a "Judy," the new dive-bomber destined to replace old droopy-drawers "Val." Our own losses were 23 planes.

The tactical dispositions worked out for these Rabaul strikes proved to be highly efficient. They inflicted optimum damage and suffered minimum loss. A typical day's work was two light bomber missions and one of mediums or heavies — Mitchells or Liberators. Separate fighter cover was assigned to each bomber formation, but all fighters combined for mutual support during the 30- to 90-minute period they were over Rabaul. The Liberators bombed and retired at 19,000 to 21,000 feet altitude; the Mitchells, approaching at 11,000 to 14,000 feet altitude, dove to pin-point gun positions,

[10] Sopac Air Combat Intelligence 22 Jan. 1944.

released at 2500 feet and retired in straggling elements between sea level and 300 feet. A typical formation of 42 bombers was given escorting fighters stacked in four levels, the P-40s close, F6Fs and Marine Corps F4Us low, medium and high. As the bombers pushed over, the two lower levels of fighters went down with and slightly ahead of them, scissoring violently in order not to get too much ahead, to provide dense cover during the period when the bombers were most vulnerable. They leveled off above the bombers and swept the route to the rallying area about 15 miles from the target. Meantime, the two high levels of fighter cover made a complete circular sweep to brush off any passing "Zekes," taking care not to be tempted by the acrobatic stunts that Japanese pilots put on to divert them. Finally they followed down behind the bombers, affording additional cover to the rear TBFs. Before the close of the campaign, Airsols tacticians invented what they called in football language the Statue of Liberty play: several fighters left the formation over the target and lay low, returning by a roundabout route to intercept Japanese planes returning from pursuit. "Many good Nips were produced by this stratagem." [11]

Despite plane losses, the Japanese continued to put up between 35 and 84 fighters to intercept each Airsols strike. They were constantly flying in new squadrons from Truk; an acceptable diversion of strength from the point of view of Fifth Fleet, then preparing to go into the Marshall Islands. Nevertheless, these late-January attacks by Airsols broke the back of Rabaul's resistance. Vessels larger than barges were seldom to be seen in the harbor, after an order by the high command prohibiting all shipping from entering the Rabaul area. [12] Very few plane replacements were flown in after 1 February. Even the "Naval Consolation Unit," Japanese euphemism for a bevy of prostitutes, was evacuated. But the tens of thousands of ground and labor troops persistently repaired the shattered airfields like ants building up a kicked-over

[11] Sopac Air Combat Intelligence "Escort Tactics of South Pacific Fighters" 1 June 1944.
[12] Kimihara Diary p. 39.

ant hill; they even began building a new strip on Duke of York Island between Rabaul and New Ireland, although the four Rabaul fields were rapidly becoming valueless for want of planes to use them.

## 3. *February Payoff*

On 1 February 1944, while the Marshall Islands operation was under way, the staff officers at Rabaul held a meeting to discuss anti-aircraft defense, the only defense of which they were capable unless the impending attack on the Torokina Perimeter should succeed in wiping out the American base on Empress Augusta Bay. For, by this time, Airsols had about 300 fighter planes and 100 light bombers based there, not to mention those on the supporting air-dromes at Barakoma and Munda.

Airsols strikes on Rabaul now became more frequent and effective, and Japanese interception grew weaker every day. Almost 3000 sorties were made over Rabaul during the first 19 days of February — almost as many as had been flown since the campaign began — and about 1400 tons of bombs were dropped on land and floating targets. On 3 February a gun near the indestructible lighthouse on Cape St. George shot down the Marine ace Lieutenant R. M. Hanson. But, as proof that the offensive power of Rabaul had evaporated, the Japanese air force made no effective opposition to our landings on Green Islands, only 115 miles away, on 15 February.

The first big air battle for almost a month, and the very last over Rabaul, occurred on 19 February. At 1030, forty-eight SBDs and 23 TBFs, escorted by 68 fighters, arrived over Simpson Harbor in search of enemy vessels. Shipping was so scarce that instead they assaulted Lakunai field with bombs and rockets. Twelve minutes after the first attack, 20 B–24s covered by 35 fighters bombed Lakunai and Tobera airfields from 21,000 feet, achieving the destruction of the one and knocking out the other with over a hundred 1000-pound bombs. Out of 50 intercepting fighters, perhaps a dozen were shot down; we lost one Corsair.

This battle over Rabaul occurred two days after the first big carrier-plane and surface attack on Truk.[13] The devastating results of that raid caused the Japanese high command to abandon the air defense of Rabaul; the vigorous interception on the 19th was Kusaka's swan song. "All our fighter planes left for Truk this morning," wrote General Kimihara in his diary for 20 February; only 30 damaged "Zekes" and 26 bombers were left. About 350 ground personnel of the air group whose "Betty" bombers had been reduced from 48 in September to 12 by February were embarked for evacuation in *Kokai Maru* and *Kowa Maru*. Both ships were bombed and sunk by Airsols planes on the 21st, and rescue tug *Nagaura* was sunk by Captain Burke's destroyers next day.

Strangely enough, General Tojo chose this critical juncture to make what he termed an "inaugural call," accompanied by Admiral Nagano, Chief of the Naval General Staff, and Admiral Shimada, Minister of the Navy. General Imamura's chief of staff found it "difficult to comprehend" the motives for this visit, as do we. One gathers that Tojo ordered Imamura to hold Rabaul at all costs, but promised him no help.

Aërial photographs of Rabaul taken on 25 February revealed only 33 grounded planes in the entire area; probably others were concealed underground. Complete mastery of the air over the Bismarcks had been won; and it was a clean-cut victory, won by superiority in pilots, planes, tactics and strategy. Rabaul was already in the red on the Japanese ledger; but much work remained to be done before it was completely written off.

Exactly how many Japanese planes were destroyed in and over Rabaul will probably never be known. The records are defective; the one trustworthy postwar interrogation gave the number as 359 from November 1943 to March 1944. Airsols "combat losses on daylight missions" in the same period were 136 planes (110 of

[13] This will be related in Vol. VII of this History.

them fighters) together with 14 operational losses. In the last nine weeks only 26 American bombers, including 3 Liberators, were destroyed, 15 of them by anti-aircraft fire.

From the numerous planes shot down on these missions against Rabaul many pilots and crewmen were rescued, some by Dumbos flown up from Empress Augusta, others by getting ashore in life rafts. As a sample of the adventures undergone by these tough young men, we may take that of 1st Lieutenant Lester V. Swenson USMCR and his two crewmen, Staff Sergeant James A. Brooks and Corporal Frederick E. Betz, who reached safety 74 days after their TBF splashed in the outer harbor on 14 January 1944. They were jumped by three fighters, made a water landing, got into their life raft and paddled down St. George Channel. That night a storm blew up and the raft capsized; but, as all equipment had been lashed down, nothing was lost. They righted the raft and covered 60 miles from Rabaul in 24 hours. Swenson hoped to paddle along the New Britain coast to Arawe. But so many Japanese planes flew overhead that the men frequently had to hide under the raft. Becoming tired of that, they decided to try their luck ashore.

Friendly natives fed the men and took them to their village, where Swenson studied pidgin English from a manual that the "teacher boy" lent him. After four days he heard that the Japanese were coming, and put to sea again. Two Australian Beaufighters spotted the raft and sent out a Catalina to pick it up; but the PBY could not find it and attracted the attention of Japanese ashore, who sent out a motor launch to search after dark. It was a very black night, and the aviators escaped. Expecting another search, they went ashore again and were helped over the coral reef by natives.

These Melanesians not only guided the Marines to the nearest American base but helped them in many ways: fed them roast pig, taro, pineapples and bananas; rolled cigarettes of native tobacco in banana leaves; threw up a rainproof lean-to every night; treated Betz's infected arm. They were thoroughly loyal and, said Swenson, were better than radar at detecting bogeys. Long before the Marines could hear anything, a "boy" would hold up his hand for silence and say something like, "Six planes — Jap — 2-engine"; and he was always right.

After three weeks' wandering through the jungle, Betz was so weak that he had to stay in a native village; Swenson and Brooks went on for 30 or 40 days more before they got into the hands of an Australian coastwatcher who took them out. Betz followed three weeks later. Swenson was flown to Washington, to report to Marine headquarters, without having had time to procure a new uniform or insignia. Someone who saw him in a Washington hotel lobby dressed in pants and polo shirt decided he was a draft dodger and called the F.B.I. Lieutenant Swenson told his story to the F.B.I. man, who replied, "Tell that to the Marines!"[14]

## 4. Rabaul Reduced to Impotence

After 19 February, the date of the last real air battle, Rabaul fell into a pattern from which it emerged only at the surrender. One game "Zeke" got into the air on 21 February, eight on 3 March and one in April, but they were the last, except that at intervals of months one or two would be patched up by "cannibalizing" the others. After using the usual fighter cover as a precaution for three weeks, Airsols for the first time on 8 March sent out an unescorted bomber strike against Rabaul. It worked, and the Rabaul bombing strikes in consequence became what the aviators called a "milk run."

Airsols now had a superfluity of fighters. Since on 24 March the Liberators were diverted to attacks on Truk, their function was taken over by Lightnings, Airacobras and New Zealand Warhawks, converted to fighter-bombers carrying two 500-pound or one 1000-pound bomb each.[15] About half of these, together with the SBDs and TBFs, were now based on the Perimeter strips at

[14] Told to Capt. Goodman by Lt. Swenson.
[15] Wing Commander C. W. K. Nicholls rnzaf "P-40(N) Fighter Bomber" 19 Apr. 1944 (Sopac Intelligence Series) is an excellent account of the performance of the New Zealand-piloted Warhawks in this campaign.

Empress Augusta Bay, the rest on Green Islands, Stirling Island in the Treasuries and Ondonga at the head of Kula Gulf. Even during the great battle for the defense of the Perimeter, 8–28 March 1944, Airsols delivered at least one strike on Rabaul every day that weather permitted. An average of 85 tons of bombs was dropped on the area daily from 20 February to 15 May — a total of 7410 tons by almost 9400 sorties.

When this final phase of the assault began, four of the Rabaul airfields were still serviceable, and the same was true almost to the middle of March. Keravat, the least important airfield of the five, was knocked out for good on 17 April. But the Japanese kept at least a part of one strip ready for use. At Vunakanau, for instance, they kept the concrete runway patched up; so it was possible, even after 1 May, for a few planes to have landed there, but the high command could spare none for a dead end.

The reason for these incessant but fruitless repairs was the expectation of a comeback. According to Tokyo propaganda, a mythical "Greater East Asia Annihilation Fleet" of the Japanese Navy was getting ready to recover the Bismarcks, Solomons and Marshalls and restore the whole outer perimeter of Japanese defense. Imperial Headquarters knew perfectly well that no such fleet existed, but they raised false hopes in order to encourage their isolated garrisons to hold out. Japanese possession of sundry islands and posts from Nauru to the Vogelkopf of New Guinea looked well on the map and persuaded Emperor and people that they were still doing pretty well in the Pacific, although it was impossible either to help these garrisons or to evacuate them.

The destruction of Japanese anti-aircraft positions continued slowly. Between 15 March and 1 May the number of effective guns observed in the area declined not more than 50 per cent. Considering the continuity and strength of our offensive, this is not a particularly brilliant score. General Imamura was very clever at moving his guns to new camouflaged positions and concentrating them on the most probable lines of approach and retirement of our planes. After a given battery had been the target in a strike, it was generally abandoned and the surviving guns were shifted to a new position. Caves were dug for the larger guns, which were sighted on the harbor to be used in case of a landing.

By 1 March, there was no shipping to shoot at, except barges and a few small cargo ships which were promptly bombed and sunk. The barge supply, however, seemed inexhaustible. A census made by photo reconnaissance on 28 February showed 235 barges in Simpson Harbor itself and 192 in Blanche Bay and around Raluana Point. But it is significant that the splendid harbor which in October 1943 had held some 300,000 tons of enemy shipping, and had sheltered powerful task forces of the Japanese Navy, was reduced to a third-rate barge depot. Even submarines, which maintained a slender supply line, dared not show themselves on the surface in daylight.

Rabaul town, which in 1943 had been a brisk little city of some 1400 buildings, in March 1944 was divided into target areas which were pulverized one by one. "More than half the city has been reduced to ashes," noted General Kimihara in his diary for 6 March. "Keep Rabaul burning!" became the Airsols slogan. By 20 April only 122 buildings were left standing, too few to bother with. The garrison by this time was housed underground.

Finally an attempt was made to wipe out the enormous supply dumps that the Japanese had heaped up in and around Rabaul in preparation for their proposed conquests to the south and east. The principal one, on the south shore of Blanche Bay, covered over a square mile and included almost a thousand buildings and tents. A systematic air attack on this area began on 10 March with a strike by 24 New Zealand Warhawks armed with 500-pound general-purpose high-explosive bombs. SBDs and TBFs joined the show, using a new incendiary bomb, a 500-pound cluster of 128 small bombs, which had a disastrous effect on supply dumps and stockpiles. In nine days, 182 tons of these incendiary clusters inflicted sixfold the damage that had been estimated for all previous attacks with general-purpose high explosives. Attention was then turned to the supply area on the northern coast of the Gazelle Peninsula.

But the large underground supply dumps were still untouched, and the large garrison never went hungry.

In addition to the beating he was taking from Airsols planes, General Imamura was smacked down in a spiritual sense. By Imperial command on 15 March, the Eighteenth Army and Fourth Air Army were transferred from his command to that of the Second Area Army in Celebes. "This seems to me to be a cruel, heartless, unreasonable measure," noted General Kimihara in his diary; and when, over a month later, he heard of our attack on Hollandia, he observed with malicious satisfaction, "I can imagine how surprised the Eighteenth Army and the Second Area Army were."

Nevertheless, General Imamura and Admiral Kusaka kept their chins up, and the morale of their forces as well.[16] When the Admiral gathered his officers about him on that fateful 20 February when the planes were withdrawn to Truk, there was some grumbling, but the conference ended with *"Shikata ga nai* — let's get to work." The garrison, some 100,000 strong (about one-third naval personnel) after troops were concentrated there from New Ireland, was kept busy strengthening fortifications, digging tunnels — practising tactics against invasion, growing fresh food in gardens and inventing ingenious weapons such as mortars for shooting converted air bombs at an invasion fleet. Shortages were felt only in proteins and medicaments. Malaria incidence became high: 30,000 cases at one time.

The garrison hoped and prayed for an invasion to repel, and when the 1st Marine Division landed on the Willaumez Peninsula in March 1944, and the Australians later went into Jacquinot Bay, they prepared for battle. Fortunate it was indeed that the Joint Chiefs of Staff never ordered the capture of Rabaul and that the

[16] This description of Rabaul from 1 May 1944 to the surrender is based on conversations in 1950 with Admiral Kusaka and Captain Sadamu Sanagi of his staff. The latter stated that 98,000 Japanese surrendered at Rabaul in 1945. A Wellington, N.Z., dispatch in *N.Y. Times* 5 Nov. 1945 states that 80,000 Army and 46,000 Navy troops surrendered in the Bismarcks and upper Solomons, and that there were still 1000 tons battle rations, 3000 tons clothing, 700,000 shells and 11 million rounds of rifle ammunition in the tunnels and underground chambers of Rabaul; Admiral Kusaka says that most of this was spoiled, and that he had set many men to work making fresh gunpowder.

by-passing strategy was employed instead. Tarawa, Iwo Jima and Okinawa would have faded to pale pink in comparison with the blood that would have flowed if the Allies had attempted an assault on Fortress Rabaul.

Thus, the Airsols campaign against Rabaul never destroyed the place as a strong fortress; it only made it impotent; but it could never have accomplished that without the amphibious operations that ringed Rabaul around with airfields and advanced naval bases. The drain that this campaign imposed on Japanese air power and, to a less extent, on surface naval power rendered far easier the advances of MacArthur along the New Guinea-Mindanao axis, and of Nimitz across the Central Pacific. Looking at the campaign from another angle, it pointed out in unmistakable terms the folly of building up a great overseas base and garrison without a navy capable of controlling the surrounding waters and air.

CHAPTER XXIV

# Northabout

*25 December 1943–20 March 1944*

## 1. Holiday Express [1]

NEW IRELAND has been likened to a sword of Damocles swung over Rabaul, Cape St. George being the hilt and the rest of the island the blade — a blade 200 miles long but only 3 to 15 miles wide. In North Cape, the sword point, Kavieng and two airfields were located, and there the Japanese garrison of about 4000 men was concentrated.[2] A great feature of Kavieng, and the wonder of the Bismarcks, was a road along the entire east coast, begun by an energetic Polish baron under the German régime, improved by the Australians. A branch ran off it to a point on St. George Channel whence a barge-ferry service ran to Rabaul. After Simpson Harbor became unhealthy for shipping, in November 1943, the Japanese began sending troops and supplies into Kavieng, where they were then transferred by truck to the ferry beachhead. In the fall of 1943, the seizure of Kavieng looked like a "must" for the Allies. In the meantime it had to be pounded. But in the end it was by-passed.

About mid-December the Japanese high command decided to send heavy troop reinforcements to Kavieng and the Admiralties. Troop-lift had become so scarce that they resorted to the unusual expedient of embarking soldiers in the superbattleship *Yamato*. It would have been interesting if this behemoth had made the express run to Kavieng and had been tackled by the aviators of carrier

[1] Rear Admiral Frederick C. Sherman's Action Report 18 Jan. 1944; recollection of Cdr. James C. Shaw who was assistant gunnery officer of *Bunker Hill*.
[2] Borpop and Namatanai airstrips in the hilt were not important.

*Bunker Hill,* whose planes helped to sink her off Kyushu in April 1945. But she was hit by a torpedo from U.S.S. *Skate* early Christmas morning, not far from Truk, and damaged to such an extent that the express run had to be postponed.

Airsols search planes got wind of this movement, and at the same time learned that the Japanese air force had a big backlog of planes at Kavieng, which as yet was too far distant for us to reach by fighter-escorted bombers. Admiral Halsey therefore planned a sort of squeeze play. In order to tempt Kavieng planes within striking distance, a bombardment of Buka was ordered, in the style to which the Japanese had been accustomed as a prelude to an amphibious landing. Their immediate and desired reaction was to stage their Kavieng air force to Rabaul for refueling and arming. These were the planes encountered by Airsols' 75-plane fighter strike on Rabaul 27 December, when as we have seen our planes formed a huge lufberry around the Japanese.

In the meantime Rear Admiral Sherman with a fast new carrier group, consisting of *Bunker Hill* and *Monterey* with six destroyers, was to catch the Tokyo Express off New Ireland, after delivering an attack on Kavieng with his planes. This Christmas Day strike was noteworthy for a quick pre-dawn launching in the dark of the moon. Before daybreak the two carriers launched 31 Hellcats, 27 Helldivers and 28 Avengers who were over the target at 0745; they completed their attack in 35 minutes and landed back on board at 1015. This attack was directed primarily at shipping in Kavieng harbor, for which the TBFs carried skip bombs; one of these disposed of a 5000-ton freighter; another freighter was damaged and a 500-ton minesweeper sunk. But there were disappointingly few targets.

The enemy counterattacked that night with 4 "Bettys," 7 "Kates" and his usual display of pyrotechnics; but Admiral Sherman well knew how to meet a night bombing attack with radical evasive maneuvers, and no damage was sustained.

This carrier task group kept the sea, outside the range of Japanese snoopers, in the hope of intercepting troop-laden ships between Truk and Kavieng. Two groups, one of heavy cruisers *Kumano* and *Suzuya*, the other of light cruisers *Oyodo* and *Noshiro*, each managed to make its scheduled run and retire. At o611 on New Year's Day, when the task group reached a launching position 220 miles east of Kavieng, it sent up a five-plane search. One plane sighted the light cruiser convoy returning to Truk, and an air strike was promptly launched to take care of it. The Japanese, who were on to this New Year's party that the carriers had planned for their benefit, had a thick combat air patrol of "Zekes" over their convoy, which threw up an intense anti-aircraft fire and maneuvered rapidly and skillfully as our carrier planes pressed their attack. Highly enthusiastic reports of damage inflicted were brought back by the planes. But all that actually happened was that *Noshiro* lost 10 men and the use of one turret temporarily, *Oyodo* lost two men; destroyer *Yamagumo* had an oil tank flooded.

A third strike on Kavieng was made by Admiral Sherman on 4 January. Two Japanese destroyers were encountered retiring at high speed, but only slight damage was inflicted on *Fumizuki*. Although the task group was well within the range of Rabaul, with fair weather and a bright moon until 0200 next morning, no counterattack developed because Admiral Kusaka was then concentrating his planes on the Cape Gloucester beachhead. Sherman retired deliberately to Espiritu Santo where his carriers prepared to join their sister ships for the attack on the Marshall Islands.

## 2. Occupation of the Green Islands,
## 10 January–15 February [3]

After the Bougainville and Cape Gloucester landings, the next operations initiated by the Joint Chiefs of Staff to throw rings around Rabaul were the occupation of the Admiralty Islands and

[3] Three reports by Rear Admiral Wilkinson: (1) Seizure and Occupation of Green Islands 16 Apr. 1944, (2) "Recording," Office of Naval Records and History, and (3) Letters of 27 Mar. 1944; conversations with him and other participants. Principal Japanese source is "Southeast Area Operations" Part 3 (Navy).

of Kavieng, New Ireland. Owing to the involvement of the Pacific Fleet in Micronesia, adequate naval support for these landings could not be promised by Admiral Nimitz before 1 April at the earliest. That was too long for Admiral Halsey to wait. A three months' interval with no forward movement was repugnant to his temperament and at variance with his conception of Pacific strategy.

Accordingly, in early January Halsey decided to do something useful between the Cape Gloucester operation and the Admiralties-Kavieng drive, to "keep the offensive rolling" and secure ground for another American airfield close to Rabaul and within range of Truk, as well as an advanced base for light naval craft such as motor torpedo boats.

A study of the map indicated that the Green Islands filled the bill. This group of small coral atolls lies 37 miles northwest of Buka and 55 miles east of East Cape, New Ireland. Nissan, the largest atoll, eight miles long, was useful to the enemy as a relay station on the Rabaul-Buka barge line. To us it looked like a worth-while acquisition because an airfield built there would be 220 miles from Kavieng, 115 miles from Rabaul and 720 miles from Truk, and therefore of material help in the air bombing of those enemy bases. Moreover, Nissan was near enough to Torokina to permit fighter planes to cover the occupation.

Could LSTs and other beaching craft get through the shallow passes into the lagoon? That question was answered after a reconnaissance by four PTs of the Torokina squadron, under Lieutenant Commander L. Taylor, on the night of 10–11 January 1944. Casts of the lead showed that 17 feet of water could be carried through the pass on the south side of Barahun Island; and that was plenty.[4]

With this information on hand, a reconnaissance in force was planned for the night of 30–31 January to find out how many Japanese were there, and whether there was land enough on Nissan to permit the construction of a proper airfield. Captain Ralph Earle commanded this enterprise in destroyer *Fullam; Guest* and *Hudson* came too. Three hundred troops of the 30th New Zealand

4 *Mosquito Bites* (the organ of Commo. Moran's PTs) 1 Mar. 1944.

Battalion commanded by Lieutenant Colonel Cornwall, and part of a United States naval base unit with hydrographic, air, motor torpedo boat, landing craft, intelligence and communications specialists attached, were brought up in three of Commander Sweeney's destroyer-transports. *PT–176* and *PT–178*, which had made the preliminary soundings, led the way for the APDs' landing craft as they entered the lagoon at night with troops and specialists embarked. The APDs and escorts, after seeing the boats safely through the channel, stood out to sea in order to escape possible air attack from Rabaul, returning next midnight to re-embark the landing party. In the meantime, air specialists located a promising site for an airfield; the lead-line boys reported the lagoon to be clear of coral heads; the Navy men found the finest kind of landing beach on the lagoon side opposite the pass; and the Intelligence sleuths, by some mysterious method of computation that is their trade secret, estimated that the Japanese defense force numbered no more than a hundred — actually there seem to have been 102. They also found the Green Islands to be inhabited by some 1200 Melanesians, who were so friendly to us and so hostile to the Japanese that in the operation plan the usual preliminary naval and air bombardment was omitted.

These scouts found Nissan Island so ripe for the plucking that Captain Earle was eager to pull it down then and there, as happened in the Admiralties a month later. But, as plans were not ready for the reinforcement, supply and defense of this island, which was vulnerable to air attack from Rabaul, the Captain re-embarked his raiders and retired. On their return passage, 31 January, *Guest* and *Hudson* depth-charged and sank submarine *I–171* thirty miles west of Buka Passage.

Upon receiving the reconnaissance report, Admiral Halsey designated Rear Admiral Wilkinson, Commander III 'Phib, to command the operation in person, and set D-day for 15 February in the hope that by that time the Rabaul air force would be sufficiently reduced to leave Nissan alone. The attack force was composed of APDs, beaching and light craft exclusively, divided into echelons of varying speeds. Small units of the "Bougainville Navy" went along too. Ample coverage was furnished by Comairsols, "Tip" Merrill's Task Force 39 (*Montpelier, Columbia* and five destroyers) to the east and north, and "Pug" Ainsworth's Task Force 38 (*Honolulu, St. Louis* and five destroyers) to the south. The ground forces consisted of New Zealand troops, under Major General Barrowclough, formerly of the Treasury and Vella Lavella occupation forces.

### GREEN ISLANDS ATTACK GROUP
Rear Admiral T. S. Wilkinson in *Halford* [5]

*Main Body*

First Transport Unit, Captain Ralph Earle

DDs FULLAM, GUEST, BENNETT, HUDSON, HALFORD
APDs STRINGHAM, TALBOT, WATERS, NOA, Cdr. J. D. Sweeney
APDs KILTY, CROSBY, WARD, DICKERSON, Cdr. D. L. Mattie

Second Transport Unit, Captain Jack E. Hurff [6]

DDs WALLER, PRINGLE, SAUFLEY, PHILIP, RENSHAW, SIGOURNEY; 12 LCIs
2 Aircraft Rescue boats; tug MENOMINEE

Third Transport Unit, Commander James R. Pahl

DDs CONWAY, EATON, ANTHONY, WADSWORTH, TERRY, BRAINE; 7 LSTs; tug SIOUX

Fourth Transport Unit, Lieutenant B. W. Pattishall

4 LCTs, one LCM rigged as bowser boat; 4 Patrol Craft and APcs

Minesweeping and Landing Support Unit, Lieutenant J. Chevalier

3 Motor Minesweepers and 2 LCI Gunboats

Landing Force, Major General Barrowclough NZA

3rd New Zealand Division (less certain detachments in later echelons), 967th Coast Artillery Battalion; Naval Base Unit No. 11, including 33rd, 37th, and 93rd Seabees, PT Boat Base, Hydrographic Survey Unit, Boat Pool, Argus 7, Acorns 9 and 10, etc.

Second Echelon, Rear Admiral George H. Fort

Included Main Body APDs commanded by Cdr. E. B. Taylor in ANTHONY, 4 DDs already mentioned, and LST–LCI Unit commanded by Capt. Ralph Earle in FULLAM. Cdr. Roger W. Cutler USNR commanded the 10 LSTs. Also 2 LCIs, DEs MCCONNELL and BARON; one PC. The Landing Unit was a Detachment of 3rd New Zealand Division, Seabees, and a Naval Base Unit.

---

[5] CTF 31 (Rear Admiral Wilkinson) Operation Order No. 2, Feb. 5, 1944, enclosed with his Action Report.

[6] Capt. Hurff also commanded the screen, consisting of all the DDs. These destroyers were used again to escort successive echelons.

Third Echelon, Captain Grayson B. Carter
10 LSTs and 3 LCIs, under Cdr. Vilhelm K. Busck, escorted by Captain Hurff's
destroyers. Landing Unit of detachments similar to those above.

MTB Squadrons, Lieutenant Commander L. Taylor
18 PTs from Torokina, including Squadron 10, Lt. Cdr. J. E. Gibson

This operation was planned to the last detail and executed with the precision, enthusiasm and smooth team play that characterized everything that Admiral Wilkinson undertook. When "Ping" led, every man jack knew exactly what he had to do, which was the best means to ensure that he did it. He himself regarded this as the neatest landing that III 'Phib ever pulled off.

The echelons departed Vella Lavella and the Treasuries on 12–13 February, timed to meet off Bougainville. During the night of 14–15 February, the formation was heckled and harassed by Japanese planes more than had been anticipated, considering the way Rabaul had recently been pounded; Kusaka sent out 32 planes for this attack. No damage was done to the destroyer-transports and beaching craft. But Ainsworth's covering force, when south of St. George Channel at dusk, was attacked by ten "Vals" which made one hit and three near misses on cruiser *St. Louis* that killed 23 and wounded 28 men. Captain R. H. Roberts had the fire under control shortly after midnight. Between that time and 0500 February 15, these ships were attacked several times but baffled the enemy by high-speed maneuvering under a generous and effective use of smoke. Kusaka lost 12 of his 32 planes that night.

The destroyer-transports arrived off Barahun Island at 0620 and promptly lowered their landing craft fully manned. Thirty-two Airsols fighter planes were already weaving overhead. At 0641 the first wave of landing craft left the line of departure about half a mile outside the channel. A few minutes later, a formation of 15 "Vals" appeared and attacked the beaching craft which were outside the channel waiting turn to enter. Fortunately these bombers had no fighter cover, which made them "duck soup" for the Marine fighter patrol that had flown up from Torokina, and the barrage balloons streaming out in the trade wind on 300-fathom cables from the LSTs spoiled their aim. Only damage to the task force was a near miss on Commander Roger Cutler's baby, *LST–446*, the pioneer Love-Sugar-Tare of the Pacific.

This was the last air opposition encountered by the Green Islands landing force, except for single night bombers. That so numerous a fleet could set thousands of troops ashore with impunity only 115

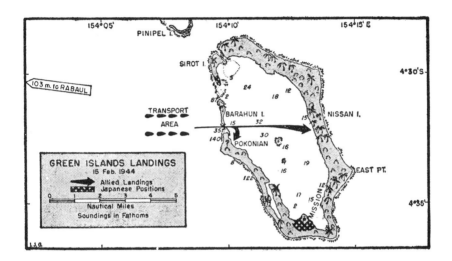

miles from Rabaul proved what good work Airsols had already accomplished. Inability to do anything about it was a source of great chagrin to Admiral Kusaka.

Only 15 minutes after the landing craft hit the cross-lagoon beaches, twelve LCIs were proudly steaming through the pass, crammed to the gunwales with New Zealanders. In half an hour's time they too were beached; ten minutes later they retracted; at 0905 they stood out of the lagoon, and within another half hour all LCIs had formed up and were hot-footing it back to Guadalcanal. As soon as the LCIs retracted, LSTs of the Third Transport Unit beached. Assault waves had already brought in a couple of bull-dozers which performed the grading necessary to fit beaches to the choosey bottoms of LSTs. Pontoon sections slung along their topsides were not needed. Captain "Chick" Carter beamed delightedly as a large, enthusiastic and hard-working beach party jerked the trailer-loaded cargoes ashore in jig time. Long before nightfall every LST had bulk cargo as well as trailer loads on the beach, and was on her way home to Purvis Bay escorted by destroyers and accompanied by Admiral Wilkinson in *Halford*. The Fourth Transport Unit of LCTs stood into the lagoon at 1357 and beached; these craft remained to serve the new Commander Naval Base Green Islands. All New Zealand combat units were ashore within two hours after the initial landing; 5800 men were landed during D-day, 15 February.

As the "Kiwis" fanned out along Nissan Island on the 16th, about 70 Japanese were encountered at the south point of the island. There was the usual rat-catcher action, which cost the New Zealanders three killed and eleven wounded. On the 19th, the 102-man Japanese garrison signed off on their radio and put up one last, tough fight; but by 20 February, when Rear Admiral Fort's Second Echelon arrived, organized resistance had ceased.

The Green Islands, easy to take, proved to be a very useful link in the ringing around of Rabaul. A PT operating base was set up on Nissan 17 February, and Squadron 10 (Lieutenant Commander J. E. Gibson) at once began getting acquainted with the neighboring shores and waters. This base enabled the PTs to extend their patrol range to New Ireland and along the outer coast of Bougainville to Choiseul. One of these, *PT-319* (Ens. Richard H. Lewin), was the first Allied vessel to "show the flag" in Simpson Harbor, in the early hours of 1 March — but she didn't stay long.

The Marine Ventura night fighter squadron's shore-based radar with its own fighter-director crew was set up on Nissan Island. This enabled the night-fighting PVs to fly up from Torokina and maintain effective combat air patrol. During the first week there, they shot down two or three Japanese bombers, which were the only missions sent against the island from Rabaul or Kavieng.

What now could be done with the friendly natives, whose taro gardens and coconut groves we were about to turn into airfields? The answer was a temporary evacuation to Guadalcanal. This was explained to the natives' head men, and, as the Melanesians are born rovers, the prospect of a boat ride to the Solomons and free food there was highly pleasing. Accordingly, "Grandpa" Roger Cutler's LSTs of the Second Echelon took on the function, new even for Love-Sugar-Tares, of evacuating natives; and so well was this done that by the time the flotilla of Melanesian Mayflowers reached Guadalcanal the 1147 embarked had increased to 1148.[7]

One month after D-day, seven echelons had discharged 16,488 men and 43,000 tons of supplies on the Green Islands. Seabees under Commander Whyte of the Navy Civil Engineering Corps had been working to such good purpose that as early as 4 March an emergency landing was made on the new fighter strip. On that day, command of the Green Islands passed from Admiral Wilkinson to General Barrowclough of the New Zealand Army.

With the completion of this airdrome, Kavieng for the first time came within range of Airsols fighters and light bombers. This was important because the Japanese air force continued to reinforce Kavieng airfields after it had given up attempting to supply Rabaul. On 16 March, Airsols SBDs and TBFs based on Nissan delivered their first attack on Kavieng. Reinforcements were flown in to the enemy base from Truk during the moonlight nights of 7–10 April, so the good work had to continue. Nissan field carried the ball until the strips at Emirau were ready in May.

## 3. Destroyer Raids, 17–29 February

Although the results of Sherman's carrier strikes on Kavieng were disappointing to us, they evidently warned Admiral Koga not to press his luck by sending warships to the Bismarcks. And by next month Halsey was ready to send warships there himself.

Between 17 and 29 February Destroyer Squadrons 12 (Captain

[7] The natives were accommodated on the top deck, with plastic toilet seats rigged outboard for their use. They refused to use them, however, until the Commander had given a demonstration.

Rodger W. Simpson in *Farenholt*), 22 (Captain W. F. Petersen in *Waller*), 23 (Captain Arleigh A. Burke in *Charles Ausburne*) and 45 (Captain Ralph Earle in *Fullam*) penetrated the Bismarcks six times, bombarding both Kavieng and Rabaul on three occasions.

Five destroyers of Captain Simpson's Squadron 12 threw the first ship bombardment into Rabaul on the night of 17–18 February. Under a heavy cloud-wrack and through frequent rain squalls the destroyers, guided by SG radar (that great gift of God and the double-domes to mariners), entered St. George Channel before midnight, steamed around Duke of York Island in search of shipping, and fired 3868 rounds of 5-inch on Rabaul town, installations and supply areas during the midwatch of 18 February, while steaming 20 knots under a smoke screen. They also launched 15 torpedoes against shipping in Blanche Bay. Shore batteries opened up on the destroyers about five minutes after the bombardment commenced, but made no hits. After this exhibition of courage and good seamanship, Simpson retired at 30 knots.

Admiral Halsey, as we have seen, when once he started "pushing the Japs around," liked to keep them rolling. Captain Burke's "Little Beavers" got only 13 hours' rest in Purvis Bay between bombardment missions, and most of that time was spent in fueling and provisioning. Tanker *Kankakee* was sent up to lat. 3° S, long. 156°30′ E, to give the "cans" a last drink at 0530 February 21. From that point the squadron steamed in a wide circle north of New Ireland, encountering nothing until the morning of the 22nd, when a large Japanese Navy tug named *Nagaura* was encountered and sunk. Seventy-three survivors, mostly aviation personnel being evacuated to Truk, were picked up from the water, and imparted valuable information.

Squadron 23 then split into its two divisions. Division 46 (*Converse* and *Spence*, Commander R. W. Cavenagh) bombarded Kavieng that afternoon, while Division 45 made for the south side of Steffen Strait between New Ireland and New Hanover, hoping to catch retiring enemy shipping. On its way, just before dark 22 February, Burke's division caught a minelayer and sank it on the shoals west of New Hanover; and after dark the three destroyers, *Charles Ausburne, Dyson* and *Stanly*, operating separately, picked up on their radar screens and sank by gunfire a small freighter and a few barges. They then closely followed the southwest coast of New Ireland looking for shipping; encountering none, they fired 1500 five-inch shells into Duke of York Island in order to damage the airfield under construction. Heavy overcast made plane spotting impossible, and as the ranges were selected by plotted positions of the targets this bombardment probably did little damage. Unfortunately Captain Burke did not know that General Tojo and suite were then making an "inaugural call" on Rabaul, or he would have given that place his very best attention. The two divisions rejoined off Cape St. George and then, as Admiral Halsey expressed it, "retired to stud in the lush fields superintended by 'Ping' Wilkinson."

Squadron 12 made a similar sweep between February 23 and 25. It is sad to relate that even in 1944 plane- and ship-recognition devices did not always work. The squadron was attacked intermittently for over two hours, on the night of 23–24 February, by an American bomber which did not show IFF and failed to recognize the destroyers' signals. Neither side hit the other, but the plane reported that she had expended all her bombs on an enemy convoy and made a direct hit. Enemy shore batteries at Kavieng really warmed up on this occasion and made hits on *Buchanan* and *Farenholt*, killing one man and wounding eight.

Finally Captain Earle's Squadron 45, thoroughly fed up with "milk run" duty in the III Amphibious Force, was let into the bombardment game. The full squadron left Purvis Bay 23 February, fueled at Stirling Harbor and entered St. George Channel at 2330 on the 24th. East of Cape Gazelle the senior division continued in a westerly direction along the southern coast of New Ireland, while Commander E. B. Taylor's division (*Anthony*, flag) headed straight in for Rabaul. Between 0030 and 0100 February 25, Taylor made three runs across the front of Vunapope area, where military stores were stacked high and deep. Coastal batteries replied, but made no hits. Although a certain number of fires were lighted and explosions were observed, later air photographs proved that this vast stores area was practically intact after the bombardment. Very little could be effected by 2200 rounds of 5-inch shell, compared with the effects of day-after-day heavy bombing to which Vunapope was subjected by Airsols during the following month.

In the meantime Destroyer Division 90 was killing time off the south entrance to Steffen Strait, between New Hanover and New Ireland, waiting for the junior division (*Conway*, flag) of Captain W. F. Petersen's Squadron 22 to drive shipping through from Kavieng. The expected game was not flushed. Division 44 subsequently bombarded the wharf area of Rabaul from the north side of Crater Peninsula on the night of 29 February–1 March. The PT squadron based on Green Islands then made a follow-up sweep of all Rabaul anchorages. They found only three barges, and sank them, while Division 44 fired some 1150 rounds into Duke of York Island before retiring. Captain Petersen's division had a go at Borpop airfield in the southern part of New Ireland, and made two bombardment runs on the Namatanai airfield across the neck before retiring to Purvis Bay.

These destroyer raids in enemy waters were regarded as very nice work. Admiral Nimitz expressed his admiration for the "bold, skillful and effective manner" in which the South Pacific Force carried out one operation after another, the latest being these sweeps around the Bismarcks; and General MacArthur, describing the raids as "daring and successful," declared that they were "conceived and accomplished in the best Farragut manner."

In retrospect, the damage they effected, though never carefully assessed, was not significant; nor was it expected to be. The main object of these raids was to demonstrate to the Japanese that Rabaul was doomed. If the United States Navy could steam at will around the Bismarcks, throwing shells ashore as it passed, the days of *Festung Rabaul* were numbered.

## 4. Occupation of Emirau, 20 March[8]

Until a month after the Green Islands were secured, it was assumed that Kavieng, New Ireland, would be occupied by the South
Pacific Force on 1 April 1944, the same date that the Southwest
Pacific was to move into the Admiralties. Owing, however, to a
growing conviction on the part of Cincpac staff that the Airsols
campaign against Rabaul would render the occupation of Kavieng
unnecessary, Admiral Nimitz appealed to the Joint Chiefs of Staff
who, on 12 March, canceled the Kavieng operation altogether.

Since Admiral Halsey had already assembled at Guadalcanal the
men who were to invade Kavieng, and the ships to take them there,
he wished to use them in some other way. Emirau Island of the St.
Matthias group, situated about halfway between Kavieng and the
Admiralties, was ideally situated to drop into place alongside them,
as the last link in the ring around Rabaul. On 14 March Admiral
Wilkinson received the order "to seize and occupy Emirau" at the
earliest practicable date, not later than 20 March.

One part of the Kavieng operation was saved – a preliminary
bombardment by the old battleship group of the Pacific Fleet, *New
Mexico, Mississippi, Tennessee* and *Idaho*. Accompanied by two
escort carriers and 15 destroyers and commanded by Rear Admiral
Robert M. Griffin, they bombarded Kavieng and nearby airfields
on 20 March. The Japanese reported this bombardment as "de-
moralizing," [9] and it created the desired impression that a landing
on New Ireland was imminent.

While the Kavieng area was being plastered with 1079 rounds
of 14-inch and 12,281 rounds of 5-inch shell, Emirau, a verdant and
beautiful island which the Japanese had never entered, was being
peacefully occupied by the 4th Marine Regiment, core of an amphibious operation commanded by Commodore Reifsnider. Within

---

[8] Rear Admiral Wilkinson's Report on Emirau Operation 7 Apr. 1944 (later
superseded by a shorter but less interesting one dated 16 April).
[9] ATIS Docs. Nos. 16948, 17895 B.

a month 18,000 men and 44,000 tons of supplies had been landed on Emirau, and it had become a motor torpedo boat base. Shortly after 1 May the first airstrip was completed.

Emirau's particular function in breaking the Bismarcks Barrier was that of a base from which the north coast of New Ireland could be kept under surveillance.

CHAPTER XXV

# The Battle of the Perimeter [1]

## January–March 1944

IT MUST NOT be assumed that Bougainville became an area
of military inactivity as soon as the Perimeter was secured and
the three airstrips were built. During January and February 1944
the Japanese were deploying ground forces along jungle trails, and,
with less success, by barge, all aimed at wresting the Torokina
Perimeter from the Americans. In the first week of March, they
attacked. If this assault on the Perimeter had succeeded, it would
have cut the most important link in the Allied armed chain around
Rabaul.

That struggle for the Perimeter went almost unnoticed outside
the Pacific. War correspondents had abandoned Bougainville for
other areas more fruitful in "stories," the public cared to hear no
more about the Solomon Islands; and armchair strategists accused
the armed forces of getting "bogged down in Bougainville." Yet
Americans were being killed every day on that island to keep up
the air attack on Rabaul, and in the Battle of the Perimeter they
fought superbly to protect the airdrome.

Japanese ground forces on Bougainville, as we have seen, were
largely divided between Buka and Buin, with headquarters and the
heaviest concentration in the south. Lieutenant General Hyakutake
of Guadalcanal fame commanded the Seventeenth Army, number-
ing about 40,000 men. Besides troops evacuated from Guadalcanal,
Munda and Kolombangara, he had Lieutenant General Kanda's

[1] Gen. Griswold's personal Narrative of the Battle of the Perimeter, which
he kindly allowed us to use; Hq. XIV Corps G–2 "History of the 'TA' Operation" 21 Apr. 1944 by Capt. John C. Guenther USA and Capt. Jack M. Tucker USA
in *Infantry Journal* Feb. and Mar. 1945. Many of the sources mentioned in chap.
xxii footnote 1 are also useful here.

6th Infantry Division, commonly regarded as the toughest outfit in the Imperial Army. In addition to the soldiers, the 20,000 sailors in southern Bougainville were under Vice Admiral T. Samejima, Commander Eighth Fleet; but for all intents and purposes the Japanese naval commander in Bougainville was Rear Admiral Isamu Takeda, charged with the defense of Choiseul, of the Shortlands, of the Kieta district on the northeast coast of Bougainville, and with barge traffic. No Army reinforcements got into Bougainville after 1 November, except the few hundred men sent into Buka, and the only reinforcements that got through came in a few sub-marines and float planes.[2]

General Hyakutake would not be convinced until the end of December 1943 that the Americans really intended to stay at Torokina. He insisted that they would either attempt a forward landing at Buka Passage, or make a frontal assault on his Kahili airdrome in the south. This fortunate miscalculation gave Major General Oscar W. Griswold USA, commanding the XIV Army Corps at Torokina, plenty of time to prepare for the assault that he knew would eventually be made. With only two divisions at his disposal, it would have been folly to send men out looking for trouble,[3] and it was out of the question for the Navy to mount a big amphibious operation to take the Buin region. By fortifying the Perimeter and letting the enemy attack him, he had the choice of weapons and terrain, a wide-open sea entrance and exit, and superiority in strength at the point of contact, all of which advantages would have been dissipated if he had sent troops chasing the Japanese through the jungle. General Griswold, it will be remembered, had fought through the Munda campaign, and he wanted no more of that.

The Perimeter on 1 March 1944 differed very slightly in size

[2] ATIS Doc. No. 14294-B, Admiral Takeda's story of the campaign.
[3] The only exception he made was to send a battalion of the Royal Fiji Infantry, commanded by Captain Taylor NZA, over the Numa Numa Trail to establish an observation post on the eastern slope of the Crown Prince Range, in early January. These stout, bushy-haired Fijians were excellent jungle fighters, but the Japanese concentrated against them and forced them back to the Perimeter on 19 Feb. 1944.

from what it had been in December 1943; an area shaped roughly like a West Pointer's shako, the brim represented by about seven miles of beach; the crown about 9000 yards from the sea, and the periphery about 23,000 yards long.[4] Only the east front had been straightened out to the line of the Torokina River. This seemed to many a dangerously small area for defending the three vital airstrips; but the Perimeter was well served by a network of roads permitting prompt concentration on any point attacked, and defense in depth was carefully organized with pillboxes, lanes of fire, and the like.

During the two months that elapsed between New Year's and the opening of the Perimeter battle, the Navy made every effort to prevent the Japanese from using the sea to move up troops. Most of the work was done at night by the PTs aided by Black Cats, rooting out and shooting up barges. Admiral Takeda boasted that, in spite of them, he managed to boat 1400 men up to Empress Augusta Bay. That is probably correct, for the enemy established two supply and concentration points near the mouths of the Reini and Jaba Rivers (the next two streams east of the Torokina) which were maintained throughout the campaign. Airsols made routine sorties to ensure that the Japanese airfields on Bougainville were kept pounded down; Ainsworth's cruisers, Simpson's, Burke's and Hurff's destroyers, and Commander Edmund B. Taylor's new Desdiv 90 (*Anthony*, flag) made sweeps of Bougainville Strait and bombarded Buka and the Shortlands. During the first five days of February there were three bombardments of Buka by two destroyers each, and one of Choiseul, whence Kolombangara evacuees were still being ferried to Buin in barges. The PTs, LCI gunboats and Black Cats, alone or in combination, had 12 fights with enemy barges, bombarded shore positions 13 times and performed many other services such as boating patrols along the coast, all during the month of February.

General Hyakutake named his all-out effort to capture the Perimeter in March the "TA" operation. On the assumption that

[4] See map in chap. xxi, above.

Griswold had only one division to defend the Perimeter, Hyaku-take sent about 12,000 combat troops (including the whole 6th Division) and 3000 reserves, under the command of Lieutenant General Kanda of the 6th, to attack the Perimeter in three columns. One approached by the Numa Numa Trail and attacked on the northwest; the other two attacked from the north and from the east. Their first objective was the "Piva Uncle" strip; their final one the Torokina fighter strip, where they anticipated celebrating a glorious victory on 17 March. Even the spot where General Griswold's unconditional surrender would be accepted was marked out on their maps, one of which was brought to the General by a patrol before the end of February. Kanda, before the attack, delivered an exhortation to his troops, which he thought so eloquent that he had it printed on leaflets.[5]

General Griswold now had about 27,000 combat troops, comprising General Beightler's 37th Infantry Division, General Hodge's American Division, and the 3rd Marine Defense Battalion (Lieutenant Colonel Edward H. Forney USMC) which, with the 49th Battalion Coast Artillery United States Army, was assigned to beach defense. His "Bougainville Navy" now comprised six destroyers of Squadron 22 (Captain Wallis F. Petersen in *Pringle* with Commander James R. Pahl of Division 44, *Conway* flag); Motor Torpedo Boat Squadron 20 under Lieutenant Commander Thomas G. Warfield, several LCI gunboats and armed landing craft. Captain O. O. Kessing, who commanded the advanced naval base, acted informally as the General's chief of staff for naval operations, and Colonel David F. O'Neill USMC of the Airsols Strike Command (32 TBFs, 64 SBDs) as his chief of staff for air operations.

---

[5] "We must fight to the end to avenge the shame of our country's humiliation on Guadalcanal. . . . There can be no rest until our bastard foes are battered, and bowed in shame — till their bright red blood adds yet more luster to the badge of the 6th Division. Our battle cry will be heard afar, and strike fear in the hearts of the bold as we proudly attack Torokina Bay and crush our opponents forever. We excel each foe in our strength and might; from each battle we rise the victor. . . ." Quoted from captured document in Gen. Griswold's Bougainville Narrative.

In addition to his combat troops the General could, at a pinch, count on his base and service forces, especially Naval Construction battalions. During the battle, these Seabees serviced planes under fire, filled up holes in the airstrips made by Japanese artillery and manned defensive sectors along the beach. Small parties of Seabees, of Airsols personnel and even of naval hospital corpsmen were continually visiting infantry front lines "to get themselves a Jap." General Griswold said that for the first time in his experience it became necessary to organize a sort of straggler line in reverse, to prevent volunteers from *going* to the front. Not much like Munda!

With infinite difficulty the Japanese had brought in along jungle trails the greatest concentration of field artillery that they had yet got together anywhere in the South Pacific. These guns were well placed on commanding sites, outside the Perimeter, which General Griswold did not have sufficient troops to occupy and defend. He knew that these steep hills and knife-edge ridges, resembling the "razorbacks" common in the Appalachians, and separated from one another by swampy ravines, would be an asset in enemy hands; but he had to accept the risk rather than spread his forces thin.

On 9 March the first main attack opened, and before the end of the day the enemy had a toe hold on Hill 700. Next day he reinforced his position there, and attacked another hill in the vicinity. The best regiment of the 37th Division, fighting hard and bitterly, was unable to dislodge the enemy from Hill 700 until the afternoon of 12 March. Commander Pahl fired 400 rounds of callfire from destroyers *Sigourney* and *Eaton* into enemy positions.

These two destroyers, and also *Conway* and *Pringle*, had been pounding enemy supply dumps and concentrations near the mouth of the Reini River every day since 3 March, and so continued until the 16th. General Griswold gave them credit for preventing the development of any attack from that quarter. Every night the destroyers and PTs were out hunting for barges, since it was known that Kanda planned a counterlanding on the Torokina beaches.

The second big enemy thrust, which through bad coördination failed to jump off with the first, began on 12 March. It was directed against the 37th Division center on the northwestern sector of the Perimeter. Here the terrain leveled off to a jungle-covered flat traversed by a number of small creeks, and a deep ravine offered the enemy a well-protected avenue of approach to the American lines. "Piva Yoke" fighter strip was only 2000 yards distant. The enemy's purpose was to seize this and "Piva Uncle," reorganize and drive on to the Torokina strip. His artillery fired intermittently on all three until silenced by Airsols dive-bombers on 13 March. He managed to penetrate the Perimeter at this point for several hundred yards, but General Beightler threw in a number of Mark-4 medium tanks which worked closely with the infantry and threw back the enemy by the end of the 13th. A third attack near the same place on the 15th was defeated by the same means, as was a fourth on 17 March. The Japanese now withdrew to reorganize.

On the night of 23–24 March they made their last attempt, penetrated to within 25 yards of a battalion command post, but were thrown back by the early afternoon. On the 27th the Japanese were expelled from Hill 260, about half a mile outside the Perimeter; and with that the battle was over. The enemy lost 5469 dead by actual count in the Battle of the Perimeter, as against 263 American soldiers killed, missing or died of wounds.

Kanda's attack never had a dog's chance against Griswold's well-organized defense, supplemented as it was by naval gunfire and a highly active and efficient air striking force, locally based. Without air or naval assistance, the famous and hitherto unbeaten 6th Infantry Division of the Imperial Army was but a one-legged stool.

Despite this signal defeat, General Hyakutake planned a new offensive in May. He continually reshuffled forces in the interior, and Admiral Takeda sent his barges bustling along the Bougainville coast. The PTs and Black Cats kept right after them, while destroyers and LCI gunboats, aided by a few armed patrols boated in landing craft from the Perimeter, shot up every small group of

Japanese soldiers that managed to reach the shores of Empress Augusta Bay.[6]

By 1 May, however, the Japanese forces on Bougainville were completely sealed off from any significant part in the war. The rice ration of the soldiers, which had been 700 grams daily before the Americans landed at Torokina, was cut to 250 grams in April and to nothing in September. Hyakutake had to employ a large part of his force in raising foodstuffs. Morale fell deplorably, from the Japanese point of view, after the loss of the Battle of the Perimeter; Admiral Takeda, in his narrative, notes robberies, insubordination and even mutiny. Hundreds of soldiers deserted and wandered through the jungle, living on anything they could find, even on snakes, rats and crocodiles.

One can find no better example than Bougainville of what want of sea and air power does to a military force. Yet, even without these indispensable legs of the military tripod, General Kanda's forces could have captured the Perimeter and the Torokina airdrome, wiping out the gains of the Bougainville campaign and raising new hopes at Rabaul, but for the stern resistance offered by the infantry and artillery of the XIV Corps. The fine fighting qualities of that Corps were ably supported by Colonel O'Neill's Airsols Strike Command, and by the valiant "cans," "Prep-Tares" and "Elsie Item gunboats" of Captain Kessing's "Bougainville Navy." General Griswold paid this tribute to the men who worked with him: "Never was a more loyal or coöperative group of officers and men from the Navy, Air and Marine Corps assembled than in my command at Bougainville." [7]

[6] One of these, located near the mouth of the Jaba River, never was disposed of. They drove off a battalion of Fijians in June and were being bombarded as late as 5 August 1944 by destroyer-escort *Bowers*.
[7] Note to the writer 10 March 1946.

# CHAPTER XXVI

# Admiralties Annexed[1]

## 29 February–1 May 1944

### 1. "Reconnaissance in Force"

NEXT on the order of business was the occupation of the Admiralty Islands. They were wanted not so much as another link in the chain around Rabaul, as a substitute for Rabaul. General MacArthur had given up hoping to wrest Rabaul from its 100,000 or more Japanese defenders by direct attack; a military sterilization of the base by Airsols and the South Pacific Force served equally well. But he wanted an advanced base where facilities could be developed comparable to those that the Japanese had formerly enjoyed on the Gazelle Peninsula. As early as July 1943 the Joint Chiefs of Staff suggested that the Admiralty Islands were the answer. This group had everything that a strategist would seek from nature and geographical position. Manus, the largest island in the group, 49 miles long by 16 wide, rugged, volcanic and heavily covered with tropical rain forest, had ample space for military installations. Seeadler Harbor, 15 miles long by 4 wide, could accommodate a large task force; Los Negros Island, which forms the eastern half of the harbor, contained plenty of level land on which a first-class airdrome could be rapidly constructed. Any power holding the Admiralties with strength would be capable not only of denying his enemy access to the Bismarck Archipelago

---

[1] Material for this chapter was gathered by Lt. Salomon at the Admiralties and Brisbane in June and July 1944. The first draft of the 1st Cavalry Division "Historical Report of the Admiralty Islands Campaign" also was consulted. Japanese records on these islands are scanty; some were used in the excellent War Dept. pamphlet *The Admiralties* (1945).

but of dominating the 1000-mile square whose corners are Bougainville, Truk, the Palaus and Biak. Situated as they are athwart the New Guinea-Mindanao axis, the Admiralties could be made the center of an air web. Their two airfields were about 75 miles nearer Truk, 190 miles nearer Saipan, and 530 miles nearer Palau than those of Rabaul.

Discovered by the Dutch in 1616 and named by Captain Philip Carteret RN in 1767, the Admiralties were annexed by Germany in the 1880s and mandated to Australia in 1920. But they remained almost completely undeveloped; only 44 white men, mostly managers of coconut plantations, were living there in 1939. The climate is too hot and the rainfall and humidity too heavy for the taste of Europeans, but they suited the 13,000 natives, whose primitive manners and customs made the islands a happy hunting ground for anthropologists.

In 1942 the Japanese occupied the Admiralty Islands as incident to their southward sweep, and in 1943 built the Momote field on Los Negros and the Lorengau field at Seeadler Harbor, but failed to develop them as plane-ferry stops between Saipan, or Truk, and New Guinea. And they neglected defense, since grandiose plans called for bases farther down the line. Hence, when we were ready to go in, the Admiralties had no defense facilities comparable to those of Kavieng, Rabaul and Kahili. The estimated 4600 Japanese in the Admiralties were poorly equipped to beat off a determined amphibious operation; and by February 1944 the military situation made these islands ripe for picking.

Occupation of the Admiralties was directed by the Joint Chiefs of Staff during the summer of 1943, with an original target date of 1 January 1944. If the decision had been made to leapfrog Cape Gloucester, that target date might have been met. The operation was delayed also by the difficulties of planning, and of straightening out the command question between General MacArthur and Admiral Halsey. The Southwest Pacific command would have to supply the ground troops, Seventh Fleet the ships and V Army Air Force the planes for an operation mounted in New Guinea;

but only Admiral Halsey could provide Seabees and service troops necessary to build up Seeadler and Los Negros as a naval and air base. Not until the day before the assault, 28 February (W. Longitude date), did General Marshall suggest to General MacArthur that he delegate the development of base facilities to Admiral Halsey, "in accordance with plans approved by you and acceptable to Nimitz."

After much flying by staff officers between Nouméa and Brisbane, an operation plan was drawn up at General MacArthur's headquarters and dated 22 February 1944. It provided for simultaneous seizure on 1 April of the Admiralty Islands and Kavieng by Southwest and South Pacific forces respectively. Barbey's VII 'Phib was to transport elements of the Alamo Force (units of the Sixth Army) to Seeadler and support them in securing the Admiralties; III 'Phib was to seize Kavieng for an air and light naval base; Fifth Fleet, Airsols and V Army Air Force, were to cover both.[2] The Kavieng part, as we have seen, was unacceptable to the Joint Chiefs of Staff, and when they canceled that, they stepped up the date of the Admiralties operation to 1 March.

The 1st Cavalry Division United States Army had already been chosen for the assault. "The complete plan in the form of a field order, together with the naval support and the air support plans, had to be in the hands of the Commanding General, Alamo Force, on the 27th of February. It was indeed a race against time." [3]

The V Army Air Force made several bomber strikes on the Admiralties in late January and on 6 and 13 February 1944. On the 22nd a B–25 flew an ineffective air reconnaissance. After flying low over the islands for an hour and a half, the pilot observed no signs of occupation and his photographs revealed no evidence of human activity. Although other intelligence indicated that there were between four and five thousand Japanese in the Admiralties, with no shipping to evacuate them, it was now assumed that the

[2] Op Plan 2–44, 22 Feb. 1944, derived from GHQ Southwest Pacific Operations Instructions No. 44, 13 Feb. 1944.
[3] Gen. Swift's "Diary of the Admiralty Islands Campaign," consulted at his Los Negros HQ.

enemy had pulled out. On this basis General MacArthur decided that an immediate reconnaissance in force would be a good gamble. Accordingly, on the afternoon of 25 February, he issued orders for units of the 1st Cavalry Division to land on Los Negros on the 29th. For, if no Japanese were left there, there was no sense in waiting a month for a formal occupation; the reconnaissance in force would be the occupation.

If, however, the General had waited two days for a report from a later reconnaissance, made by 2nd Lieutenant J. R. C. McGowen of the 158th Infantry on 27 February, he might have decided differently. This officer with five enlisted men was dropped by a Catalina 500 yards off the southeastern shore of Los Negros at 0645 February 27. He went ashore in a rubber boat, pushed halfway across the island, saw plenty of the enemy, and at 1600 got through to the plane the following message, which was relayed to headquarters at Brisbane: "Could not get to river. Lousy with Japs." The men spent the night ashore and at 1600 February 28 were taken off by the Catalina. But it was too late to change the plan.

Admiral Kinkaid and staff had to do some quick thinking and take some lively action. The Admiral first learned of the General's decision at 1500 on the 25th. Rear Admiral Russell S. Berkey, commanding Cruiser Division 15, and Captain Noble of cruiser *Phoenix* happened at that moment to be in his office at Brisbane, where the ship had called on her return from a ten-day liberty in Sydney. Admiral Kinkaid told them that the ship must reach Milne Bay by noon on the 27th to do her part. All liberty was at once canceled, patrols were sent to round up 300 *Phoenix* bluejackets already ashore, and trucks equipped with bull horns raced around the city broadcasting the code word for the recall. At 1709, exactly two hours after the Admiral had passed the word, *Phoenix* got under way from Newstead Wharf, Brisbane, with only 22 men missing. Several of these chased her down-river in small boats, waving frantically, and were taken on board under way; the rest were flown up to Milne.

*Phoenix* steamed up to Milne at 27 knots, launching aircraft before entering China Strait in order to fly staff officers to Buna to confer with Admiral Barbey. She anchored at 1209, only nine minutes late. That afternoon General MacArthur and Vice Admiral Kinkaid came on board with their aides and staff. The General knew he had ordered a risky operation, and had gallantly determined to share the risk and see it through.

Kinkaid issued his operation plan by dispatch on the afternoon of 26 February. He ordered Barbey to transport and land the reconnaissance force, provide close fire support, and be prepared either to commence immediate reinforcement or to embark and withdraw troops when reconnaissance was completed or defeated. Cruisers *Phoenix* and *Nashville* and destroyers *Daly, Hutchins, Beale* and *Bache,* under Admiral Berkey, were to cover the approach and conduct bombardment as directed. Air support and cover were to be supplied by the V Army Air Force; Admiral Barbey to conduct the landing; Brigadier General William C. Chase USA, to take command when his forces were established ashore.

On the eastern shore of Los Negros is the small Hyane Harbor with a treacherous, 50-yard wide entrance between two high points of land that dribble off in coral reefs. Momote airstrip, which touched the south shore of the harbor, could be seized immediately if a landing were effected there; but the shores of the harbor, except for the airstrip landing, were a mass of tangled mangrove. Kinkaid's staff strategists decided that we would land there because it was not an obvious place to do it. That was a good idea; since the whole operation was a gamble anyway, one might as well be consistent!

Admiral Barbey placed the attack group under the command of his deputy, Rear Admiral W. M. Fechteler. It comprised our old friends, Captain Jesse H. Carter's destroyers *Reid, Flusser, Mahan, Drayton, Smith, Bush, Welles* and *Stevenson,* and Lieutenant Commander F. D. Schwartz's three APDs, *Humphreys, Brooks* and *Sands.* On the afternoon of 27 February 1026 troopers were embarked in these ships at Cape Sudest near Oro Bay.

Each APD took 170 men, and each destroyer an average of 57. General Robert E. Lee, who had once been colonel of the 5th Cavalry, would certainly have been astonished to see what his troopers were riding now.

Colonel Yoshio Ezaki, who commanded the local garrison, learned what was coming by intercepting the messages of some talkative United States submarines then patrolling south of the islands. But he was perfectly certain that we would come into Seeadler Harbor, or use the good beaches on the southeast coast of Los Negros.

## 2. *Momote and Los Negros*

The attack group sailed from Cape Sudest, New Guinea, at 1600 February 27, preceded by *Phoenix, Nashville* and four destroyers, who maintained position approximately eleven miles ahead. They arrived off Hyane Harbor shortly after 0700 February 29, without incident and apparently undetected.

Small as this operation was, it had some distinguished observers. General MacArthur and Vice Admiral Kinkaid viewed it from the bridge of cruiser *Phoenix*, standing off Hyane, but they scrupulously left Rear Admirals Berkey and Fechteler in full charge.

At 0723, when the harbor bore due west, distant six miles, Admiral Fechteler signaled "Deploy." The APDs proceeded to their transport area 5000 yards off the harbor entrance, while the destroyers took position in assigned fire-support areas. Five minutes later three Army Liberators were dropping bombs around Momote airfield; they were the only ones of 40 planes that got through bad weather. At 0740 destroyers opened fire on assigned targets. Now the first wave of landing craft charged with troops was nearing the line of departure 3700 yards off shore. It took the enemy less than ten minutes to react. Machine-gun fire opened on the landing boats, which maneuvered radically as they stood in. Heavier shore batteries opened on the destroyers and on the *Phoenix* group to the south. Immediate counter-battery fire was ordered, and a 4.7-inch naval gun on the southeastern point was knocked cold on the third salvo.[4] Close support was rendered by the destroyers which moved within a mile of the shore as the landings progressed. The plan called for stopping naval gunfire at 0755 in order to permit low-level bombing and strafing, but at that time no B–25s were in sight, so naval gunfire continued until 0810. The flagship then fired star shell as the signal for strafers to deliver their attack if any were on station. Shortly thereafter about nine B–25s strafed and bombed. Air and surface bombardment enabled the first three waves to round the southern point of the harbor and reach the beach.

The first three waves landed between 0817 and 0835. No opposition was encountered at the beach and Japanese shooting from the headlands was inaccurate; only four of the twelve boats were damaged by gunfire, although every one had to make repeated trips. Of these small-boat sailors Admiral Fechteler said, "The success of this operation was due more to the courage, skill, determination and devotion to duty of this group of officers and men than to any other single factor."

By 0950 the troopers had captured Momote airstrip and were proceeding to establish a perimeter around it. It had not been used for a long time, and was overgrown with weeds and pocked with muddy bomb craters. By 1250 the last destroyer had completed unloading, and only sporadic fire came from an area north of the airfield. So smoothly had the operation rolled along that General MacArthur and Admiral Kinkaid came ashore at 1600 to inspect the airfield and the perimeter. General Chase assumed command ashore, and at 1729 Fechteler's task group pulled out, leaving only *Bush* and *Stockton* to furnish call-fire to the ground troops. Fewer than a thousand cavalrymen were left with very meager supplies and the support of two destroyers to fight over 2000 Japanese in the immediate vicinity.

---

[4] Admiral Kinkaid told us that this performance so impressed General MacArthur that he (Kinkaid) thereafter had to argue on the limitations, not the capabilities, of naval gunfire.

A real fight was yet to be. Troopers scouting among the Momote revetments found a Japanese battalion headquarters, three big kitchens, a warehouse full of supplies, and other evidence that Lieutenant McGowen had been right when he reported Los Negros to be tenanted. Very few Japanese had been killed on the

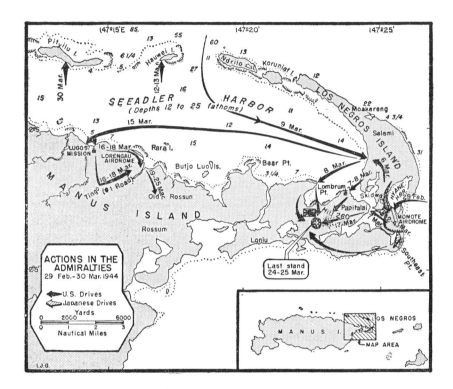

29th; it was certain that they had withdrawn to reorganize and counterattack.

Colonel Ezaki, declaring his indignation at "the enemy's arrogant attitude," ordered Captain Baba's battalion to "annihilate the enemy" that night. He might have succeeded if General Chase had not taken the precaution to narrow the perimeter, withdrawing his troopers to a line a little over 1500 yards long. It began at the beach in the harbor, followed the eastern edge of the airstrip for half its length, and then bent eastward to the sea.

During the night the enemy infiltrated, and spasmodic close-in fighting occurred. But something went wrong with the enemy's plans; there was no counterattack until the darkness before dawn. Captain Baba tried again on the afternoon of 1 March, and came close to capturing General Chase; but he failed again and committed suicide along with 15 other officers and noncoms. During the following night the Japanese launched a real counterattack, but the short lines held firm.

The next echelon to follow up this "reconnaissance in force," consisting of six LSTs each towing an LCM, escorted by destroyers *Mullany* and *Ammen* and minesweepers *Hamilton* and *Long*, and commanded by Captain Richard M. Scruggs USN. These, plus *Warramunga*, brought up important reinforcements — the rest of the 5th Cavalry and the 99th Battalion Field Artillery United States Army, together with 428 officers and men of the 40th Seabees (Commander I. S. Rasmusson USNR). As the leaders of this echelon had heard only overoptimistic accounts of the landing on 29 February, they were surprised to find a serious situation on their arrival off Hyane Harbor at 0900 March 2. They observed B–25s strafing and bombing all around the beachhead, and the enemy right then was bringing up forces from other parts of Los Negros. The LSTs kept right on going into Hyane Harbor, the narrow entrance of which was marked by two landing craft; and as they beached they came under Japanese mortar fire. Coastguard-manned *LST–202*, the nearest to the enemy, opened up with her 3-inch and 40-mm guns, as well as the .50-caliber machine guns that she was carrying topside as freight. The other five LSTs did the same. In the midst of this brawl their bow doors opened, ramps were lowered and unloading began. And after seven hours of the hottest, most grueling work anyone present had ever experienced, the six LSTs were completely unloaded by 1700. This process was greatly facilitated by B–25s and P–40s of the V Army Air Force which bombed and strafed all around the beachhead until 1500.

From noon on the Seabees' mobile equipment cleared and graded the taxiways between beach and airstrip, and at 1600 the 5th

Cavalry dug in for the night on the western edge of the strip, from which the Seabees' graders started clearing weeds and top soil. "One fifty-year-old operator drove his grader the full length of the strip three or four times, drawing sniper fire from the coconut grove. When he came in he said, 'I'm sure glad Mother let me come this time; you know, she wouldn't let me go to the other war!' " [5]

There was not a quiet minute on the beachhead during the night of 2–3 March. The enemy was jabbing all around it, hoping to find a soft spot, but not one could he find.

During 2 March the escort destroyers stood by to deliver call-fire, while two minesweepers escorted by destroyer *Mullany* were sent around the north end of Los Negros to force an entrance to Seeadler Harbor and commence sweeping inside. Fortunately the commanding officer of *Mullany*, whose name by a curious coincidence was Baron J. Mullaney, decided to precede the sweepers through the 1500-yard-wide entrance between Hauwei and Ndrilo Islands, with the idea of provoking enemy fire. In this the destroyer was very successful. The shore defense guns opened up with heavy and accurate fire, straddling her continually. Mullaney maneuvered his ship violently while he and the two sweepers covered their retirement with rapid fire. [6]

Captain R. M. Scruggs, the task group commander, brought up *Ammen, Bush* and H.M.A.S. *Warramunga* at 25 knots and closed *Mullany*. The destroyers immediately took the harbor defense batteries under fire, shooting 100 rounds per ship with no visible effect or response. When *Mullany* and the two sweepers again tried to enter Seeadler Harbor, they met the same reception from the island and again cleared the area at high speed, once more escaping damage. So the sweep was called off until heavier fire could be brought to bear on the islands. All ships then returned to their patrol stations off Hyane Harbor and awaited call-fire requests.

During the night of 2–3 March, *Bush* and the two minesweepers

<hr />

[5] Cdr. Rasmusson's Report of Combat and Construction Operations 9 Apr. 1944.
[6] Com VII Amphibious Force letter of 13 April 1944.

escorted the LSTs of the Second Echelon back to New Guinea while the four remaining destroyers, *Warramunga, Mullany, Ammen* and *Welles*, patrolled 15 to 20 miles northward of Hyane Harbor to intercept possible enemy raiders or reinforcements.

A 75-mm howitzer battalion which arrived with the support echelon was of great assistance on 3 March, when the 5th Cavalry took the offensive shortly after noon. The westernmost taxiways and revetments of the airdrome, previously the enemy's front, were occupied and secured by nightfall. The Seabees "after working all day and fighting all night, still found time during their few hours of leisure off duty to rout out small bands of the enemy, locate and report pillboxes, and otherwise carry the offensive to the enemy's positions. . . . In particular, the operation of the bulldozers into the teeth of the enemy's positions was most inspiring and heartening, and created an immediate resurgence of the offensive spirit in weary troops." [7] If God, as one sailor remarked, was on the side of the most bulldozers in this war, the Seabees were "God's own chill'un."

A counterattack developed around 1900 over and around the narrow "skidway," a causeway that the natives used to pass from the Momote area to the northern part of Los Negros. General Chase sent an urgent request to the destroyers for gunfire support. *Warramunga, Welles, Mullany* and *Ammen* in succession steamed up to the harbor entrance and delivered intense rapid fire with 40-mm and 5-inch guns, for which cavalry officers spotted. This bombardment broke up the Japanese counterattack, and General Chase thanked the destroyers and requested them to stand by to deliver call-fire during the night of 3–4 March. At about 0200 March 4, after the moon had set, *Mullany* and *Ammen* went on a barge-hunting mission requested by General Chase, while *Warramunga* and *Welles* closed Hyane Harbor entrance to support the cavalry by another bombardment of the skidway. They killed a large number of the enemy in that area, and on that "hot corner" defeated the most serious counterattack of an unusually hellish night.

[7] Presidential Citation of the Seabee outfit.

While the Navy afloat hurled shells onto the skidway, the Navy ashore, represented by the Seabees, supported the troopers in the heaviest fighting on Los Negros. The 5th Cavalry were well dug in in their new perimeter, with the Seabees in line on the northwestern part; land mines had been laid, lanes of fire bulldozed out, trip wires strung. The attack was intended to be a three-pronged affair; but, as earlier on Guadalcanal, troops advancing down different sectors through a jungle could not coördinate. The Americans for the most part sat tight in the trenches and foxholes, mowing down the enemy with rifle and machine-gun fire. An amusing feature of an otherwise grim night was the enemy's propaganda. He set up a sort of public-address system which played such tunes as "Home Sweet Home" and, appropriately, for a large part of the troopers hailed from the Lone Star State, "Deep in the Heart of Texas." Front-line soldiers heard the Japanese yelling such messages as "If you want to see your wife and babies you better retreat!" "You'll never see San Francisco," "Roosevelt is making a fool of you." They tapped the telephone wires connecting the mortar batteries with forward observers, and a clear voice in perfect English called, "For God's sake, lift your fire; you're hitting your own troops!" It even ordered the commander of the mortar platoon, by name, to retreat; unfortunately he did.

More reinforcements were already on their way. The 7th Cavalry, General Custer's old regiment, was embarked 3 March at Cape Sudest in the same three APDs that had taken part in the original landing, and in nine destroyers. This Third Echelon, with Captain Jesse H. Carter as commodore in *Flusser*, arrived off Hyane Harbor at 0750 next morning. By noon all troops were ashore, the boats had been recovered and some of the destroyers had departed for Cape Sudest, but *Wilkes, Nicholson, Swanson* and *Smith* under Commander A. J. Greenacre stayed. As one of the troopers said, "It was a joy to know that the destroyers were in back of us. It was music in our ears."

By the time this echelon was ashore in the morning of 4 March, the backbone of enemy counterattack had been broken and the moment had come to launch a strong offensive. The 7th Cavalry relieved the men who had been fighting for four days and nights. These troops eliminated Japanese from the peninsula on the north side of Hyane Harbor, distributed supplies including ammunition dropped by B–17s (95 per cent recovered) and prepared to push on. That night the enemy attacked with diminished strength and were held completely at bay by our outer defense line.

Major General Swift USA, Commander 1st Cavalry Division, arrived with his staff on the morning of 5 March with the Fourth Echelon — five LSTs escorted by destroyers *Reid, Hobby, Kalk, Gillespie* and *Gilmer.*

We shall have to leave it to the Army historians to chart the day-by-day progress of the troopers on Los Negros, supported almost constantly by call-fire from the destroyers. By 9 March the Japanese on Los Negros were in retreat, leaving large supply dumps intact. About half the island, including the vital sections enclosing Momote Field and facing Seeadler Harbor, was in Allied hands. American losses so far were 116 dead and 434 wounded; Japanese killed numbered 1288. No prisoners were taken, except 68 Sikhs of the Indian Army who had been captured at Singapore two years earlier and impressed as labor troops.

## 3. *Seeadler and Manus*

Task Force 74, commanded by Rear Admiral Crutchley RN in H.M.A.S. *Shropshire,* with U.S. cruisers *Phoenix* and *Nashville* and destroyers *Daly, Beale, Hutchins* and *Bache,* passed Cape Sudest, New Guinea, on 2 March to establish a covering patrol between the Admiralty Islands and the equator. This patrol was maintained from 3 to 7 March, except for interruptions due to foul weather and bombardments. Guns on Hauwei and Ndrilo Islands, at the entrance to Seeadler Harbor, had driven off the mine-sweepers. *Nicholson* cleverly ferreted out and destroyed these concealed batteries. That did the trick. Next day, *Long* and *Hamilton* escorted by *Wilkes* and *Swanson* entered the harbor. Everyone had a fine time pitching shots into Japanese machine-gun positions. The sweepers swept up eleven of our own mines which had been laid by Southwest Pacific planes in May 1943. These ships were followed in by a procession of LSTs and cargo ship *Etamin*, which landed troops on Lombrum Point, Manus, and on the back side of Los Negros.

Lorengau Village, on Manus Island almost directly opposite the entrance to Seeadler Harbor, had been the seat of government and the location of a commercial airstrip. Apparently this field was never used by the Japanese, but about 900 of their occupation forces were concentrated in the area and it was our job to get them out so that the Navy could use Seeadler Harbor as an advanced base.

After a two-day attack by B–25s on Lorengau targets, the cavalry, counting on good artillery support, was ready to assault the place. A shore-to-shore operation, of the type often practised in the Southwest Pacific, took place on the 15th. The troopers were embarked at a beach on the harbor side of Los Negros in 20 landing craft and one LST carrying seven amphtracs, supported by three PTs, three rocket-equipped landing craft and four destroyers. They landed at Lugos Mission, two miles west of the Lorengau airdrome, at 0830. Both field and village were secured by 18 March. The enemy rallied at a place called Old Rossun south of the village, but was obliterated by an attack on 25 March. That ended all organized resistance on Manus Island. Armed patrols were then organized which hunted Japanese in the jungle like so many animals.

There was still a strong enemy force on the western part of Los Negros Island, in a rugged terrain covered with dense jungle. Here, around a hill that we called 260 from its approximate height in feet, the Japanese took their stand. Getting them out proved to be a difficult operation for the troopers, since the area between Papitalai Harbor and Hill 260 was covered with dense jungle in which the Japanese had set up a strong defense in depth. The men advanced at snail's pace, supply was difficult and the enemy proved tenacious as usual. Progress was slow and painful; terrain and tactics alike resembled those of the Battle of the Perimeter then going on at Bougainville, with the rôles reversed and the attack succeeding. For ten days, 14–23 March, the 5th Cavalry fought over 1200 yards of jungle terrain. The 12th Cavalry had already launched an attack from the other side, and on 24 March the troopers broke Japanese resistance on Los Negros.

Motor Torpedo Boat Squadrons 18 and 21 (Lieutenant Commander H. M. S. Swift USNR and Lieutenant Paul T. Rennell USNR respectively) were operating all this time from their tender *Oyster Bay* in Seeadler Harbor. Both squadrons were New Guinea veterans, but their work in the Admiralties was new for they belonged to the cavalry's "sneak and peek" organization, acting as the troopers' messenger boys, seagoing ambulances, salvage tugs, hydrographers, pilots, even command vessels for cavalry generals. The PTs gave infantry close support with machine guns and 81-mm mortars. Marksmen in *PT-363* at the Lugos landing knocked a sniper neatly out of his nest; *PT-323* located a Japanese observation post complete with radio and ladder in a tree on Rara Island on 16 March, and "fixed it up."

One enemy strong point remained — Pityilu Island on the barrier reef, just west of Hauwei, about two and a half miles long and 700 yards wide. Destroyers bombarded it almost daily from 13 to 24 March. On the 30th the 7th Cavalry Regiment (Colonel Glenn S. Finley USA) prepared to land. P-40s and Spitfires of the R.A.A.F. blasted the beach for 20 minutes. Next, the 105-mm howitzers of the 61st Field Artillery Battalion opened up from Lorengau. The landing was made on the harbor side of Pityilu at 0845 from LVTs and LCMs. The troopers met determined opposition from a strong garrison and overran the island only on the last day of March.

Although two small islands remained to be taken, and there were still several hundred Japanese in the interior of Manus, the Admiralty Islands were to all intents and purposes under Allied control by 3 April. Naval support, no longer needed, was withdrawn. On these islands, which the scouting airplanes had reported to be free of Japanese, almost 4000 were accounted for by the end of the campaign, and it is anyone's guess how many were still lurking in the interior. Our ground forces had lost 294 killed, missing or died of wounds, and 977 wounded. Naval casualties, as yet uncompiled, were relatively slight. The Seabees, who had taken the rap in the fight at Momote, had lost 10 killed, and 59 wounded of whom 20 returned to duty.

General Swift made a handsome acknowledgment of naval support in this operation: —

The bald statement, "The naval forces supported the action," appearing in the chronology, is indeed a masterpiece of understatement. When asked regarding the effect of naval gunfire support the commanding general of one brigade made the laconic reply, "The Navy didn't support us, they saved our necks!" All commanders firmly believe that, especially during the initial phases, the balance of war was tipped in our favor by the superb support rendered by the naval forces.

Several days after the initial landing, he adds: —

The bulk of the naval force moved to the south. From these positions they laid a heavy barrage on the enemy positions. So cleverly was this barrage placed and so devastating its effect that the Japs were forced out of their positions right into the waiting bands of automatic fire of the dismounted cavalrymen. And the reports state, "The Naval forces supported the action." Indeed! Without the Navy there would not have been any action.

By the middle of the year, Seeadler Harbor, Lorengau and Moakareng on the northwestern arm of Los Negros were activated as naval and air bases. "Manus," as these were collectively known in the Allied forces, became very valuable for staging the landings in Palau and Leyte, and for keeping the remaining airfields on New Guinea and in the Carolines pounded down. The interior wilderness became known as "the Reservation," since the Japanese still subsisting there furnished good practice for green infantrymen before they were sent to battle areas.

So, when all's said and done, the Admiralties gamble was a brilliant success; MacArthur's decision was justified.

Generally, in an expeditionary force, a 3-to-1 ratio of superiority over the defending enemy is considered indispensable; and often in this war, as at Munda and Tarawa, that proved to be not enough. Here, the ratio at the start was about 1 to 4. Why then did the venture succeed? Simply because the United States and Australia dominated that stretch of the ocean and the air over it. The enemy had so few boats and barges that he was unable to apply his 4 to 1 superiority against the Cavalry-*cum*-Seabee spearhead. The Navy not only provided the Army with seagoing artillery but brought up troopers, beans and bullets in greater and greater numbers; while the Japanese were as completely sealed off from help as MacArthur's forces had been on Bataan early in 1942.

Thus, for the neutralized but virtually impregnable Fortress Rabaul, the Allies substituted a better base behind the Bismarcks Barrier, farther advanced along the New Guinea-Mindanao axis, more useful to the Allies and dangerous to the enemy. Algernon Sidney's motto, *Manus haec inimica tyrannis*, "this hand, enemy to tyrants," applied to a Manus that he never knew; for Manus in the Admiralties proved to be one of those air and naval bases, like Saipan and Okinawa, whose possession by the Allies rendered the defeat of Japan inevitable.

# Index

# Index

Names of Combat Ships in SMALL CAPITALS
Names of Merchant Ships, lettered Combat Ships like I-boats and
PTs, and all Japanese *Marus*, in *Italics*

In the following Task Organizations, only the names of Flag and General Officers
are indexed:

Invasion of New Georgia, pp. 144–6; Landings at Torokina, p. 297; Rear
Admiral Montgomery's Carrier Strike on Rabaul, p. 331; Landings at Cape
Gloucester, pp. 381–2; Occupation of Green Islands, pp. 415–16.

## A

AARON WARD, 123
Adachi, Lt. Gen. H., 55, 255, 390
ADHARA, 123
Admiralty Is., 418, 432–3, 439 (chart);
in strategy, 92n, 369–70, 432; opera-
tion, 433–48
AGANO, 71, 306, 321, 328, 332, 341
Ainsworth, Rear Adm. W. L., 106, 209;
support and bombardment missions,
113–16, 119–20, 123, 146, 156–8, 178–9,
363–4, 415, 427; Kula and Kolomban-
gara Battles, 180–96
Air bases, Solomons, 91 (chart); New
Guinea, 254–6
Air search, 105
Air Solomons Command, 99n, 290–2,
350n, 353; strength and losses, 292,
395, 402–5; strike command, 428
Aircraft, Australian, Kittyhawk, 37–8;
PBYs, 58, 208, 435; Beaufighter, 59, 65
Aircraft, Japanese, production, 22n, 117;
types, 91, 400; carrier planes sent to
Rabaul, 118, 127, 284, 336, 347, 398, 400
Aircraft, New Zealand, Warhawk, 319,
405–7
Aircraft, U.S., numbers and types in
Sopac, 90, 99; types – A-20: 59; B-17:
58–61; B-24 (PB4Y): 58, 90, 118–19,
191–2, 206–7, 287–8, 323–4, 350, 396–
404, 407; B-25: 59–60, 256, 287–8, 376;

F4U, F6F and TBF: 90–1, 118–20, 150,
206–7, 325–7, 363, 398–402, 407; F–5:
104–5, 120; P–38 and P–40: 59–60, 118–
24, 287–8, 376, 385; PV–1: 291, 346;
SB2C, 332; SBD: 115, 206–7, 325–7,
398–402, 407; Night Fighters, 290–1,
346, 418; Black Cat, 291n, 110–12, 115,
183–4, 190, 206–7, 219, 242, 363, 374,
427–30; Dumbo, 397, 404
*Aiyo Maru*, 56
AKIGUMO, 75, 244
AKIKAZE, 208
Akiyama, Rear Adm. T., 162–3, 174
ALBACORE, 68–9, 71
Aleutians, 6, 226–7
Allen, Cdr. B. C., 261
ALOE, 121
*Aludra*, 141
AMAGIRI, 162, 167–8, 172–5, 211,341,353–8
AMERICAN LEGION, 303
AMMEN, 391, 440–2
Ammunition expenditure, in bombard-
ments, 116, 321; Kolombangara, 184n;
Emp. Aug., 321; 11 Nov. air attack,
335
Amphibious commands and training, 97,
131–2
"Anakim" Operation, 6–7
Anderson, Capt. A. B., 297, 343
Anderson, Capt. Bern, 15, 130n, 131, 271
Angau, 28, 42, 48
ANTHONY, 342–3, 421

AOBA, 125
APACHE, 295, 303
APC (Coastal Transport), 134*n*, 376–7
ARASHI, 39, 214–21
ARASHIO, 56, 61
Arawe, 372–7, 385
ARIAKE, 208, 256
Armstrong, Lt. Cdr. H. J., 308, 354
Armstrong, Lt. W. W., 113*n*
Army Air Force, U.S. Fifth, organiza-
  tion, 64–5; *see* Kenney, G. C.
Army, Australian, 36–50, 136, 258, 269–
  75, 389
Army, New Zealand, 239, 243, 289*n*, 294,
  361, 413–19
Army, U.S., Engineers, 36–9, 137, 258*n*,
  262; 1st Cavalry Div., 133, 373–7, 434–
  48; XIV Corps, 198–206, 364, 426–31;
  Paratroops, 266; Infantry divisions –
  Americal: 364–5, 428; 25th: 22–3, 229,
  238; 32nd: 42, 45–50, 132, 389–90; 37th:
  344, 348, 364, 428–30; 41st: 50, 137, 258;
  43rd: 98, 144, 148, 155, 177, 198–206;
  Alamo Force, 379, 434; 61st and 99th
  Bn. F. A., 440, 446
Arnold, General H. H., 3
Arundel Is., 222–3
ASAGUMO, 56–9, 62–3
ASASHIO, 56
Ashmun, Capt. G. M., 398
ATAGO, 323, 328
Atkins, Lt. Cdr. B. K., 61, 136–7
Austin, Capt. B. L., 11*n*, 307–18, 354–8
AUSTRALIA, 39, 130
AWAHOU, 121

B

BACHE, 436, 444
BAGLEY, 39. 134
Bairoko, 116, 157, 176, 202–3, 222
BALAO, 70–1
BALLARAT, 47
Ballentine, Capt. J. J., 331, 334
Barakoma, 228–32, 240, 290, 350, 396, 399
Barber, Lt. R. T., 128
Barbey, Rear Adm. D. E., 97, 130–3,
  131*n* (*biog.*); Lae, 261–6; Finsch., 269–
  74; N. Britain, 372–6, 378–81; Saidor,
  389; Admiralties, 434–8
Barges, Jap., 48–9, 53, 210–51, 239–43,
  255, 274, 407, 426–7; *see also* Daihatsus
Barker, Capt. H. B., 284
Barnett, Lt. M. E., 184

Barnett, Paul T., 327
Barr, Lt. Cdr. E. L., 74–5
Barrowclough, Maj. Gen. H. E., 239,
  415, 419
Battleships, 31, 106, 423
Baylis, Lt. (jg) J. S., 61
Beaching Craft, 32, 42, 131; *see* LCI,
  LCT, LST
BEALE, 390–1, 436, 444
Beatty, Capt. F. A., 308
Beck, Cdr. E. L., 242
Behrens, Capt. B. S., 283–4
Beightler, Maj. Gen. R. S., 289*n*, 364,
  428, 430
Beisang, Lt. R. E., 170
Bena Bena, 255, 258, 272
BENALLA, 134
Benn, Maj. Wm., 57–8
BENNETT, 360
Bergin, Ens. E. R., 61
Berkey, Rear Adm. R. S., 344, 435
Berlin, Ens. Theodore, 329
Berndtson, Lt. A. H., 210
Betz, Corp. F. E., 404
Bieri, Rear Adm. B. H., 9
BILLFISH, 79–84
BILOXI, 341
BIRMINGHAM, 341, 344–5
Bismarck Archipelago, 371 (chart);
  plans, 369–72; campaigns, Part IV
Bismarck Sea, Battle of the, 54–65
Blackburn, Lt. Cdr. J. T., 331–3
Blackett Str., 112–15, 209–11, 223, 364
BLACKFISH, 71, 74
Blamey, Lt. Gen. Sir Thos., 34, 256
Blanche Bay Channel and Harbor, 147–
  8, 230, 293–4, 326, 407, 420
BLUEFISH and BLUEGILL, 74, 80
Bock, Lt. Cdr. B. N., 121
BONEFISH, 79–80
Bostock, Air Vice Marshal W. D., 64
Bougainville, 285 (map); directive, 96;
  campaign, Part III; description, 279–
  81; Jap. forces on, 281, 300, 425–31;
  airfields neutralized, 291–3, 350; *see
  also* Buin, Kahili, Perimeter
Bougainville, Jap. "air battles" of, 328–9,
  344–7, 351, 360–1
"Bougainville Navy," 364–5, 428
BOWFIN, 79–85
Boyd, Capt. C. A., 176
Boyington, Maj. Gregory, 396–8
BRAINE, 360–1
Branson, Cdr. G. C. F., 51–2, 126

Brantingham, Lt. L. J., 210
Brantly, Capt. N. D., 384
BREESE, 112–14, 308
Briscoe, Capt. R. P., 107, 110, 308
Brockway, Lt. C. W., 122
BROOKS, 261–3, 267, 269*n*, 436
Brooks, Sgt. J. A., 464
BROOME, 47
Browning, Capt. Miles, 7, 13, 93
BROWNSON, 385–6
BUCHANAN, 149, 182, 421
Buin, 94, 234, 362, 425–6
Buka, 90, 118, 280–1, 291–2, 341, 350, 353–4, 362, 425–6
Bulkeley, Lt. Cdr. J. D., 47, 209, 247
Bulkley, Cdr. R. J., 41*n*, 209*n*
Buna, occupied by Jap., 33; Allied base, 262, 272
Buna-Gona campaign, 33, 41–50; map, 44
BUNKER HILL, 331–6, 411
Burke, Capt. A. A., support missions, 203–4, 289, 292, 360–1, 427; Battle Emp. Aug. Bay, 307–18; Battle C. St. George, 353–9; Kavieng, 420–21
Burma, 4–8, 25
Burns, Eugene, 327*n*
Burns, Col. F. L., 36
Burrough, Capt. E. W., 9
Buse, Lt. Col. H. W., 387
BUSH, 391, 436, 441
BUSHNELL, 36
BUTTERNUT, 121

**C**

CABRILLA, 85
Caldwell, Cdr. H. H., 325–7
Calhoun, Vice Adm. W. L., 11*n*
Callahan, Cdr. J. W., 182
Campbell, Capt. Colin, 161, 167, 181
Cape St. George, Battle of, 352–9
Carey, Lt. (jg) J. L., 137
Carney, Rear Adm. R. B., 13*n* (biog.)
Carpender, Vice Adm. A. S., 32, 47, 50, 58, 97, 132, 259, 262, 372
Carter, Capt. G. B., 228, 230, 237–8, 337–9, 351, 417–18
Carter, Capt. J. H., 259–63, 272–4, 390, 443
CARTER HALL, 374–5
Casablanca Conference, 4–7
Cassady, Capt. J. H., 325
Cavenagh, Cdr. R. W., 308, 420

Cecil, Capt. C. P., 161, 170–1, 191, 196
*Celeno*, 140
Central Solomons Operation, plans, 94–6; conclusion, 224; *see* New Georgia
Chandler, Cdr. A. D., 242
CHARLES AUSBURNE, 241, 308–18, 354–6, 420–1
Chase, Brig. Gen. W. C., 436–48
CHEVALIER, 113*n*, 156–8, 234–6, 244–5, 248–50
Chew, Lt. Cdr. J. L., 171*n*, 191–2
Chiang Kai-shek, 3, 8,
Chichi Jima, 94
CHIDORI class, 79
CHIKUMA, 323
Childs, Lt. (jg) R. L., 61
Choiseul, 239–43, 293, 295–6
CHOKAI, 323, 335
Christie, Rear Adm. R. W., 67*n*, 75–6, 83
Christoph, Capt. K. J., 131
Churchill, Hon. Winston, 4–6
Cincpac-Cincpoa Staff, 10–13
CLAXTON, 241, 308–21, 354–8
CLEVELAND, 106–7, 292, 308–21
Clifton, Cdr. J. C., 325
Clowes, Maj. Gen. C. A., 37–8
CLYMER, 300
Coastwatchers, 115, 120, 141, 192–3, 208, 211, 228, 296, 405
COLAC, 47
Collins, Maj. Gen. J. L., 222
COLORADO, 106
COLUMBIA, 106*n*, 241, 292, 308–21, 346, 415
Combat Information Center, 108*n*
Combined Chiefs of Staff, 3–10
Combined Fleet, Japanese, 18–21, 23, 229, 285–6, 323–4
CONFLICT, 121–2
CONVERSE, 308–18, 354–8, 420
CONWAY, 230–2, 303, 422, 429
CONY, 230, 242, 295
CONYNGHAM, 98*n*, 260–1, 269*n*, 376, 390
Cook, Lt. Cdr. Charles O., 169–70
Cooke, Rear Adm. Charles M., 9
Cooke, Capt. W. R., 228, 237, 242
Corey, Lt. Cdr. H. G., 262
Cornwall, Lt. Col., 414
Corrigan, Flight Lt. J. A., 159
Cory, Lt. G. L., 266
*Couch*, 328*n*
Cowdrey, Capt. R. T., 294
Coxe, Lt. Cdr. A. B., 113*n*
Coye, Cdr. J. S., 70

Craig, Col. E. A., 347
Craig, Lt. Cdr. J. R., 107
CRAVEN, 98*n*, 214–16
CRESCENT CITY, 98*n*, 303
CROSBY, 152, 295
Crudele, Anthony P., 248
Crutchley, Rear Adm. V. A. C., 39, 51, 130, 380, 383, 390, 444
Curran, Lt. J. A., 157
Currin, Lt. Col. M. S., 152
CURTISS, 139*n*
Cutler, Cdr. R. W., 339, 417–19

D

DADAVATA, 141
*Daigen Maru*, 74
*Daihatsus*, 208–10, 221, 236
DALY, 386, 436, 444
Dampier Str., 27, 254–5, 260, 271–3, 369–71, 379, 383–5
Davis, Signalman C. L., 273
Davis, Cdr. J. W., 71–2
*Deimos*, 141
Delany, Capt. W. S., 11*n*
DENT, 142, 148, 193–4
DENVER, 106–7, 292, 308–22, 346
Destroyer raids, 419–22; tactics, 212–14
Dillard, Lt. R. W., 265
Dobodura, 42–3, 46, 125, 255, 259–60, 286, 328, 376, 381
Dragon's Peninsula, 159, 175, 222
DRAYTON, 98*n*, 262, 390, 436
DRUM, 69
Dubose, Rear Adm. L. T., 289, 341, 344–5
Dudley, Capt. Roy, 262
Duke of York Is., 402, 420–2
Dukws, 375–6, 385
DUNLAP, 214–18
Dupuy, Lt. R. F., 303
Dykers, Cdr. T. M., 84
DYSON, 241, 354, 421

E

Earle, Capt. Ralph, 343, 413–14, 420–2
EATON, 230–2, 337, 429
Ebert, Lt. Cdr. W. G., 69–71
Eichelberger, Lt. Gen. R. L., 46–9, 132
ELLET, 193
Emirau, 370, 423–4
Emmons, Ens. J. W., 61
Empress Augusta Bay, 281–4, 299; land-
ings at, 298–304; Battle of, 305–22
Enogai Inlet, 175–6, 200, 203
ENTERPRISE, 106
Erickson, Frederick, 265
ERSKINE PHELPS, 121–2
Espiritu Santo, 103–5, 330; air raids on, 139*n*, 241
ESSEX, 331–6
ETAMIN, 445
Evans, Sub-Lt. A. R., 115
Ezaki, Col. Y., 437–9

F

FARENHOLT, 149, 151, 325, 421
Farrington, Lt. Cdr. Roberts, 325*n*
Fechteler, Rear Adm. W. M., 436–8
Fellows, Lt. Cdr. J. B., 182
Ferguson Passage, 113*n*, 115, 209*n*, 211
Field, James A., 128*n*
Fife, Capt. James, 67, 142
Finley, Col. G. S., 446
Finschhafen, 52, 136, 261, 269–71
Firth, Robert, 192
Fitch, Vice Adm. A. W., 90, 104, 139, 146, 281
Fleet numbers, 97
FLETCHER, 107, 116
Flittie, Lt. W. J., 61
Flood, C. A., 191
*Florida Maru*, 125
FLUSSER, 261, 267, 270, 384, 390, 436, 443
Foley, Cdr. R. J., 73
Fort, Rear Adm. G. H., 121, 145–6, 294, 415
FOOTE, 241–2, 308–22
Forney, Col. E. H., 428
Foster, Capt. F. F., 339
Freeman, Wing Cdr. T. O., 396
Frey, Lt. (jg) H. W., 329
Friend, Col. D. G., 102
Frisbie, Col. J. W., 385
FUJINAMI, 328
FULLAM, 360, 413, 420
FULLER, 344
FUMIZUKI, 125, 244, 412
FUYO, 75

G

GAMBLE, 112–14, 308
Gano, Cdr. R. A., 308, 354
Gash, Lt. R. W., 171*n*
Gasmata, 372

GATO, 73–4, 280–4
Gazelle Peninsula, 370, 393 (chart), 407, 421
Geiger, Maj. Gen. R. S., 282, 348, 364
Germany and Pacific strategy, 3, 115–16
Gibson, Lt. Cdr. J. E., 418
Giffen, Rear Adm. R. C., 106*n*
Gilbert Is. operation, 289, 324, 330
Gillan, Capt. M. J., 241
GILLESPIE, 444
GILMER, 133*n*, 261–3, 267, 269*n*, 444
Gizo, 213–15, 230, 239
Gloucester, Cape, 208, 256, 258, 370; capture of, 378–89; task organization, 381–2
Gona, *see* Buna
Goodenough I., 38–40, 374, 380, 389
Goodman, Capt. W. H., 279*n*
Gordinier, Cdr. V. F., 182
*Gorgon*, 126
Gould, Lt. Cdr. F. G., 214
GRAMPUS and GRAYBACK, 107
GRAYLING and GRAYSON, 85, 98*n*
Great Britain, and Pacific strategy, 4–8
Green Is., 331, 370, 402, 406, 412–22; chart, 417
Greenacre, Cdr. A. J., 443
GREENLING and GRIDLEY, 193, 293
Griffin, Rear Adm. R. M., 423
Griffin, Ens. W. F., 229
Griffith, Lt. Col. S. B., 103, 175–6
Griffith, Lt. Cdr. W. T., 80–4
Griswold, Maj. Gen. O. W., 198–202, 223, 364, 426–31
Guadalcanal, struggle for, 18, 22–3, 31–2, 89; as base, 94, 100–3, 140, 282; air raids, 120–2, 229, 328*n*
GUARDFISH and GUDGEON, 77–9, 85, 284
GUEST, 360–1, 413–14
Gunn, Maj. P. I., 57
GWIN, 149, 158, 182, 189

**H**

HAGIKAZE, 214, 216–17
HAGURO, 305–12, 321
HALFORD, 418
Haines, Capt. J. M., 67*n*
Hall, Lt. Cdr. Madison, 181
Halsey, Admiral W. F., staff and plans, 13, 93–7, 281–3, 289; quoted, 89, 96, 110, 129, 303, 329–30, 421; relations with SWPac, 94–5, 433–4; decisions and orders, 112, 119, 138, 155, 160, 180,

190, 284, 292, 320, 324–5, 333, 353, 411–14, 419, 423
Hamacheck, Lt. (jg) R. E., 61
HAMAKAZE, 37, 162, 174, 181, 234–6
Hamberger, Cdr. DeW. C. E., 308, 354
HAMILTON, 440–4
Hanson, Lt. R. M., 402
HATSUKAZE, 306, 312, 315, 318, 322*n*
HATSUYUKI, 162, 167, 172, 206
Harding, Maj. Gen. E. F., 47
Harmon, Maj. Gen. M. F., 7, 198, 205
Hayler, Capt. R. W., 161, 181, 184, 189
HELENA, 120, 156, 161–171, 191–4
HELM, 39, 134
Henderson, Capt. George, 325
Henderson Field, 101, 120, 207
HENLEY, 39, 134, 269*n*, 272–3
HENRY T. ALLEN, 131
Hernan, Lt. E. N., 222
Herring, Ens. J. W., 61
*Hie Maru*, 68
Higgins, Cdr. J. M., 182
Hill, Lt. Cdr. A. J., 161, 174, 181
Hill, Rear Adm. H. W., 106
Hill, Capt. T. B., 11*n*
HILO, 47, 53, 127
Hine, Lt. R. K., 129
Hirohito, Emperor, 18
HIYO, 118
HOBART, 39, 130
HOBBY, 444
Hodge, Maj. Gen. J. R., 364
Hogan, Lt. Cdr. T. W., 79–80
Hollander, Lt. F. H., 341*n*
Hollandia, 32, 391
HONOLULU, 113*n*, 120, 156, 161–8, 181–90, 363, 415
HOPKINS, 152
Horaniu, 233–9; chart of action at, 235
Horii, Gen. T., 33, 44
HUDSON, 342–3, 413–14
HUMPHREYS, 133, 261–3, 267, 269*n*, 374, 436
Hunter, Lt. O. D., 231
HUNTER LIGGETT, 297, 304
Huon Gulf and Peninsula, 135, 254–61, 271–2, 378
Hurff, Capt. J. E., 337, 427
Hutchins, Johnnie D., 265
HUTCHINS, 385–6, 390, 436, 444
Hyakutake, Lt. Gen. H., 425–31
Hyane, 436–44
Hydrographic surveys, 290, 298–9, 338

**I**

"I" Operation, 18, 117–27, 143

I-boats, *–20*, 242; *–36*, 286; *–168*, 68–70; *–171*, 414; *–177*, 391; *–182*, 75

IDAHO, 433

Ijuin, Rear Adm. M., 234–6, 252, 306–10, 321*n*

Imamura, Lt. Gen. H., 49, 54, 92, 136, 233–52, 261, 265, 342, 348–9, 403, 408

Imperial Headquarters, 17; orders, 22, 233, 260, 284, 345, 406

INDEPENDENCE, 331–6

Inglis, Capt. T. B., 344

ISOKAZE, 234–7, 244

ISONAMI, 75–6

ISUZU, 323

*Isuzugawa Maru*, 80

Iverson, Lt. Cdr. Clifton, 214–15

Izaki, Rear Adm. S., 181, 183

**J**

JACK, 84

Japan, strategic plan for defeat of, 7–8; command and planning system, 15–26; New Operational Policy, 22–26, 284; defensive perimeters, 24–26

Jenkins, Capt. D. R., 346

JENKINS, 116, 150, 153, 161–2, 166–8, 181, 186, 190, 193

JINTSU, 181–7, 190, 193–4

JOHN PENN, 229

Johnston, George H., 41*n*, 45

*Johore Maru*, 70

Joint Chiefs of Staff, 3–12, 93; directives, 96, 132, 139, 281, 320, 412, 423, 433–4

Joshima, Rear Adm. T., 98

Josselyn, Henry, 192–3

JUNYO, 118

**K**

Kagawa, Capt. K., 333–6

KAGERO, 115

Kahili, 90, 111–12, 118, 120, 128–9, 206, 230–2, 240, 245, 280–3

Kaiaput, 271–2

KALK, 444

*Kamakura Maru*, 78

KAMOI, 83–4

Kanaoka, Capt. Y., 244–5

KANAWHA, 121–2

Kanda, Lt. Gen., 425–30

KANKAKEE, 324, 420

*Kashima Maru*, 79

Katz, Lt. Col. B., 181, 244

Kavieng, 208, 323, 369–70, 383, 390, 410–11, 419–23; occupation canceled, 423, 434

KAWAKAZE, 214, 218–9

KAZAGUMO, 112, 244, 247

*Keisho Maru*, 275

Keliher, Capt. T. J., 11*n*

Kelly, Maj. B. T., 192

Kelly, Lt. Cdr. R. B., 151, 155

*Kembu Maru*, 55–6

Kennedy, D. G., 141–2

Kennedy, Lt. J. F., 211–12

Kenney, Maj. Gen. G. C., 27*n*, 39, 44; Bismarck Sea, 57–64; Rabaul, 90, 275, 286–78, 320, 328; misc. ops., 125, 136–7, 208, 260; Lae-Salamaua, 256–9, 262–3; New Britain, 372–6, 381–3; Admiralties, 434

Keravat, 392, 406

Kessing, Capt. O. O., 102, 181, 190, 365, 428, 431

KIDD, 334

Kiland, Capt. I. N., 98–9

KILTY, 152, 295

Kimihara, Maj. Gen., quoted, 390, 399, 400, 403, 407–8

Kimura, Rear Adm. M., 55–63

*Kinai Maru*, 37

King, Admiral E. J., 3–5, 9–10, 60, 93*n*; orders, 97–8, 130–1, 226

Kinkaid, Vice Adm. T. C., 97, 385, 435–8

*Kirishima Maru*, 79

Kiriwina, 132–4

KIYONAMI, 181, 191*n*, 207

Knoertzer, Cdr. H., 243*n*

Koga, Flt. Admiral M., 23–4, 129, 139, 156*n*, 271, 284–6, 305, 323, 336, 390, 419

Kojima, Capt., 200–2, 205

*Kokai Maru*, 403

Kokoda Trail, 33–4, 42–3

Kolombangara, 90–4, 190, 225–7; Battle of, 180–91; blockade of, 239–43

Koromokina fight, 341–2

*Kowa Maru*, 403

K.P.M. ships, 36–7, 46–7, 125–7, 130; losses, 127*n*

Krueger, Lt. Gen. Walter, 15, 274, 374, 380–1

Kruesburg, Lt. H. F., 237*n*

Krulak, Lt. Col. V. H., 296

Kula Gulf, 115, 156–8; Battle of, 160–75
KUMANO, 207
KURASHIO, 115
Kurita, Vice Adm. T., 323, 328, 330
Kusaka, Vice Adm. J., 54, 63, 92, 118, 136, 140, 149–50, 207, 233, 237–8, 261, 320, 328, 332–6, 352, 362, 383–5, 408, 412
*Kyokei Maru,* 80
*Kyokusei Maru,* 56–8

**L**

Lae-Salamaua, 261, 264 (chart); reinforcement of, 52–55, 58, 136, 257–8; campaign on, 254–68
Lajeunesse, Lt. Cdr. R. W., 237
Lake, Capt. B. G., 15*n*
Lake, Lt. Cdr. R. C., 68–9
Lampman, Cdr. L. R., 308, 317
LAMSON, 262, 386, 390
LANG, 214–21
Lanphier, Capt. T. G., 124, 128
LARDNER, 98*n*
Lark, Lt. Cdr. J. A., 308
Larson, Cdr. H. O., 242, 244–7, 250
LAVALIETTE, 244, 251
Layton, Capt. E. T., 11*n*
LCIs, types, 134*n*; in Solomons, 152, 230–2; Lae, 263–4; gunboats, 294–5, 427, 430
*LCI-68, –70,* 329; *–339,* 263–4
LCTs, at Tulagi, 121–2; Finsch., 269; Arawe, 376–7; Green Is., 417–8
Leahy, Admiral W. D., 3
LEANDER, 178–9, 181–3, 186–90
"Leapfrog" strategy, 225–7, 239
Leary, Vice Adm. H. F., 31–2
Leary, Ens. Leo, 390
Leavey, Maj. Gen. E. H., 11*n*
Lee, Rear Adm. W. A., 106
Lewin, Ens. R. H., 418
LIBRA, 151
Liversedge, Col. H. B., 102, 156–8, 175–80, 198, 202, 222
Lockwood, Rear Adm. C. A., 67, 82
LONG, 440–4
Los Negros, 432–48
Loud, Cdr. W. R., 297, 344
LSDs, 338*n*, 374
LSTs, problems of, 338–40; use of, at Vella Lavella, 228–33, 237–8; at Lae, 264–6; Finsch., 269–71; Torokina, 337–

40, 352; Green Is., 417–19; Admiralties, 440–5
*LST-340,* 140; *–449,* 123; *–446,* 417
LVTs, 360, 374–5, 386, 445–6
Lynch, Ens. R. J., 48

**MAC AND MC**

MacArthur, General Douglas, 3–4; staff, 15; problems and strategy, 31–3, 225–6, 254–5, 269, 369–72; Milne, 35–7; Papua, 41–50; Filipino guerrillas, 85; relations with Sopac, 95–7, 433; Nadzab, 266; Bougainville, 282–3; N. Britain, 369–74, 380–1; quoted, 422; Admiralties, 432–8, 448
"MacArthur's Navy," 32, 130–1
MCCALLA, 151, 242
MCCAWLEY, 147, 151
McClure, Brig. Gen. R. B., 229, 233
McCormick, Capt. L. D., 10, 11*n*
MacDonald, Lt. Cdr. D. J., 161, 166, 181, 244, 248–52
McFall, Rear Adm. A. C., 146
McGee, Cdr. H. F., 261
McGowen, 2nd Lt. J. R. C., 435, 439
McIlhenny, Cdr. H. H., 272
McInerney, Capt. F. X., 110*n*, 161, 166, 168; Kula G., 171–4; Kolombangara, 181–8; rescue, 193–4
MCKEAN, 294–5, 351
McLean, Cdr. E. R., 158
McMahon, Cdr. B. F., 69
McMorris, Capt. C. H., 10–11
McQuilkin, Ens. M. W. T., 248

**M**

Madang, 52, 261–2, 271, 383, 390–1
MAHAN, 260, 262, 267, 384, 390–1, 436
Maher, Lt. Cdr. J. B., 386
Malaria, 35, 104, 408
Mallard, Capt. J. B., 261
Manchester, Lt. R. C., 246, 251
Mansergh, Capt. C. A. L., 181
Manus Is., 432–48
Marilinan, 255, 259
Marine Corps, Defense Bns., 98, 428; Raider Bns., 98, 139, 142, 152, 347; Aviation, 111, 122–4, 139–40, 150, 176, 230–2, 290, 362, 401, 418; 1st Div., 274, 380–9, 408; I 'Phib, 289, 296, 364; 3rd Div., 296, 337–42, 351–2, 362–5; Dog

Platoon, 302; Engineers, 387; *see* Liversedge

Marshall, Gen. G. C., 3–5, 256, 434

Martin, Brig. Gen. C. D., 390

Mason, Rear Adm. C. P., 99*n*, 118

Matsuda, Maj. Gen., 383, 387–8

MATSUKAZE, 181, 244

Matsumoto, Capt. K., 56

MAURY, 98*n*, 182, 193, 214

MAYA, 323, 328, 335

Mercer, Capt. P. V., 11*n*

Merrill, Rear Adm. A. S., 106*n* (biog.); 6 March action, 107–10; support and bombdt. missions, 142, 146, 177–9, 203, 209, 241, 292, 337–8, 345–6, 415; Emp. Aug. Bay, 305–22

Merritt, Brig. Gen. L. B., 323*n*

Mikawa, Vice Adm. G., 22, 118

MIKAZUKI, 162, 174, 181, 186–7, 190*n*, 208, 256, 384

Miller, Col. A. M., 373

Miller, Cdr. Harry F., 161

Miller, Cdr. Henry L., 325

Milne Bay, 28; Battle of, 34–7, 35 (chart); base, 47–8, 51–3, 68, 126–7, 380, 390, 435–6

Milner, Samuel, 34*n*, 41*n*

MINAZUKI, 181

MINEGUMO, 107–10

MISSISSIPPI, 423

Mitchell, Maj. Gen. R. J., 350, 395

MOA, 121–2

MOBILE, 341, 344

MOCHIZUKI, 162, 174

Momote, 437–41

MONTEREY, 411

Montgomery, Rear Adm. A. E., 330–6

MONTPELIER, 307–22, 363*n*, 414

Moosbrugger, Cdr. F., 212–21

Moran, Commo. E. J., 209

Mori, Rear Adm., 267

Motor Torpedo Boats, in Buna camp., 47–9; Solomon and Bismarck Seas, 52–4, 62, 136–7, 257, 273–4, 391; Cent. Solomons, 151–5, 209–13; Vella Lavella, 227–9; Boug., 341–3, 354, 427–30; C. Gloucester, 379; Green Is., 413–14, 418, 422; Emirau, 424; Manus, 445–6

Mullaney, Cdr. B. J., 441

MULLANY, 391, 440–4

Mumma, Cdr. M. C., 53, 61, 136, 372

Munda, 147; value of, 90–1; in U.S. plans, 93–6, 106; bombardments, 116,

179; land campaign, 153–5, 198–206; base, 222–4, 350, 396

MURASAME, 107–10

Myhre, Lt. Cdr. F. B. T., 182

MYOKO, 305–13, 321

**N**

Nadzab, 266, 272

NAGANAMI, 306, 341

Nagano, Admiral O., 17–18, 403

NAGARA, 208

NAGATSUKI, 162, 168, 172–5

NAGAURA, 403, 420

Nakano, Lt. Gen., 55

Nakayama, Capt. S., 244, 251

*Nankai Maru*, 37–8

NARWHAL, 85

NASHVILLE, 113*n*, 116*n*, 320, 436–7, 444

Nassau Bay, 136–7, 255–6

Naval gunfire, 194; *see* Ammunition

Naval shore bombardment, problems of, 177–9, 203–4; Lae, 259–60; Boug., 292–3, 361; Bismarcks, 418–23; Admiralties, 438–48; *see* Ainsworth, Burke, Merrill

Neale, Cdr. E. T., 47

Netherlands ships, *see* K.P.M.

New Britain, 369–88; *see* Rabaul

New Georgia, 147; plans, 96, 138–9; charts, 143, 201; task org., 144–6; land campaign, 140–59, 175–7, 198–206, 222–4; naval and air actions, 160–91, 206–22; secured, 223–4

New Guinea, 27–32; charts, 29, 133; campaigns, 33–65, 125–37, 254–75, 389–91; air attacks on, 125–7

New Guinea-Mindanao axis, 6–7, 369, 448

New Ireland, 399, 410; attacks on, 418–23

NEW MEXICO, 423

Newell, Lt. Cdr. James, 325*n*, 328

Newton, Lt. Cdr. R. A., 214

NIAGARA, 121–2, 139*n*

*Nichei Maru*, 323

NICHOLAS, 107, 110*n*, 116*n*, 157, 161–3, 166–74, 181–3, 193, 234–5

Nichols, Wing Cdr. C. W. K., 405*n*

NICHOLSON, 443

Nickelson, Cdr. W. D. R., 335*n*

NIIZUKI, 162–3, 166–70, 172–4

Nimitz, Admiral C. W., quoted, 9, 31, 94, 116, 129, 191, 220, 422; staff and

plans, 10–13, 93–5; decisions and orders, 128, 226–7, 286, 289, 330, 434
Nishimura, Rear Adm. S., 206
NISSHIN, 207
*Nissho* and *Nisshun Maru*, 69, 323
Noble, Capt. A. G., 435
*Nojima*, 55–8
Nolan, Lt. J. C., 191–2
NOSHIRO, 328, 412

O

O'BANNON, 107, 113*n*, 119, 156–8, 161–3, 166–7, 181–2, 193, 234–5, 244–52
Ofstie, Capt. R. A., 331
*Ogurasan Maru*, 81
Ohmae, Capt. T., 19*n*, 327*n*
*Oigawa Maru*, 56, 61
Oikawa, Admiral K., 17*n*
Omori, Vice Adm. S., 305–22, 341
ONAMI, 353–6
Ondonga, 332, 396, 406
O'Neill, Col. D. F., 428–31
*Onoe Maru*, 72
Orita, Capt. T., 152–3, 174, 181
Oro Bay, 46–7, 125, 380
ORTOLAN, 123
OSHIO, 68–9
Osugi, Rear Adm. M., 306, 312, 341
OTORI class, 79, 81–2
*Oyama Maru*, 69
OYASHIO, 115
OYODO, 412
OYSTER BAY, 446

P

Pacific Military Conference, 7
Pahl, Cdr. J. R., 229, 428–9
Painter, Cdr. William, 374
Papua, 28–30; charts, 28, 134; campaign, 31–66; air raids on, 118, 125–7
PATHFINDER, 363
Pattee, Richard S., 66*n*
PATTERSON, 242
Patton, Richard, 273–4
PAWNEE, 151
Pearl Harbor, Jap. recco. of, 286
Peck, Brig. Gen. DeWitt, 13, 93–5
Peckham, Lt. Cdr. G. E., 244–6, 251
*Penang Maru*, 76–7
Perimeter, Torokina, 348–52, 360–5, (map), 361, 369, 405; Battle of, 425–31
Perkins, Lt. Cdr. V. O., 345*n*

Petersen, Capt. W. F., 420, 422, 428
Peyton, Maj. M. K., 139
Pfeifer, Lt. C. F., 246
PHILIP, 230, 237, 295, 337
Philippines, supplied by subs., 78, 85
Phillips, Cdr. R. H., 375, 386
PHOENIX, 39, 130, 435–7, 444
Photo interpretation, 104–5
Pineau, Lt. Roger, 21*n*, 54*n*, 287*n*
Piva, 347, 352
"Piva Uncle" and "Yoke," 365, 394–9, 429–30
Planning, strategic, Allied, 3–8; U.S., in Pacific, 9–15; Japanese, 15–26
*Polaris*, 46
Pollock, Lt. Col. E. A., 381
Pongani, 43, 46
Port Moresby, 30–1, 33–4, 125–6
Porter, Lt. Cdr. G. E., 80
"Postern" Operation, 256
Post, Lt. Cdr. W. S., 77–9
PREBLE, 110–14
PRESIDENT ADAMS, 98*n*
PRESIDENT HAYES, 98
PRESIDENT JACKSON, 98*n*, 300
PRINCETON, 324–31
PRINGLE, 320, 429
Privies, "Battle of," 364
*PT–64*, *–318*, 354
*PT–66*, *–67*, *–68*, *–121*, *–128*, *–143*, *–149*, *–150*, *–151*, *–152*, 61, 137, 257
*PT–107*, *–109*, 157, *–159*, *–162*, *–171*, 210–12
*PT–110*, *–325*, *–327*, 379
*PT–114*, 48, 62
*PT–120*, 49, 137
*PT–121*, *–122*, 47–8
*PT–128*, *–194*, 273–4
*PT–146*, *–320*, *–323*, 391
*PT–163*, *–169*, *–170*, 251, 343
*PT–167*, 329
*PT–168*, 137, 229
*PT–176*, *–178*, 413–14
*PT–319*, 418
*PT–323*, *–363*, 446
Puruata Is., 300, 340–1
Purvis Bay, 102–3, 321, 337–8; ditty, 363
Pye, Admiral W. S., 305*n*, 358

Q

Quackenbush, Cdr. R. S., 104–5
Quadrant Conference, 8
Quinby, Lt. (jg) W. C., 61

## R

Rabaul, 392–4, 393 (map); Allied objective, 6, 93–7, 281; as Jap. base, 23–5, 37, 55, 92, 117–8, 406–9; aircraft at, 93, 118, 258, 286–7, 347, 395, 398, 400; naval forces at, 143, 394, 407; land-based air strikes on, 208, 275, 286–8, 393–409; air counterattacks on, 303, 319–20, 328–9, 333–6, 343–7, 362, 376–7, 385–6; carrier strikes on, 323–36; troops at, 370, 394, 408; a day's work, 400–1; town, 408; naval bombardment of, 420–2
Radar in subs., 68; cruisers, 108, 163, 183, 195; Australia, 384
Radar Detecting Device, 183–4
RADFORD, 107, 110–14, 154, 158, 161–3, 167–74, 181, 186, 193
RAIL, 122
RALPH TALBOT, 151, 157, 182, 189, 242–4
Ramey, Lt. Cdr. R. L., 351
Ramsay, Cdr. Alston, 308
Ramsey, Rear Adm. DeW. C., 106, 146
Rankin, Lt. D. W., 232
Rasmusson, Cdr. I. S., 440–1
RATON, 71–2
REID, 265, 269–72, 390, 436, 444
Reifsnider, Commo. L. F., 297–8, 303–4, 313n, 318, 323, 423
Rekata Bay, 90, 239
Rendova, 147–55, 209–10
Rennell, Lt. P. T., 446
RENSHAW, 308, 337, 354, 360
Reynolds, Cdr. L. K., 308, 354
Rice Anchorage, 156–8
RIGEL, 133, 381
"RO" Operation, 284–8, 346–7
RO–34, 119; –103, 141–3; –107, 179; –113, 112
Roberts, Capt. R. H., 416
Rocket guns, 375, 385
Rodgers, Capt. R. H., 150
Romoser, Cdr. W. K., 114, 154, 161, 167–9, 181
Roosevelt, President Franklin D., 4–6
Rosecrans, Col. H. E., 387
Royal Australian Air Force, at Milne, 37–8, 52; Bismarck Sea, 64–5; see Aircraft, Australian
Royal Australian Navy, 46–7; see Admiralties, C. Gloucester, Lae
Royal New Zealand Air Force, 100, 392n; see Aircraft, N. Z.

Royal New Zealand Navy, see LEANDER, MOA
Royle, Admiral Sir G., 51
Rupertus, Maj. Gen. W. H., 378–89
Russell Is., 94–100, 120, 139–40, 190
Ryan, Capt. T. J., 149, 181–2, 186–7, 193–4, 235–6

## S

Saidor, 389–91
ST. LOUIS, 113n, 116, 120, 161, 163, 167–8, 181, 187, 190n, 363, 415
Salamaua, see Lae
Salomon, Lt. Cdr. H., 279n, 323n
Samejima, Vice Adm. T., 118–19, 210, 305–6, 323, 426
SAMIDARE, 119, 244–8, 306, 311, 315–17, 341
SANAE, 75
Sanagi, Capt. S., 408n
Sanananda, see Lae
SAN DIEGO and SAN JUAN, 325
SANDS, 133n, 261–3, 267, 269n, 374–5, 436
SANGAMON class, 106
SANTA FE, 341, 344
SARATOGA, 106, 292, 324–31
Sasaki, Maj. Gen. N., 150, 177, 180, 198–206, 222, 225, 242
Satelberg, 271–4, 389
SATSUKI, 162, 168, 181
SAUFLEY, 242, 337
SAZANAMI, 68, 234–5
SC–699, –742, –743, 375–6
SCAMP, 69–71
Schultz, Lt. Col. D. E., 175, 222–3
Schwartz, Lt. Cdr. F. D., 436
Scruggs, Capt. R. M., 440–1
Seabees, 98, 102, 105, 153–4, 222; at Vella Lavella, 233, 237–8; Treasuries, 295; Boug., 350, 361, 429; C. Gloucester, 387; Green Is., 419; Admiralties, 440–2
Seeadler Harbor, 432–4, 441, 444–7
Segi Point, 139–42, 153, 333
SELFRIDGE, 39, 244–51
SENDAI, 220, 306–17, 322
Seton, C. W., 290
Seventh Fleet, 97, 130–3; see Carpender, Kinkaid
Shaw, Cdr. J. C., 143n; account of carrier strike, 331–6, 410n
SHAW, 375, 385–6
Shepard, Capt. A. G., 308

Shepard, Lt. Cdr. R. D., 244
Sherman, Rear Adm. Forrest P., 7, 10, 11*n*
Sherman, Rear Adm. Frederick C., 106, 292–3, 324–31, 411–12, 419
SHIGURE, 214–20, 234–6
SHIKINAMI, 56, 62–4
Shimada, Admiral S., 17, 20, 403
Shimai, Capt. Y., 181, 187–9
*Shinai Maru,* 56
SHIRATSUYU, 306, 312, 315–17, 341
SHIRAYUKI, 55–6
Shock, Capt. T. M., 100–2
SHOKAKU, 286, 332
Shortland Is., 207–8, 283
*Shoyu Maru,* 83
SHROPSHIRE, 384
SICARD, 308
Sieglaff, Lt. Cdr. W. B., 76
Sigel, J. F., 237*n*
SIGOURNEY, 337, 351, 429
Simpson Harbor, 288*n*, 326, 392, 398, 407, 419
Simpson, Capt. Rodger W., 214, 218–21, 325, 364, 420–1, 427
Sims, Cdr. G. L., 182, 214
Sio, 267, 389–91
SIOUX, 303, 321, 346
SKATE, 411
Skip-bombing, 57–60, 288*n*
Smith, Lt. Cdr. J. M., 294
SMITH, 260–2, 267, 272, 390, 436, 443
Sonsorol, 74–5
South and Southwest Pacific Areas, 13–15
SPENCE, 241, 308–22, 345, 354–8, 420
Spruance, Vice Adm. R. A., 7, 97
STACK, 214–21
STANLY, 308, 421
Steele, Capt. J. M., 10–11
Steffen Strait, 420
Steinke, Lt. Cdr. F. S., 113*n*
*Stella,* 46
STERETT, 214–21
STEVENSON, 436
STEWART, 83*n*
Still, Harold L., 237*n*
STINGRAY, 67
Stirling Is., *see* Treasury Is.
STOCKTON, 438
Stout, Cdr. H. F., 308, 354
STRONG, 110*n*, 113*n*, 116*n*, 119, 157–8, 195–6
Submarines, U.S., score of sinkings, 24,

68, 75, 84; in support of Fleet, 42; in SWPac, 66–85
*Sumatra Maru,* 79
SUWANNEE, 140
SUZUKAZE, 162–3, 167, 172
SWANSON, 443, 445
Sweeney, Lt. Cdr. J. D., 193, 414–15
Swenson, 1st Lt. L. V., 404–5
Swett, 1st Lt. J. E., 122
Swift, Lt. Cdr. H. M. S., 446
Swift, Maj. Gen. I. P., 444; on naval support, 447
*Sydney Maru,* 82

T

"TA" Operation, 427–30
*Taimei Maru,* 56
TAKAO, 323
Takeda, Rear Adm. I., 426–31
TALBOT, 147, 351
TALLULAH, 98*n*
TAMBOR, 85
Tanaka, Rear Adm. R., 22, 181
TANIKAZE, 37, 162–3, 167, 172
Tankers, Jap., 84, 323
TAPPAHANNOCK, 123
TATSUTA, 33, 37–9
TAUTOG, 76–7, 85
Taylor, Cdr. E. G., 421–2, 427
Taylor, Lt. J. G. G., 231–2
Taylor, Lt. Cdr. L. T., 413
Taylor, Lt. Cdr. R. L., 244
TAYLOR, 110*n*, 113*n*, 121, 179, 181, 193, 234–5, 251, 292–4
*Teibi* and *Teiyo Maru,* 55–8, 80
TENNESSEE, 423
TENRYU, 33, 37
TERRY, 242, 360
THATCHER, 308–18
Theiss, Capt. P. S., 140–1
Theobald, Lt. Cdr. R. A., Jr., 273
Third Fleet, 97; *see* Halsey
Thompson, Capt. E. M., 341, 344
THRESHER, 85
Thurber, Capt. H. R., 13, 93, 226
Tidball, Ens. J. M., 263–4
"Toenails" Operation, 138
*Toho Maru,* 78
Tojo, General H., 17–20, 23–4, 33, 225, 403
TOKITSUKAZE, 54–5
Tokuno, Lt. Cdr., 109–10
Tomioka, Rear Adm. S., 18–19

Tomonari, Col., 200, 205
*Tonan Maru*, 82
Torokina, Cape, 283–4, 301 (chart); landings, 297–304, task org'n, 297; position, 299*n*; Jap. counter-landing, 306, 341–2; securing beachhead, 337–40, 347–9; fighter strip, 350, 361–2, 394. *See* Perimeter
Torpedo boats, Jap., 79*n*
Torpedoes, U.S., 76, 196*n*, 329*n*; Jap. "long lance," 195–6, 213; reloading device, 172
Towers, Rear Adm. J. H., 323*n*
Toyoda, Admiral S., 17*n*
Treasury Is., 293–5, 294 (chart), 396; base, 406
Trident Conference, 7
Trobriand Is., 95–7, 132–4
TROUT, 85
Truk, 6, 84, 284, 400, 403
Tulagi, 67, 102, 161; air attacks on, 120–2
TULSA, 47–8, 53
Turnage, Maj. Gen. A. H., 289*n*, 297, 360
Turner, Rear Adm. R. K., 9*n*, 14, 97–100, 129–30, 142–52, 155, 180, 189–90
Twining, Maj. Gen. M. F., 290–1, 324, 348
Twitty, Brig. Gen. J. J., 11*n*

U

Ugaki, Vice Adm., 129
UMIKAZE and URAKAZE, 37, 68, 71
URANAMI and UZUKI, 56, 353–8

V

Vandegrift, Lt. Gen. A. A., 281, 289, 296–8, 304
Van Every, Lt. S. A., 376*n*
Vasey, Maj. Gen. G. A., 46, 266–7, 272
Vella Gulf, 114–15; Battle of, 212–21
Vella Lavella Is., 192–4, 221, 227, 240 (chart); campaign for, 226–39; Battle of, 243–53; base, 291; *see* Barakoma
Vila, 90, 93, 107–10, 115–16, 119, 156, 222, 239
Villella, Lt. William, 140
VIREO, 123
Viru, 152–3
Vitiaz Str., 254–7, 260, 271, 369–71

Vlasich, P. L., 189
Vose, Lt. Cdr. J. E., 331–2

W

WADSWORTH, 303
WAGGA, 127
WAKATSUKI, 306, 328, 341
Wake Is., 286
Walker, Capt. F. R., 241–52
WALLER, 110, 237, 337, 420
WARD, 295
Warfield, Lt. Cdr. T. G., 428
WARRAMUNGA, 440–2
WASHINGTON, 106
Watanabe, Capt. Y., 129
"Watchtower" Operation, 6, 95, 281
WATERS, 142, 148, 193–4
Wau, 52, 54, 136, 256, 258
WELLES, 436, 442
Wellings, Cdr. J. H., 157–8
Wendell, Capt. W. G., 279*n*
West Cactus, 36
WESTRALIA, 374–6
Wewak, 52, 258–9, 262, 373, 383, 390
Wheatley, Norman, 147
WHYALLA, 46
WICHITA, 106*n*
Wickham Anchorage, 152–3
Widhelm, Cdr. W. J., 291
Wilfong, Cdr. J. L., 214, 219
WILKES, 443, 445
Wilkinson, Lt. Cdr. R. H., 228
Wilkinson, Rear Adm. T. S., 13–14, 97, 282*n* (biog.); N. Georgia, 144, 203–4; Vella Gulf, 212–13, 221; "leapfrogging," 226; Com III 'Phib, 227; Vella Lavella, 227–34, 241, 244–5; Bougainville, 281, 289, 298, 300–4, 348; Green Is., 415–18; Emirau, 423
Willoughby, Brig. Gen. Charles A., 27*n*, 259
Wilson, Lt. Cdr. G. R., 244, 248, 250
Wiltse, Rear Adm. L. J., 11*n*, 325
Windeyer, Brigadier J. V., 269–72
Woodlark Is., 132–4, 328, 373
WOODWORTH, 123, 153, 182
Wootten, Maj. Gen. G. F., 267

Y

Yamada, Maj. Gen., 270–4
YAMAGUMO, 412
Yamamoto, Capt. C., 19

Yamamoto, Fleet Admiral I., strategy, 18–19, 92–3, 117–27; alleged boast, 128$n$; death, 128–9
Yamashiro, Capt. K., 162–3, 167–8, 172–3, 353–5
YAMATO, 410–11
*Yamayuri Maru*, 400
Yano, Capt. M., 38
Yasuda, Capt. Y., 39, 44, 50
*YMS-49*, 384; –50, 376
Yokoyama, Col. Y., 33, 44
Yokoyama, Rear Adm., 21

YUBARI and YUGIRI, 74–5, 112, 353–7
YUGUMO and YUGURE, 181, 191$n$, 207, 247–51
YUKIKAZE, 54–5, 58–9, 62, 64, 181, 187, 189$n$
YUNAGI, 181, 244

Z

Zanana, 155–6, 177, 199–202
ZANE, 147–8
ZUIHO and ZUIKAKU, 118, 286